A JOURNAL

of my

JOURNEY TO PARIS

IN THE YEAR 1765

By the

REV. WILLIAM COLE M.A. F.S.A.

Edited from the original MS. in
the British Museum
by

FRANCIS GRIFFIN STOKES

SOMETIME POSTMASTER OF MERTON COLLEGE OXFORD

With an Introduction
by

HELEN WADDELL

LONDON

CONSTABLE & CO LTD

1931

PUBLISHED BY

Constable & Company Limited
London W.C. 2

.

BOMBAY
CALCUTTA   MADRAS

Oxford University
Press

.

TORONTO

The Macmillan Company
of Canada, Limited

.

NEW YORK

Richard R. Smith Inc

PRINTED IN GREAT BRITAIN BY ROBERT MACLEHOSE AND CO. LTD.
THE UNIVERSITY PRESS, GLASGOW.

CONTENTS

NOTE ON MAP

THE map which will be found at the end of this volume is reproduced from Plate XI. of Turgot's *Plan de Paris*, drawn by Louis Bretez, engraved by Claude Lucas, and published in 1739 under the auspices of Michel-Etienne Turgot, whose name it bears. It was a return to the old bird's-eye view, abandoned by most eighteenth century map-makers, and a magnificent specimen of its kind : " in no way geometrical," said a contemporary, "but rather for curiosity than utility : it was sent as a present not only to all the Courts of Europe and all the Savants, but also to Constantinople and to China." It is to be remembered that Bretez puts the west at the bottom of his map, so as to show the façade of the churches. It is almost possible to identify Walpole's lodging "almost the first House in the next Street [to the Rue des Petits Augustins at the bottom of the map] called the Rue du Colombier, opposite the high dead Wall of the Royal Abbey of St. Germain des Prés." Mr. Cole's " Apartment was beautifully situated just above the Duke de la Rochefoucault's Garden . . . with a small oval Pond, in which was a single Swan" [this the only detail M. Bretez has omitted], and so near M. Walpole "that I could see into the Courtyard of his House, and see when his Coach was going out with him, from a back Window of my own" (pp. 37-38, 52-53).

EDITOR'S PREFACE

THE *Journals* of William Cole fill the folio volume numbered 5835 in the Catalogue of "Additional Manuscripts" in the British Museum. This is lettered on the back: *Journals kept by Mr Cole, 1765-1770. Vol. xxxiv. Mus. Brit. ex Dono Test. Gul. Cole, A. M. 5835. Plut. clxxxi. F.*, and contains 469 numbered pages, with three flyleaves on which appear a few notes. The *Paris Journal*, reproduced in the present volume, occupies pp. 1-253 of the original MS.

The handwriting, which is for the most part distinct and rather large, becomes small and crabbed from about p. 332 onwards, while the last forty-nine pages are legible with difficulty, and are written in French—of a rather macaronic kind, for when Cole cannot, apparently, think of a French equivalent, he uses the English word. His reason for thus abandoning more or less plain English is obscure, for there is nothing of peculiar interest, or of a very private nature, in this latter part of the diary.

Whether Cole ever contemplated the ultimate publication of his *Journal*, it is hard to say: some phrases used by him seem to show that he did—others have a contrary implication. In either case revision to-day is clearly inadmissible, and in preparing a transcript of the MS. for the press I have simply aimed at reproduction, *verbatim et literatim*, of the original, with all its oddities of spelling and obscurities of style.

With regard to orthography, Cole evidently held views which he carried out with much consistency. The most obvious peculiarity is the invariable substitution of *ei* for *ie* (*freind* for *friend*, *cheif* for *chief*, and so on), and although he might have produced many early instances in justification of this practice, it was certainly almost obsolete in his day. Attention is occasionally drawn in the footnotes to other examples of the employment of rare, but not wholly unjustifiable, modes of spelling.

Proper names, however, stand on a different footing. With regard to these, even after making an allowance for the laxity then prevailing in the matter, Cole cannot be acquitted of carelessness. Different spellings of a name too often occur in the same paragraph, and here and there I have corrected obvious slips of this kind *sub silentio*.

The few omissions made in the text fall under three heads: (*a*) certain monumental inscriptions which Cole has admittedly copied, not from the originals but, from Germain Brice's *Description de Paris* and Montfaucon's *Monumens de la Monarchie Françoise*. In such cases I have given, within brackets, precise references to the book quoted, so that the reader may readily recover the inscription if he desires to do so.

(*b*) Descriptions of a few coats-of-arms, accompanied by coloured sketches in the original MS.

(*c*) Two brief interpolations of irrelevant matter, due no doubt to the temporary use by Cole of his diary as a note-book.

It should be added that in every case where an omission has been made the fact is indicated. Readers of the *Journal* will recognise that it was not wholly written, in its present form, during Cole's journey or his residence in Paris. During the last three months of 1765 he made, it is true, daily notes, but these were revised and considerably expanded in the Spring of the following year, after his return to Bletchley (see, for instance, pp. 61 and 87), while a few entries are of a still later date (see pp. 118, 153).

In supplying notes, I have steadfastly resisted the temptation to over-annotate; but what constitutes defect or excess of annotation in a book of this nature must always remain a matter of individual opinion.

The *Index* will, I trust, be found complete so far as the names of persons and places are concerned—except that repeated mention of certain well-known streets in Paris, without comment or information, seemed scarcely to call for record.

It may be mentioned that the *Index* frequently supplies corrections of the spelling of personal names as they appear in the text. In this connection I have often made use of the elaborate *Table des Noms* appended to Mrs Paget Toynbee's edition of *Lettres de la Marquise du Deffand à Horace Walpole* (3 vols., 1912).

F. G. STOKES

INTRODUCTION

"A JOURNAL," wrote the Reverend William Cole, antiquarian and rector of Bletchley, " being, as some one justly enough calls it, the Importance of a Man to his own Self, I shall, till I am tired of it, transcribe from my Almanacks the Contents of them, and so run over the last Year, and be ashamed of the Manner in which it has passed." He entered that resolution on the 1st of January, 1766, the day of his return from his travels in France to his parish of Bletchley. His " fat little Dun Horse," by far the most considered person in the parish, had met him at Dunstable, and brought him to the parsonage, about three o'clock, to Dinner. The Ringers did him the Honour to ring the Bells on his Arrival, and they all eight came into the Kitchen and drank as much as they pleased, in Reason and Sobriety: he wrote to Mr Walpole, whom he had left behind him in Paris: sent a French Snuff-Box to Mr Pomfret, and Earrings of Firestone and Marcasite to his Niece Apthorp, and a Tooth Pick to her Father, " being Paris Presents": noted the gardener's brother all Sunday afternoon and evening "in the Kitchen with my Cook whom he courts": grumbled at the bill of £21 3s 6d for last year's malt, " though I never touch a Drop of Ale myself": caught cold watching Tansley lop the trees in the churchyard: married John Hinchley and Eliza-beth Crane in the church, but had them into the Par-lour to sign the Book, it was so cold: where they brought out the Child to be baptised, and that done, the mother begged that he would church her, which seemed to him Absurd to do in a Parlour, but there is no Parleying with your Parishioners in any Point of Discipline, thanks to the Practices of the Dissenters. Mrs Holt and her daughter Mrs Goodwin, came and drank coffee with him on the Saturday: "they both cried, and told me of Mr G's ill-humours at Home, except with the Maid, who was going away with Child. I gave them a Neat's Tongue I had brought with me from Paris, and a Snuff Box for him, which I had on Purpose bought for him as a Present, on which was painted Turtle-doves Billing." Letter from Mr Masters, fellow anti-quary, "desiring me to search my MS. Collections concerning his Parish of Waterbeche, he having a Lawsuit with Mr Peter Stanley of Paxton, about Tithes, and to send him an Extract from Doomday Book about that Parish." Very angry to find not one Onyon or Potatoe left, though the Gardiner had bought in 3 Bushells of the last and 1 of the former for the Winter's Use. In short, Goodman Frog, as Walpole calls him, was home again.

It was not, however, till May 9th that Goodman Frog sat down to sort out the notes made during his stay abroad, which result in this, the first volume of his Diary: and a fortnight later he is still lamenting his slowness. " At the Rate I go on, I shall be longer in writing out my Journal than I was in taking my Journey: for when I first sat down to enter it from my Pocket Book, I thought I should only have the Trouble of transcribing from that a few Inscriptions and other trifling Observations . . . but I now see no End of my Labours, for the most minute Hint is liable to draw me into a Dissertation of two or Three Pages. However," says he, manfully averting his eyes from the unfitness of Dr Foster to be headmaster of Eton (he being more of a Scholar than a Gentleman, and thought to write in too dogmatical and pert a Manner for so young a Man, against the University of Oxford, on Account of the Greek Accent) "however, I will endeavour to be less Diffuse, that I may once again get into my own Parish and enjoy the Sweets of my Garden, much more to the Purpose of benefitting my Health than thus sitting scribbling in an Elbow Chair."

For Mr Cole, like his friend Mr Betham of King's, was a passionate gardener, and even in that antiquaries' paradise of Strawberry had eyes for other things than Mr Walpole's Magna Charta and the warrant for King Charles' execution, hung on either side his bed: in May 1773 he is writing for a root of the pale yellow Mortigan or Crown Imperial, now that it is out of Blow: " you have two of them in one Plat or Bed on the left Hand going from the Castle to the Cottage." He had a great deal of talk with the French King's Gardener (a well looking old man who has a son in England and is acquainted by Correspondence with Mr. Miller) as they travelled in the Coach to Versailles, about winter Sallads and Broccoli: and Mr Cole especially admired an enormous kind of Water-Melon or Pompkin, which he feared there was not sun enough in England to ripen. However, it goes into the Hot Bed at the Parsonage, till the first frost comes that killed the late Tuberoses and flagged the Leaves of the Pompkins: next year seeds of it go to Mr Betham at Cambridge, who plants them with excitement in the Physics Garden, thinking it a pity to lose so great a Rarity in his own small plot: and he returns it with convolvulus seed from China, and " Ptolemy's beloved queen Berenice," prosaically acknowledged by Mr Cole as the stellated scabious:

"which rather touched me," says Mr Betham, who was very romantic for "an old Senior Fellow .... such an awkward one as I muſt be at beſt." There were other things, too, felt Mr Betham, on which Mr Cole was not quite sound : he might be passionate for Chartularies and Bishop's Regiſters, but he was casual, not to say careless, about fossils. They had good moments, as when Mr Cole found a *cornu ammonis* and invited Mr Betham to the parsonage, and after an evening of Cambridge gossip " reposed in elbow chair [that elbow chair in which Mr Cole sat over much, for at forty-nine he was over 14 ſtone], with a pipe of the beſt British," Mr Betham ſtole downſtairs early before his friend was awake, " to take a view of my *cornu ammonis*. How was I ravished in admiration of it! I measured it with astonishment, turned it about and about, would have secured it in my pocket, but it was too big. That other Fossil too I wishfully eyed." Mr Cole reports another, lighthandedly, and Mr Betham is in a fever—"you talk of such a treasure with so much calmness and indifference that I shall be in continual fears and apprehension while they continue in your hands"—and finally when Mr Cole moves from Bletchley to his damp little house at Waterbeche ("I am very sorry for the fever you have had," writes Horace, "but, Goodman Frog, if you will live in the Fens—") and discovers yet another fossil at his doorſtep, Mr Betham is all in a twitter till he can come to fetch it. True, it may serve as a neſt-egg to breed more, "but I can't say I overlike it lying so publick at your door."

Mr Gray of Pembroke sometimes came out with Mr Betham to sit in the smoky parlour at Waterbeche: came at eleven one morning and ſtayed till seven. Mr

Gray's recipe for pot-pourri is on a fly-leaf of one of the folio *Collections*, " I having seen and smelt the odoriferous Jar in his Chamber the year before"; but Mr Cole's man Tom brought him "Siringo" flowers to put in it one June, which spoilt it. They had been at Eton together, though Gray was two years younger: "his manner from a boy disgustingly effeminate, finical and affected," writes Mr Cole, who has sudden violences, and whose trick of talking to himself in manuscript as he emblazoned coats of arms and copied epitaphs made his Collections the terror of his contemporaries: one of them, as he calls to mind in his *Paris Journal*, was so uneasy at a note recording "the ancient blood of the Hanmers to be mixed with that of a little trading Presbyterian" that he gave Mr Cole no rest till he scratched it out, and even one day "was so earnest as to desire to see whether I had really done as I promised." The notes on Gray, his interleaved Linnaeus, and the parody of the epitaph from the *Elegy*, and the neat bloodstone seal always on his inkstand, are embedded among the antiquities and monuments of the church at Burnham (Bucks.), two epitaphs from the pen of Mr Gray being sufficient circumstance for pages of digression. Mr Gray followed Mr Cole to Cambridge, where Mr Cole was first a Pensioner and later Fellow-Commoner, at Clare Hall: and where he "had the Happiness to become the Friend of my dearest Friend, Thomas Western of Rivenhall in Essex." There were ten of them, all merry, who lived in each other's pockets and breakfasted in each other's rooms, but Mr. Western was the most for frolic of them all. Mr Cole sat for his picture in a conversation piece with Mr. Western, and his mother, and Charles Plumtre,

not yet archdeacon, to Mr Hogarth [1] "at his house in
a square at the west end of the town," Mr Cole then
being twenty-two, and painted playing on the harpsichord: and in the same year 1736 "Mr Western sat to
him for a full-length picture for me, which I have now
in my Gallery [Molly called it the Passage], and is one
of the most resembling Portraits I ever met with."
It was painted in Mr Western's rooms at Clare Hall,
"over the Arch, towards the River," and as the chimney
could not be got into the picture, "Mr Hogarth has
drawn a Cat sitting near it, to express the Situation,
agreeably to his Humour." Then Mr Western married,
which altered his Disposition, and Mr Cole moved into
those rooms but had no pleasure in them: and finally his
solitariness drove him, without prejudice to Clare Hall,
to take rooms in "the new Buildings" at King's, where
his half-brother, Stephen Apthorp, was Senior Fellow:
"the second Apartment of the first Staircase nearest the
Chapel, on the Ground Floor." He kept them for seven-
teen years, from 1736 to 1753, and had reached the
fourth volume of his MS. *History of King's College* when
Mr Browne Willis the antiquary, commonly called The
Old Chariot by reason of the extreme antiquity of his
coach and its perpetual motion with him upon the roads,
presented him to the living of Bletchley, "and so," says
Mr Cole, writing a mournful note on the fly leaf of his
unfinished MS. in 1782, thirty years later, "lost fifteen
Years of the best part of my Life for Disquisitions of this
sort." It had been Mr Cole's intention to keep his rooms
at King's and still spend at least six months of the year
at "my beloved Cambridge," but Mr Browne Willis

---

[1] Mr Cole's sister Catharine, a spinster, "was much acquainted
with his Wife, and was often at Chiswick with them."

had other views for him. It was his habit to send to every person to whom he had done a favour an "Exclamation" on the divinity of Gratitude taken from the works of his favourite divine, and specially printed for this purpose: and he had already worn out five rectors, chosen for various reasons, Mr Cole's predecessor, for instance, because he did not wear a wig ("Sir, Your wearing your own hair is a circumstance so very agreeable to me that it has determined me to offer you . . ."). Mr Cole indeed wore a wig, but he was a Fellow of the Society of Antiquaries: here, felt Mr Willis, was the heaven-sent coadjutor in his colossal task, the *History of the Hundreds of Newport and Cotslow in Buckinghamshire*. Mr Cole was safe in the trap before he suspected it; found that to spend a night out of his parish beyond what the canons allow would mean prosecution: and settled down to make the best of a situation that was not without its humours. He missed none of them: did his duty doggedly by his parish and his patron: and when the massive figure in its three greatcoats and the Boots

> . "from that Cow's Hide
> By Guy of Warwick slain . . .
> By Spelman, Camden, Dugdale worn,
> And then they came to Herne,"

no longer blocked his doorway of a morning, and Mr Cole sat by his deathbed to hear the old man say things to him that he could not for modesty record, he had no malice in retrospect. Indeed, by 1763 the wags of the University are suggesting that the famous Boots have found another wearer: and he comes to Cambridge himself an "Antiquarian of the first Magnitude." "Had you not stole out as you did," says Mr Betham, "I can't

b

say what might have followed. You might have been addressed. The wool-combers were ready."

Browne Willis died in 1760: after this, the visits to Cambridge are more frequent, and in 1761 Mr Cole made the great discovery, that in spite of the Beauty and judicious Elegance of Mr Gray's poetical Compositions, he had also condescended to look into the Study of Antiquities. "Dining in his Rooms at Pembroke Hall the laſt Time I was in Cambridge, *viz.* one Day the Beginning of this very Month, Dec. 1761, he told me that he was deeply versed in Dugdale, Herne, Spelman and others of that Class, and that he took as much Delight in that Study as he did in any other." Twenty years later, Mr Cole sat down to make a sadder entry on the blank page opposite. "Tues. July 30, 1771, Mr Essex calling on his way to Ely told me Mr Gray was thought to be dying: so I sent my Servant in the Evening to Pembroke Hall to enquire, but he was then going off, and no Message could be delivered: he died that Night." Then follows a copy, in Cole's hand, of the shaken letter from Horace Walpole in Paris, asking if the news can be true: a hurried reply from Mr Cole confirming it: and a day or two later another letter to Mr Walpole, for meantime Mr Cole has been in Cambridge and had gone "to drink my Tea" with the Maſter of Pembroke, and hear all about "poor Mr Gray." Another note, in 1772, that the Maſter, by this time Vice-Chancellor, has called on Mr Cole to ask his acceptance, on behalf of himself and Mr Mason, of a large embossed silver Snuffbox, or rather Tobacco-Box, seemingly by the figures on the lid made in China, for a memento of Mr Gray. And finally, in a feebler hand, that " in 1774 I gave this silver Box to my brother Apthorp, who is

a great Smoaker of Tobacco, which I never could
conquer."

Mr Cole liked and admired Mr Gray, but he loved
Mr Walpole: and the sketch to which he was moved by
the sight of Mr Walpole's legs wrapped in flannel,
that firſt morning in Paris, is the greateſt of the Digres-
sions. Mr Cole's lodgings in the Rue des Petits
Auguſtins were near Mr Walpole's, "indeed so contiguous that I could see into the Court Yard of his
Hotel, and see when his Carriage was going out with
him, from a back window of my own." Mr Walpole's
man was with Mr Cole before he was up; and going
to him after breakfaſt, he finds him very lame with the
Gout, an impertinent Diſtemper in that meagre Frame,
which was, thinks Mr Cole, so oddly come by, considering the bulk of the late Sir Robert, and that
"very luſty well-looking woman his Mother, whom I
remember very well also, when I have had the Honour
of visiting him often at Chelsea, when I was a Schoolboy:
. . . never liable to catch cold: & I have seen him at his
House at Strawberry Hill in the Parish of Twickenham
in Middlesex, in the Months of October and November,
when the Dew was quite wet upon the Grass, go out
into his Garden, & all over the Grass, without so much
as a Hat on his Head, a light silk Waiſtcoat, & thin
Slippers, not thicker than good subſtantial Brown
Paper, to feed his Poultry of all Sorts, after his
Breakfaſt: & all this without the leaſt Inconvenience,
when I have been muffled up in a Cloak & forced to
change my Shoes as soon as I got into the House."

Mr Cole's own greatcoats, which multiplied with the
years (though there is an agreeable Pickwickian episode
on the river near Wicken where Mr Cole was fishing

and fell in), were one of the ſtanding jokes between him
and Mr Walpole, along with Mr Cole's leanings to
Popery ("as true a Roman Catholic as it is possible for
a Proteſtant clergyman to be, and there is but a very
nice diſtinction between them, especially when they are
antiquaries"), and his indifference to any gossip later
than the Reformation. The Duchess of Kingſton is
being tried for bigamy: "I don't tell you a word of it,"
writes Walpole, "for you will not care about it these
200 years." Therein Mr. Walpole erred: to judge from
Mr Cole's diaries at Bletchley and Waterbeche, he
would have made a good third to Mr Woodhouse and
Miss Bates: and his bag of six Saxon Bishops and one
Duke of Northumberland unearthed at Ely Cathedral
("you have had good sport this season," says Horace
impishly) makes less figure in the journal than the whole
Sauce Boat of Oyſters and Butter Sauce for a Turkey that
Mrs Plumtre spilt on Miss Rachel Gooch's red Silk
Gown. Mr Eyles comes to dine at half paſt Twelve, and
"told a great deal of Scandal of other People, and forgot
how the World talks of him"; how Mr Goodwin lay
with Mrs Holt, and what Mrs Goodwin said to Frank,
and how Mr Knapp and his wife had not spoken for 3
weeks together, and how the Widow Woods was a kept
Miſtress, and how Mr Pitts had said that none of his
neighbours (Mr Cole being one), except Dr Pettingal,
was anything of a Scholar. "So I told him of Mr Pitts'
former Behaviour to me and his Talk with Mrs Willis
about my Resignation, and he seemed delighted with
the Acquisition," says Mr Cole, with the fine dry malice
that went out with snuff. Mr Cole's flavour was not loſt
on Mr Walpole: every morning of his ſtay in Paris,
Mr Walpole sent to invite him to dine, and Mr Cole

sent his excuses, for Mr Walpole dined at three, and Mr
Cole was anxious to see Paris so long as the November
daylight laſted, and only came home, tired with walking,
at four, "at which Hour I always ordered my Dinner at
a Traiteur's to my own Chamber, and there enjoyed
myself as if I had been at home, in my Night Cap,
Night Gown and Slippers by a good Fireside." Mr Cole
was indeed too fond of his fireside for Mr Walpole's
pleasure. He is for ever, especially as they both grow older,
inviting him to Strawberry, "almoſt the laſt monaſtery
left, at leaſt in England": the two old pieces of antiquity
can have their talk together, unmocked of that generation
that thinks George I lived in the time of the Crusades.
Mr Cole did go sometimes: has even left a short diary
of an elderly visit there, and the "squat gummy appearance" of Mr Walpole's half-siſter, whom Bishop Keene
was to have married in return for his presentation to a
living, but reneged at the laſt (here Mr Cole shows
sympathy for the Bishop); and he copies out a blotted
sheet of verses lying on Mr Walpole's desk, a laughing
mock-epitaph for Kitty Clive, with whom Mr Walpole
had spent laſt evening;

> "Ye Smiles and Tears, still hover round,
> This is Mirth's consecrated ground."

"You know," wrote Walpole, pleading for a visit,
"I am a brother monk in everything but religious and
political opinions." Mr Cole was a High Churchman
and a High Tory, Mr Walpole a railer upon Bishops
and his father's son ; and though Mr Cole's heart
warmed to hear him one evening in Paris hot in defence
of eſtablished religion, it saddened again at the knowledge that he spoke from his sense of political expediency

rather than conviction. If Mr Cole's religion was not
experimental, and he had small sympathy with " Mr.
Bull's Nocturnal Exercises"—"Few that are really Fervent in Prayer care to talk of it. Those that do are
very much to be suspected," says he in an acid gloss on
his folio *Life of Mr Richard Baxter*—it was no less profound: its basis a sober conviction of his own short-
comings, and of the mercy of God. He listens all evening
to Mr Walpole and Madame Geoffrin exchanging
scandals about Lady Mary Wortley Montagu: "I
hope this Account may be exaggerated," says he, "in
Pity to Human Nature, and in regard to a Person of
so great Talents and Abilities: if it is not, I should rather
impute it to another Cause, than the Badness of her
Heart." Two pages of unusually stern indictment are
levelled against Mr John Whaley, corrupter of youth,
Epicurus his Disciple, "round and sleek as a Mole."
"I have been the more particular in my Account of this
Man as I have ever looked upon him to have been
throughout Life, one of the worst Men I ever was acquainted with." But the steady charity that underlies
the admirable dryness wells up again: "Pray God have
Mercy and Compassion on his Soul. Amen."

" I hold it as a Truth," he confessed in his old age
to Dr Michael Lort, "that all true genuine Antiquaries
have a Spice or Dash in Favour of Mother Church."
With him, religion and politics were one with the pro-
foundest passion of his nature: his sense of the past.
Dr Kippis the Dissenter asks him to contribute to
his new edition of the *Biographia Britannica*, but Mr
Cole refuses. "His Worthies were such as had no Niche
in any of my Temples," he wrote to Mr Walpole, and
Mr Walpole commends him with his uncanny lightning

flash of perception: "Bishop Laud and William Prynne could never agree." It was a jeſt, but a true one, for Mr Cole, in all but girth, was Laud. He judged the Church of England more beholden to him than to any of its Metropolitans since St. Auſtin: and when St. Mary's in 1781 brought in a grace againſt the keeping of Saints' Days, the world to him had come to such a pass that he could rejoice at his soon leaving of it. The Devil and Oliver Cromwell, Mr Pitt and Mr Wilkes (whose father Mr Cole when rector of Hornsey once saw in church there, though characteriſtically it was only to uphold his right to a pew), Deiſts and Dissenters, were all one to him: and though he insiſted on his loyalty to the Church of England, which he held to be "a very safe and orthodox Body," he saw "Popery," with all its faults, as "the laſt Bulwark of Chriſtianity": and the Tillotsons, Burnets and Hoadleys rejoicing at its undermining in France as blind to the landslide that would take firſt the older faith, then the Church of England, and then "all that we now hold to be essential to Chriſtianity" into the abyss. "That restless republican Spirit of Calvin," said he, "will never be at Quiet till the Monarchy and Hierarchy are laid level with their Idol of Equality." Paris, to which he had come with such ingenuous anticipation, was haunted for him, and it is a deeper malaise than his dislike of the naſtiness of its manners and the dampness of its beds, or even the indisposition of "my Stomach which was very much out of order," and which he attributed to his discovery of "a species of Burgundy called *Vin de Beaune*" which he relished exceedingly and of which he drank near a Bottle a Day. Already in 1765 he is sensitive to the menace that

Sterne had no feeling for: "France to me," says he, "has much the Appearance of being soon the Theatre of a Civil War."

He had hankered after France for years: and visiting the English Benedictine Priory in the Rue St. Jacques, he confesses that he has always had a secret inclination in favour of that House and Order, once so flourishing in England: and that while he was still at King's, he had begun to sound the Prior as to whether it would be allowed for a clergyman of the Church of England to have a lodging in their convent: and only for the intervention of Mr Browne Willis, he might have been fixed there for life, he says, a little sadly, never having had "any other Views in life, than to live retiredly and quietly, and pretty much to myself, after the monkish manner." His old friend, Father Charles Bonaventure Bedingfield, chaplain to Mrs Markham in Lincolnshire, was indiscreet enough on his return to suggest that Mr Cole had gone to France for the purpose of changing his religion there, and Mr Cole is very tart: yet the hankering persists, and when in a year or two the old Friar is heading "in vast Spirits" home to the Recollet house at Douai, Mr Cole's letter of farewell betrays him. He knows that it is not for him: he has been bred to too much Latitude ("for Dinner a most noble Trout, and Lobsters from London") and "what is worse, has no Religious Call or half Virtue enough for the Profession": and yet if one could have a Lodgin near the Convent with one's Books and Conveniences about one, it would be a happy way to end one's days. France had cured him for a while of that nostalgia: he found it easier to daydream at home than where the religious orders were hooted in the street, and a dirty oil pot set on the

Tomb of one of Charlemagne's queens, and he was
bothered for sous for his seat at Mass, and his fellow
worshippers hawked and spat upon the floor: Yet the
humanities of old religion, every rapport between the
great English Catholic families and the ancient houses of
the faith kindles him: the grave of a Bourke of Clanricarde
in the Cordeliers, the arms of James Beaton, Archbishop
of Glasgow, in the Scots College Chapel, and Walter
Montagu, Abbot of Pontoise, and his own remote
kinsman, William Herbert, Marquis and Duke of
Powis, and Bishop Giffard's portrait that he knew very
well, having seen a copy of it "at my friend Mr Throckmorton's at Weston Underwood hanging up in a
chamber which I have often lain in": and the tomb of
Elizabeth Theresa Throckmorton, whose picture as
an old abbess is, he thinks, in the dining parlour at
Weston Underwood (did Cowper and Mrs Unwin dine
under it?); and he goes to visit a young Throckmorton,
pensionnaire at Port Royal, who cried and hoped her
Mama would not let her stay long, and Mr Cole
comforts her and urges her improvement in the French
Accent. Long after, when he has come back to England
and is settling down in the "goodnatured" little house
at Milton, he writes to thank Mr Walpole for the
stained glass he has sent him, packed with his own
hands, from Strawberry. Ananias and Sapphira complete are very handsome in a window: and the *Memento
Mori* "is a most suitable Piece for my Cell or Hermitage:
and though the Inhabitant is not a Carthusian, yet he
wishes to be as like one as his Frailties and Profession
allow of."

It was Mr Walpole who urged the final argument
against his Hermitage abroad ("I had much rather find

you one in the neighbourhood of Strawberry"), when
he reminded his friend that should he die in France, all
his goods would forfeit by the *Droit d'aubaine* to the
French Crown, including the precious *Collections*, that
magpie hoard which had been accumulating ever since
as a schoolboy he had tricked out his firſt coat of arms
in glass from a window in Baberham church. He had
the notes ſtill by him in 1771. For though he himself
published nothing, giving away his own grubbings and
findings with both hands to any fellow antiquary who
asked for them, he felt that at leaſt he might leave
behind him ſtuff that another man might use. Four years
before his death, he reads Dr Johnson's rebuke to the
ſterile labours of the antiquary, and his conscience
smites him: yet, says he, "there may be many Pallia-
tions in Favour of the Dilatory Antiquary. . . . He
would make his Work as perfeƈt as he could, colleƈt all
the Material necessary for that Purpose: in the mean
Time Years slide from under us and we leave our Col-
leƈtions to others to piece together, who have not had the
Drudgery to colleƈt, but have all ready to their hands.
This is exaƈtly my own Case. . . . I hope my Induſtry
may fall into the Hands of a judicious Brother Antiquary who will make a proper Use of them when I am
no more." The disposal of them after his death gave
him much exercise of mind. To leave them to King's was
to throw them into a Horsepond, so conceited were the
Fellows of their Greek and Latin, said Mr Cole, who
had copied out the simple medieval Latin of the epitaph
on Adam of St. Viƈtor's tomb as a teſtimony againſt
the "Ciceronian Jargon of this enlightened Age":
added to which, the new Provoſt was, he says roundly,
"a snotty-nosed Blackguard," with a Bursar like unto

him. So in the end the Collections, about a hundred folio volumes, went to the British Museum, which Mr Gray had once taken rooms to be near, with instructions that they were not to be opened for twenty years: for in his sixty-eighth year the memory of those marginal indiscretions weighed heavily on the old man, knowing that he had gossipped to his MSS. as to no living creature except "my man Tom." The proviso made some stir: "peculiarly cruel and ungenerous," said his surly brother antiquary, Mr Masters, proceeding to give a brief and acid account of the passions and prejudices of the last forty years, "to prevent any mischief that may arise hereafter from his unwarrantable prejudice." Mr Master's conscience was not easy: yet if he had known, his one-time neighbour had spoken more kindly of the living than himself of the dead, and one of the most agreeable portions of the diary is the account of how Mr Cole brought Mr Wells out of Cambridge to copy Langdon's maps of the parish of Gamlingay as a little present for Mr Masters, and how he painted them himself with tubes of colour also brought from Cambridge. These tubes were a new toy to Mr Cole, and when the maps are finished he goes through all his Collections, industrious and happy, painting all his drafts of monuments and coats of arms, including his own. For though the Coles had lived only in "a reputable farmerly way" at Ashden in Essex (it was through his mother Catherine Tuer that Mr Cole claimed kin with George Herbert the poet, and even that "the Blood of the Barons Fitz Hugh flows in my Veins"), they had their arms in a west window in the North Aisle at Steeple-Bumstead Church, " in a glass Coat of at least 400 years Antiquity; argent: a

Cheveron gules with three Scorpions sable." What would not Mr Masters have said of the Scorpions?

The MSS. are still in the British Museum, a quarry for the antiquarian: his annotated copy of Bentley's *Milton* shows a memory of the classics that might have surprised them at King's, and a sensitiveness to the association and the beauty of words a little astonishing in this scholarly crustacean. Walpole's letters to him, all carefully kept, have been used again and again in successive editions of the *Letters*, but the Diary has been left untouched. Young Nichols (of the *Progresses*) had a considerable twinkling respect for the old man, with whom he had begun to correspond the year before his death, and wrote a very tolerable account of him in his *Literary Anecdotes*: but he could not do with the Diary. "Truly laughable," says he; "it is worse than honest Humphrey Wanley's," and proceeds to give examples "*e.g.* Jan. 25, 1766. ' Foggy. My beautiful Parrot died at ten at Night, without knowing the Cause of his Illness, he being very well last Night ' . . ." Nichols misjudged posterity: the accident that happened in the Kitchen to the Parlour Cat moves us as much after a hundred and sixty years as the "inconceivable News" that Mr Wilkes is elected Member for Middlesex. "Time that will make all we now contend for nothing" has a way of dissolving the important and embalming the little. Mr Pitts losing at cards, "horrible black, envious, and out of humour," Dr Pettingal proving by a quotation from Hierocles that the Greeks were fond of Toasted Cheese, Tansley cutting in the Clay Pit Close, very drunk and in his Haytime and Harvest airs, these also have their immortality. And this is perhaps the reason why the diary form has a secret enchantment beyond any narrative: it has the mystery of arrested action. Mr Cole and Mr Cartwright are still dining on a brace of very fine Trout under the Walnut Tree in the Yard, the Hay being then putting on the Cock: February 2nd is still so Summer warm that the Blackbird sung out so as to be heard upstairs before Mr Cole was up: April 1st still has the largest Blow on the Apricot Trees that ever one remembers, it being rainy soft Weather: and Molly and Catherine Giffard for ever picking Pagles, which are Cowslips, in fields that still are fresh and green, and still are filled with flowers.

So with the *Paris Journal*, though here the interest is more various and the substance more solid, its final charm is not its curious resurrection of pre-Revolution Paris, so that the Paris which we know becomes suddenly ghostly beside it, like the skeleton scaffolding that Mr Cole saw on the high corner roofs of the Louvre: not that he saw the tombs of Adam and Hugh of St. Victor in churches now razed to the ground, and of John Scot the Subtle Doctor and our Countryman Alexander Hales the Irrefragable Doctor, and the gravestones of old canons of Notre Dame ranged against the walls to make room for the new pavement, and the grave of Rabelais, and James II quiet beneath his tattered pall, and just missed seeing those Stuart MSS. of the letters of Mary Queen of Scots and Charles II, whose losing is as tragic a fairy tale as any of that house. It is in its glimpses of himself, from the first page to the last: refusing to go to *The Beggar's Opera* because he must catch the coach at four in the morning: conversing with two young ladies in the Dover coach, of the name of Bannister and Shove, the latter newly married to a tradesman in London: valiant on deck without his greatcoat, and every passenger sick except himself: anxious in bed at Lille, remembering the £40 note in the toe of his boots, gone downstairs to be cleaned, and the loose conversation of the young Player at supper, whom he and the Abbé Maguire had rebuked, "perhaps the first Time that a Popish and Protestant Priest agreed amicably together to preach Morality in the same room": ordering his flowered black velvet waistcoat and his Great Coat of a Pompadour Colour, but not full-trimmed with Buttons, lest he should have to go into mourning for the Dauphin: observing Madame Geoffrin's lack of stays: buying coffee cups and a neat Sugar Dish with Mr Walpole in "a dangerous Shop" in the Rue St. Honoré, where the mistress was as tempting as the China, and might, though almost forty, have played havoc with a younger Man than myself: walking gingerly on the waxed floors of the Palais Royal: or, as on October 31st, "enjoyed myself by not stirring out all Day." A very sober mole going its obscure ways among grave stones and epitaphs, beside Walpole's fire-fly glancing. Yet the one is the complement of the other: and the letters that passed between the oddly assorted pair, of which only Mr Walpole's have so far been published, are the documents of an inveterate friendship.[1] Mr Walpole is never perhaps quite so likeable as when he is writing to Mr Cole. It was to him that he wrote, sharp with anxiety, when he heard a rumour of the death of Mr Gray: to him he pours out his wrath when some one throws a stone at the memory of Sir Robert—"you allow me," says he, "to open my heart to you when it is full." It was Mr Cole

[1] The complete correspondence, as well as the Diaries kept at Bletchley and Waterbeche, will be published later.

who got the story of how *The Castle of Otranto* came to
be written, and Mr Cole for whom Walpole kindled into
that melancholy bale-fire of remembrance, when they
would have him admire newer authors: "Recollect that
I have seen Pope, and lived with Gray." They both perhaps thought too well of each other: Mr Cole, that Mr
Walpole was one of the greatest characters of the age,
and Mr Walpole, that Mr Cole was the only real
philosopher he knew; and when Conway is thought to
be dying, he writes pages to his oldest friend, "you
who are full of nothing but gentle and generous senti-
ments." Diverse as they were in faith and politics, they
never had the shadow of a quarrel. If they could have
fallen out, it might have been over Mr Cole's obstinacy
in refusing to wear the Bootikins that had cured Mr
Walpole's gout: but it was his view that gout was a
poison in one's system, and that to drive it from the
legs might be to send it where it might do more harm.
That Mr Cole loved a little the better of the two is true,
but it is the way of lovers: and it must have been
with a secret warmth of pleasure that he copied Mr
Walpole's last letter of Nov. 6th, 1782, almost as sharp
with anxiety as that long ago letter about Mr Gray.
For though Mr Cole's handwriting had been growing
very shaky, and he has to apologise for failing in some
request because of his "poor shattered head," it was not
till October of 1782 that he had a physician and a surgeon, for the first time in his life, and is a little low. However, in his interest in Dr Lort on the Brink of Matrimony
in Savile Row, and his wrath at the attack upon Tom
Warton and the Bishop of Dromore, he is himself
again: is even contemplating with a wry face com-
mencing author at the age of sixty-eight, in publishing

those 1000 separate papers of the Old Chariot's *Two Hundreds of Bucks* which had hobbled him for the laſt forty years. Walpole clutches at comfort. "The writing is much better than in moſt of your lateſt letters. If your pains were not ceased, you could not have framed your letters so firmly and diſtinctly. I will not say more leſt I should draw you into greater fatigue. Let me have a single line in answer. Yours moſt cordially, H. W." Mr Cole copied that letter, as he had copied every one of Mr Walpole's letters and his own replies for more than twenty years, but the old exactness is wavering. He ſtumbles a little at the signature: the initials are not, as usual, a faithful copy of Horace's own. After that, the page is blank. Whether or not Mr Walpole ever had that single line of reassurance there is no knowing: at any rate, Mr Cole took no copy of it: and on the 13th December he died. In his will he left £10 to buy a black marble slab to cover the grave, in St. John's College Ante-Chapel, of Mr Thomas Baker, over whose MSS. his brother antiquaries ſtill were squabbling, but no man cared for his grave. It was to have Mr Baker's arms upon it, these detailed by Mr Cole, who would truſt that task to no other: but the epitaph to be composed by some better hand, "and no mention of Me in it." His own epitaph he had already written: it implored Chriſt's mercy for a Fellow of the Society of Antiquaries and the chief of sinners.

HELEN WADDELL

A JOURNAL
OF MY JOURNEY TO PARIS
IN THE YEAR 1765

May 9, 1766. Having been twice in my Life in
Flanders & Artois,[1] I had a great Desire to see Paris, &
its Curiosities: that being generally esteemed the Centre
of Taste, Magnificence, Beauty & every Thing that is
polite. However, to be ingenuous, I had another, &
more substantial Reason, than barely to gratify my
Curiosity, in undertaking this Journey; which was this:
As I had Thoughts of retiring from the Care of a Parish
in about 2 years' Time, a Way of Life I never was
calculated for, & which I never relished, I conceived
the Climate of France, with their way of Living, I mean
as to Eatables and Drinkables, would wonderfully
accommodate both my Constitution & Fortune: for as
a more mild & moderate Air would probably agree well
with a Person turned of 50, as the Wine also might be
cordial to that Age,[2] so the boasted Cheapness of that
Country I thought would equally suit my private Fortunes, which would be reduced to a Moiety of what I
was used to live on, when a Parish Priest. On these
Motives I was much disposed to pick out some agreable
Retreat, either in Flanders, Artois, or Normandy, where
I thought I could with Comfort & Satisfaction finish
my earthly Pilgrimage, & yet be near enough my native

[1] In 1736 and 1743.
[2] Though C. was very abstemious; *cf*. p. 166 *infra*.

A

Island, as to be able, if my Relations & Friends would
not come & see me, to cross the Sea, & go to see them:
for to pretend to live in England, upon a Footing one
would chuse, was, by the exorbitant Taxes, continually
encreasing, even in Times of Peace, a Thing almost
impracticable, without running into Debt, for a Person
of a moderate Fortune, & who would do as his Neighbours.[1] These were the principal Considerations of my
Journey to Paris: besides the common ones, of satisfying
one's Curiosity & the Hopes such a Jaunt & so much
Exercise & change of Air, would all contribute to better
a Constitution, rather injured by sitting too much at my
Books & using too little Exercise.

[1]In 1764 C. asked Horace Walpole to look out a residence for him in
France, and H. W. writes in reply: "I am a bad commissioner for search-
ing you out a hermitage . . . and I had much rather find you one in the
neighbourhood of Strawberry". *Letters of Hor. Walpole* (Toynbee), No.
968, July 21, 1764.
    But on March 9, 1765, Walpole warned C. that if he settled in
France, "the King of France is heir to all strangers who die in his
dominions, by what they call the Droit d'Aubaine". (*Ib.* No. 1012.)
C. found this objection fatal to his project.

A DIURNAL OR JOURNAL
OF MY EXPEDITION TO PARIS IN 1765

On *Monday, October* 14, 1765, being a very fine Day, having parted with a Pair of old Coach Horses to my Neighbour Mr Hanmer of Simpson, knowing I should have no great occasion for them 'till towards the following May, I set out from Blecheley in Buckinghamshire, with my faithful Servant Thomas Wood,[1] in my Neighbour Mr Goodwin,[2] Rector of Loughton, his[3] Chaise & Horses, which conducted me as far as Dunstable, to Breakfast, where I easily got a Place in one of the Chester Coaches, in which were 2 Men Passengers, (one the Brother of Mrs Weekes of Fenny-Stratford, who lived, I think, in Warwickshire), & after dining at Markyate Street, arrived in London about 5 o'Clock in the Evening at the *Crane with* 2 *Necks*[4] in Lad Lane, where I took a Place in the Dover Coach for Wednesday: from hence I took a Coach & called on Mr Cartwright, at Mr [James] Rowley's, Linen-Draper in Ludgate Street, & from thence to Mr Roger Mawdsley's, Nephew to my late Brother[5] Mr Hector Mawdsley, in Bishop's Gate Street, where my Sister Catherine Cole was come to meet me, by Appointment, from

[1] Son of the Parish Clerk of Bletchley.
[2] Thos. G., Trin. Coll., Camb., *ob.* 1785.
[3] *I.e.* "Mr G.'s"; C. was fond of this mistaken form of the genitive.
[4] A slip for "The Swan with Two Necks".
[5] Brother-in-law.

3

Hackney: here both she & myself lodged, after supping with Mrs Draper, Sister to Mr Daking, Partner with Mr Mawdsley: they being the most considerable Cheese-Mongers in London, or England: as may be seen in Maitland's Survey of London.[1]

Tuesday, Oct: 15. Fine Day. I breakfasted with my Sister at Mr Draper's, where were his Brother-in-Law Mr Carter Daking, Mr Mawdsley & Mrs Townshend, who came from Hackney to meet me. We all agreed to go together to the Play, " The Beggar's Opera" :[2] but I being to get up by 4 o'Clock next Morning, I afterwards excused myself. Here I gave my Sister a Discharge for the 50 Pounds which Mr Mawdsley was so kind to leave me as a Legacy to buy me Mourning: tho' I took not the Money, but left that in my Sister's Hands to be divided between her & my Sister Jane Cole, at Bath: but as my Sister Catherine was Executrix, with my Brother Dr. Apthorp,[3] it was necessary to give a Receipt, in order to settle her Accounts with my Nephew Newcome of Hackney, who had married my Sister Mawdsley's only Daughter & Heir. From Bishop's Gate Street I went to Mr Cartwright's who changed me a 40 Pound Bank Bill, & also took out the £100 I had in the Funds, & got it changed into Ten Pound Bank Bills, for the convenience of Carriage: we dined together at Mr Rowley's,[4] & after Dinner I took a Coach & called on Father Wyburne the Provincial of

[1]"I applied to Mr Abraham Daking (who undoubtedly is the greatest dealer in Butter and Cheese in the Kingdom, and probably in the Universe)." W. Maitland, *Survey of London,* 1760, vol. ii. 758-9.

[2]At Covent Garden, with Shuter, Beard, and Miss Brent in the principal parts.

[3]Son of C.'s mother by a former marriage.

[4]John R., of Ludgate St.

the English Benedictines, & late Prior of the English
Benedictines at Paris; which Place he was obliged to
quit on Account of his Health: I found him at his House
in New Ormond Street, Bedford Row, & very much out
of order with the Gout: this Gentleman I was recomended to by my Friend Father John Sympson of Lancashire, a Benedictine of the English Priory in Lorain, &
now Chaplain in the Family of my late much honoured
& esteemed Friend George Throckmorton of Weston-
Underwood in Buckinghamshire Esq., eldest Son to
Sir Robert Throckmorton,[1] Baronet. Father Wyburne
was so kind as to write to his House at Paris to supply
me with what money I should have occasion for, & gave
me several useful Hints in Respect to my Journey thro'
France, & Continuance in it. I then called at Mr
Walpole's House in Arlington Street to know if his
Servants had any Letters that I could carry to their
Master at Paris,[2] & took some; & so to Mr Rowley's in
Ludgate Street to drink Tea, where was Mr Harper, a
young Clergyman, whose Father was one of the
Assistants at the British Museum,[3] & who was lately
of Trinity College in Cambridge: I then took leave of
the Company, & went with Mr Nathaniel Cartwright[4]
to my Inn at Lad Lane, where we supped, & I went
early to Bed.

Wednesday, Oct: 16. Fine Day. I set out in the Dover
Coach at 4 o'Clock in the Morning, & breakfasted at
Rochester; but being pressed for Time, had no oppor-

[1]4th Bt., *ob.* 1791; succeeded by his grandson.

[2]Walpole had reached Paris on Sept. 12.

[3]Opened, at Montague House, five years before.

[4]Nathl. and James C. were lace-buyers, who lived alternately at
London and Bletchley.

tunity to give a Peep in to the Cathedral, which seemed to be repairing, by the Scaffolding at the West End. Two young Ladies were set down at Sittingburn of the name of Banister & Shove; the last lately married to a Tradesman[1] in London. I dined at Canterbury & went after Dinner to look into the Cathedral, where the Dean, Dr Friend,[2] was carried in a Sedan Chair in his Surplice & Scarlet Hood up into the Choir, as he was very lame of the Gout. It was a Fair Day at Canterbury, & a great many Stalls were erected in the College Court just before the South Door of the Nave of the Cathedral: they were then going to begin Vespers when I went into the Church: but I had no Time to stay, but getting into the Coach arrived in the Dark at Dover about 7 o'Clock, where I lodged at the *King's Head*, & where a Custom House Officer came & searched my Portmanteaus.

Thursday, Oct: 17. Very fine Day. At 10 o'Clock in the Morning I went aboard the Pacquet Boat, & arrived at Calais in 3 Hours & 4 or 5 Minutes,[3] during which Time every Passenger was sick except myself, it being a rough Sea, tho' an exceeding fine Day: so that I sat upon Deck without my great Coat all the Passage. We had about 20 Passengers, English, French & Germans. After being examined immediately on Landing, before an Officer, (to whom you are carried by a Couple of Soldiers), who only requires Your Name, Business in France & occupation, you are dismissed, & may go where you please; only the Baggage is sent to the Custom House, with your Servant & Porters, to be

[1]A John Shove had a shop in Cannon St.

[2]William Freind, 1715-66. The consistent perversity of C.'s spelling is noticeable, since he always writes "ei" for "ie".

[3]A very quick passage; Gray took 5 hours, with a stiff breeze; see *Letters*, (ed. Tovey), i. 16.

searched for Contraband Goods. As the 2 great Inns at
Calais, the *Lion d'Argent* or Silver Lion, & the *Hôtel
d'Angleterre*, or the English Inn, have Servants ready
on your getting out of the Ship, to conduct you to either
of these Houses, we were at no Loss to find our way to
them: both being on the other side of the Square or
Market Place. I went to the " Silver Lion," as I had
been there several Times before, where I found Mr
Grandsire, the Landlord, just laid up with a broken Leg,
& his Son just married but a few days before: here two
English young Merchants, Brothers, in deep Mourning, who came over in the same Pacquet with me, &
who were going to Paris for about a Fortnight, proposed
to me to dine together: & as they were going Post, &
would be in Paris some 10 Days or a Week before me,
I begged they would take charge of Mr Walpole's
Letters; which they accordingly very safely delivered,
they setting out for Boulogne about 4 o'Clock in the
Afternoon, when I took a Walk to view the Parish
Church of Calais, which is a very large & spatious
Gothic Building, with a Spire & Ornaments on the
Tower: but it was too dark to see the inside perfectly:
tho' I formerly remember to have observed several old
mural Monuments & others, with English Names,
probably of such as were settled there before we lost
that Town in Queen Mary's Reign. Over the Gates of
the Town, carved in Stone, I observed the Arms of
Cardinal de Richelieu, ensigned with his Cardinal's Hat
& ornamented with Marine Ensigns, as the Anchor
&c, he being High Admiral of France. [Arms deline-
ated.]

    Friday, October 18. Fine Day. After Breakfast I hired
a Chaise with a Pair of Horses, & Driver on a Sort of

Box, tho' the Carriage had only 2 Wheels, to carry me
to St Omer for a Guinea or French *Louis d'Or*, which
goes for the same, they giving you 24 Livres, or 4
double Crowns of 6 Livres each, for either of them. I
dined at Ardres, a poor wretched fortified Town, where
all the Neighbourhood was at Mass at the two Churches
on the Market Hill, (one of which was a Conventual
Church), it being St Luke's Day: here I got an indifferent Dinner at a miserable Inn, the best in the Town,
which is about 8 Miles English from Calais, thro' a very
flat & fenny country: from Ardres to St Omer is about
12 Miles, cheifly a low & flat Country: at a little
Village called La Rècousse[1] my old Chaise broke down,
& with Difficulty it was set to Rights to go thro' to St
Omer; so that I gave over all Thoughts of taking it with
me to Lille, as I had agreed with the Man. Near La
Rècousse is a Toll Gate, where the King has some
Officers to search all Passengers for Contraband Goods:
as I knew they only wanted to squeeze something out of
me under a Pretence of looking into my Portmanteaus
for run Goods, & would have been contented to have
let me pass had I given them a Livre, yet I was so
provoked with their Impertinence, (having paid a Livre
or two in coming out of the Gates of Calais for the same
Affair), that I told them I would give them nothing, but
that they were at Liberty to search my Valise: accordingly they set about it, & I had like to have suffered for
my Refusal: for the first Thing they lit upon in opening
my Servant's Portmanteau were a Pair of new Boots
which he had never put on his Legs: these they presently
seized, as pretending no new Goods were suffered to
come into the Kingdom without paying Duty: but I,

[1]Near Tournehem; still a mere hamlet.

resolutely telling them that they might take them at their Peril, as they were the only Boots he had to make use of, after some Altercation, & no Bribe, went off much to their Dissatisfaction. I was set down at the *Poste Royale* at St Omer, a very noble Inn, where I arrived at 3 o'Clock & bespoke my Supper, & discharged my old Coachman, or whatever he called himself: but going to the College of Louis le Grand, formerly belonging to the English Jesuits, but lately bestowed, (since their Expulsion 2 or 3 years ago, when the whole Order of Jesuits was banished France) on the English Secular Priests, for the Education of Youth of our Nation in the Roman Catholic Religion, I was most earnestly pressed by the President, Mr Alban Butler,[1] to whom I had Compliments from Fathers Sympson & Wyburne, to sup with him, as also to take my Lodging there also. I was no ways squeamish about it; tho' perhaps I was the first Clergyman of the Church of England who ever laid in that College: but the President's general Character, & his open unreserved Behaviour, were such as gave me no Reason to distrust his Hospitality & good Will: After shewing me all about this truly royal College, founded or rebuilt by Lewis XIV for the English Jesuits, & nobly seated in the middle of the Cheif Street, about mid way between the Cathedral & St Bertin's Abbey, with a magnificent Front of Stone, (as are all the Buildings I saw in France, except a very few of Brick), with their Chapel, which is small, & not at all equal to the Rest of the Building, in the middle of which was lately deposited, & covered by a white Marble, an English Priest of the Name of

[1] 1711-73; author of *The Lives of the . . . Principal Saints* (1756-9); chaplain to the Duke of Norfolk.

Wilson, as well as I remember, for I would not presume
to take Notes either here, or any where else in France,
where the Churches, open all Day, have always People
in them at their Devotions; after shewing me every
Thing curious in his College, which I had indeed seen
twice before, while the Jesuits were Masters there, the
President walked out with me to see the most noble &
venerable Abbey of St Bertin, a short Account of which
is in my vol: 2. p. 93.[1] of these Collections, taken when
I was here in the year 1743. We examined at our Ease
the rich Altar of pure Gold & Silver; the Images in
Miniature, tho' antique, are exceedingly well executed
both in the Drapery & every other Part: the Treasury
was open, which we also examined, there being 2 or 3
Gentlemen & Ladies, with 2 or 3 Nuns, or Beguin[e]s,[2]
also, looking at the venerable & rich Contents of it.
From this superb & elegant Gothic Church, built by the
English in Henry VIth's Time, or thereabouts, we
walked by the English College, up a rising Part of the
City, to see the Cathedral Church, but that being shut
up, & it being also rather darkish, I would not give Mr
Butler the Trouble of having it opened, as I had formerly seen in it more than once; the last Time 22 years
ago [Arms depicted.] The See was then vacant, the late
Bishop bearing an excellent Character, & much beloved
in his Diocese for vigourously opposing some late
Endeavours of inclosing what was used to be open and
common. The Pile is very large & in a much heavier
stile than the Church of St Bertin's Abbey. When we
came back we sat in the Parlour, a very elegant square

[1]*Add. MSS.* 5803, p. 91.

[2]A semi-monastic sisterhood, bound by no vows, but devoted to works
of charity.

Room, (handsomely wainscoted, with a fine Marble
Chimney Peice), in which hung the Pictures of Lewis
XIV, King James II & his Queen, & other Portraits,
the lofty Ceiling being ornamented with Crowns &
Cyphers of their Names. It being a Fish Day, we had a
very elegant Supper of Fish, Omelette, Sallads & other
Things of that Sort in the same Room, where 3 young
English Priests, whose Names I don't recollect, Sir
Piers Mostyn,[1] Baronet, a young Gentleman of about
17 or 18 years of Age, thin & seemingly not very
healthful, who was there for his Education, & a thin tall
Gentleman of Durham, who had lost one Eye, of the
Age of between 30 & 40, as I judged, & a great Talker,
but whose Name I heard not, supped & spent the
Evening with us. There was also an Irish Priest, who
was called in a Certificate I saw in his Hand, the Abbé
Morison, who that Day brought from Lisbon 2 Young
English Merchant's Sons to be put under the Care of
Mr Butler. I was very hospitably & agreably entertained, & slept in a very neat & pretty Apartment,
purposely kept for Strangers: my Servant also lodged in
the College, the Servants of which undertook to get me
a Place in the Lille Diligence for the Morrow: as it set
out by 4 in the Morning, I took Leave of the President
& the other Gentlemen by about 10 that Evening, with
many Acknowledgements of their kind & civil Treatment. Mr Butler had shewed me his private Apartment,
formerly belonging to the Rector of the College, in
which I observed a great many Prints of our Antiquary
Society, & others of that Sort, which indeed determined
me to call upon him, having heard, as well as observed
from his Writings, that he had a good Turn for Anti-

[1]1749-1823; 6th Bt., of Talacre (Flint); properly "Pyers" M.

quity; he also shewed me his private Library belonging to himself, where he had many curious MSS. & a good Collection of choice Books in the historical way: & as he told me he had been collecting materials towards a Life of that worthy Bp of Rochester, Cardinal[1] John Fisher, I made him an offer of such Notes as I had by me relating to him ; which I since sent to him: but I much doubt whether he will have the Courage to print a Life of that excellent Person, since even Mr Butler himself, an harmless & inoffensive Man, & who could give no Umbrage in Respect to the Disputes relating to Mr Phillips's late Life of Cardinal Pole,[2] yet could not escape the abusive Pens of your Neve's, Ridley's, Pye's, Stone's & Critical Reviewers. merely for Mr Phillips's having somewhere in that Life, spoken of him with Esteem, as a learned Man & his Freind. But as I have said a great Deal of Mr Butler in my Vol. 25. p. 16, &c,[3] I shall say no more here. The City of St Omer is large, well built with Stone, Streets large, well paved & clean, but there does not seem to be any great Traffick in it. The first Time I ever came to this City in the year 17—, as a Jaunt of Pleasure, with my Brother Stephen Apthorp, then Fellow of King's College in Cambridge, & now of Eton College, near Windsor, & D.D. I hired a Servant at St. Omer to go back with me to College, one Bernard Dessonville, a quiet honest young Man; for whom I made much Enquiry when I was here, but could hear no news of him: he quitted my Service on Account of his utter Inability to learn the English Language.

[1]But he never wore the hat sent him by the Pope, for, in fulfilment of Henry's bitter jest, he had no head to wear it on when it arrived.

[2]*The History of the Life of Reginald Pole*, Oxford, 1764, 4to.

[3]*Add. MSS.* 5826 and 6400.

Saturday, Oct: 19. Fine Day. I set out from St Omer
in the *Diligence*, or Stage Coach, with 9 other Persons in
it, my Servant included, at 4 in the Morning, & got to
Lille by about 6 at Night. There were 2 or 3 Abbé's or
Secular Clergymen in it, the Rest seemed Tradesmen
& a Couple of Women. We dined at Béthune, as well
as I can remember, & stop'd in the Afternoon at a little
low Place called La Bassée, all thro' a marshy flat
Country. Mr Morison, who had Business at Lille, was
one of the Company, & by his Recommendation I went
to an Inn, in a Street which was open to the Grande
Place, called the *Nouveau Monde*; which altho' no very
elegant or showy Inn, was a very clean one, & both
Master & Mistress very obliging. An odd Accident
happened to me here, which gave me for a Time much
Uneasiness: for the Abbé Morison & myself supping
together in the common Dining Room, two young
Players of Lyons seated themselves at Table with us, &
as they were lively & chearful in their Conversation,
their Company was entertaining enough; bating that
towards the latter End of the Evening, one of them, a
very handsome young Fellow, began to talk very loosely,
& gave us such an Account of his abandoned & leud
way of Life, in which he seemed to glory & take Pride,
that both the Abbé & myself were much scandalized at
it & took the Liberty very seriously to point out to him
the wretched & miserable way of Life he was then
engaged in, & the shocking consequences, both in this
& another Life, that would certainly attend his Continuance in it. Perhaps it was the first Time that a
Popish & Protestant Priest agreed amicably together to
preach Morality in the same Room. The Scene was so
striking, that the young Comedian, for he was well

ascertained of both our Characters, could not help remarking the Singularity of it, by observing, That how well soever both of us might mean for his Advantage, yet he was only the more confirmed in his own way of Life, in persuing[1] Pleasure wherever it was to be met with, as the Doctrines of Protestantism & Popery were so discordant & damnatory one to the other, as made indifferent People suspect that there was nothing in either of them. This was the first Sample that I met with of that general Spirit of Infidelity & Scepticism so prevalent thro'out France. When I was got into my Bed Chamber a Servant of the House pulled off my Boots, & I got into Bed: but awaking at 4 in the Morning, I recollected that by way of Security, I had put my 100 Pound in Bank Notes at the Bottom of one of my Boots, & being uncertain whether the Servant had taken them down Stairs, or left them in the Chamber with me, made me so uneasy that I could not rest 'till I had got up, & called my Servant, who lay just by my Chamber, to be satisfied about it, (for it was too dark to see any Thing in the Chamber), & when he assured me, that the Servant had taken them down Stairs, I began to think my 100 Pound in a very bad Situation; especially if they should have been dropped out of the Boot on the Staircase, & picked up by either of these Players, who lodged in the House: which was by no means an improbable Supposition. However I had no Remedy but Patience, & to stay 'till Day Light appeared; which was to me a very irksome Hour: for I did not chuse, on many Accounts, to disturb the Family upon this Accident: but had I lost my Bills, [I] was determined to have said nothing about them, & made the best of my

[1]A spelling adopted by Johnson in *Rasselas*, xxx.

way back into England; having still in my Pocket above 40 Pounds: besides that the Count de Vignacourt,[1] a Flemish Nobleman, laid in the next Room to me, whom I was unwilling to disturb. I laid till 5 o'Clock, when Day began to appear, & then sent my trusty Servant down Stairs, to see what Discoveries he could make; who, by his quick & sudden Appearance gave me no small Hopes that all was well. Accordingly he found my Boots cleaned, & set, by the Servant, in a Manger, in the Court Yard, close at the Foot of the Stairs, & with my Notes safe in the Foot of one of them; [the boots] being left there by the Servant in order to bring them up in the Morning, having cleaned them at Night. The Escape was extraordinary, & much pleased was I at it. Had the Servant in cleaning the Boots either felt the Paper at the Bottom, or let them fall out in tumbling them about, the Temptation of so much Money would probably have got the better of his Integrity; as Notes on the Bank of England are changeable any where, & no where sooner than at Lille: but I thought myself in much more Danger had they fallen into the Hands of my young Comedian.

Sunday, Oct: 20. Fine Day. The Abbé Maguire, an Irish Clergyman, [had] settled at Lille, where formerly my Neighbour at Blecheley, Mr Richard Cartwright, being in some Difficulties in Regard to his Lace Trade, & being assisted in the same by this Abbé, (who was Interpreter for him, Mr Cartwright not speaking French), my said Neighbour was so grateful for the Obligation, that he sent over one of his Nephews, my Neighbour Mr Nathaniel Cartwright, to be educated

[1]Presumably Adrien de la Vienville, Comte de Vignacourt, novelist, *ob.* 1774.

under him in every Thing but Religion. On my leaving
Blecheley Mr N. Cartwright desired me, if I went to
Lille, to call & see Mr Maguire: accordingly I sent to
him as soon as I got to my Inn; but he sent an Excuse,
as he was an old Man, & did not chuse to come out so
late. When he called upon me at 9 this Morning, he
made an hundred Scruples of coming into the Inn, as
the Bp of the Diocese had published an *Ordonnance*,
that no Clergyman should go, on any Account, into
public Houses, within such a Distance of their Place of
Residence, except on a Journey. I sent therefore for a
Coach, & went with him to see the Churches of St
Peter, St Saviour, & two other large & beautiful
Churches, where they were all at their Devotions. As I
could not persuade the scrupulous Abbé to dine with
me at the Inn, he called upon me after Dinner, &
taking a Coach, we went to the abovesaid Churches, &
then to a Place of public Resort called the *Ramponneau*,
where was a public Garden & fine walks at the Extremity of the Town, with a Chocolate & Coffee House,
where the Abbé would not be persuaded to sit down &
drink a Dish of Chocolate, 'till the Waiter assured him,
that many of the Clergy frequently did the same. In a
Range of Apartments above the Coffee Rooms, where
were Assemblies for Cards, was a large & curious
Collection of Curiosities, natural & artificial, in every
kind: this I went up with the Abbé to look over; &
afterwards to a Banker's, one Monsieur Rousse, who
changed me 20 Guineas into so many *Louis d'Or's*.
From hence I went with him to his own Lodgings, at
one Mr Launoy's in the Marché au Verjois, to drink a
Glass of Wine with him: his Landlord, poor Man,
seemed to be in a dying Condition. As the Abbé would

not accompany me to the Comedy, I was forced to go there by myself; but was little entertained, as I could not enter into the Spirit of the Performance. When I came Home, I found the Abbé Morison[1] at Supper with the two Players, to whom I joyned myself, & we spent the Evening very agreably together.

Monday, Oct: 21. Some small Rain all the Day. Messieurs Maguire & Morison after Breakfast at the Inn accompanied me in a Coach to the Water Side, where I got into the Passage Boat for Douay: it was a large unweildly Vessel, but perfectly commodious. There were aboard 3 Capuchin Friers, several Abbés & many Trades-People bound for Douay. The Passage was slow & unlively, as the River was without any Stream or Current, & thro' a very wretched Flat, low, & fenny Country. I dined on Board, the Dinner being provided by the *Patron*[2] of the Vessel: but I dined by myself, as every Passenger had brought his own cold Provision & Bottle of Wine in his Bag, or *Sac de Nuit.* We saw several Hares by the Side of the River, & the *Patron* of the Barque shot one from on Board, as also several Fen Birds peculiar to that Country: at least I never had seen any like them. It was quite dark, near 7 o'Clock, when we landed at Douay, & being recommended to the *Croix de Bourgogne*, I found it a quiet & still Inn, tho' not much frequented.

Tuesday, Oct: 22. Fine weather. After Breakfast I went to see the large Church of St James, which is not near so elegant as that of St Peter,[3] tho' a spatious & handsome Building: on the North Side of it is the grand & elegant front of the English College for Secular Priests: it is a large & modern Range of Building of

[1]Moryson (MS.).   [2]Master.   [3]At Lille, presumably.

B

good Stone: the Inside Courts of the College are very
poor & mean, & some much decayed. I was recommended to the President of the College, Dr Green, a
large & oldish Man, much afflicted with the Gout, who,
as he could not shew me about himself, turned me over
to one Mr Gibson, Professor of Theology in the College,
who shewed me almost every Apartment in the College:
the Chapel was neat & small: the Tabernacle on the
Altar was made at London by one Mr Lovet, consisting
of white Marble with Pillars of *Giallo antico*:[1] their
Gardens were commodious, full of Fruit & Legumes,
but by no means handsome: the Parlour where the
President received me, was an handsome Room, with
the Pictures of Cardinal Howard,[2] Bp Gifford[3] &
several modern Bps of the Church of Rome of English
Parentage. The President did not seem to me to be a
man of much Address, or Behaviour, & was very well
represented by Mr Gibson, who had no great matter to
say for himself. While I was there the Students were all
very busily employed in taking down & brushing their
Books & Shelves in their Library; which was a very
elegant Room. The President was so obliging as to send
a Servant of the College with me to shew me the way to
the Convent of English Benedictines, whither I was
recomended by Mrs Throckmorton to see her 3 Sons,
who were all sent to me by the Prior's Order to his
Apartment: I found them all very well, & much grown.
The Prior, (brother to Sir John More, of Berkshire,
Baronet), was a very large tall black Man, had lately

[1]A richly coloured marble, found only among Roman ruins.

[2]Probably Philip Thomas H. (1629-94).

[3]Bonaventure Giffard (1642-1734); for a few months President of
Magdalen Coll., Oxford; he bequeathed his heart to Douay College.

been in England to attend a Chapter of his Order, &
having had a very bad Passage over, in which he was
very sick, had hardly recovered himself when I was with
him. He was very civil, pressed me to dine in the
Convent, tho' he was obliged to go out to Dinner on
some particular occasion: he seemed to be about 50
years of Age, a man of no striking Address or Behaviour,
but rather of a rough & clownish Carriage. The Church
belonging to the Convent, stands by the River, & is a
very elegant Pile of Building in the modern stile, with
2 Ranges of high Pillars to support the Roof: the High
Altar is not yet rebuilt, it being lately removed into the
middle of the Church, & the Stalls & choir of the
Religious placed in its Room quite up to the East End
of the Choir: their present Altar in the middle of the
Church being an ordinary extempory one, 'till a grander
can be finished, which is in Hand: so that the Choir will
then be behind the Altar: this Taste & Fashion is now
very prevalent in France, where the Altars are removed
into the Middle of the Church, from the East End, to
imitate the Position of the High Altar of St Peter's
Church at Rome, which is so placed. As this is the
Practice of the Church of Rome, unhappily for the
Presbyterians, their old objections about the Popery of
the Church of England in placing their Communion
Table Altar-Fashion, against the East Wall of the
Choir, are no more: & if it was worth while to retaliate
so ridiculous an Argument, against so perverse a Sect,
one might observe, that their Table in the middle of
their Meetings, if it is so placed, is more consonant to
the Popish Church than our own. My Freind the late
Mr Throckmorton's 3 Sons were all dressed in close
black Cassocks, being the common Habit of Students:

being a very modest, decent & becoming Dress. Here I
sent for a Coach, not knowing that they plyed about
the Streets of Douay before, or should have had one at
my first going out in the Morning, to conduct me to the
English Franciscans, which was not far off. The Father
Gardien[1] was one of the most lively chatty Men I have
met with, extremely polite & well bred, & most extraordinary obliging: his Name was Cock or Cox, a well
looking Man, about the Middle size, plump & jolly &
seemed to me about 40 years of Age: he had been
Chaplain in Sir Harry Inglefeild's[2] Family in Berkshire,
one of whose Brothers, a Frier of this Convent, who was
Chaplain in Mr Paston's Family in Gloucestershire,
(Father to Mrs Throckmorton, as she informed me,
since my Return), is going to end his Days in his own
Convent, having been in so declining a way for so long
a Time, & now despairing of any Releif on this Side of
the Grave, that he is determined to seek it only in
Religion among his own Brethren. With the *Gardien*
was also another Frier, aged 40 years, as he told me
himself, who had taught Theology 15 years in the
Convent, & was a very well looking Man & very civil
& obliging: I think his Name was Jennings, & that he
was a Londoner. It was on my Friend Brother Charles
Bonaventure Bedingfeild's Account, that I visited this
Convent, he having been formerly a *Recollet*[3] Frier
therein, & now Chaplain in Mrs Markham's Family,
& now settled with her at Somerby Hall in Lincolnshire, near Grantham, but about six years ago removed
to that Place from my Parish of Blecheley, where they

[1] The Superior.

[2] Sir Henry Englefield, 6th Bt., of White Knights (Berks); *ob.* 1780.

[3] Follower of an especially strict rule.

resided many years. I am sorry I did not recollect, when
I was in the Convent, that there was a young Lad, a
Student therein, one Charles Simpson, of Lincolnshire,
a Godson of Mrs Markham, & her Servant, tho' very
young, when she lived at Blecheley, & a great Acquaintance & Playfellow of my Servant. This Lad's Father
was a Carpenter, as I have heard Mrs Markham say, &
that as she had a Value for the Family, which was
numerous & poor, she was at the Expence of his
Education, sent him to a Dame's Schole at Blecheley,
(where I suppose he was also further instructed by Mr
Bedingfeild), & then sent him over to Douay, in order
for the Mission. About 4 years ago Mrs Markham sent
to Mrs Page, Grandmother to my Servant Tho: Wood,
& Tenant of a Farm of near 100 Pounds per an. under
Mr Willis, to send her Grandson James Wood, (then &
before & now living with me also, & at that Time about
8 years of Age), to her, to live with her a few years, &
then to be disposed of in the same way.[1] Mrs Page
shewed me the Letter, to consult with me what to do in
it : I told her, I was sorry that she had applied to me, as I
could only give her Advice, as I was Parson of the
Parish, not to let him go to be bred up an idolatrous
Popish Priest, but that I must needs tell her, that had I
not stood in that Capacity, I did not know how she
could dispose of him better : especially as the Father,
who had 8 young Children, & might have more, had no
Place to stow them & himself & Wife, but in her
House : besides that his being so drunken, there was no
great Probability, (now he was Bankrupt in his little
Shop in the Parish), that he would ever be able to
provide in the least for them. I suppose Mrs Page was

[1]Sentence rearranged.

disposed to have sent him, had not the Father, Wm
Wood, an honest quiet Man, (whom I made Clerk of
the Parish out of Compassion to his Circumstances,
when the old one was sent to Aylesbury Gaol for a
Robbery, & whom I did not then know to be half so
sottish as he appeared to be afterwards), been utterly
against His Son's being brought up a Roman Catholic:
for that, it seems, was a necessary Condition of his going
to serve her: & tho' this Wm Wood, whom Mr
Thomas Willis, Son to Mr Browne Willis, brought out
of Lancashire with him, as his Foot Boy, & [who was]
somewhat related to the Family of his Wife, (of the
Name of Hulme, whom he married in that Country),
while Mrs Markham lived in the Parish, & bought
most of her Goods in his Shop, before he broke, was
willing that his 2nd Son Thomas, now my Servant, as
he has been these 8 Years, should have served her in the
same Capacity, & under the same Conditions, as he has
since told me, had it not been for his Wife, Mrs Page's
Daughter; yet the same Wm Wood, now Clerk of the
Parish, & so belonging to the Church, tho' ten Times
more drunken than ever, had Scruples of Conscience
about his Son's Future well-being. So inconsistent, so
contradictory are our Actings at various Times, even in
the highest to the very lowest Situation in Life! But to
return from this long Digression. The well-bred & easy
Father *Gardien* shewed me all about his Convent, which
seemed to be small & confined, & nothing worthy to be
remarked in it: tho' they were then altering & fitting up
a very neat & elegant Parlour or Common Room, tho'
small, in the English Fashion, with a neat Ceiling of
Stucko: for the French Ceilings are rarely any Thing
besides plain Rafters: but however deficient in Point of

Ornament their Convent might be, it was amply made
Amends for by the Beauty and Elegance of their
Church, which was entirely built for them by the
Charity & Bounty of Sir Henry Fletcher, Baronet,
Grandson of that Sir Henry Fletcher of Hutton in the
Forest, in Cumberland, Baronet, (as I suppose), who
was created a Baronet in 1638, (as I also guess), by King
Charles the first, whose eldest Daughter Barbara, was
the Wife of Daniel Fleming of Rydal Hall in Westmor-
land, Esqr; which Sir Henry the elder, being a Colonel
in the Service of King Charles I, engaged so heartily &
valiantly in his Service, as he raised a Regiment of Foot
for his Majesty, & assisted in the Defence of Carlisle,
during the whole Time of that memorable Seige; & was
afterwards slain, with many other noble & loyal Persons,
on the King's Side, in the Battle of Rowton-Heath,[1]
within 2 Miles of Chester, 24 Sept: 1645; *v.* Gwillim's
Display, p. 429, Edit: 1724. His Grandson, (as I conceive), the younger Sir Henry Fletcher,[2] was educated a
Member of the Church of England, & lived many years
in that Profession: but at length becoming a Catholic,
he left England, & retired to Douay, where he fitted up
for himself a small Apartment, adjoyning to this
Convent, where he died May 19, 1712, in the 54th year
of his Age, & lies buried on the North Side of the Choir
before the High Altar, having an handsome mural
Monument of Marble against the North wall, just above
where he lies buried. The Guardian showed me the
Windows of a little Apartment, just above the Organs
at the West End of the Church, (which were large &
handsome), where Sir Henry used to live, after he had
built the Church, which is elegant & moderately large,

[1]Routon-Heath (MS.).   [2]3rd, and last, Bt.

with 2 Ranges of Pillars to support the Roof of the
Nave; at the East End of each Ile is a neat Altar. The
High Altar is very elegant, ascended by Steps, & the
Sanctuary, which encloses a good Part of the Choir, or
all of it, [is] surrounded with an elegant Ballustrade of
Marble about 3 Feet high, the Top of which is entirely
covered with Brass: on each Side of the Altar are 2
capital large Pictures, covered with Curtains to preserve
them, & just above the Altar is a large opening in the
Wall, thro' which you discover a large Crucifix behind
it, which stands in the middle of the Friers' Choir,
behind the Altar, & to which you ascend by 20 or more
Steps, & where they chant their Service: This Contrivance has a very good Effect, especially from the Bottom
of the Church, where the Crucifix is seen to great Advantage. In every Window of the Church are the Arms,
painted on Glass, of Sir Henry Fletcher [Arms
described]. One of the Friers shewed me in the Vestry,
an *Antependium* or Fore-Front of an Altar, made of a
Petticoat of Queen Elizabeth, which was just finished
by one of her Ladies at her Death, & never used: it was
richly worked in Gold & Silver. The Guardian much
pressed me to take my Dinner at the Convent; but as I
was to go to Cambray that Afternoon, & it was 12
o'Clock when I was with them, & knew not which way
I was to get thither, I took Leave of their Reverences,
with many Thanks for their civil & very obliging
Behaviour: which I took the more notice of, as it was
least to be expected from religious Men of their
abstracted & retired way of Life: besides that the
Character of that Order, as it is generally talked of in
the World, gives no great Prejudice in Favour of their
Politeness. But there are exceptions to all Rules: besides

that the World is now got so infidel, sceptical, conceited
& puffed up with Maxims little in Favour of Monkery
of any Sort, & of Recluseness of any Kind, that even
the Common Duties of Christianity in the ordinary way
bid fair to be soon thrown aside: so that it is no wonder
that the old fashioned & antiquated Rules & Garbs of
St Francis, St Dominic or St Benedict are lightly
esteemed, when even Christianity itself is in so great
Danger of being thrown out of Doors, by the zealous
Endeavours of such Preachers in France as Voltaire,
Rousseau & D'Alembert, who are now retailing to the
French the Doctrines of our Apostles, Shaft[e]sbury,
Hobbes, Tindal,[1] Toland, Collins,[2] Morgan[3] & Boling-
broke:[4] & by what I could observe, by the little & few
Opportunities I had of conversing with them, the Soil
seems by no means ungrateful to such Cultivation.

From the *Recollets'* Convent I went in a Coach to an
excellent Inn on the Market Place, or *Grande Place*, a
Square very spatious & well built, where I got an excellent Dinner, & at one o'Clock got into the Diligence,
which was going from that House to Cambray, in
which were only 2 young Men of that Country, & got
to Cambray by 6 o'Clock: but it was too dark, tho' a very
fine Moon, to see the City to any Purpose, which is
built on rising Ground: however I walked across the
Grand Place or Market Hill to give a Look at the
venerable large Gothic Cathedral, by which stood the
Arch-Bishop's Palace: but as the Church Doors were

[1]Matthew T. (1657-1733); author of *Christianity as Old as the
Creation*, 1730.

[2]Anthony C. (1676-1729); author of *Discourse of Freethinking*, etc.

[3]Thomas M. (*ob.* 1743); deist and pamphleteer.

[4]Bullingbrook [MS.].

shut, I had no opportunity of seeing the Inside of the Cathedral, so returned to my Inn, where I supped with about 15 or 16 French People, most of which were to go with me to Paris to Morrow: however there was one very civil Gentleman, whom I had met at Mr Rouci's[1] the Banqu[i]er at Lille, & his Brother-in-Law. who reconnoitred[2] me, but was unfortunately going another Route. Among others of the company that was to go to Paris with me, were: 1st, The Count de Mornay, Knight of the Order of St Louis, a well-behaved, well-looking Man of about 50 & 60 years of Age: 2nd, The Chevalier Pomeroy, a blustering & hectoring Officer, & Knight of St Louis, who was going to Strasbourgh, & came from Dunkirke: he seemed to be aged between 40 & 50, & could hardly be civil, so great was his Choler against the English: 3rd, A young Merchant of Holland, named Moliere, going to Paris for a Week or two; his Mother being a Parisian: 4th, Mons. Theodore Eynhouts, of Eyndhoven in Holland originally, but long settled at Paris, where he married a Parisian: he was Cousin to Mr Van Mouselle of Antwerp, whom I have seen at Mr Cartwright's at Blecheley, he dealing with him for Thread & Lace; Mr Theodore was a vast large & corpulent Man, a great Smoaker, & probably by his Colour, as great a Drinker: [5th, Mons.] Bertrand, a Lace Merchant at Paris of about 60 years of Age, who lived, as well as Mr Theodore Eynhouts, in the Rue de Bussy at Paris, & both dealt in the same Commodity, *viz:* Linen, Lace &c: 6th, A lively talkative little Man of Auvergne, a Tradesman seemingly, whose Name I heard not: 7th, a Jew of Leghorn: an 8th Person whom I have forgot, & myself made the

[1]Rousse, p. 16.   [2]"Recognized".

9th, for Tom & Captain Pomeroy's Servant rode on the *Imperiale*, as they called the Top of this great lumbering Coach, which was to hold 10 Persons, but which was sufficiently crowded with 8 or 9. On the Top of this great awkward Machine was laid Straw for them to lie on: it had no Coach Box, but 2 Postilions rode upon 2 of the 8 Horses that drawed[1] it, which were often changed, & considering the Clumsiness & Weight of the Carriage, with its Contents, went at a very tolerable good Rate, as it was a good paved way the whole Route. At Supper the French all talked very freely, loosely & licenciously, both of their Religion & Clergy: abused the Jesuits, for whom nothing was too bad, & seemed to think that their Banishment was only a Prelude to that of the other religious Orders: & as their Abuse of the Clergy was exorbitant, so their Commendations & Panegyrics of Voltaire & Rousseau were in the highest strain. For my Part I was only a silent Observer: for as the French did us then the Honour heartily to envy & hate us, so one of that Nation, which had so lately mauled them in allmost every Quarter of the Globe, could not expect to be much caressed by them: & this I must needs say, that, notwithstanding all their boasted Politeness & good Manners to Strangers, during the whole Time I had any Opportunity to experience it, I never could see the least Advance or civil & obliging Behaviour of that Sort: but rather the Reverse, in a stiff & reserved Distance of any civil Communication. Perhaps I may have given the Reason of it already: & perhaps my Character of an English Clergyman, (which, tho' I never declared, yet never took the least Pains to disguise, going without Ruffles, & in every Part of my

[3]A recorded form (*O.E.D.*).

Dress, as if I was travelling in England), might occasion the Shyness I have observed: but methinks, considering how loosely any Sort of Religion sat upon them, this ought not to have been regarded. That I was taken for a Priest is most certain, as the Count de Mornay the Evening I met him at Cambray, on sitting down to Supper, addressed himself to me, by the name of Monsieur l'Abbé, as did several other People at Paris & elsewhere: but my French Servant I hired at Paris had not been with me 2 Days before he asked if Monsieur was not *un Ministre*; & the French Taylor I employed, upon my desiring the black Coat he was making for me might be quite plain, took the Liberty of asking me the same Question. But I forget my Journal.

Wednesday, Oct: 23. Small Rain all the Day. I got into the Cambray Coach at 5 in the Morning with 7 other Passengers only, & was fortunate enough not to pick up any more on the Road, as the Vehicle was full enough already, & People seemed to be disposed to be sufficiently out of Humour with one another for want of Room, & that they could not contract themselves into a narrower Compass: it was so very troublesome, that I was determined to return in a Post Chaise by myself to avoid the Inconvenience of such a Conveyance; as before the End of the Journey I fully experienced the French *Politesse*: for altho' I was Complaisance itself both in commending their Country, (more than it deserved), & cried up their Wine & Provisions, & said & did every Thing that I thought would flatter their Vanity, & occasion a free Conversation, yet all was thrown away, by their sole Talk among themselves, a contemptuous Reserve in Respect to myself; & tho' they were not absolutely rude, yet the French Officer

could not contain more than once having a malitious
Fling at the English Nation, & at Mr Pitt in particular.
Indeed, when one considers this coolly & without
Passion, one ought to excuse it: for what Liberties do
we not take in our Turn, in both speaking & acting
against the French? This is so true & remarkable, that
I remember the young Player I met with at Lille, had
conceived such a Notion of our Barbarity & shocking
Abhorrence of the French, that he supposed it a Fact
not to be denied, That a Frenchman, known to be such,
in London, could not with safety, & without being
pulled in Peices, or stoned by the Mob, pass the Streets,
or go about his Business. When a People have got such
a Notion among them, (& it cannot be denied but that
there is too much Truth in it), one cannot with Reason
expect much Advances of Civility from them. As the
Morning did not appear 'till towards 8 o'Clock, & as
the Rain occasioned the Shutters to be drawn up, or the
Leather Curtains to be drawn over them (for there were
both of these Elegancies, & no Glass) I could make no
Judgement of the Face of the Country, except in
General. The whole from Cambray to Paris, & from
thence to Calais, seemed an open Champaign Country,
without much Wood & no Hedges, & had the Appearance of that Kind of Country which is about my Lord
Godolphin's at Gogmagog Hills in Cambridgeshire, &
like many Parts of Hertfordshire adjoyning to Cambridgeshire, as Royston and Baldock, being a chalky
Country thro'out; except when you get nearer Paris,
you pass thro' a fine Wood or Forest, belonging to the
Prince of Condé, called the *Bois de Senlis*. From Cambray to Peronne, where we dined, is the distance of 4
Posts, which, allowing 5 or 6 English Miles to a Post

makes about 24 miles, thro' Bons-Avis, one Post, Fins, a
Post & an half, & from Fins to Peronne a Post & half:
Peronne is a little neat fortified Town, very strongly
situated & defended; & because it has been often
attacked & never taken, they call it Peronne *la Pucelle*,
or the Virgin. The Coach carried us to the Custom
House, where all our Portmanteaus were taken out &
searched, & walking over the Way to the Inn, where
we dined, [we] got into the Coach, after Dinner, at the
Custom House, & travelled that Afternoon as far as
Roye, where we lodged at a very good Inn on the
Market Place. (From Peronne to Marché le Pot is a
Post & half; from thence to Fonches, one Post, & from
Fonches to Roye one more Post; in the whole 3 Posts
& an half, or about 20 Miles). As we got here in very
good Time, I had an Opportunity of walking about the
Town, which is but ordinary, & ill built: it is a small
Town, & was formerly fortified, but now quite dis-
mantled: I walked on the ruined Ramparts, from
whence you discover the neighbouring Country, & the
Gardens below them look very pretty: on the other Side
of the Town, as we entered it from Cambray, there was
lately erected a very superb & large Calvary on the
Ramparts, being our Saviour on the Cross, with the
Ornaments[1] of the Crucifixion about it, & where many
People were at their Devotions. I then went into 2 of
the Churches: that of St Florent's on the Market Hill,
near our Inn, was tolerably large, but very gloomy, &
not handsome or ornamented: the Front of the West
End was in the modern Stile, but nothing elegant: near
this Church stood the Convent of the Minims. St
Peter's Church, nearer the Calvary, was larger & in a

[1]Accessories.

better Stile of Gothic Architecture: it was very dark &
gloomy, occasioned cheifly by the painted Windows,
which were quite perfect & very beautiful: among other
Arms in the Windows I observed those of Half France
impaling Anne de Bretagne. In this Church was a
Funeral going to be solemnized. Here is a great
Stocking Manufacture. I bought a Sample, but it was
not to be compared to our own. We had a very good
Supper, & good Wine, & all the Company, after
sitting together about an Hour, except the Jew, who
always retired to a Room by himself, agreed to go to
Bed early, as we were to arise so soon in the Morning.

Thursday. Oct: 24. Rain. We set out from Roye about
2 o'Clock in the Morning, & made our first Meal, an
early Dinner at Pont St Maixence, which is pleasantly
seated upon the River Oise, over which a large & very
high Bridge[1] carries you into the Town. The River was
full of Boats & Barges with Corn, it being reckoned one
of largest & best Corn Markets in France: the Market
Day is on Friday. (From Roye to Conchy-les-Pots was
a Post & an half; from thence to Cuvilly, one Post;
from Cuvilly to Gournay, one Post; from Gournay to
Bois de Lihen, one Post more; & from Bois de Lihen,
to Pont Saint Maixence, a Post & an half: in all, 7
Posts & an half, about 45 Miles English). From Pont
St Maixence to Senlis was a Post & an half: here we
stop'd, as the Comte de Mornay quitted us at this Place,
which did not seem to be very considerable: the Cathedral Church seemed to be small, & had a Tower, & Sort
of Spire[2] on it, at the West End: but I had no opportunity of getting a Sight of the Inside. The Situation,

[1]Replaced in 1785.
[2]The spire of Senlis Cathedral is, however, renowned for its beauty.

however, was pretty, as it was somewhat elevated, & its
Neighbourhood to the Bois de Senlis, or the Forest of
Senlis, thro' which are many beautiful Ridings & Cuts,
must make it a very agreable Place to live in. Not far
from Senlis we left on our Left Hand a very elegant &
modern built House, in a most wretched, flat & moorish
Country, belonging to Monsieur Villette, round about
which we saw plenty of Pheasants, Partridge & Hares;
which grew more common & plentiful the nearer we
approached the Metropolis. From Senlis to La Chapelle,
was only one Post: from La Chapelle to Louvres, a Post
& a half; from thence to [Le] Bourget, another Post &
half, & from thence to Paris, leaving St Denis on the
right Hand, a *Poste royale* or single Post next the
Metropolis; making in all 6 Posts & an half; about 38
English Miles. So that from Cambray to Paris, according to this my Computation, makes in all about 137
English Miles. We got in to Paris about 7 o'Clock in
the Evening, & were set down at the Custom House or
Bureau de Roi, where my Portmanteaus were again
rummaged over & searched, & where I paid my Fare
for my Passage from Cambray to Paris, for my Self &
Servant; which cost me about 3 Guineas. In the Custom
House Yard, as soon as I had paid, & been dispatched
at the Bureau, I was accosted by a French Valet, who
offered his Services to me: but as I knew nothing of him,
I was desirous to have one recommended to me by the
Person to whose House I was recommended by Mr
Hinde, the Master of St. John's Hospital at Bedford,
who had been at Paris about 3 years before: however,
though I told the Man over & over that I had no Occasion for him, yet he was so officious about me, that I
could not get rid of him; & getting me an Hackney

Coach to carry me to my Lodgings, in the Rue des
Petits Augustins, at the *Hôtel d'Orléans*, in the Fauxbourg St Germain, he jumped up behind the Coach,
where I should not have known that he had been, had
it not happened, that the Portmanteaus being put into
the Coach with me, one of the Doors of the Coach flew
open, & let one of them fall into the Street, & upon my
calling out to the Coachman to stop, he was ready to
pick it up. In short, there was no saying him Nay; for
he would follow me to my Lodgin[g]s, where, finding
it absolutely necessary to have a French Servant, as my
own knew not a word of the Language, I consented,
thro' his Perseverance, to accept of his Service: he was
a Man of about 40 Years of Age, a Burgundian, whose
only Name that I could get from him was La Pierre: it
is probable that he had a Family one, but this, out of
Pride possibly, (for he had no small Share of it, without
a Groat in his Pocket, with a Wife & Children to
maintain), he would not discover. He had served above
20 English Gentlemen, but had not acquired a single
Word of our Language, except the word "Clock," which
he always mistook for a Watch: & I never undeceived
him. I agreed with him to serve me for a Livre per Day,
as Mr Hinde told me he had given no more: yet after he
had been with me 3 Weeks, & I was going to pay him,
he made a Demand for 30 Sous, which is 10 Sous per
Day more than he had agreed for: he asking no more
than 25 Sous per Day, as I well remembered; but upon
my remonstrating that my Friend gave no more than
one Livre, or 20 sous, & that I would give no more, &
he perceiving that I was resolute, he acquiesced in my
Terms: tho', I believe, at an under Rate, being determined to make it up some way or other upon his

c

Knavish Demand, I sent up for the Mistress of my Lodgin[g]s, as it was before her that I made the Stipulation;
but as she either did not, or would not remember any
Thing of it, (there being a Sort of mutual good understanding between these Letters out of Lodgin[g]s &
occasional Servants), & upon my being determined to
have no further Dealings with, & not to give him more
than his original Demand for 25 Sous, except I was
forced to it by the Magistrate, & desiring the Mistress
of the House to get me another Servant, which she
pretended to do, but came & told me that all her
Endeavours were in vain, [and] as the Man made the
most abject Submission & begged my Pardon, offering
to serve me at any Rate rather than be discharged, & as
my Design was not to stay much longer in Paris, I was
contented to let him stay: tho' I had no opinion of him,
nor did I at all like his Drunkeness; which was very
Disagreable, especially when I was out with him, in
looking over Churches & going about the City, (as he
was to go about with me, & to inform me of such
Particulars as I wanted to be informed about.) That this
was no unusual Practice of these French Valets, I had
occasion to be a Judge of, as the Paris Valet, La Jeunesse,
as he called himself, a very clever & creditable Servant,
which my honoured Friend, Mr Horace Walpole,
youngest Son to the first Earl of Orford of that Name,[1]
after some two Months Service with him, gave him to
understand that he expected to be paid in another way
than the usual Rate of Servants. And that Sottishness is
not peculiar to the English Servants, was evident, that
this Servant attending his Master, when he did me the
Honour to take me in his Coach with him to St Denis

[1]The 1st E. of Orford was Edward Russell (1653-1727).

—this Man, as we were walking round the Church &
Convent, would be for ever talking to me, when he had
an Opportunity, & making his Observations: which
he would not [have] presumed to have done, had he
been sober; for he was in general a very well behaved
Man: but I afterwards observed by his Gait & Behaviour that he was quite drunk. I will just set down
another observation to shew how Alert the French are
to take all Opportunities to cheat, & make the most of
the English, (& other Foreigners, no doubt), who come
to make but a short Stay among them. Madame Mean,
the Mistress of the *Hôtel d'Orléans*, with whom I
lodged, after I had been in her House just a Month, on
my sending for her to be paid according to my Agreement, at a Guinea, or *Louis d'Or*, per Week, pretended
that I owed her 5 Louis, tho' I had been there but 4
Weeks; because, said she, when you took the Lodgin[g]s at a *Louis* per Week, you did not stipulate to take
them for a Month; & therefore, according to their
constant Custom, they always charged a Week before
hand: it is probable she might mean, that if I had agreed
to have taken them for a Month, supposing that I had
come the 1st Day of it, yet I should not have paid more
than 4 *Louis*, even if I had staid 'till the last Day, *viz:*
the 30, which is more than 4 weeks, by 2 Days. However, whatever was her Meaning, she was positive in her
Demand; which I finding ridiculous & without Reason
or Foundation, plainly told her, that Paris was the
first Place that ever I heard of, where a Month was
lengthened out to 5 Weeks: which, if it was the constant Practice & Custom, (which however I ought to have
been apprized of at my first taking her Lodgin[g]s), I
would certainly, tho' unwillingly, comply with; but as

I was going out to Dinner, I would inform myself of this Matter, & not pay her 'till I returned. But on her leaving me, finding that I was determined not to be thus imposed upon, & that I should make such enquiries, as would not be much to her Credit, & the Reputation of her House, she soon returned, made an Hundred Apologies for the Mistake she had made, begged my Pardon, hoped that I would not take Notice of it, & desired me to stay in my Lodgin[g]s as long a Time as I pleased, by the Day if I chose it, at the Rate of a Guinea a Week, or 4 Guineas a Month. This Madame Mean was a very well-behaved civil Woman, aged about 50, & very thin; had 2 or 3 Daughters grown up & very well-looking young Women, & 2 Sons, I think, one at Schole, & the other an Apprentice. Her Husband, to whom I was recommended, had been dead about 4 Months, & was a Barber & Perri-Wig Maker of some Reputation. Mrs Mean told me he had left her in but indifferent Circumstances; but as her Parents,[1] who were in good Credit at Paris, were not very helpful to her, what she seemed to dread most was a rupture with England; for her whole Dependance was in letting Lodgin[g]s to them [the English]; & in Case of a War, she should be ruined & undone. The Apartment I chose was up two Pair of Stairs; it consisted of a little Bedchamber for my Servant in the Passage, or little Gallery to my own, where an elegant & lofty Crimson Damask Bed was at the further End, raised on a Step, & floored with Oak, & had an Extempory Partition, if I chose it, to divide it off from the other Part of the Room; which was paved with neat small octagon red Bricks, never washed, but frequently rubbed with a

[1]Relations.

waxed Brush to keep them polished: the common Flooring both above & below Stairs in Paris, & thro'-out all France. The Room was furnished with a Bureau, half a Dozen elegant & sumptuous elbow-Chairs & a Sopha of the same Sort, of the Tapestry of their own Manufacture, a *Cuvette* or flat-bottomed awkward Bason to wash Hands in, with the Fire Furniture, as Shovel, Tongs, & Pair of Dogs to burn Wood on; which with a Towel to wash your Face with, & another for Breakfast, & a miserable little Deal Table, was all the Furniture I found in the Room: the Rest, as a Glass to shave with, Tea Equipage of all Sorts, even to the Kettle to boil the Water in, Glasses to drink out of, &c, I was forced to purchase on the next Morning: together with Tea, Sugar & other Necessaries, which the French Valet was very expert in procuring. The Apartment was beautifully situated just above the Duke de la Rochefaucault's Garden, which was very large & elegant, with a small oval Pond, in which was a single Swan: at the other End was the Duke's Hôtel, a large Range of Buildings, & handsome, according to the Notions of French Architecture, which was not at all suited to my Ideas of it. The Gardens were disposed in Grass Plots, Gravel or Sand Walks, with Trees all round it, whose Heads being cut off & otherwise mutilated,[1] disfigure the Trees, & take away their whole Beauty from them: but this Taste prevails universally thro' the Country. From my Chamber Window I could see, just across the Duke's Gardens & very near me, the beautiful Dome of the *Collège de Quatre Nations*[2] or Cardinal Mazarin's

[1]"Trees cut into fire-shovels and stuck into pedestals of chalk, compose their country" (Walpole to Gray; Nov. 19, 1765).

[2]Now the *Palais de l'Institut*.

College—on the other, or left Hand, the awkward Dome & Part of the Convent of Petits Augustins, & above the Roofs of the Houses, I could easily see, at no very great Distance, the ridiculous Corner Roof of the Louvre, nearest the *Samaritaine* on the Pont-Neuf, of a most preposterous Height, called Roofs *à la Mansarde* :[1] the other Parts of the Roofs of the Louvre & Thuilleries I could also discover from my Window: but this Corner Roof, *à la Mansarde*, was very conspicuous. I suppose they begin to see the Absurdity of such high Roofs, as the other Parts of the Louvre are lately reduced, & this that remains, by the Scaffolding, seems to be condemned. As I could see so many fine Objects, so the Situation was the more agreable to me, as I could hear 3 large Clocks always very distinctly, *viz:* the Mazarin College, the Petits Augustins, & that of St Germains des Près, which was as near me, tho' on the other side. The Duke de la Rochefaucauld suffered a Passage to be made into his Garden for the Duke of Bedford, as there was one already out of Mrs Mean's Court Yard, when that English Duke lodged at her House about 2 or 3 years ago, since he was Embassador in France. The first Floor of this Hôtel was very magnificent, then occupied by Mr Matthews, an English Gentleman; as the Apartment above him, & opposite to mine, was by an Irish Roman Catholic Gentleman, whose Name I have forgot, nor whose Person did I know all the Time I was there: tho' it is probable I saw him several Times, tho' I might know him not. There was a great awkward Country Maid, who came into the Chamber once a Day to bring fresh Water, & empty

[1]From François Mansart (1598-1662), but used in the Louvre as early as 1550.

the Bason, & to make my Servant's Bed: as to mine it
was made by the Porter of the Hotel, La Pierre, a young
stout Savoyard, who wanted very much to get a place in
England, and requested me, if I would not take him
myself, to recommend him to some of my Acquaintance: his Name was Pierre Durand, & came from about
Chamberry :[1] of him I bought my Wood every Morning
as I wanted it: which came to about the same Price was
I to have bought it at Home, it seeming to be about
10d. or 1s. a Hundred of dry Billets; of which I con-
sumed about 5 or 6 Hundred Weight every Week. As
my Stay was so short, I did not think it worth while to
send for a Cart Load to the *Chantier*, or Magazine of
Wood, by the Side of the River, for it. I had most
excellent Butter, fresh every Morning, in 2 or 3 small
Pats, with Cream & French Rolls, from the English
Embassador's *Crémier* or Dairy-Man, & at an easy Rate:
so that I found no Difference here or at Home, in my
Breakfast, except that here the Butter & Bread were
better. As to my other Meals, a *Traiteur*, or Cook, lived
opposite almost to the Hotel, from whence I had any
Thing I had an Inclination for, & in the best Manner:
& a Wine Merchant was near as nigh, from whence I
had such Wines as I chose. I had 3 or four Things from
the *Traiteurs* at about 5 Livres; which was enough for
me & my 2 Servants. Hares, Partridge, Woodcocks, &
Turkeys were in such abundance, as to see the Quantities of them hanging up as one passed along, & in
their Markets, one would think they almost lived on
nothing else. Pheasants were to be had: I cheapened
one near St Thomas de Louvre, which they asked 7
Livres for. As for Woodcocks, it is incredible the

[1]Chambéry (Savoy).

Quantities I every where saw, both at Inns on the Road,
& at Paris: but as it was a remarkable plentiful year for
them in England also, there was no judging of their
Commonness of them in France by this year's Appearance: they were sold at the *Traiteurs* at about 3 Livres
the Brace, & Partridge the same. I had the red-legged
Partridge sometimes, to try the Difference: but could
perceive none in the Taste. Geese in the Markets made
a wretched Appearance, being not half fatted, & black;
indeed it is only the very ordinary People who eat them.
I saw whole strings of Robin-Red-breasts hung up in
the Markets, like Larks, to be sold. There is no want of
Fish of all Sorts in the Fish Markets, both River & Sea
Fish: I had fresh Salmon & Cod-Fish, & saw Pla[i]ce,
Herrings & Soles in Abundance: Pikes, Eels, Carps,
Tench, Perch & other Fish are sold alive & exposed in
the Markets to such as buy them. Beef, Mutton & Veal
I saw as good as need to be in the great *B[o]ucherie* near
the Châtelet: so that there is no more want of the good
Things of this Life, for those that can purchase them,
in this City, than any where else. Their *Poulardes* are
beyond any Thing of the Sort I ever saw: indeed they
ought to be excellent in their Kind considering how
they are sold. I was charged for a single *Poularde* 5
Livres at Versailles: & the Price I observed at the
Traiteurs at Paris was 3 Livres for a Fowl: indeed they
are as much beyond an English Fowl, both in Taste,
Whiteness, Moistness & Fat, as a common Hen is to a
fine Pheasant.   They put no other Sauce to it than
Water-Cresses, which they have all the Winter Months:
& in general they send no Gravy or Sauce up with any
of their Poultry or Game. The Grapes were so incom-
parably good, so sweet, so well ripened, so luscious, with

such a fine Russet Colour on them, as will make me look
with Pity on our best ripened Fruit with us: the Cressan
Pears also had such a Flavour, as was unknown to me
in that Fruit at Home: in short, we have not Sun enough
to give a true Flavour to most of our Fruits: but we
have, thank God, what is much more valuable, a more
beautiful Country, even in Winter, a Climate more
moderate & such a Verdure as is unknown to the very
best spots they have in France. The Wine they cheifly
drink at Paris is Burgundy: that which I drank commonly, mixed with Water, was at 1 Livre 10 Sous per
Bottle, & was exceedingly good: a smaller Wine for my
servant cost 12 Sous the Quart: I gave also for incom-
parable Champaign, sparkling, or as the French call it
Moussir,[1] also for the non-Moussir Champaign, or what
did not sparkle in the Glass, for each, 3 Livres a Bottle:
what we call Claret, or Bourdeaux Wine, I could not
relish at all at Paris: it had quite another Flavour in
England. These were the only Wines I tasted in France,
& were quite sufficient, as nothing could be better to
my Palate. Most excellent Cyder from Normandy, &
the *Cydre d'Issy*, is about a Groat a Bottle; but it is rich,
high-flavoured & admirable. They have Beer in plenty
at Paris, & thro' all the Parts of the Country I passed;
but as I never in my Life could drink any Beer in England, except now & then small Beer, when it is excellent
of the Sort & very fine, so it was impossible to think of
tasting their thick muddy *Bièr[e] de Mars*,[2] or their
White Beer in Flanders, the very look of which is
sufficient to disgust an Englishman; & the Taste, as
they told me, is full as bad as its Looks. The Water of
the River Seine is as thick & muddy as the Channel of

[1]For *mousseux*.   [2]*Cf.* our "October".

the Severne which comes up to Bristol: so that to drink
such Water is not practicable: besides they say it is very
unwholsome, creates Gravel, & is very purgative,
especially to Strangers: so that they carry clear Water
about in Pails & Vessels, & sell it by the Quart or
Gallon, at a very extravagant Price. I have seen People
on the *Pont-Neuf*, with a large Copper Vessel on their
Backs, with a Cock to it, selling drinking Water to the
Passengers. Even the Water they carry about for use in
Meals is supposed not to be very wholsome: at least for
Strangers; who generally in about a Week or 10 Days
after their Arrival at Paris, are troubled with a Dysen-
tery; occasioned probably by the Water, Change of
Climate, & Manner of Living: if Fruit is in Season, a
too great Quantity of it will certainly occasion this
Disorder; & a too free use of Water, without Wine is
not advisable. Notwithstanding the Beastliness & Filth
of the River Water, both Sides of the Seine in the City
of Paris, are covered with large covered Boats, or rather
Water-Houses, in which live all the Washer-Women of
Paris; who hang continually over the Sides of the Boat
& so beat the Linen with flat Peices of Wood to get
them clean; from whence they are sent out to the
neighbouring Feilds to be dried: & this is all the cleaning they have: & their Ironing is full as bad as their
Washing: so that it is no wonder that your Linen comes
back torn to Peices, dirtier than when it first went there,
& just of the nasty dirty yellowish Colour of that beastly
River. It is Pity they should have much good Linen to
spoil: as to their own, it is no great matter what becomes
of it; for it is generally both very coarse & of a bad
Colour. The poor People, I fancy, fare hard enough, &
the better Sort of Tradesmen, I am told, live very

meanly. Bread & Apples, with Fruit, being no uncommon Dinner with them. I saw in the Season I was there,
an enormous Kind of Water Melon, or Pompkin, as
yellow as the yellowest Melon, Rinde & Inside: this the
poor People make Soup of, & otherways dress it for
themselves: I saw it sold in Peices all over the City of
Paris in October & November, but was told it was a very
insipid poor Sort of Fruit. I got some of the large Seeds
of it, & have raised several Plants in my Hot-Bed, (I
write this on May 20, 1766, Whitsun-Tuesday) in
order to see whether they will ripen with us: they are
as big again as the largest Pompkin I ever saw. It is
probable we have not Sun enough to bring it to Perfection.[1] I was told a very singular Thing by the French
King's Gardiner, (a well looking old Man, who has a
Son in England, & is acquainted by Correspondence
with Mr Miller), as I travelled with him in the Coach
from Paris to Versailles, That, notwithstanding the
great advantage they had of a nearer Sun, & warmer
Climate, yet several Things which we have in Perfection, as Winter Sallads & Greens, will not stand or bear
that Season with them: he instanced particularly in
Broccoli, which, he said, always went off after the first
sharp Frost: whereas with us, it is never good 'till after
a good sharp Frost has mellowed it. As to their Trees,
as I before hinted, they are miserable Things for
certain :[2] I don't positively know that I saw, during the
whole Course I travelled thro' France, what may be
called a fine Tree: tho' you travell generally thro' a
Range of them on each Side of the public Roads: they

[1]C., however, was successful in raising them, as he tells us. *Add. MSS.*
5835, 322.
[2]*Cf.* p. 37 n.

are all stunted, starveling Things, of no Size or Beauty:
even those on each Side of the Road from Paris to St
Denys, or from Paris to Versailles, are nothing of Trees:
there were some in the Gardens of the Thuilleries which
were the best I saw there: the other Plantations in Paris,
as before the *Invalides*, & some other public Buildings,
look more like a Plantation of Orange or Lemon Trees,
than a fine & stately Parcel of Oaks, Elms or Ash, such
as we have in Common with us in England: & as these
are the great & natural Ornaments of the Face of a
Country, none can be said to be handsome without them.
When you ask for the Beauties of the Environs of Paris,
they immediately point out to you the miserable, dreary,
barren, sandy & brown Hill of Mont-Martre, with a
great Number of Windmills upon it, to add to its
natural Deformity: it has more the Look & Appearance
of an artificial Hill, raised out of the Dirt & Filth of the
neighbouring City, than of a beautiful rising Ascent,
covered with green Hedges, Grass, fine and stately
Timber, & well cultivated Feilds, & here & there
interspersed with good Houses, & fine Gardens; as
about London, & indeed almost every Part of the
Country in England: on the contrary, this Hill of Mont-
Martre can't be so well compared to any one Thing I
know, as the great Dirt Hills about Pancras or White
Chapel, made from the Filth which is carried out of
London: except that these Dirt Hills have an Advantage,
which never happens to Mont-Martre & its barren Soil,
that they are in a good Measure covered with a fine Coat
of Grass, to hide their original Meanness. Neither are
the Outskirts of Paris worthy to be mentioned, except
to be laughed at. No elegant neat Boxes:[1] no beautiful

[1]Small country-houses.

& pleasant Gardens to divert the Eye of the Passenger, as you meet with in every Outlet for Miles from London: but on the contrary, even on the 2 great & royal Roads from Paris to Versailles & St Denys, the Moment you leave the Metropolis, you meet with, on the St Denys Road, a Village with Houses on each Side for a Mile perhaps, but wretched Stone Buildings, more like Stables, than elegant Retreats, & most of them have more the Appearance of Ruins, than inhabited Houses, as they really are. God Almighty has been in no one Thing more gratious & good, than in thus scattering promiscuously his Favours on all Mankind in just Proportion. What he has denied to one he has made up in another: was France equally happy in every, as in some of its best Endowments, the Rest of the World would be miserable 'till they had got an Establishment therein: I was one who thought a reasonable Settlement there, would be a most desireable Situation: I went there, & was happily undeceived. Hardly a Cow to be seen for Miles, & when you do see them, they are poor starved Creatures, of about half the Size of our own. Yet the People, amidst all their Beggary, Poverty & Misery, seem to be happy & contented. It is incredible how troublesome the Beggars are to you: if you stop in a Coach, or Post Chaise, you have presently 10 or a Dozen about you: if you go into a Church, you are not more quiet; for here even tolerably gentile-dressed People will come, & ask you privately to give them Charity; & the common Beggars at the Church Doors, & in the Church are so tormenting, that was it not for Duty & Curiosity, one would not enter them at all.

The Buildings at Paris, in my Eye, are very mean & contemptible; all built of Stone, & mostly very lofty:

but all the lower Story being for the most Part Ware-Houses, & ordinary Shops, & the Windows of no Symmetry or just Proportion, with bad Glass, altogether have a very mean Appearance. I must except some of the Hôtels of the Nobility, which, however, altho' cheifly situated in good & spatious Court Yards, yet are Constructed in a Taste of Architecture whose Stile I am not enough acquainted with, to be pleased with. The Streets in general are very narrow, & no Place for Foot Passengers, except in a very few, so that they are also very dangerous to walk in; tho' they are well paved: yet most abominably lighted up: perhaps 3 or 4 round Lanthorns of Lead & greenish Glass enlighten one Street, being flung across a Rope which crosses the Street, & so hang in the middle of the Street from the Rope. The 2 or 3 great or principal Streets which cross the City, are barely tolerable for width; as the Rue St Honoré, St Antoine in some Parts of it, & very few others: so that upon the whole, it is one of the most dreary & gloomy Cities I have been in:[1] & was it not for the Prejudice People are in in Respect to Paris, & the Fashion of going so many miles to see it, & Train[2] one is in to call it the Capital of Europe for Beauty & Elegance, I am sure it would be seen in its true & only Light, the Metropolis indeed of a great Kingdom, but a City of no real Beauty to recommend it, except some few artificial Perfections, in a few public Buildings, situated on a dirty nasty Ditch of a River, & in a Country that has nothing remarkable to recommend it, even in a very indifferent Situation. And this is my real, true, faithful & unbiassed Opinion of this much extolled City &

[1]"It is the ugliest beastly town in the universe", Walpole to Gray (Nov. 19, 1765).   [2]Habit.

Mile End Library

Queen Mary, University of London
Reading Week 18th - 24th February

Extended Reading Week loans
One Week Loans borrowed or renewed
from Thursday 14th February
will be due back on Monday 25th February

Borrowed items 26/02/2013 16:21
XXXXXX5092

Item Title	Due Date
Paris : biography of a city	04/03/2013
Death in Venice and other st	04/03/2013
* The great partition : the ma	05/03/2013
* The partition of India	05/03/201

* Indicates items borrowed today
PLEASE NOTE
If you still have overdue books on
you may have more fines to pay
Don't forget to renew your loans
if you are going away for Reading

Country about it. Others may see it in a different Point
of View. I went prejudiced in its Favour: consequently,
with a view to be pleased, had I found it pleasant: on
the contrary, I experienced I had left, in my native
Island, Beauties of every Kind, as much exceeding those
of France, as I can conceive France to exceed Spain, &
its more barren Climate. The price of Hackney Coaches
seemed to me to be no otherwise than at London: and
the whole Equipage, meaning Coachman, Horses,
Machine & Harness much worse: for nothing can be
supposed to be dirtier & more shabby than them all:
indeed they are easier than ours, being hung lower than
ours, & upon Leather in a different Manner, & as their
Streets are so well paved that the uneasy Joltings of
London Streets, which are yet unpaved in the new way,
are not felt here. As squallid & forlorn as these Hackney Coaches are, those belonging to the Nobility &
Gentry, & those also which may be hired by the Week,
Month or longer at Paris, are as splendid, beautiful &
elegant: the Varnish which covers them is beyond any
Thing we have yet been able to find out,[1] & their Taste
in making them, lining them, & otherwise finishing
them is equally inimitable: tho' Mr Pascal, a very
considerable Coach-Maker in the Rue Guenegaud, of
whom I hired my Post Chaise to carry me to Calais, on
leaving Paris, very ingenuously owned to me, that their
Workmanship, was in Reality much inferior to ours in
Point of true Workmanship, & real Strength, as theirs
exceeded ours in Shew & Fashion. They now have left
off putting any Arms on their Equipages, the Pannels
being either painted with Festoons or Groups of

[1] C. took a supply of French varnish back to England, and praises it
in his " Home Journal."

Flowers, or else an uniform plain Colour, as Purple, Green, Blew, Ash-Colour, or the like: but the Varnish that covers them is of a most exquisite Polish. I did not observe that there were any Wherries or small Boats to carry People backwards & forwards on the Seine, to different Parts of the City; but all was a still Scene upon that dirty River, except the cleanly Sight of the Washer Women, with their nasty Shirts, & a large Boat or two plying to carry Passengers across it. The Bridges over the Seine at Paris are about 5 or 6, & nothing remarkable for their Beauty: tho' to hear the Descriptions of the Pont-Neuf, & the Pont-Royal, one would suppose that there were not two such Bridges to be met with any where. The Pont-Neuf is built over a Part of the River where a small Island divides it about the middle; so that it has an Advantage that none of our most noble, truly royal, & excellently constructed Bridges over the Thames at London & Westminster, had in their Formation: they being all founded in the Bed of the River. The Pont-Neuf has about 12 small Arches, & the Pont-Royal, which is the more elegant of the two, has, I think, fewer Arches: the End of it abuts upon the grand Entrance of the Gardens of the Thuilleries. The Horse upon which the Statue of Henry the Great is placed, is a dull heavy Animal, without Life, Spirit or Fire; but the King's Figure & Attitude are admirable.[1] On the same Side of the Bridge with this Equestrian Statue, at the lower End, next the Cheif Front of the Louvre, is another great supposed Ornament of this ordinary Bridge, called the *Samarita[i]ne*;[2] being a small

---

[1]The statue was designed by John of Bologna, the horse being given by Cosmo II, grand Duke of Tuscany.

[2]Erected in 1603, demolished in 1813.

Building, of no Beauty, containing Water works to supply some Part of the City with Water, & because there is a large Clock with Chimes, & before it in Front some Clock-work representing the Story of our Saviour & the Woman of Samaria at the Well, (at which the People stand staring in Admiration, in the same Manner as the Country Bumkins, just come to London, do at the Giants in Guild-Hall, or rather at St Dunstan's Clock in Fleet Street), they call it *La Samarita[i]ne*, & by their Expressions about it, seem to think it a wonderful Matter. The other Bridges are not worth mentioning, one of which, nearest the Pont-Neuf, is built upon, with very high lofty houses, in the same Manner as our London Bridge was before its late ornamenting about 10 years ago, when all the Houses were taken down. How must a vain & fantastical Frenchman be inwardly chagrined, mortified & struck dumb, on taking a Boat on a fine Day & being rowed from Westminster down the River below London Bridge! If such a Sight will not make him blush at his Vanity in supposing Paris the Centre of every Thing great & noble: if Truth will not make him acknowledge the *Petitesse*, the Littleness, the Nothingness of Paris in Respect to the Beauty, Grandeur & Superiority of London, he must be ashamed of nothing; indeed a very Frenchman. At the Foot of these Bridges stand some of the most whimsical Conveyances I ever saw; very little superior to a Wheel-Barrow, supposing it had a Top to it: it is a little, low Sort of dirty Sedan Chair, covered with ordinary black Leather, & being someway placed on two very small Wheels, it is drawn along the Streets by a single Man: I suppose few make Use of them, but Women only. As to the elegant, rich &

D

beautiful Sedan Chairs, such as you see commonly about London, I never saw any of them: what I saw, were miserable dirty, paltry Things, such as a Person of any Fashion would be ashamed to get into at London, with short Poles, I suppose for the Convenience of turning up their narrow Streets, consequently can't be very easy. I make the longer Stay upon these Trifles, to shew that these great Regulators of Europe in Point of Trifles, are even outdone by those they affect to treat with Contempt, & call Savages. I will venture to say, that I will produce as great Instances of Barbarous Cruelty in the French History, as Voltaire has pretended to single out in ours; & thereby to fix the Character of a savage Ferocity on the English. In good Truth, both D'Alembert & Voltaire, notwithstanding their Pretences to Philosophy, can't help shewing their Envy at a Superiority, which they are unwilling to allow: & I wish it does not run thro' the whole People.

The Shops at Paris are the poorest gloomy Dungeons you can possibly conceive, however rich their Contents may be: as the Brillancy & Shew of ours in London make one of its cheif Beauties & Ornaments, so the dead Gloom of the City of Paris is nothing beholden to its Tradesmen in shewing their Goods to the best Advantage: you here & there see a Shew-Glass about the Size & Appearance of what a ragged Jew carries before him, by the Help of a Cord thrown over his Shoulders: and however they may figure away, when they are from Home, & make their Boasting & Vaunting of the Elegance, Beauty & Deliciousness of Paris, a good cleanly English Stomach in passing thro' any of their Streets, at first coming among them, would be apt to convince them of their Nastiness, by not being able,

without being sick, to pass by so much Carrion, hung
up in their Shops, as eatable Victuals. It has been as
much as I could do to forbear putting my Head out at
the Coach Window many a Time in the Streets, the
principal Streets of this Glory of the World, to bring up
the Contents of my Stomach, when I have passed by so
much Liver, Lights & other Offal, cut out in Slices &
sold on small Tables in almost every Street: whether it
is for Dogs, Cats or themselves, it is equally offensive:
the monstrous black Sausages in great Guts, or Blad-
ders, hanging by many of their Shop Windows;
Quantities of Sheep's Heads boiled & partly dried, in
Heaps on Stalls, are all such odious & indelicate sights,
as would turn any other Stomach but that of a Frenchman. All these Delicacies & Elegancies you perpetually
encounter; & while Monsieur le Parisien, & Madame
la Parisienne with their Heads most elegantly *frisez* &
poudrez, & their Tails bedaggled & full of Holes &
all over Rags, cheapen, with a watery Mouth, some of
these *bons Morceaux*, without any Difficulty, where all
Live alike, would perhaps, at a Distance from Home,
equally turn up their Noses at such Rarities & the
Indelicacy of English Roast Beef. Poverty, Rags & a
poor mean way of Living, are by no Means the proper
Subjects of Ridicule, when unavoidable: but when
Vanity, with a Contempt for the Manners of other
People, are joyned to them, then surely there cannot be
a more proper Subject to laugh at.

But it is high Time to return to my Journal: I said
that on the steady Perseverance of my French Lackey,
I was contented to hire him, on my getting to my
Lodgings at the *Hôtel d'Orléans* in the Little-Austin's
Street. I forthwith had occasion for his Assistance: for

one great Inducement to my going to Paris at this Time, was the Certainty of finding my very good Friend, the honourable Mr Horace Walpole there, who went before me about 3 Weeks or a Month:[1] I had received a Letter or two from him from Paris, before I left England: but as he then was lodged at his first Cousin's, the Earl of Hertford's, our Embassador, who, tho' himself had left Paris, yet his Countess was still there, but since her Departure also for England, [H.W.] was got into other Lodgings, which I knew nothing of. I immediately dispatched La Pierre to Mr Foley,[2] an English Banker, settled at Paris, who, I knew, was acquainted with Mr Walpole's Situation, for Information: however, I was not able to get this Information, as Mr Foley was, within these few Days, gone to England for a short Time: on this Disappointment, my French Valet undertook to bring me certain Intelligence, by the Time I should be stirring next Morning: so I made myself easy with a good Supper from the *Traiteur's*, after a very fatiguing Day, with hardly any Sleep the Night before, I went to Bed very early, & slept very comfortably.

Friday, Oct: 25. Fine Day. Mr Walpole's Swiss Servant Louis, who had lived with him many years,[3] was with me before I was up. La Pierre the more easily found him out, as the Hôtel du Parc Royal was almost the first House in the next Street, called the Rue de Colombier, opposite the high dead Wall of the Royal Abbey of St Germain des Prez. This Rue de Colombier,

[1]He arrived Sept. 12, 1765.

[2]Friend and correspondent of Sterne.

[3]"My rough savage Swiss", W. calls him: *Letters of Hor. Walpole* (Toynbee), No. 871, Ap. 8, 1763.

& the Rue Jacob make one long Street from the Rue du
Seine quite down to the River; & the Rue des Petits
Augustins, where I lodged came into this long Street,
near the Joining together of the Rue de Colombier &
the Rue Jacob. It was very fortunate that my Lodgings
happened to be so near those of Mr Walpole; indeed so
contiguous, that I could see into the Court Yard of his
Hôtel, & see when his Coach was going out with him,
from a back Window of my own. I went to his Lodgings
at the Hôtel de Parc Royal, after Breakfast, & found
him very lame with the Gout:[1] a Distemper so much the
more impertinent, as he had never done any Thing to
deserve it: nay so far from it, that had he been intitled to
an hereditary Gout, his Way of Living from his Infancy
to this Time was such, that one would have concluded
it would have sheltered itself in a Body more adapted to
its Ravages, & where it might have had more scope to
have displayed its malevolent Influence; & not have
taken Possession of one of the most puny, thin, delicate
& meagre Constitutions & Frame of Body this Day in
England. This was his Constant Habit of Body from a
Child: Tea & Bread & Butter half his Sustenance:
rarely any coarse Meat & never any Thing salted; &
water, with a little, & very little indeed, Wine, mixed
with it, his constant & habitual Beverage. With such
a regular Way of Life could one have conceived that the
Gout, which loves good Nourishment of both Eatables
& Drinkables, would have condescended to have been
acquainted? yet such was its whim, that the preceeding
Summer, for the first Time,[2] it gave Mr Walpole such

[1] v. *ibid.*, No. 1063, Oct. 16, 1765.

[2] This is an error: Walpole mentions his first attack of gout in a letter
to Richard Bentley, Nov. 16, 1755.

an unwelcome Visit, as to confine him to his Bed for some Months: & the Hopes of finding Relief from Change of Climate, was one of the Things that determined him to spend his Winter at Paris. Before this Fit of the Gout, which made great Havock in his slender Habit of Body, by making him excessively tender, he was used to be remarkably hardy, notwithstanding his puny Constitution: never having had a Great Coat in his Life, (& indeed there was the less Occasion for one, as neither Himself, nor his Friend Mr Gray, the Poet, ever were on an Horse's Back in their Lives:) never liable to catch Cold:[1] & I have seen him at his House at Strawberry Hill in the Parish of Twickenham in Middlesex, in the Months of October & November, when the Dew was quite wet upon the Grass, within these 2 or 3 Years, go out into his Garden, & all over the Grass, without so much as an Hat on his Head, a light Silk Waistcoat, & thin Slippers, not thicker than good substantial brown Paper, to feed his Poultry of all Sorts, after his Breakfast; & all this without the least Inconvenience, when I have been muffled up in a cloak & forced to change my Shoes as soon as I got into the House.[2] His Father the late right honourable, Sir Robert Walpole, Earl of Orford, was a very Corpulent, lusty Man; & his Mother, whom I remember very well also, when I have had the Honour often of visiting him at Chelsea, while I was a Schole-Boy, was a very lusty well-looking Woman: so that how this meagre Frame

[1]"I have persisted through this Siberian winter in not adding a grain to my clothes, and in going open-breasted, without an under waistcoat". Walpole to Gray, 25 Jan., 1766.

[2]John Pinkerton, writing more than twenty years later, uses almost the same words: "Sometimes a walk in the grounds would intervene, on which occasions he would go out in his slippers through a thick dew; and he never wore a hat."

fell to his Lot, I know not. Certain it is, after this Fit of the Gout, which added ten years to his Age, as he said, he was forced to suffer a Great Coat to be made, & grew otherwise so tender, as to be a great Mortification to think of it. At Noon he was disposed to take an Airing, in order to better his Health, & to shew me about the City of Paris: so wrapping his Legs in Flannel, & being helped into his Coach, or as they call them half-Coaches, which hold but 2 Persons, who set opposite one to the other, (his *Vis-à-Vis*), he carried me all over that whole Quarter of the City which is called the Faubourg St Germain, reckoned the politest Part of the Town, & where all the Hôtels of any Consequence are situated, & where all the Foreigners of any Distinction are lodged: from thence we crossed the River over the Pont Royal, to the good Street of St Honoré, went into the Place Royale, to the Hotel de Luxembourgh, to the Pont-Neuf, to the Place de Vendosme, to the Place de Louis quinze, & other remarkable Places, which we might see without getting out of the Coach, for he was too lame to walk. In the Fauxbourg St Germain he stopt at the Houses, & sent in his Compliments, not being able to get out, to the Duke de Nivernois,[1] late Embassador in England, Mr Wilkes, late Member of Parliament for Aylesbury, then in Banishment for seditious & blasphemous Writings, & who had been to visit Mr Walpole, & [it was] therefore necessary to return his Visit, & to many other People, both English & French. I forgot to mention in its Place, that Mr Walpole's Picture by Richardson,[2] from which there is a Mezzotinto Print in

[1]"The Duc de Nivernois is inexpressibly good, and has scarce missed a day", writes Walpole to Lady M. Coke (Oct. 15, 1765).

[2]An error: this portrait was by Reynolds.

1757, by Mac-Ardal, standing in a pensive Posture, by a Table, on which is his fine Antique Eagle in a Print, is very like him, except that it is a little too plump for him. Monsieur le Baron d'Olbiach,[1] a German Nobleman, settled at Paris, where he had married a French-Woman, came in after Dinner to Drink a Dish of Tea with Mr Walpole; as did Dr Burrell, of Doctor's Commons, with whom I was a little acquainted, as well as with his Brother, Peter Burrell Esqr[2] formerly of St John's College in Cambridge: the Doctor came to take his Leave of Mr Walpole, being to set out for England to Morrow.

This Day, according to a Letter to me from my Brother, Stephen Apthorp, D.D. & Fellow of Eton College, before I left England, was fixed for the Election of a Provost of that College, void by the Death of Dr Stephen Sleech, the late Provost & Rector of Worplesdon[3] near Guilford in Surrey, a Living about 400 Pounds per Annum. My Brother wrote me Word the very Day before I set out from Blecheley, for France, that as it was probable that he should succeed to Worplesdon, as all the Fellows of the College were well provided for by Livings, so he would have me consider whether I should think it worth my while to succeed him at Burnham: as he supposed he should have Interest enough with the Society to procure it for me. As the Situation of Burnham, in a delightful clean Country, within 2 or 3 Miles of Windsor, the Garden of England, & within a Mile of the Thames, a River

---

[1]Paul-Henri Thiry, Baron d'Holbach (1723-89); born in Baden; famous for his dinners; author of *Sytème de la Nature*.

[2]"Old Peter Burrell who was attached to my father". Walpole to Mann, July 9, 1779.

[3]Warplesdon (MS.).

which exceeds all others in the World, for Beauty, made
this a most desirable Place to sit down in for Life, tho'
a Vicarage of no great Value, being about 150 Pounds
per Annum, I was delighted with the Thoughts of it:
consequently was very indifferent about looking after,
or enquiring about a Situation in France, which had
been my first Motive for this Journey. But behold the
uncertainty of human Events![1] Dr Barnard was
elected Provost on this very Day, according as my
Brother had foreseen: but his Hopes about Worplesdon[2]
had been too sanguine, as I had foreseen, & had told
him, in Answer to his Letter: for altho' the Vice-
Provost, Dr Burton,[3] a very old Man, who had the
Vicarage of Maple-Durham, (a most sweet Situation on
the Banks of the Thames, with an admirable House, &
worth above 200 Pounds per Annum), yet he could not
resist the Temptation of a double Income, even at his
advanced Age, & no Family to provide for: my Brother
upon this might, had he chosen it, have removed to
Maple-Durham: but as he had, soon after his Election
to a Fellowship at Eton, resigned two Livings in
Hampshire, (Monkston, given to him by King's
College in Cambridge, & Steventon, presented to him
by Mr Knight), in order to take the Vicarage of Burnham, by which he lost in Income above 100 Pounds
per An., to be within a Ride of Eton College, so the
same Motive determined him not to accept Maple-
Durham in Oxfordshire, tho' at no great, yet at too great,
a Distance from the College, to be consistent with his
Plan. He then advised me to try my Interest with the

---

[1]C. became (non-resident) Vicar of Burnham in 1774, and held the
living for the remaining eight years of his life.

[2]Warplesdon (MS.).   [3]John B. (1696-1771).

Society for Maple-Durham, as none of the College would accept of it: but altho' it would have been very agreable to me to have gone there, yet I declined the Offer, as not being made in the least for briguing[1] & caballing: & who has that Living now I know not, or whether yet disposed of I am equally ignorant; having never once enquired about it since: for soon after, within a week I believe, my Arrival at Blecheley, about the first Week of this year 1766 [I wrote this May 22] my Brother wrote me Word, that the Society had now since the Election of Dr Barnard[2] to the Provostship, come to a new Determination in Respect to their Disposal of their College Preferments: for whereas before on the Vacancy of any Living, it was the Provost & Fellows, (that is cheifly the Provost himself), who had the Disposal of it, they now had come to a Resolution, that the Provost first, & then every Fellow in his turn should present to the Livings as they became vacant: which would put an end to all caballing about them with the Society in general, as every Member would, by this Means become a private Patron himself. Indeed, I am so little made for Preferment hunting, that had not the Motion been made from my Brother to me, I should never have thought of any such Thing myself. Dr. Barnard was the Son of Mr Barnard, Vicar of Luton in Bedfordshire, & being educated at Eton Schole, & superannuated, was entered of St John's College in Cambridge, where he became Fellow, & had from it the Vicarage of Ospring[3] in Kent; he afterwards went Assistant to Eton Schole, where his

[1]Intriguing, especially with the object of getting votes.

[2]Edward B. (1717-81); headmaster, 1754; provost, 1764.

[3]Ospringe, near Faversham.

Scholarship & Disposition for that Kind of Life were
so conspicuous that on a Vacancy he was preferred to
the Head-Mastership of that Royal Schole: which, by
his great Learning, superior management & exact &
nice Discipline, he soon brought to that Eminence, as
never had been Known before: for the Number of
Scholars by a great many exceeded 500, during all the
Time he was in that Station: so that I am credibly informed, that his own Emolument as Head Master was
every year above 1500 Pounds, by the flourishing State
he had brought the Schole into: so that a Man of his
great Parts & Reputation could not, in his Situation, be
long without such Preferment as he chose: accordingly
he was made King's Chaplain, & had a Canonry of
Windsor, reckoned one of the most gentile Preferments
of the Sort, in the Kingdom, conferred upon him. As
Dr Sleech, a Bachelor, & not an old Man, had been in
a very declining way for years before his Death, so it
gave a fair Opportunity for those who had Pretensions
to ask for this desirable Preferment of 700 Pounds a
year, to be early enough in their Applications after it:
accordingly my Freind Dr Lyne, one of the Fellows,
had the Promise of it, & would certainly, without the
greatest ill Fortune, succeeded to it, had not the Earl of
Sandwich, his great Freind & Patron, & who had got
him the Promise of it, in case he continued in the
Ministry, been, with his Cousin the Earl of Halifax,[1]
just then turned out from being the two Secretaries of
State: & at this Critical Juncture, the worthy Marquis
of Granby, equally a Freind of Dr Barnard, had so
much Interest with the New Ministry, to get him

---

[1]"Halifax, Sandwich, and general warrants are sent to the devil".
Walpole to Mann, July 12, 1765.

elected: to the extreme Mortification of Dr Lyne.[1] Dr Barnard was always a little lame, wearing an Iron to strengthen one Leg or Foot: he is a thin Man, pitted with the Small Pox, of a most lively & piercing Eye, sufficiently indicative of his lively & sprightly Genius: too apt, as I have been told by those who know him better than I do, to dwindle now & then into Sneer & Sarcasm: tho' always esteemed a very good tempered Man. While he was Master of Eton Schole, he married a West India Lady, of a good Fortune, but who lived with him not many years: his Father also left him, according to Report, 10,000 Pounds; so that his Income is very ample: I have heard about 2000 Pounds per Annum. His Successor in the Head-Mastership is Doctor Foster,[2] late Fellow of King's College in Cambridge, the Son of a Bricklayer of Windsor, a very ingenious Man, & a great Critic & Scholar in the learned Languages: but as he is supposed to be too profound a Critic, & more of a Scholar than a Gentleman, (for they should be blended in the Character of a Head Master of such a Schole as Eton), it is supposed that the Reputation of the Schole will hardly be equal to what it was in his Predecessor's Time. I am not much acquainted with Dr. Foster, he being greatly my Junior in the University: yet I have very often met him, as he was private Tutor, even while Scholar of the House, to my Lord Montfort's only Son, the hon: Mr. Bromley, who then boarded in the Family of my late most worthy & amiable Friend the late Dr Conyers Middleton[3] at

[1]Whose death was even attributed to this cause. *Add. MSS.* 5835, p. 361.

[2]John F. (1731-74); Canon of Windsor, 1772; wrote controversial works on Greek accentuation.

[3]*Ob.* 1750; the famous latitudinarian divine and antagonist of Bentley.

Cambridge, where as he used to attend his young Pupil,
& as I used to spend most of my Evenings with the Dr.
& his Wife, with such other Company as usually met
there, I had frequent Opportunities of being with him:
as well as at Horseth Hall,[1] the Seat of my most worthy
& much lamented Friend the late right Hon: Henry
Bromley, Lord Montfort: but as far as I could observe
by his Behaviour then, at both Places, he seemed to be
of a silent & reserved Disposition, (which, however,
might be proper enough in his Situation, & as a very
young Man) & too much given up to Books, ever to be
much conversant with Mankind. He was then a very
handsome Man, tall, thin, black Hair & large black
Eyes, but not very healthy, from his too great Application: he afterwards went Assistant to Eton Schole, had
a Living in Shropshire, given to him by his Pupil my
Lord Montfort, I think of that Name also, being the
Town [Montford] from whence he took his Title, & is
since lately married. About 4 or 5 years ago he was
thought to write in too dogmatical & pert a Manner,
for so young a Man, against the University of Oxford,
on Account of the Greek Accent: when he was promoted
to the Head Mastership of Eton Schole, it was thought
proper that he should be doctorated: accordingly he
had, together with Dr Hurdis,[2] Canon of Windsor &
Chaplain to our Chancellor the Duke of Newcastle, a
Royal Mandate for his Doctor's Degree in Divinity,
about a Fortnight ago, at Cambridge. (I write this on
May 23, 1766.) At the Rate I go on, I shall be longer in
writing out my Journal, than I was in taking my Journey:
for when I first sat down to enter it from my Pocket-
Book, I thought I should only have the Trouble of

[1]Or, Horseheath.   [2]Thomas H., *ob.* 1784.

transcribing from that, a few Inscriptions, & other trifling Notes & Observations I occasionally put in it: but I now see no End of my Labours, for the most minute Hint is liable to draw me to a Dissertation of 2 or 3 Pages. However, I will endeavour to be less diffuse, that I may once again get into my own Parish, & enjoy the Sweets of my Garden, much more to the Purpose of benefitting my Health, than thus sitting scribbling in an Elbow Chair.

Saturday, Oct: 26. Tolerable fine Day. Not very well, having had little or no Sleep in the Night, so I did not stir out 'till 3 in the Afternoon, when I went to Dinner at the Hôtel du Parc Royal with Mr Walpole, whom I found very much indisposed, having been very early disturbed by Drums & Trumpets, to welcome the Arrival of his Grace the Duke of Beaufort,[1] who came the Evening before to Paris in his way Home from off his Travels, & was lodged in the Apartment immediately under Mr Walpole. The Duke gave 25 Guineas per Month for his Apartment, being only one Pair of Stairs; & that above it, where Mr Walpole was lodged, was at the Rate of 14 Guineas per Month; containing a Vestibule with a Fire Place & Dutch Stove, for the Servants to sit in, thro' which you passed to a very handsome Dining Room with 3 sashed Windows, out of which was an elegant Bed Chamber, & small Closet in it: together with a Bed Chamber for a Servant at the other End of the Vestibule or Servant's Hall. After Dinner, Monsieur le Chevalier de Lorenzi,[2] an Italian

[1]Henry Somerset, 5th Duke. On Nov. 15, Walpole complains of the disturbance caused by a ball given by the Duke to which "I was forced to go in my own defence". *Letters of Hor. Walpole* (Toynbee), No. 1068.

[2]Brother of Count Lorenzi, French Minister at Florence. Of the Chevalier, Walpole writes to John Crauford (March 6, 1766), "Lorenzi blunders faster than one can repeat".

Nobleman, of Florence, (I think, Knight of some Order, as a very rich Diamond Cross hung before him), aged between 40 & 50, as it seemed to me, came in to drink Tea with Mr Walpole, & presently afterwards the Chevalier de Dromgould,[1] Knight of the Order of St Lewis, a very pretty Gentleman of much the same age, dressed in a Military Habit: he was thin & well shaped, as the Chevalier de Lorenzi was rather of a clumsy make: Some Time after came in one Doctor Gem,[2] an English Physitian, lately established at Paris, being a very tall awkward kind of Man, of a solemn Figure, & no great Conversation. The two Knights spent the greatest Part of the Evening with Mr Walpole, but Dr Gem did not stay above half an Hour. I had more Entertainment from this Evening's Conversation, than from any Thing I met with during my Stay at Paris: for the Subject falling upon the famous Mr Rousseau, who had just about this Time drawn some Censures upon himself, from his libertine way of Writing, against the Establishment of his Country, & indeed of Christianity, a great Part of that Person's Character was laid open to me, & the Merits of his Cause very freely debated, with no less Spirit & Vivacity, than Candour & Moderation. Dr Gem, it seems, was fallen into the modish French Taste, in philosophizing Revelation out of Doors; tho' he was in a Manner quite silent in the Debate: but this I could discover by the little he did say, & from what

[1]Described by Dr Johnson, who met him in Paris, as "Colonel Drumgold, a very high man, Sir, head of *L'Ecole Militaire*, a most complete character, for he had first been a Professor of Rhetorick and then became a soldier." (*Boswell*, 1766.)

[2]Jem (MS.). On first meeting Walpole, G. observed, "Sir, I am serious, I am of a very serious turn!" *Letters of Hor. Walpole* (Toynbee), No. 1077, Dec. 2, 1765. See also *Add. MSS.* 5819, p. 190.

others said of him afterwards. But this is the *Ton des François* now almost universally among Men of Fashion, & not uncommon among the Ladies. As I have elsewhere [*Add. MSS.* 5824] spoken of this Man [Rousseau] & his Singularities, I shall have the less Occasion to say much of him here: yet shall not omit some Particulars which Mr Dromgould mentioned of him in this Evening's Conversation: especially as the Man is since come into England,[1] where all new Things are greedily admired: he was then supposed to be *incognito* at Paris. The Cavalier Lorenzi was a bigoted Admirer of Rousseau, & his Tenets, & seemed to be sunk into the very Dregs of Deism & French Philosophy: but happily for Revelation, there was only an Inclination, without any Power to do Mischeif: for tho' he had a great Flow of Words, & Vehemence of Elocution, yet they were but words only: for there was no Reason in any of his Arguments: nor could Mr Rousseau have fallen into the Hands of a worse Advocate. Indeed he was esteemed but an absurd Sort of a Character: & some Stories he told of himself, very sufficiently proved him to be so.[2] Mr Dromgould was of a good Irish Family drove away from his Country by the Rebels in Oliver's Time, & ever since established in France. About 22 years ago, when Mr Walpole was before at Paris, he was acquainted with him, when he was a young Man of about 19 or 20 years of Age, a Student in the Sorbonne, & designed for the Church: at which Time he had a very pretty Turn for Poetry: a Specimen of which may be seen in

[1] "I hear he does not succeed in England, where singularities are no curiosity". Walpole to Cole, Feb. 28, 1766.

[2] *See* De la Lande's *Voyage d'un François en Italie*, 1769, ii. p. 362, for Mr Lorenzi [C.].

the 2nd Collection of Whaley's Poems, pp. 174-7, printed in the year 1745, the same year in which the Author, (if he may with any Propriety be called so, when his 2 volumes contain more of other People's Genius than any of his own, particularly Dr Davies of Kingsland in Herefordshire, who has contributed largely to the first Volume), died at Norwich; where is a French Translation into Verse of Satan's Speech on his being cast into Hell, from Milton's *Paradise Lost*, Book 1. verse 242.[1] It was given at that Time to Mr Walpole by Mr Dromgold, & Whaley having Occasion to make up a Book, to supply his Necessities, was glad to beg it might be put, with the Rest, into his Collection, which he inscribed to Mr Walpole.[2] It is there said Mr Dromgold was a Student in the Jesuits' College at Paris : it may be so; tho' I have minuted it down in my Pocket Book, the Sorbon[ne]. I think the other is more probable: & this only shews how diffident one ought to be even of one's own Notes, taken from common Conversation, where many Things are often advanced, & believed as Truths, which will not bear a nice Scrutiny. I beg that what I write & have written, may have the Benefit of this Observation: as I am firmly persuaded no one will have more Occasion for a candid Indulgence than myself. "Mr Romgold", as he is called in the said Poems, (tho' I always hear Mr Walpole call him Dromgold, perhaps adding the French De to the Name, as thus, " De Romgold", the French, & then others, might call him Dromgold,) afterwards quitted

---

[1]"Traduction de Milton Liv. 1. Discours de Satan precipitè du haut de Ciel à la vue de l'Enfer: by Mr Rumgold, a Student in the Jesuit's College, at Paris."

[2]Whaley had been Walpole's tutor at Cambridge.

E

his Design of entering into the Church, & having a
Commission in the Count de Clermont's Regiment, he
now resides in the Abbey of St Germain des Prez, of
which the said Count is Commendatory Abbat, tho' a
Military Man :[1] but being a Prince of the Blood Royal
of France, this rich Abbey was given him to support his
Dignity: yet I have several Times met this Lay Abbat
in his Coach, dressed in a Clerical Habit, having a
Cassock & Cloak over it, in his own short Hair, with a
Cross before his Breast, as a Prelate; being a fat, jolly,
well looking Man. As Mr Dromgold is a Favourite of
his, he is lodged in the Abbey, & attends him also when
he goes to his Regiment. This mixing religious &
military Characters together, let the Persons who bear
them be ever so unexceptionable, can never be for the
Credit or Advantage of Religion: it must at Length
undermine all Notions of the use of religious Societies:
better surely, if the Riches of the Endowment are a
Temptation to give it in this Manner, to reduce the
regular Abbat's Income! Mr Dromgold is, as I observed, a very well looking Man, turned of 40, very
lively, & speaks English perfectly well for one who has
always lived abroad: he is an excellent Scholar, a Man
of fine Parts, of a good Taste & had no small Genius
& Talent for Poetry; as may be observed from the
Specimen I mentioned, at the age of 19 years. He is
descended from our great old English Poet Gower, &
therefore had much studied his Works, as well as those
of Chaucer, & being related to my Lord Gower,[2] his
Lordship has lent him a MS. containing the Works of

[1]Louis de Bourbon-Condé (1709-71); see *Lettres de Mme Du Deffand*
(Toynbee), ii. 260 *n*.

[2]2nd Earl; afterwards Marq. of Stafford.

their common Relation, many Parts of which, with those of Chaucer, & some of our best English Poets, he has translated into French Verse, in order to give that Nation some Idea of our antient Poetry, & to convince them, that we were not such Barbarians as their Politeness is apt to suppose, so many Centuries ago, when they may be difficulted[1] to produce such Specimens of true Genius & exalted Poetry among themselves. Mr Dromgold could not with Patience mention the Character of John-James Rousseau, who did his Endeavour in every Country he came to, to unhinge & unsettle People's Minds in Respect to their Religious Principles, thereby rendering them unhappy & miserable from their State of uncertainty, when before they were contented and happy in their national Establishment; all which could bend to no good Purpose, but only to the creating in People's Breasts Doubts & Difficulties, & loosening in Time the strongest Bonds of all civil Society: for according to his own System, no real outward Advantage to mankind was to accrue from this Philosophic Religion: which, however it might do for Men of Superior Understandings, was by no means calculated for the Vulgar: for if the present Sanctions to Virtue, Honesty & civil Society, from the united Force of Religion, offering Rewards & Punishments, with those of the Laws of one's Country, by present Execution, are found by Experience to be insufficient to restrain & keep Men in due Bounds, what may be expected when all these Ties are unloosed, & every Man left at large to persue the Bent of his own Passions without Controul? The Consequences are natural, frightful & alarming. The same Arguments were

[1]See *O.E.D.*

enforced by Mr Walpole, who thought it the most ridiculous Thing in the World, to endeavour the Destruction of a religious Establishment, which on all Hands, even by these Philosophers themselves, as they affect to stile themselves, was allowed to have a most excellent Tendency in promoting Virtue, all the Benefits of civil Life, & keeping Mankind in a due & proper Subordination one to the other: (for without this the Savages in America are an unhappy People): & at the same Time that they were pulling down this allowed useful, if not absolutely perfect Fabric, they had agreed upon no Plan to substitute in its Room, no new Religion to give a Check to the boiling human Passions, impossible to be kept in due order by natural Religion alone & the Force of Reason. I was not a little pleased to hear my Friend argue so warmly in Defence of Religion; & should have been completely so, had it proceeded, as in Mr Dromgold's Case, who was a zealous Catholic & Christian, from a Conviction of the Truth of Revelation, than merely from Political Considerations. It was observed also by Mr Dromgold, that even in England, where Prejudices in Favour of Revelation were daily dying away, & among the politer Sort were in a Manner totally extinguished, yet even the Parliament, so lately as within these 2 or 3 years, had made an Example of a crazed Kind of Enthusiast for religious Liberty, (as Deism is now called, forsooth), who had taken it into its Head to write an Abuse upon Moses, & had ordered him to be pilloried, & confined in Prison: he observed therefore very justly, that if the Parliament was so alert in Defence of the Jewish Legislator, they would hardly allow of a Toleration for Rousseau & his Disciples, who was then preparing for

England, as his System was utterly subversive of
Christianity, the Established Religion of the Country.
It was also taken Notice of by Mr De Romgold, that
notwithstanding all these Pretences to Philosophy, &
the Good of Mankind, yet it was much to be suspected
that a Man, who out of Pride & Vanity would not
own & cohabit with the Woman he had married, could
have no very honest Principles at the Bottom. Reason,
as well as natural Religion would condemn such a Man
as unjust, dishonest & cruel, even if Christianity was
out of the Question. Yet this was the Religion of the
wonderful Mr Rousseau, who, from a very low & mean
Extraction, had Pride enough, after he had gained a
Reputation in the World, from his Writings, which also
had greatly enriched him, & consequently had puffed
up his weak & trifling Mind, to disown his Wife, &
make her live with him as a Servant: he being too
highly exalted in Life to acknowledge her as his Consort
& Equal, who, at their first setting out in Life together,
never dreamt of any Disparity between them. If I do
Mr Rousseau any Injustice in this Representation, I
am to throw the blame of it upon Mr Dromgold, who
related the whole, as I have represented it, to the
Chevalier Lorenzi, who made no Objections to the
Truth of it, tho' his great Admirer: & therefore I the
more confidently report it. But methinks I need not be
so scrupulous: for notwithstanding the boasted Pretences to a sublimer Virtue among these Sort of Gentry
of the Infidel Stamp, their known and avowed Examples
are a full & sufficient Proof of the Falsehood of them.
The Luxury of Voltaire's Life, with his famous Proof of
the Being of a God, from the sole Act of Generation, is a
sufficient indication of the Looseness of his Morals, as

well as of the extreme Grossness of his Ideas. But we need not go in Quest of modern French Philosophers for the Proof of their dissolute Doctrine & abandoned Morality: our infamous Lay-Sacheverell, (as I have heard him improperly called, to stigmatize him for a factious, & seditious Blower up of Tumults & Uneasinesses in his Country), the late banished Member for Aylesbury,[1] tho' bred up a Presbyterian, (his Father being a very eminent Distiller,[2] & had a Country House in my Parish of Hornsey, where I once however saw him at Church, while I was Rector of that Parish,[3] in Order to keep up his Right to a Pew therein,) in all their formal & solemn Cant: with all their Hatred, inward Malice & Abhorrence for the established Religion of his Country: who married the Daughter of a Presbyterian Minister, of the Name of Mead, with a Fortune, as it is said of between 20 & 30,000 Pounds; a Woman of an excellent Character, & by whom he has an only Daughter: this said precise Gentleman, of a Presbyterian rigid Education, the Son-in-Law of a formal Dissenting Teacher, is the Author of a blasphemous Book,[4] for which he was expelled the House of Commons, together with other aggravating Circumstances, but also used his Wife so ill, to whom he was so much beholden, that they were forced to be parted: but what is still more incredible, & shews the Integrity of this great Patriot, espoused by the great Mr Pitt, Earl Temple, & such Patriots, when the poor Woman was reduced by him to apply for a Common Maintenance, which the Laws of

[1] John Wilkes.   [2] Israel W., of Clerkenwell, *ob.* 1761.

[3] The statement in the *D.N.B.* that Cole "never resided" at Hornsey must not be taken quite literally.

[4] *An Essay on Woman*, 1763.

his Country had fixed to £200 per an., he had the
Villainy to force the Tenant, (one Bernard Fountaine,
of Eaton Lays, in or close to my Parish of Blecheley),
to pay him the Money, by which means the poor
Woman was left in a starving Condition; while He &
his Whores were rioting in Plenty, sometime in Italy,
& other Times at Paris. Yet this was the Man, who for
a Time was an Idol in England: & is now, as I hear,
suffered to return into this Country, with a Pension of
£500 per an. from the Government: as my Lord Cam-
den has given it as his Opinion, That general Warrants
are illegal, & the Parliament has confirmed that
Opinion, This late Idol, on his Return, may chance to
be hosannaed, or pelted by the Mob, as the Humour
may happen to be: certain it is, that a more barefaced &
abandoned Fellow had never the Impudence to assume
the respectable Character of a Patriot & Lover of the
Good & Prosperity of his Country, than this Man. It is
more than probable, that his good Friends, other Patriots
like himself, our great Demagogues in both Houses,
who only made a Tool of this Fellow, & raised a Blaze
& Faction in the Nation, to serve their own infamous
Purposes, & beggar their Country; it is probable, I say,
that these Gentry, being tired with the Expence of
keeping by Contribution such an extravagant Wretch
abroad, were willing that he should come back again, &
be saddled upon his Country, rather than [paid] out of
their own Pockets: for I heard grievous & lamentable
Complaints from that Quarter last year, how expensive
he was to them & how unmercifully he drew Bills upon
them from Paris, at 3 or 400 Pounds at a Time. I gave
a Shrewd Guess then, that they began to be tired of him,
now he had served their Purposes. Pity it is, that they

who made such a Market of him, were not obliged to
keep him & his Appendages for Life. I have lived long
enough to see, what I long suspected, as it is an old
Observation, that what was originally intended for the
Safeguard of the Constitution, was the likeliest Thing
to be the Destruction of it: for let such Law-Givers,
Legislators, or whatever high Titles they may please
lavishly to bestow upon each other, or in the mightiness
of their Power & Authority as lavishly to throw out
their Censures upon particular Professions, such as
Divinity, Law & Physic, (the 2 last of which, God
knows, have but too great Occasion for it) yet it is my
firm Belief & most assured Persuasion, from what I
have been able to observe, that could a large Cast-Net
be thrown over any great Company of Men in this our
Islet, & let them be of whatever mixed Degree, Profession or Calling you please, & another of the same
size & Capacity thrown over a certain congregate Body
in a certain famous House or Chapel, met together
under the Pretence of the Public good, & almost the
whole of them striving only how to amass for themselves
regardless of what they were sent thither for; I must
repeat it, I say, it is my most firm Belief, that you would
meet with more Villainy, Meanness, Knavery & Deceit,
under all the specious Disguises & Pretences of
Patriotism, Public-spiritedness, National-Welfare, Com-
merce, Liberty of the Subject, & an hundred other
fine spun Arguments, in the one, (but which I shan't
say), than in the other Body of Men. Not but what I
think there are some very honest Men to be met with
in the Society I speak of, & who act & mean well for
the Service of their Country: but the Number is so
inconsiderable, as to be hardly worth mentioning. I

speak this with Sorrow & Concern, & am ashamed that so much Infamy should be cast in the Teeth of my Country: but while the present System of ridiculing all Religion, & an utter Contempt for the Truths of Christianity, is the prevailing Fashion, it is no wonder that there is so little Decency in even appearing to be an honest Man, a Man of Virtue & Integrity. Morality alone is not sufficient to answer the Purposes of civil Life: without Christianity it is ten to one but we become a Voltaire, a Wilkes or a Rousseau: which brings me to where I left off: the Affectations & Singularities of this Citizen of Geneva: who not only affected to give the Preference in his Writings to the Savage State of Mankind, above the Civilized; with Paradoxes equally absurd & glaring, & obtruded upon the World more to be admired at, than to be believed, but also from the same vain Principle of Ostentation & Singularity, affected to appear in the cheif Metropolises of Europe in an Eastern or Turkish Habit: if it was not to hide the Deformity of a Rupture, as some reported.[1] But to have done with Persons of such worthless Characters, when I have said a word or two about a Person mentioned 2 or 3 Pages before; & with whose Character I was too well acquainted, as to be deceived in drawing it up. I mean Mr John Whaley, cited at p. 65 of this Volume. He was the son of a Tradesman of Norwich, whose Father dying when he was young, left him to the Care of his Mother, a very sensible, active & stirring Woman, who following her Husband's Profession, entered with such Spirit into it, & encreased it to so great a Degree,

[1]D. Hume writes, "His Armenian dress is not an affectation. He has had an infirmity from his infancy, which makes breeches inconvenient for him."

that she was nick-named at Norwich, Jack-of-all-Trades, dealing very largely in the Haberdashery Way, & mixing other Professions with it: & tho' she was said to have a great Run of Business & got a great Deal of Money, yet the Extravagance of her Son at last put her to the utmost Difficulties. She at first sent him to Eton Schole, where he was observed to be a Boy of a sprightly & toward Genius, & as such, encouraged by Dr Bland,[1] the Master, who was beneficed in Norfolk [and] closely connected with the Minister, Sir Robert Walpole, who readily patronized, upon political Motives, his own Countrymen. Soon after his Removal to King's College in Cambridge, he began to indulge his Propensity to the Muses, such as it was; but much more his Turn for a dissolute & debauched Kind of Life—which appeared to be his Taste very early, at Schole, but which blazed out with more Fire when he was his own Master at College, after his first 3 years of Scholarship was over: yet as he was reckoned a Man of Genius & a Poet, a good Jolly Companion, a Singer of a good Song, & rather a gentile Person, his Company was sought after, & he spent his Time in a continual Scene of jovial Amusements & mirthfull Society: nor was this Train of Life at all altered, when he became the private Tutor in College of John Dodd Esqr, the present Member for Reading,[2] a young Gentleman of excellent Parts, lively Genius, & uncommon understanding, who had been educated at Eton, & coming Fellow Commoner to our College fell into his Hands by some Recommendation or other: & had it not happened

[1]Head-Master of Eton, 1719; Provost, 1732; *ob*. 1746; a schoolfellow of Sir Robt. Walpole.

[2]*Ob*. 1782; of Swallowfield, Berks. Walpole mentions that he died "not of cold water".

that this young Gentleman was the Master of as good a
Judgment, as his Parts were lively, it could not have
been but that his Tutor would have ruined him for ever:
for so indecent was his Behaviour in Respect to his
Pupil, that the whole University cried out Shame upon
it. Indeed, it was so notoriously scandalous & shameful,
that a Tutor should thus publicly not be ashamed to
bebauch his Pupil's morals, that few people were so
abandoned as not to be scandalized at it. Excessive
Drinking, high & luxurious Eating, & other riotous
Behaviour was the daily & common Way of Life with
Mr Whaley, at his Pupil's Chambers, & his own, which
were opposite to one another, on the Ground Floor, on
the other Side of the Arch in the New Buildings of the
College; & if I was now & then of the Party, I speak it
to my Shame, as well as Reputation; I never came from
it, but with the utmost Contempt for the Author of such
Shameful Proceedings: whom every Body must condemn in their own Minds, however a Love of Society,
their Youth & Inexperience might tempt them sometimes to be present at them. To such an Height of
Luxury had he brought his own Taste, that he could
rarely dine in the College Hall, with the Rest of the
Society, where the frugal, tho' sufficient, Provisions
were too flat & insipid for him, but 2 or 3 Days in a
Week had Entertainments at his or his Pupil's Chambers, where many of the University were invited, & at
which all the Delicacies & Niceties in Season, which
could be collected, were sure to be met with: & the
Common Wines of Spain & Portugal too gross &
indelicate for his refined Taste: for he would hardly
ever condescend to drink any other than French Wine,
on which the Duty was so heavy as to make it come

to 6 Shillings a Quart, or Bottle: to such an Excess
of Extravagance had his Taste brought him! I well
remember, that about the year 1737, a certain honourable Friend of mine, then a Nobleman of our College,
writing to me to come & meet him at Hockerill, near
Bishop's Stortford, where we were to lodge, as half way
between London & Cambridge; (for then the use of
Post-chaises was not introduced, & the Method of
Flying on the Road was not yet found out); & he would
bring me back again in his Chariot to Cambridge, as I
was to go on Horseback to meet him: I happening to
mention this to Whaley, he immediately catched at it,
& making a Party to fill a Coach, offered to carry me as
a 5th Person in it, as I was to return with my honoured
Friend, more than once mentioned before in this
Volume: the Party was, a right rev: & hon: Bp of our
present Bench, one of a most excellent & most amiable
Character, then Fellow of Christ's College, whose
Acquaintance with Whaley, was the greatest Apology
in his Favour that can be produced: Mr Dodd, his
Pupil, & Mr Belcher, a Fellow of the College, & a most
intimate Acquaintance of Whaley, but a dull, heavy,
formal Fellow; one, whose Ambition it was to be
thought a Man of Parts & Vivacity, but who in Reality
mistook his Talent: for he was by Nature design'd to
have been a low Mechanic, at the Time when his
Father aimed to have bred him a Scholar: this Father of
his was a very reputable Man in his Way of Life, being
the Master of a very large & creditable Inn at Kingston
in Surrey; one of whose Sons, I think, is his Successor
in the said Inn; another was a Surgeon of good Credit &
Reputation; & a 3rd was a Banker, & Member in one
or more Parliaments, for the Borough of Southwark,

with whose Wife my Sisters were well acquainted. Our
Mr Belcher, was for some years one of the Bursars of
the College, but living too high, outrun his Income, &
by aiming at the same way of Living with his Friend
Whaley, without having the Resource of a Mr Dodd's
Pocket to have Recourse to, he ran himself so into Debt,
that in the French War, about 1745, (he not having
entered into Orders) to extricate himself out of them,
he left his Bursarship, & took Part of a Privateer; &
being taken by the French, was carried in to Port
l'Orient, where he soon after died. The Occasion of my
mentioning this Party, was to shew the Extravagance
of Mr Whaley's Disposition, who had the ordering of
the Supper when he got to the Inn, where what with
French Wine, & Eatables according, our Bill the next
Morning, only for Supper & Breakfast, was exclusive
of Horses & Servants, to each Person 17 Shillings:
about double to what ought to have been for reasonable
People. By this extravagant way of Living he very much
injured his Fortunes, & distressed his Mother, who,
often, in her Way to & from London with a female
Companion or two, would call upon her Son, & lodged
in the College for several Days, where they were
junketted from Chamber to Chamber, for she was of
the jovial Sort; & [he] not only spent his Money thus
idly, but by his immoderate Eating, being one of Epicurus his Disciples, so blew himself up, that he could
hardly walk about conveniently for Fat; being as round
& sleek as a Mole. In 1732, before he had taken his
Degree in Arts, he had collected together & published
in an 8vo volume, A Collection of Poems,[1] in order to

---

[1]Mentioned by Allibone, but not by Watt. There is no copy in the
British Museum.

put a little Money in his Pocket, by solliciting Sub-
scriptions: the Best Part of which Collection was furnished by his Friend, the present worthy Archdeacon of
Derby, the rev: Dr Sneyd Davies,[1] (Rector of Kingsland in Herefordshire & Chaplain to the hon: & rev:
Dr Cornwallis Bp of Lichfeild & Coventry), who had
as true & genuine a Taste for Poetry, as Whaley's was
supposed to be false & spurious: however, these Poems
gave him a Name, & might be his Ruin; as it gave him
an idle Turn, & introduced him too much into Company. Mr Dodd's Father, I think, had kept an Inn at
Chester, but was a Descendent from Judge Dodd,[2]
whose Estate, for want of Male Heirs, descended to
him. As there was a long Minority, & a great Deal of
Money had been saved, & as there was no Family Seat,
as soon as Mr Dodd was of Age to look out for one,
which was while he was at College, the Estate & House
belonging to Russell, Earl of Orford[3] at Chippenham
in Cambridgeshire, (afterwards purchased by the late
George Montgomery Esqr) was offered to be sold by
my Lord Sandys: & as Mr Dodd had been introduced
into the Acquaintance of the late Lord Montfort & Mr
Sam: Shepheard, Member for Cambridgeshire, who
both would have had Mr Dodd have made that Purchase, & by that means have made an Opening for him
to have represented either the Town or County of
Cambridge, as occasion should offer. But this was a
Plan by no means suitable to Mr Whaley; who did not
chuse to have his Pupil under any other Direction than
his own, & thought my Lord Montfort too shrewd &
discerning as not soon to perceive the Tutor's Designs

[1]1709-69.   [2]Sir Samuel Dodd, 1652-1716; Lord Chief Baron, 1714.
[3]Edward Russell (1653-1727); Admiral, etc.

& Views, & consequently too honest & generous not to
advertise him of them. Accordingly Whaley dissuaded
him from this Purchase, & soon engaged him in that
of Swallowfeild near Reading in Berkshire; where he
also very early entangled him in a disputed Election for
that Borough, & where he had an opportunity to display his Genius for Drinking & Party: for one of Mr
Whaley's cheif qualifications, was his distinguishing
himself as a violent Whig, & Partizan for the Hanover
Family. Here he seemed placed in his Element: for Mr
Dodd had taken him with him from College, on his
Settlement at Swallowfeild. But the Ruin of this Felicity
may be dated from Mr Dodd's Marriage with a young
Lady of the Name of St Leger, who being a Person of
Family & not relishing the Behaviour of such a loose
Moralist where she was concerned, as his Faults indeed
were not to be overlooked in a decent & well-ordered
Family, he was given to understand, before the Year
was at an End, that Swallowfeild was no Place for his
Residence: & to make the Disgrace more tolerable, Mr
Dodd, who was Generosity itself, settled an Annuity
upon him, I think, of 50 Pounds a Year for Life: This
however he afterwards sold, in order to supply his
Necessities; & to compleat the Scene some Time after
retired to College, & took Orders, that he might in due
Time accept a College Living, to keep him from
starving at the latter End of his Life. However about
1744, his Finances being very low, & his Annuity
Money spent, he again sollicited another Subscription
for a new volume of Poems, which he entitled, *A
Collection of Original Poems & Translations*,[1] which were

[1]Cole's copy of this book is in the British Museum, and contains some
MS. notes by him; (11631. d. 60).

printed in 1745, at London in 8vo, & inscribed to Mr
Dodd's particular Friend, my most worthy & esteemed
Friend the honourable Horatio Walpole Esqr, Usher
of his Majesties Exchequer. How long this last Effort
subsisted him I know not; for he soon after fell ill at
College, which, turning to a melancholy Madness, he
was sent in a Coach to his Mother at Norwich, where he
died in December in the year 1745, & was there buried.
I have been the more particular in my Account of this
Man, as I ever looked upon him to have been thro' out
Life, one of the worst Men I ever was acquainted with.
Pray God have Mercy & Compassion on his Soul. Amen.

The Occasion of this long Dissertation, was the Conversation at Mr Walpole's on the Subject of Rousseau.
The same Evening I heard there that as the Duke
of Richmond's [1] Pack of Dogs were come over this
Day from England to Paris, it was not to be reasonably
expected that his Grace would be long behind: he was
expected on Thursday or Friday following. The Duke
of Buccleugh,[2] & the Earl & Countess of Fife,[3] who
came last from Spa, arrived at Paris this Day.

Sunday, Oct: 27. Foggy weather. I did not stir out
'till 3 o'Clock, when I went to dine with Mr Walpole,
who was better. After Dinner his Grace the Duke of
Beaufort, with his Governor Mr Lyte,[4] together with
my Lord Wm Gordon,[5] (Brother to his Grace the Duke
of Gordon), came to pay a Visit of Ceremony for half an

[1]Charles Lennox, 3rd D. of Richmond and Lennox (1735-1806);
Ambassador to Paris, 1765.
[2]Henry Scott, 3rd D. of Buccleuch (1746-1812).
[3]James Duff, 2nd E. of Fife (1729-1809) and his wife: see G.E.C.,
The Complete Peerage, (1926), V. 378.
[4]Henry Lyte, Fellow of Queens' Coll. (1749-63).
[5]2nd son of the 3rd Duke.

Hour to Mr Walpole. The Duke is an Handsome, well built young Man, of 21 years of Age, with an aquiline Nose, with a Colour in his Face, which looked as if he was no Enemy to a Chearful Glass: his Grace talked but little; so the Conversation was cheifly filled up by Mr Lyte, a Middle sized Man, & fat, & much belaced, so [I] suppose he was not a Clergyman, & seemed to be aged about 35 years, & was a well-behaved Man. He afterwards told Mr Walpole that it was with the utmost Difficulty that his Grace could be prevailed upon to stay at all at Paris, & [that he] could never get him to converse in French, but that his whole Conversation & Acquaintance was with the English. It is probable that the Hurry his Grace was in to be in England, was from some Attachment he had there: for it was not above 2 Months after his getting Home, before he was married to his present Duchess, Daughter to the late Admiral Boscawen, Son to Lord Viscount Falmouth, a match highly disagreable to his Grace's Mother, Sister to the Lord Botetort,[1] as the Lady had no great Fortune, which was almost necessary, as his Grace's Estate was much encumbered. My Lord Wm Gordon was a tall, spare young Man of about 20 years of Age, of a civil & obliging Behaviour, with a good Person. After this Company was retired, came in an elderly French Lady, of about 60 years of Age, to drink Tea with Mr Walpole, tho' no French custom: her Name was Madame Geoffrin,[2] a widow Lady, very rich, a great

---

[1] Norborne Berkeley (*ob.* 1776), cr. Baron Botetourt in 1764.

[2] "Geoffrain" [C. throughout]; Marie Thérèse, *née* Rodet, a rich widow at this date 66 years of age. She presided over a *salon*, and was at daggers drawn with Mme Du Deffand—"ou crois que je hais cette femme", writes the latter to Walpole. *Lettres de Mme Du Deffand* (Toynbee), i. 444.

F

Protectress of the Party of Philosophers, & was herself a *Bel Esprit*, or Free-Thinker: when she came in, she immediately flung herself carelessly into an Elbow Chair, almost half reclined, with one Leg thrown over the Knee of the other, & so she sat for 2 or 3 Hours; & being without Stays, in the loose, easy & negligent Dress of the French Women, she had more the Appearance of a Person just got out of Bed, with a Night Gown flung hastily over her, than a Person dressed to make a Visit in an Evening. However, her Company was very entertaining & her Conversation spirited & agreable; especially as she had been acquainted with 2 or 3 English Ladies of Fashion & Distinction, & was a particular Friend of the present Lady[1] Hervey, Mother to the Earl of Bristol, whom she talked of visiting this Summer in England. But the cheif Part of her Conversation turning upon 2 remarkable English Ladies, that she was very intimate with, & whose Characters are worth dwelling upon, my Curiosity was raised in Proportion as I was not much acquainted with either of them; tho' both pretty much known in the World. The one was the late old Countess of Sandwich,[2] Daughter of the Famous witty Earl of Rochester, of the name of Wilmot; & the other the very witty & sprightly Lady Mary Wortley Montagu,[3] Daughter of the Duke of Kingston, & Mother to the present Countess of Bute, whose Fame has been much extended in the Writings of Mr Pope. This Lady Sandwich was Elizabeth the youngest of the 2 Daughters of Wilmot, Earl of Rochester, whose Son dying in his Minority about the

[1]"Molly Lepell"; Mme Du Deffand disliked "Milady Hervey", as being "admiratrice et imitatrice de la Geoffrinska". *Ibid.*, i. 219.

[2]Elizabeth Wilmot, *ob.* 1757.   [3]Mountagu [C.]

latter End of the Reign of King Charles the 2nd his 2 Sisters became his Heirs: one of which marrying the Earl of Sandwich, on his Death she retired to Paris, where she lived all the Rest of her Life; dying in a very advanced Age, in that City, she neither relishing the Air nor the Politics of her Native Kingdom: & what was very extraordinary, tho' she had lived almost all her Life in France, so that she might in a Manner be looked upon as a Native of that Country: [and] tho' what happened after her Death was partly foreseen, & therefore Application made in Time to those in Power, to prevent it: & altho' her Grandson, the present Earl of Sandwich, was a Person of that Distinction in the Court of England, as, if not actually, yet soon after, to be one of his Majesty's Principal Secretaries of State: yet notwithstanding all these Prerogatives & Advantages, on her Decease, which happened about 5 or 6 years ago at Paris, that inhospitable, barbarous & Gothic Law of the *Droit d'Aubaine* immediately took Place, notwithstanding all the Precautions made use of to prevent it; & several of the Civil Officers of the Police belonging to the King of France, the Moment she was dead, broke into her House, & fell to rifling & rummaging her Boxes & Furniture, for the use of that King as an Escheat which was fallen to him.[1] By this *Droit d'Aubaine*, the Personal Effects of most Strangers, (for some Nations are exempt) who happen to die in the King of France his Dominions, fall of Right to that Sovereign. So that it behoves every Foreigner, Englishmen in particular, to be very cautious how their Effects

---

[1]Sterne inserted this note on p. 2 of the *Sentimental Journey* (1768): "All the effects of strangers (Swiss and Scotch excepted) dying in France, are seized in virtue of this law, tho' the heir be upon the spot—the profit of these contingencies being farm'd, there is no redress."

are deposited, in Case of Accident which may threaten their Life: & great Pity it is, considering the Inhospitality of such a singular & barbarous Law, that so many of this Nation, who generously spend their Money among them, to the great Enrichment of their beggarly Country, should be tempted to hazard the Loss of what may be very considerable to their Families in England, by crouding in such Numbers to see a City much inferior to what they left behind them, & a Country & People highly ridiculous! Should such a Law in England subsist against the French, what an Outcry of Barbarity & Gothicism should we hear against us from Voltaire & his Compatriots? What Savages, Brutes & Barbarians should we be called by these affectedly polished more than Savages? Does any Nation in Europe serve them in the way they take upon them to treat other People? I am sure such a Law is sufficient to stigmatize them for greater Barbarians & more inhospitable Savages than any of their Neighbours round about them. This Law seemed to me to be so unjust & inhuman, that it in a Manner determined me to get out of their Country as fast as I could. But to return to the Account Madame Geoffrin gave of this Countess [Sandwich]: she remembered her above 40 years ago, when she was neither handsome nor pretty, but was remarkable always for a starched & settled Formality, keeping a most forbidding Distance to those of her Acquaintance that would submit to it, being one of the most haughty & proud Women she ever remembred; & yet, what seems a Contradiction, but is always Part of the Character of a very Proud Person, she was meanly condescending to those whom she courted, & thought her Superiors. Of this she [Mme G.] gave this

Instance, that happened one Day while she was present.
The Princess de Carignan[1] had paid a Visit to the
Countess & was taking Leave of her, when Madame
Geoffrin was just coming in upon the same Occasion, &
in the Hurry of Ceremony was not observed: but when
the Countess came back, & observed that that Lady
had been a Witness, not only of attending the Princess
to the very last door, but also, at Parting, had taken up
Part of the Princess's Robe, & kissed it, in Token of
the great Honour she thought she had received by that
Visit, she was ready to burst thro' Chagrin & Mortification, as Madame Geoffrin easily perceived by her
faltering Excuses & consequent Behaviour. Another
Instance she gave, of her treacherous, deceitful &
ungenerous Carriage towards the Duchess d'Aguillon,[2]
a Lady with whom she had always lived in the utmost
Intimacy & Friendship, & who had been as a Nurse
to her, in a Manner, in her last Illness, & attended &
waited upon her as one of her Servants, with the
greatest Tenderness & Affection: for she has always
flattered her with the Notion of making her her Heir:
accordingly the very Night she expired, she sent for her
in an Hurry, protested she had left her every Thing,
embraced her in her dying Arms, & expired in them.
When the Will was opened, it was found, that she had
not left her a single Farthing, but had made her Grandson, the present Earl of Sandwich, her universal Heir;
a Person she always abhorred, & heartily detested. So
utterly unaccountable are the Actings of weak Mortals!
One can hardly suppose that any one can be so entirely

---

[1]Presumably, wife of Louis (*ob.* 1778), the 4th Prince de C.

[2]"Frank, and jolly, and handsome and good-humoured, with dignity
too" (Walpole to Selwyn, Dec. 2, 1765).

void of all the good Principles of common Honesty &
Integrity, as designedly & on Purpose to leave the
World with a Lye in One's Mouth, & a full Design to
impose on one's Friend: one can hardly suppose any
Creature to be so uncommonly base: one must therefore
seek after some other Reason for so much Disingenuity:
it is possible, she might not think her end so near, &
might really Design, what she so often had promised:
or possibly the great & ruling Passion of Pride; in the
Augmentation of her own Family's Wealth, might
extinguish the less violent one of Freindship, & even
get the better of the inveterate Hatred to her Grandson:
agreable to the Practice of many great People, who
heartily hate their own Children, & yet love their
Posterity with an Affection that can only be accounted
for but from a Principle of Pride & Vanity.

Lady Mary Wortley Montague was a Daughter of
the Duke of Kingston, & Wife to Edward Wortley
Montague Esqr, Grandson to the first Earl of Sandwich: so that this Lady & the last mentioned Character
were Cousins by Alliance. In 1716, she went with her
Husband in his Embassy to Constantinople; a very
agreable Expedition for a Woman of her lively &
romantic Turn of Mind, & which gave her an Opportunity to display that sprightly Genius in a Series of
most entertaining & elegant Letters, descriptive of the
Manners of the People she conversed with, during her
Travels, wrote, I suppose, as to the greatest Part of
them, to her Sister, the Countess of Mar, & published
about the year 1763, soon after the Death of the Author
of them. I am sorry the Prefaces to these Letters give a
Testimony of that Lady's Character that must be dis-
proved, if the following, which I heard from Madame

Geoffrin & Mr Walpole, who knew her well, deserves any Credit, who represented her as the vilest & most worthless of Womankind: notwithstanding, her Talents for Wit, Vivacity, Genius & Elegance of Taste were unexceptionable.

As a Specimen of her Style & Manner of Writing, I shall enter here a very elegant & ingenious Epistle of hers to a young Lady, written, I suppose, on some Eclipse of the Moon, & published this Month in the *Whitehall Evening Post* of May 3, 1766, which, in order to preserve it, I copied into a blank Leaf of my Edition of the abovesaid Letters, & for the same Reason give it a Place here:

"An original Letter from Lady Mary W. Montague
    to Miss . . . .

"My Dear Girl,
    "I have so violent a Cold, that I never was less qualified in my Life for inspecting the heavenly Bodies, & must content myself with the vulgar Warmth of my Dressing-Room Fire, to a Corner of which I am confined all this Evening, & very glad to see you, if you can attend me any Time after your most learned Employment.
    "If the Moon is inhabited by Mortals like us, & the most important Transactions among them, are nothing more than Kingdoms turned into Common-Wealths, & Common-Wealths into Kingdoms; & these mighty Events are produced there, as they are here, by Tyranny or lust, I have no Desire of being acquainted with its Inhabitants: but can look down upon them, as they do upon us. I have peeped behind the Scenes here, more than contributes to my Ease, & by examining the Wires & Mechanism of the Shew, the Entertainment has long since ceased. Who is any longer entertained with a Hocus-Pocus Man, when he knows how the Tricks are performed? In short, my dear Girl, our most pleasing Pursuits become Carrion by the

Time they are hunted down. I would not put you out of Conceit with the World you are but just beginning to enter into; but to prepare you to bear those Disappointments, common to all, but most severely felt by those of your Cast & mine: for I would willingly tack myself to any Thing that is half so good as I know you to be, & wish myself."

This witty Lady was formerly exceedingly pretty, had a fine peircing Eye, was rather under-sized, & pitted with the Small-Pox; but altogether a very agreable Person, as well as the most accomplished. With so romantic a disposition, it is no Wonder she had a Turn for Gallantry. She had an Affair with a French Nobleman, whom she afterwards enticed to follow her to London, where, under the Pretence of greatly encreasing his Fortune by some Project or other, she cajoled him out of 2000 Pounds: soon after this, she gave him to understand that her Husband had got some Intimation of their Amour, & threatened to have him assassinated: on which Intelligence the Nobleman fled over to France in all Haste; but on his getting there & hearing nothing from her after repeated Addresses to her, & gaining some Light into her real Character, & guessing at her Design to trick him of his Money, he made Interest in England with those who could redress him; & she finding that the Thing was in a Train to become public, to her Disreputation, she refunded the Money, to her no small Regret.[1] Mr Walpole had been much acquainted with her at Florence about the year 1743 or 1744, where she long resided, & where she was reputed to be one of the most wicked, malitious &

[1] A libellous story. A Frenchman, named Rémond, who had pestered Lady M. with love-letters, sent her money to be invested for him in South Sea Stock. When the stock fell he demanded his money back in full and threatened her with blackmail in default of receiving it.

envious Persons in the World:[1] her whole Employment
being to make Mischeif, & never better pleased than
when she could set Friends at variance, & raise
Squabbles & Jealousies among Acquaintance. She
afterwards turned out one of the most wretched,
miserable & avaritious Creatures upon Earth: to such
a Degree, as to employ the Dregs of the People,
Kennel-Sweepers & such Gentry, to pick up old Nails
in the Gutters & Streets of London, & to buy old Iron
& other vile Materials, of which she had Magazines, in
order to sell them again by the Great.[2] A Thing
incredible had I not heard it averred for Truth, by those
who knew her well. She afterwards went again to live
abroad, where her nearest Relations would fain have
persuaded her to have remained; they being ashamed
both of her Character & Practice; but could not prevail
with her: so accordingly she came over, & took
Lodgings in London, where Mr Walpole saw her about
3 years ago, going to pay his Respects to her as an old
Acquaintance, & found her, agreably to Mr Pope's
Description of her, for it is her whom he means when
he says:

". . . Sapho's Diamonds, with her dirty Smock,"[3] all
over dirt, in Cloaths not fit for a Common Servant to be
seen in, slipshod, in a pair of tattered old Slippers,[4]
mending, by the Light of 2 Tallow Candles, her own
Stockin[g]s, in a very ordinary & wretched Lodgin[g]s.
I hope this Account may be exaggerated in Pity to

---

[1]"Her dress, her avarice, and her impudence must amaze any one
that never heard her name"; Walpole to H. S. Conway, Sept. 25, 1740.

[2]Wholesale.   [3]*Moral Essays*, Ep. ii. 24.

[4]See a letter of hers in the *Annual Register* of 1766, p. 218, relating to
slippers [C.].

human Nature, & in Regard to a Person of such great Talents & Abilities: if it is not, I should rather impute it to another Cause, than to the Badness of her Heart. It is well known that the Family from whence she was descended have an hereditary Malady in it, which is more to be pitied, than condemned. Her Sister, the Countess of Mar, was long confined in Ampthill Manor House, where her Daughter, Lady Fanny Erskine,[1] had the Management of her: who also told the Gentleman, from whom I had the former Part of her Story, that altho' her Circumstances in Life could not well afford it, as her Sister had what was allowed to maintain her, yet Lady Mary's Covetousness was so excessive, as almost to starve her Mother: upon which she offered to keep her for nothing; which, as it suited that Lady's known Disposition, was freely accepted: tho' I believe Lady Frances had afterwards a full Allowance for keeping her. Another Instance of the same unhappy Disorder was also in my Neighbourhood of the same Family, Lady Frances Meadowes, Sister to the present Duke of Kingston;[2] & who lived many years, often confined, in that Duke's House at Hanslop near Newport-Pagnel in Buckinghamshire. Which noble Duke, living many years at Paris, fell in love there with a French Banker's Wife, one Madame La Touche,[3] with whom he lived many years after she retired with him into England; but afterwards parting, She, out of Conscience, as it was said, turned Protestant, & bore a very good Character: his Grace then, being one of the

[1]*Ob.* 1776.   [2]Evelyn Pierrepoint, 2nd D., *ob.* 1773.

[3]C. refers to Justamond, *Life of Louis XV*, (transl.) 1781, i. 264, but here it is merely stated that "she forsook her husband to follow a gallant into England in 1737."

most personable Men in England, lived altogether with Miss Chudleigh, who is since parted from him, & gone Abroad; & whether his Grace has any other Attachment to supply the Place of these two Ladies, I know not, he being never married.[1] The mention of Madame La Touche's turning Protestant puts me in mind of a similar Case in point of a Conversion for Conscience, told me by Mr Walpole about this Time, which was, That he was very well informed, & from undoubted Authority, that the eldest Son of the old Chevalier de St George, out of Principle & Conscience, had actually lately abjured the Roman Catholic Religion for that of the Church of England, in St Martin's Church in London,[2] under the Name of Charles Stuart, but not known to be who he was by the officiating Minister, who supposed him to be a Common English Catholic: he said moreover, that he was much given to Drink; that the French made a mere Joke of him; & that he had declared, that he would never marry, in order to put an End to the Troubles & Disgraces of his own unhappy Family, & those of his Friends. Since the Death of the old Chevalier at Rome, about 3 Months ago,[3] there were some Hints of this Sort in the public Papers, which, however, are of no Authority whatever: but how this agrees with his Reception & Residence at Rome, I leave others to judge.

After Madame Geoffrin had left Mr Walpole, as soon as the French Comedy was over, his Servant came into the Room, & said that Mr Wilkes was coming in to pay

[1] He married Miss Chudleigh (but bigamously, as it turned out), in 1769.

[2] This is the account given by Walpole to Mann on Aug. 12, 1765.

[3] This must be an addendum, for the Old Pretender died Jan. 1, 1766.

him a Visit. I was all Expectation to see this famous, or rather infamous Man: when, behold, instead of a squint-eyed ugly Fellow, with hardly a Tooth in his Head, a tall, well-made & handsome young Gentleman, of about 21 years of Age, was introduced. Both he & Mr Walpole laughed heartily at the Servant's Mistake; tho' I question whether the Earl of Ossory[1] was pleased at the Bottom to be taken for so worthless a Character, & ill-looking a Fellow. Mr Wilkes had never been but once at Mr Walpole's,[2] & having pretty much the same Sort of Coat as his Lordship then wore, occasioned the Mistake. Lord Ossory had been expected in England, & had fixed his Departure 2 or 3 Times: but a little Attachment at Paris chained him there, where he staid 'till after I left it. A pleasant Story was mentioned in his Company, which, for its Wit & Liveliness, I will give a Place here: it was a smart Saying of the present Viscountess Dowager Townshend,[3] Etheldreda Harrison, who is as remarkable for saying as many good Things, & doing as many improper ones, as any Lady in England. This Lady being walking in Ranelagh Gardens one Evening of the last Season, met there, as usual, in all Places of public Resort, their Royal Highnesses the Dukes of York & Gloucester; as soon as she had passed them, she said to the Company she was with, This is surely the dearest Family to keep, & the cheapest to see, of any that ever was in England.

[1] John Fitzpatrick (1745-1818), 2nd E. of Upper Ossory; "Modest, manly, very sensible, and well-bred", *Letters of Hor. Walpole* (Toynbee), No. 1060, Oct. 15, 1765.

[2] But, "Wilkes is here and has been twice to see me in my illness", Walpole to G. Montagu, Oct. 16, 1765.

[3] Widow of the 3rd Visct.; mother of Charles Townshend, the statesman.

Monday, 28 *Oct. St Simon & St Jude.* Fine Day. My Taylor, one Mr Schelling, a Brandenburgher established at Paris, measured me for a Suit of black cloth Cloaths, & a Pompadour-Coloured[1] Great Coat, by Way of Morning Gown. As the Dauphin's Death was expected every Day,[2] I ordered my Coat not to be full trimmed with Buttons, that it might serve me without making up fresh Mourning. The Dauphin's Disorder was a confirmed Dropsy; & as the Court went a little before to Fontainbleau from Versailles, to spend a Month or 6 Weeks there, (tho' they were distressed to find Money for the Expence of it, their Finances were so disordered), his Royal Highness was willing to attend it, in Hopes that Change of Air might benefit his Complaint; tho' he was then so ill, that it was with Difficulty he could be got thither. This Prince was of a most amiable Character, an excellent Husband, tender & good Father & dutiful Son: he was a great Freind to the Church, a Protector, as much as laid in his Power, of the Jesuits: consequently maligned, hated & abused by the Deistical Philosophers & their Faction to such a Degree, as it was a shameful Sight to observe the Joy on their Countenances, as fresh Advices came every Day from Fontainbleau confirming the little Hopes of his Recovery. Nay, notwithstanding the great Silence imposed, & generally observed by the French, on any public Calamity, or any Thing respecting the Court, or Politics; where one is presently sent to the Bastile, or some Place of Confinement, for it, yet in private Society this Restraint was less, & People could not help express-

[1] C. at p. 179 describes this as "between red and purple", but in the *O.E.D.* it is "a shade of crimson or pink"; let us hope C. was right!

[2] The Dauphin (Louis) died Dec. 20, 1765.

ing their Hopes & Fears upon this alarming Occasion: for it was presumed, should the Dauphin survive his Father, the Banishment of the Jesuits would be repealed, & their Enemies, with those of Christianity, would be disgraced. But such is the Will of Providence, which knows what is best for us, tho' we may judge otherwise, that generally the Best are taken away soonest, while their Adversaries are left behind to fill the Measure of their Iniquity: & indeed to such a Pass were these Philosophers arrived, as not only in their Writings to fall foul of all Revelation, but also in private Companies to ridicule the Religion of their Country: insomuch that the Religious Orders could not pass the Streets without being pointed at, & turned into Ridicule for the Singularity of their several Habits: in the very same Manner, that the two last *Whitehall Evening Posts* (I write this May 31, 1766) have contained each a long letter to ridicule the Dress of the English Clergy, & Endeavours to persuade Mankind, that a mere Lay Habit, of any Colour rather than black, would be much more suitable & proper, than the decent Robes & Dress now in Use: for it is the self same Principle that animates the Enemies of the Church in both Kingdoms: the Jansenistical Faction covertly acting under the Auspices of their Allies the Deists in France, as the Calvinistical, Presbyterian, & Independant Faction in England unites with the Free-Thinkers in their Venom against the Established Church: & rather than their own Party should not be uppermost, would be contented that Christianity should be sacrificed to the Malice of Unbelievers. There is hardly a Paper in the *St James's Chronicle* which is not stuffed with Abuses of the Roman Catholics, by which often they spit their

Poison against the Church of England, but also the latter is as grossly abused & fell foul on, as in the years a little before & after the infamous 1640: so that it is very easy to know from what Forge such Implements are made: & if the same Spirit is suffered to diffuse its Malignity in the same Proportion among the common People, Tradesmen & smaller Gentry, as it has within these last 30 years, by the means of Magazines, News-Papers of multiplied Forms & other pestilent Books & Papers, it is easy to foresee what will become of our present Christianity & Form of Government: for that restless Republican Spirit of Calvin, will never be at Quiet 'till the Monarchy & Hierarchy are laid level with their Idol of Equality. To such a Pitch of Assurance was the French Philosophy risen, that I was told by Mr Walpole, on observing to him the few regular Clergy one saw in the Streets of Paris, that they had Orders from their Superiors to keep more within their Cloistres, not to give Offence to their Enemies, by their too open Appearance in the World: & their Ridicule had had this Effect, that many of the younger Monks of St Germain's & other Convents, had actually petitioned the Parliament for Leave to quit their religious Habit: but as the older Part of their Convents had disavowed what the others had done, it was not yet judged proper to proceed to those Lengths taken on the same Conjuncture in our Henry 8th's Time. Things were not quite ripe for it yet: however there is a Restraint laid upon receiving Religious of both Sexes under such an Age, & beyond such a Number: & so far, I think, they judge very rightly: but whether they will end as prudently, God only knows for certain; tho' one may be allowed reasonably to presume, that they will not:

considering the Temper, Disposition, & Principles of those who are likely to be the Reformers: for the Men who take the Lead in their several busy & factious Parliaments, if we may judge of all by the Specimens we have of many of them, are of too Philosophical a Turn to allow, that Reason is only an Handmaid of Revelation. In short, the present Situation of France has much the Appearance of being soon the Theatre of a civil War. I must needs own, tho' a good Englishman, & praying that he might never be an Enemy to my Country, that when the public Prayers were ordered to be put up for the Recovery of the Dauphin, as I frequently went into their Churches, where they were assembled upon that Occasion, & where I must do them the Justice to own, that they were greatly crouded, & that the People seemed very devoutly to be in Earnest for what they came thither, that I as heartily joyned my Prayers to their own, when I considered the great Accomplishments & many good Qualities of the Prince for whose sake the Congregation was assembled. For it is my firm Persuasion, & ever has been so, notwithstanding your Tillotsons, Burnets & Hoadleys,[1] that the Church has much worse Enemies than Papists to encounter with; as also that common Christianity has no good Reason to be so eager to see Popery extinguished in France or elsewhere: that many Things want Reformation in it, is too true: but that in general it is the Bulwark of Christianity, & that when the Calvinists & Deists have undermined that, the Church of England first, & then the Rest of what we have been always taught to look upon as essential to Christianity, will not be long before they must give Way to a Deistical

[1]As representing "low-churchmen".

Licentiousness. And such are the Obligations we are under to these mighty Patrons of Civil & Religious Liberty! But God, in Chastisement for the Infidelity of France, had otherwise disposed in Respect to the Dauphin, who, after suffering great Pains, died at Fontainbleau, in the Diocese of Sens, on 20th of Dec: 1765, in which Cathedral Church he desired to be interred, & not at St Denis, out of Regard to the Arch-Bp thereof, the Cardinal Paul D'Albert de Luynes;[1] & where his Wife, the Dauphiness,[2] an amiable Princess of the House of Saxony, desired also a Vault to be made for her, against the Time she should rejoyn him. But to get clear from this long Digression, which I hope will be fewer & shorter for the future, or I see no End of finishing my 6 Weeks' or 2 Months' Travels.

This Day I called about Noon on Mr Walpole, who carried me to St Roche's[3] Church, & all round the new Boulevarts, which surround half the City of Paris on the North Side of the River. We entered these Boulevarts, (being the old Ramparts & Fortifications of the City, which Lewis the 14th caused to be demolished, saying that the Capital of his Kingdom ought to have no other Defence than the Hearts of its Inhabitants), at the Port St Antoine, near the Bastile, & went all round them quite to their Extremity, at the Port St Honoré, near the Place de Louis le Grand, & the Thuilleries; great Part of which on the right Hand, nearest the Fauxbourg, is filled up with Coffee Houses, Houses of public Resort & Amusement. Rope-Dancers, Mountabanks, Slight-of-Hand People, with Music & all other Entertainment, are crouded together, & in Balconies, with

[1]1703-88.   [2]She was buried beside him two years later.
[3]Rocque (MS.).

G

Monkeys & other Animals, invite continually the
Passengers on Foot or in Equipages, to come in, &
partake of their Amusements. As it is a Place much
frequented in Fine Weather, & deserted in the Winter
Months, it is very amusing now & then to pass thro'
in airing, as the Passage is broad, & Trees in Rows
planted on both Sides: & has much the Appearance of
Bartholomew Fair, & what I remember formerly to
have seen at Sturbridge Fair,[1] when the People from
Sadler's Wells, & Collections of foreign Animals &
Wild Creatures used to be brought there, with Trum-
peters & Music constantly inviting People to come in
& see them. On the Walk for Foot Passengers on the
other Side, are Stalls with Fruit, Prints & Maps,
hanging against the Walls of the Gardens of the Houses
belonging to the City, in which are Arbours, & other
Ornaments of a most beautifull & elegant Workmanship, called Trellis Work,[2] made of thin Peices of Wood
crossing each other & painted green, & have an admirable Effect in Gardens, & are peculiar to Paris; at least
I saw none any where else. I have seen whole Ranges of
Buildings of them in Gardens, with Corinthian & other
Pillars, done in so artful & nice a Manner, as must
require great Judgment & Labour to finish them so
elegantly. Mr Walpole designs to have some of the same
Sort of Work at his Country House at Strawberry Hill[3]
near London: but I much question whether an English

[1] A very important fair formerly held in the outskirts of Cambridge.
Often "Stirbridge".

[2] C. speaks of this as though it were a novelty, but both the word and
the thing went back to the fifteenth cent.

[3] Walpole wrote to Cole, March 9, 1765, "My bower is determined
. . . I have decided that the outside shall be of *treillage*, which, however,
I shall not commence till I have again seen some of old Louis's *galan-
teries* at Versailles."

Hand will be able to do it in the Way they are finished at Paris.

As the Sun shone out, & it was a fine Day to see the Scenery of St Roche's Church to Advantage, as we passed by it in the Rue St Honoré, Mr Walpole would make me get out of the Coach, tho' he was too lame to do so himself, to go in, & view it, while he staid for me. It is a very noble Pile of Building in the Doric Stile, ascended by a very large Flight of Steps up to the Portico,[1] in a very good Situation for Paris; being in a tolerable broad Part of the good Street St Honoré, with the West End fronting it, supposing, (as I shall always suppose, to save Trouble), that their Churches are built, like our's in England, due East & West: which by the Bye, I believe they do not so much regard. From the great West Door at the Bottom of the Nave or grand Middle Ile there is the most striking Peice of Scenery that can be exhibited; there being 3 Chapels behind the High Altar, all of which are discovered at the same Time; the last of all being the Chapel of the Calvary, on the Altar of which is a fine large Crucifix of White Marble, finishing the whole; & has, indeed, more the Look & Appearance of a beautiful Scene in an Opera or Play-House, than of any Part of a Place dedicated to Christian Worship. The Altar of the elegant Church of the English Recollets at Doway, mentioned at p. 19 is in the same Taste; tho' not so magnificent. The architect has contrived that the Back Part of each Altar should be open, which, with a Cupola[2] at the Top darting the Rays of Light & Sun,

[1]Battered by artillery on Oct. 5, 1795, in the fight between Denican's forces and the troops of the Convention.

[2]Cupulo (MS.).

from some well disposed Windows, casting their Beams upon some of the principal Objects, give a Scene & Lustre not to be described on Paper: by Means of which, if the Devotion of a good & pious Catholic would be greatly improved & much elevated, the squeamish Stomach of an Huguenot would be sick to Death, & would turn away from so much Foppery, as he would scornfully call it, with Fright & Abhorrence. On each Side of the High Altar are two Marble Figures, [one] of our Blessed Saviour holding his Cross, & the other of St Roche, extremely well executed:[1] the Chapel behind this, is of our Lady, & has a most beautiful Altar, over which is represented our Lady's Annunciation, she, being on her Knees, & the Attitude of the Angel addressing her, (both admirably executed in white statuary Marble), are inimitable: & on each Side of this Altar stand two vast Figures in Brass of King David, & the Prophet Isaiah. The Paintings also in this Church are excellent: one representing the Death of St Lewis, who is giving his last Instructions to his Son King Philip the Bold, hanging against a wall fronting one of the cheif Altars, seemed to me to be a very capital Picture, [by Ant. Coypel]. There are private small Chapels on each Side of the Side Iles, very neat & elegant: but the Singularity of the different Altars, is so striking, at the East End of this fine Church, is such as must give it a Preference to most others in this City: it pleased me so much, notwithstanding all its noted Irregularities, that I went to see it 2 or 3 Times afterwards.

After Dinner, Mr Mariette,[2] Grandson of the famous

[1] By Fr. Anguier, *l'ainé*.

[2] The son, presumably, of Pierre Jean M. (*ob.* 1774), a great collector; his grandfather, Jean M. died in 1742.

Engraver of that Name, & who left his Family a good
Estate, came to drink Coffee with Mr Walpole: he is
an old Man of between 60 & 70 years of age, a great
Connoisseur in Painting, has a large Collection of them
as well as Prints; & seemed to be well acquainted with
all our best Books of Antiquity; especially such as had
any Prints in them, as Dugdale, King, &c. Between 5
& 6 o'Clock Mr Walpole lent me his Coach to carry me
to the French Comedy, which was *Le Joue[u]r*,[1] or *The
Gamester*, with a Farce, called the Frenchman at London,
Le François à Londres, where the English were well
ridiculed in the Character of Jack Roast-Beef, a
Gentleman of Fortune, but quite an Englishman, &
dressed more like a Quaker than any one else: indeed
the Character was *outre* overdone: however, to do them
Justice, the French Marquis was as extravagant a
Character; & the Winding up of the Scene acknowledged, That if the French had more Politeness, the
English had more Reason, so that upon the whole, we
had no Reason to be displeased: besides, when we
consider how we revenge ourselves on them constantly
in our Theatres in London, we ought to think ourselves
well off, in being handled so gently. Indeed, there is
some little Difference in the Case between the two
Nations: for whereas we go to Paris to spend our
Money, & fill their Pockets, it would be hardly fair, nor
would it answer their Purpose, to make us the standing
Subject of Ridicule, as we do them; they on the Contrary, never come to London, but with a Design to
advantage themselves at our Expence: which may, in
some Measure, account for our treating them in that

---

[1] A translation, by B. J. Saurin, of Edward Moore's play *The Gamester*
(1753) seems to be meant, though this was a tragedy.

Manner. Their Play-House was Handsome, longer than ours, but not so convenient: the People in the Pit all stand: I sat, in, what they called, the Orchestra; a Place, with about 6 or 7 Ranges of Seats, between the Music, (which is placed as ours is, just below the Stage), & the Pit. The Boxes all round were the same as in our Theatres. The Actors & Actresses might be very accomplished: but they did not suit my Taste, no more than their Singing: the Women were so painted with red & white & that so injudiciously, & unnaturally, as to look hideous. Their Dancers were good, & among them an Englishman exceeded the Rest. I gave 6 Francs, or Livres, for my Seat: but upon the whole was so poorly entertained, that I took my Leave of their Theatre, & went no more.

Tuesday, 29 *Oct:* Fine Day. Mr Walpole was so kind as to send his Servant to invite me to dine with him: which indeed he did regularly every Day, while I was in Paris: so will mention that Circumstance no more: however, I excused myself, as it was often inconvenient for me, (as he was disabled to go with me to Churches, Convents & other Places, as he designed, had he been well enough), to be back again by the Time he usually dined, which was 3 o'Clock: for I loved to go out after Breakfast, which I seldom got over, & dressed myself, before 11, when I sufficiently tired myself, (by walking over Churches & Cloysters, & visiting other Parts of the City, tho' always in a Coach,) by 4 o'Clock; at which Time I always ordered my Dinner at *Traiteurs* to my own Chamber, & then enjoyed myself as if I had been at Home in my Night Cap, Night Gown & Slippers, by a good Fire Side: for never eating Suppers, a late Dinner was always very agreable to me; by which

Means no Part of the short Days at this Season was lost.

The first Place that I walked to after Breakfast, with my 2 Servants, was the Convent of the *Petits Augustins*,[1] just over the Way, & a little farther up the Street near the Quay of the Mazarine College: this Convent, which gives Names to the whole Street, if one may judge of its Inside, by its Outside Appearance & Front to the Street, has nothing worthy of being examined with Attention. The principal Entrance into the Convent is by an Arched Gateway in the Street, into a small Court where Coaches may drive up to the Cheif Front of their Church: but neither the Buildings in this Court, nor one adjoyning to it, which I entered into, nor the Front of the Church is the least worth Observation: the Church itself, which is one large Nave, with an arched Roof, is dark & gloomy, & the High Altar at the End of it, seemed to be too much charged with Ornaments & Figures, & to be too large & massive to be regularly handsome: behind it was the Choir of the Religious, who are Friers of the Order of St Austin. On the right Hand of the High Altar is a round or octagon Sort of Chapel, with a vaulted Roof or Dome, but of no Sort of Beauty or Proportion: out of this Chapel is a private Door into the Street, near the End of it, towards the River. The Convent was founded by the famous Margaret de Valois, the repudiated Wife of King Henry 4, who died in 1615.

From hence I walked by the River Side, on a broad & handsome Quay, & at no great Distance from the

[1]Noteworthy as the building in which Lenoir deposited many of the works of art, and historical monuments, rescued by him during the Terror.

Convent, to the noble College founded by Cardinal
Mazarine, fronting the Louvre on the other Side of the
Water, & near the Foot of the Pont-Neuf, called *Le
Collège des Quatre Nations*,[1] the Cardinal's Intention
being to give a Gentleman's Education to a certain
Number [60] of Students of 4 different Countries,
which had been late the Theatres of War, *viz*: about
Pignerol, for Italy; Alsatia, for Germany; French
Flanders, & Roussillon, for France & Spain. The Front
to the River is truly magnificent, being a Semi-Circle,
in the midst of which is the Portico, supported by
Columns, of the Church, & the Extremities consist of
two Pavilions for Lodgings, which project out rather
too much into the Street or Quay, & hinder a fine View
all the way down it. The Cupola,[2] tho' fine, seemed to
me to be too big for the Church, which is small, & in
the Inside far from being a pleasing Building, with its
small Windows & vast naked Walls & Arches. It is
paved with Marble, but, according to the polite French
Fashion, excessively dirty, they continually hawking &
spitting, (as well in private Rooms, as in their Churches):
which is very offensive to our more cleanly Manners: &
it was a Week or two before I could at all break my
French Servant from spitting all over my Chamber,
while I was at Breakfast or Dinner: & so different are
our Ideas of Cleanliness in this, as well as in many other
Particulars, that it was beyond my Power to make him
comprehend the Impropriety of it. There were 2 or 3
Side-Chapels in the 2 Side-Iles of the Church, but
[they] did not seem to be finished. The Chapel on the
right Hand of the High Altar, or South Side, is entirely
taken up by the very fine Tomb of the Cardinal, fixed

[1]Now *Palais de l'Institut*.   [2]Cupulo (MS.).

against the South Wall;[1] but is so ill lighted & so gloomy, as to be seen to great Disadvantage. The Cardinal is represented on his Knees, in his Cardinal's Robes, in a very light & airy Manner, with Devotion towards the High Altar, & behind him is an Angel holding the Fasces, (Part of his Arms); both these Figures are on a Sarcophagus, at the Foot of which are three Virtues sitting, represented as Women, in full Proportion & highly finished, as is the Figure of his Eminence in white Marble, but soiled thro' Time & Dust, & is supposed to be very like him: at least it is very like 2 fine Prints of him in my Possession, both engraved by Nantueil,[2] one in 1655; the other a full Length, sitting in a Cabinet full of Busts, having a Plan of Fortifications in his Hand, very ridiculously, tho' dressed in his Ecclesiastical Habit. Indeed he has more to be said for him than Cardinal Richelieu & his Admiralty Insignia, as he was originally bred a Soldier: however, when he had taken so good Root in the Church, as to be one of its Princes & Pillars, it was high Time to quit his other Military Profession: but he had always the Vanity & Ridicule to be thought to excell in his first Way of Life even in the Camp with a Marshal Turenne. Just under the Arch, in a *Compartiment*, above the Monument, are placed the Cardinal's Arms, supported by 2 large Figures of Women, emblematical of the Cardinal's Virtues: On a Table of Marble just behind his Head, against the Wall is an Inscription to his Memory; which I did not take on the Spot, but transcribe it from a printed Copy. [See G. Brice, *Description de Paris*, iv. 119.]

[1]During the Revolution conveyed to the *Musée des Monumens Français*.
[2]Robert N. (1630-78).

This Church is never opened for public use, (as almost all the other Chapels & Churches are), except on 2 or 3 particular Festivals in the year: so that the way to it is to go into a Court on the left Side of it, into which is the common Entrance for the Students by a handsome Side Door, opposite the Cardinal's Monument. This first Court is small, & has nothing remarkable in it for Beauty: beyond it is a much larger Quadrangle, but of no great Beauty. The Library is reckoned handsome, is much esteemed for its Contents, as well as for its elegant Manner of being fitted up: but, on Enquiry, not finding it open, I never went again to see it. From hence I walked over the Pont-Neuf, examined the famous Equestrian Statue of Henry 4 upon it, mentioned before at p. 48, standing on a Pedestal of Marble raised very high, on an Angle of the Bridge contrived on Purpose for its Reception; so that it stands in no one's Way, & in the most public Part, & indeed the most ornamental & beautiful, of the whole City, with its Face fronting the *Sainte Chapelle* & Notre-Dame. From this Place I crossed the Pont-Neuf, by the Samaritan Fountain, & the great Front of the Louvre, which was then beautifying, the Scaffolding not being taken down, & a large Space before it, opened it, to make the Entrance suitable to it: in the Front of which, nearer to the Bridge, stands surrounded by narrow Lanes & Passages, the fine old Gothic Church of St Germain l'Auxerrois, the Parish Church of the Louvre & of all this Quarter: It is a fine old venerable Fabric perfectly regular, & very neat in the Inside, the Choir having lately newly fitted up: there is an Isle surrounds the Choir, with Chapels all round it: tho' the Church is but gloomy & dark from the painted Glass: in the Nave,

near the Choir, is a very large & expensive Pew for the
Officers of the Parish, which contributes to spoil the
Beauty & Symmetry of the Church.

I walked from hence over one half of the Pont-Neuf
to the Isle du Palais or into the City, thro' the Triangular Place called *La Place Dauphine*, just opposite to
the Statue of Henry the 4, & so to the awkward Court
in which is one Side of the elegant & neat little Church
called the *Sainte Chapelle* in which is interred the Body
of St Louis, King of France.[1] It put me in Mind of our
Magnificent Chapel of King's College in Cambridge,
which would contain, I suppose near a Dozen of this
diminutive one: but its Gothic Form, & Windows &
Spires are somewhat resembling: tho' this has a very
lofty & light Spire in the Middle of it. You ascend to it
by, as I suppose, some 30 Stone Steps, there being
another Chapel underneath it. The West Front is
adorned with many Stone Statues, of good old Workmanship. The Nave is but small, but the painted Glass
in the Windows, which are very large for the Size of the
Room, being well painted in small round, oval & other
shaped *Compartiments*, in which are represented in small
Figures the History of the Old & New Testament, are
well worth Observation, as are the Statues in Niches,
between the Windows on both Sides, of the 12 Apostles:
but over 2 old Altars on either Side of the Door into the
Choir are some large Peices of Enamel Painting representing Francis 1 & his Queen Eleanor of Austria, on
one Side, & Henry 2, with Catherine of Medicis on the
other Side, with other ornamental Peices of Enamel,

---

[1] A strange error; "his bones were preserved in a coffer, and buried at
St Denis, in France, which he had selected for his place of burial", as
De Joinville tells us. *Cf.* p. 321, *infra.*

are the most curious Things of the Sort that can be seen.[1] The Choir is extremely small, consisting of a thin Chapter, being a Treasurer, who is at the Head of it, & has the Privilege of the Mitre, with a Chanter & a few Canons: all of which have been rendered immortal by the ingenious little Poem of the *Lutrin*,[2] by Nicholas Boileau, who is interred in the undermost Chapel. There are Milliners Shops, & Shops for all Sorts of Trinkets & Toys, on the Steps & all round the *Sainte Chapelle*, & still more of them in Alleys as you pass from that to the *Salle* or *Halle du Palais*, who teize & tire you not a little by calling after you, as the Shop-keepers do in Moor-Fields, to come into their Shops, & buy Something of them. This *Salle du Palais*[3] is frequented by the Law Gentry in their black Gowns & Adonis powdered long Hair,[4] & black Cloaths, in the same Manner as our Westminster Hall is, & their Parliament House & different Courts of Law Business are all adjoyning about it. The *Salle* or *Halle du Palais* is one large and long Room, built & roofed with Stone, of no very great Height, with a Range of Stone Pillars in the midst of it to support the Roof: in this Hall, which is a gloomy, dull, heavy Room, are on all Sides of it Shops of Booksellers & Pamphlet-Sellers cheifly: at the Upper End of one Side, the furthest from the *Sainte Chapelle* & on the right Hand is an Altar covered by a Curtain, with

[1]Walpole praising the *Sainte Chapelle* in a letter to Cole (Jan. 18, 1766), adds, "You did not tell me what charming enamels I should find in the ante-chapel". They were executed by Léonard de Limoges after designs by Primaticcio.

[2]"The Reading-desk", (1674-81), a serio-comic account of an ecclesiastical squabble.

[3]The *Salle des Pas Perdus*.

[4]Presumably, hair worn after the fashion of an "Adonis wig".

a Set of Organs, where Mass is performed on the Meeting or Opening of Parliaments, where the Nobility,
Members, & Magistrates attend upon such occasions
in great solemnity. On the same Side, about the
Middle, & just fronting the Entrance into this Hall
from the *Sainte Chapelle*, is a Door thro' which you are
led into 2 or 3 different Chambers, where the Parliament assembles, & where Law Cases are debated &
Pleadings are heard: but they seemed to me to be much
too small for such Purposes, & had nothing magnificent
or grand to denote their being applied to such Purposes.
In the Chamber where the Parliament assembles, were
two small Tribunes or little Galleries for the Royal
Family: it had some raised Galleries at one End for the
Cheif Magistrates & on the Floor some moveable Seats
& Benches with a Table covered with a Carpet. Against
the Wall were a few modern Pictures, one of the present
King: but what struck my Fancy more than all were
some exceeding antique Paintings above the Wainscote
behind the principal Magistrates' Bench: one was an
excellent old Crucifix well painted on Board; another of
St Denis; besides 2 or 3 other very antient Pictures.

From hence I walked by the Châtelet[1] & Butcher's
Market to the most noble & venerable Pile of Gothic
Architecture I ever saw: tho' I think Ely is longer &
more lightsome: I mean the Archiepiscopal Church of
Notre Dame, whose grand & stately West Front strikes
one with Reverence at one's first Approach to it: tho'
many of our Cathedrals have a more airy Appearance,
this being in a clumsy & heavy Stile; yet none, that I
know of is so richly ornamented with Sculpture: there

[1]*Le Grand* and *le petit Châtelet* were, respectively, civil and criminal
courts, with a prison adjoining.

being no Part of it but what is crouded with Images &
Carving. The lowermost Story of it is the most like our
Cathedral of Peterborough, having 3 stately & magnificent *Portails*, deeply arched, & entirely fitted with
Niches in which are Images of Saints, Bishops, Angels,
Kings, Queens & other famous Personages. The Story
above these 3 Doors is taken up entirely by a Range of
Statues, containing near 30 Kings of France in Succession from Childebert to Philip Augustus, who is
supposed to have finished the Fabric of the Church in
the 13th Century. Above this is a 3rd Story, the Middle
of which contains a fine Rose or Catherine-Wheel
Window looking into the Nave, & the 2 Sides are
double Gothic pointed Windows, in the 2 Towers in
Front of the Church: the 4th Story is uniform & neat,
consisting of a Range from one Side to the other of long
pointed Arches or Niches, very light, ornamented at
Top with a neat Lattice or open work. The 2 noble
Towers terminate the Building on each Side, & are
perfectly square, with no Spires on either of them; tho'
there is a very light neat Spire on that in the Middle of
the Church. The Archiepiscopal Palace is on the South
Side of the Church, & is a modern Building, standing
close to the Church on one Side, with a View of the
River on the other, & an Entrance to it by an arch'd
Portal of Stone joyning the Front of the Gothic Cathe-
dral, in the modern Stile, which has an absurd Appear-
ance: as also the same Absurdity is visible the other
Side, where are the Canons' Houses, with an old shabby
Cloystre towards the East End of the Church, the
Pavement of which is the fullest of old Gravestones
(with the Figures of Canons engraved on them, in a
Slight Manner with long Lines, according to their

general Method), that can be conceived. The Outside also of this noble Cathedral is also the most richly adorned with Statues & Carving, in a very good Stile for the Age they were done in, that ever I saw any where: the grand North Door into the Nave & another into the Cross Isle being highly finished, & Statues & Alto-Rilievo's, containing Stories out of the Bible & other Histories, being in Niches & on Pedestals, in & about the arched Buttresses which support the Chapels of the Choir, & against the Wall about 6 or 8 Feet high of the said Chapels which surround the Choir: especially on the North Side: for I did not go round that Part on the South where the Arch Bp's Palace stood, tho' I went thro' the Grand Entrance from it to the Church, by the South Cross Isle: where I observed numberless fine large Gravestones of Marble, with old Inscriptions & the Figure of the various Dignitaries of this Church, ranged against the Sides of it, taken from different Parts of it, when they were new paving it: these probably were taken from the Nave, as they had just finished a new stone Pavement of it, which was sunk a little lower than the Side Isles, & than the Pediment of the several large Pillars of the Nave: under which they were then also making a large Vault for the Interment of the Canons. But why should we presume to turn out of Doors our Ancestors' or Predecessors' Monuments? Is it to gratify a luxurious Taste for Novelty? I wish this may not end, as it began, by a disrespectful Behaviour to the Dead, by an utter Contempt for the living Members of a Church, which can suffer such a smaller Kind of Sacrilege, under Pretence of beautifying & rendering it more handsome & elegant: whereas, in good Truth, they more frequently contribute to its

Deformity, by adding Ornaments utterly unsuitable to the original Design. I must own, other People must have a very different Idea of Beauty & Symmetry than falls to my Share, when they mix Corinthian Pillars with Gothic ornaments: which puts me in Mind of no unpleasant Story, told of my worthy good Friend & Schole-Fellow, the present Lord Bp of Carlisle,[1] who, with a very aquiline Roman Nose, has the long Neck & lank meagre Figure of his Family. The Bp. as an Antiquary, was finding Fault one Day with his Brother, the Lord Lyttelton,[2] for fitting up his Library, with Shelves & Gothic Spiral Ornaments over them, & Pediments between the Spires, on which stood several fine Roman Busts: the Bp rallied his Lordship upon the Impropriety & Incongruity of the Ornaments with the Busts; to which his Brother had nothing to reply, (for he owned the Absurdity), but this Joke, That however just the Remark might be, yet the Bp had no Title to make use of it, who, with a most compleat Roman Nose, had the most gothic Face of any in the Kingdom.

Surely an even Pavement of handsome Marble Gravestones, ornamented with the Figures & Inscriptions of many learned & pious Men, most of them desiring expressly the Prayers of their Successors in the same Dignities; many of them Benefactors to the Church & which the present Generation reap the Advantage, & all of them as handsome as any modern Stone they can put in its Room, is as congruous, proper & beautiful to a fine old gothic Cathedral, as any the

[1]Charles Lyttelton, Bp of Carlisle (1762), President of the Society of Antiquaries (1765).

[2]George, 1st Baron.

very best Stone Pavement, of equal square Figures, that can be placed in it! The Offence is not so great in such Reparations in England, tho' in my own Mind they had much better be let alone, even at York, & other Places, where the old Pavements have been thrust out to make Room for more elegant & modern ones, where the precatory Form[1] is looked upon as superstitious: but to do so in a Church whose Clergy reap so great Advantages by a Doctrine that inculcates the Benefit of Prayers for the Dead: to fling out of Doors what the Piety of their Predecessors, at their no small Expence, conceived, & they allow to be so much for the Advantage of their Souls, is such a Peice of Indecency as well as Contradiction, as nothing but a Contempt for Antiquity, & a Disregard to their own Doctrines can any ways reconcile to Reason. A Respect for the Dead is no ill Sign of an humane & benevolent Disposition. The Turks in this Respect, I wish I might say in many others also, are a Reproach to our Indecency: perhaps they may exceed the other Way. I will give an Extract of Part of one of Lady Mary Wortley Montagu's Letters on this Subject to shew the Turkish Delicacy; for I won't call it Superstition; tho' I shall make no Scruple to call our different Method of digging up the human Body before it is half turned to its Mother Earth, as is the Practice in most of our Churches & their Yards, by the Name of Irreverence, Indecency & Savage Brutality, in this Respect: it is in Letter 35 to the Abbat . . . . , Vol. 2, p. 116, where she thus writes: "A certain French Author says, Constantinople is twice as big as Paris. Mr Wortley is unwilling to own 'tis bigger than London: tho' I confess it appears to me to be so: but I don't

---

[1] *Requiescat in pace.*

H

believe 'tis so populous. The burying Feilds about it
are certainly much larger than the whole City. 'Tis
surprising what a vast Deal of Land is lost this Way
in Turkey. Sometimes I have seen burying Places
of several Miles, belonging to very inconsiderable
Villages, which were formerly great Towns, & retain
no other Mark of their antient Grandeur, than this
dismal one. On no occasion do they ever remove a
Stone that Serves for a Monument."

The same is confirmed since by Dr Hasselquist[1] in
his *Travels into the Levant*, & lately printed. It seems
very hard, that a Person, while alive, should be absolute
Lord & Master of many Hundred Acres of Land, when
dead, should be grudged a poor Habitation, 5 Feet
under Ground, & but of 6 Feet in Length! Yet such is
our Avarice, that it is more than probable, that this last
Home, as it is improperly called, will be within 20 or
30 years at furthest, irreverently intruded into, to make
Room for a new Guest; while our Remains are turned
out with as little Concern to the present Generation, as
if it was not to be their Turn to be so served after a few
years Resolution! I was led to these Reflections by the
Gravestones I saw on the Outside of the Church, in the
Passage to the Arch Bp's Palace. It is probable more
sumptuous ones were served the same Sauce when the
Choir was fitted up in the elegant Manner it now
appears, in the Time of Lewis 14: as there were many
Persons of royal & noble Extraction, with Prelates &
Dignitaries, buried there, of whom there is now not the
least Trace of any Monument to be discovered. If such
is the Fate of Kings & the Lords of the Earth, that

[1]Fredrik H. (1722-52), a Swedish traveller; the work referred to is
Voyages and Travels in the Levant, 1766.

after a Life of Vanity, even their dead Carcases are
liable soon to be kicked about like common Earth, the
Apostrophe of a very ludicrous Author of a late silly
Book, tho' much in Fashion, to a crowned Head, "O
King, thou wert a Tadpole!" is not so ridiculous, as one
is apt to imagine at first Sight. This Choir is most
sumptuously fitted up in every Part, even so as to make
one regret having said so much against introducing the
modern Taste into old Buildings: which, however, I
can't at all approve of: the Stalls all round this large
noble Choir are finely carved in Oak, & the Arch-Bp's
Throne, with another Seat of the same Sort opposite to
it on the other Side of the Choir, are very elegant: the
6 Angels, holding the Instruments of the Passion,
placed upon Pediments against the Pilasters surrounding the Round-Point, or Semi-circle of the Altar are
finely executed, as are the 2 capital Statues of Lewis 13
& Lewis 14, royally habited, kneeling on each Side of
it, on 2 raised Pediments, & turned to the Altar; which
is most highly finished, being the Figures of Our Lady
sitting with our Saviour on her Knees as taken from the
Cross, & behind a plain Cross, all in white Marble,
with Angels & Cherubims in various Attitudes about
it: these Statues & Cross are upon a second Kind of
Altar, raised above the first, & within a Niche or Arch,
above which is represented a large Glory, before which
are 2 Angels, one of whom holds by a Chain the Tabernacle, in which is contained the consecrated Hosts. The
Floor of the Choir is of Marble of various Colours, &
regularly formed into different Figures: but being
generally covered with Carpets, this Beauty is lost:
there is a very fine Eagle of Brass in the Middle of the
Choir, about which the Music, *viz*: the great Serpen-

tine Horn,[1] for the Cheif Part, (an Instrument of no great Merit or Variety) with Bass Viols, & Violins, assemble. Round the Choir, or rather on both Sides of it, are 8 most ample & glorious Pictures, in Frames of suitable Proportion & Expence, done by some of the best Masters of the French Schole, & tho' not admired by those who are better Judges of Painting than I am, yet, I must needs confess that they struck my Fancy greatly, the Colouring being light & airy, & the Figures easy & agreable: that over the Arch-Bp's Throne on the South Side nearest the Altar, is the Annuntiation of our B. Lady: the next to it, is her Visitation, painted by Jouvenet[2] with his left Hand, being paralitic in his right, & under it is wrote this, *Iouvenet Dextrâ Paraliticus, Sinistrâ pinxit*: the 3rd is our Lord's Nativity: the last on this Side is the Adoration by the Eastern Magi. The 5th, (being the first on the left Hand as you enter the Choir), represents the Purification of our Lady: the 6th, The Flight into Egypt: the 7th, Our Saviour in the Temple disputing with the Doctors: the 8th is the Assumption of the Blessed Virgin. These 8 costly & most magnificent Pictures were given to the Church by a Canon of the Church, named Anthony De la Porte,[3] whose half Length Picture is in one Corner of the Treasury, & who lies interred under a large Marble as you are going to enter the Choir from the Nave, between the two Chapels, (or rather Altars, except that they are finely railed in), of our Lady on the S. & St Denis on the N.

[1]Long used in French churches. "Even when played by a boy, it is sufficient to support the voices of twenty robust monks", Mersenne, quoted in Grove's *Hist. of Music*, iv. 723.

[2]Jean J. (1647-1717).   [3]*Ob.* 1710.

Side against the Back of the Stalls, or Staircase that leads up to the *Jubé*, or Rood Loft, which divides the Nave from the Choir. The Pillars which support the Nave are very large & Massive, as are those of the Side Isles, there being double Isles on both Sides, with Chapels enclosed next the Walls on both Sides, & all round the Choir & *Rond Point*; many of which have fine Pictures & Altar Peices; & immense Pictures all round the Nave, above the first Range of Pillars of both Sides: for there are Galleries all round the Church, as well [as] over the Side Isles, as over the Isles & Chapels of the Choir; which is very convenient on all solemn Occasions when the Church is hardly big enough to hold the Spectators. At the Entrance into the Nave on the South Side by the first Pillar is an immense colossal Statue of St Christopher in Stone,[1] by which, on a Pillar about 8 Foot high is the Statue kneeling of a Man in Armour, by whom is this Inscription: [See G. Brice, *Description de Paris*, iv. 220.]

The monstrous Statue is 28 Foot high, & his Thumb 12 Inches long. In my Opinion, tho' it has been lately brushed up & scraped so as to look new, it is a great Disfigurement & Blemish to the Church. On the same Side of the Nave by the first Pillar nearest the Choir, & opposite our Lady's Chapel stands another Disfigurement, in my Eye; I mean the awkward Figures of King Philip the Fair & his Horse, both harnessed & caparisoned in full Armour, according to the Mode of the Times, & so hid by their Armour & Housings, that no Part of the Man or his Horse are discoverable—no,

---

[1] This *ex voto* statue was demolished in 1784; it was erected by Ant. des Essarts, brother of the better known Pierre taken prisoner at Homildon.

not so much as the Horse's Legs: this stands on a
Pillar or Pedestal about 10 Feet high, & seems an
absurd Peice of Furniture for a Church: had it been
placed in a Vestry it would have been a Curiosity, &
worth being visited: but no one can suppose that the
King came on Horseback into the Church to pay his
Devotions there, in that Posture & Equipage: at least
the Horse might have been left at the Door. The Story
is this, that after the Battle of Mons en Puelle 1304,
against the Flemings, whom he vanquished, on his
Return to Paris he entered the Cathedral, dressed as I
have represented him. Upon looking into Father
Montfaucon's *Antiquitez de la Monarchie François*, Vol.
2, p. 286, I see the Horse's Head & Neck is uncovered.
He affirms that the Figure is not to represent Philip the
Fair, but Philip the 6th, or De Valois, who caused this
Monument to be erected in Consequence of a Vow
which he made to the Blessed Virgin, being in great
Danger at the celebrated Battle of Mont-Cassel, which
he gained against the Flemings in 1328. This seems
more probable than the vulgar Tradition before mentioned; especially as it is placed just before the Altar of
our Lady in her Chapel in the Principal Church of the
Metropolis of France. Father Montfaucon has given us
a Print of the Statue in the cited Place. Monsr de Saint-
foix[1] has taken more than ordinary Pains to prove what
Father Montfaucon had done before him, & has made
out his Point beyond exception. (*Essays upon Paris*, Vol:
2. p. 116. Ed: Lond. 8°. 1767, *penes me*, 1779,—
v. also p. 258, 259, &c. where more on the subject.)

Against the same great Pillar, which supports the

[1]Germain François Poullain de St. Foix (1703-76): *Essais Historiques
sur Paris.*

Middle Tower of the Cathedral, & near the Figure of King Philip, hangs a noble Picture painted by Champagne,[1] opposite the Altar of the B. Virgin, representing a Vow of King Lewis 13, royally habited on his Knees before an Image of our Lady of Pity, & offering his Crown to her. This large & fine Picture is reckoned one of the best in the Church.

The Altar of the Chapel of the B. Virgin, on the right hand as you are going to enter the Choir, is really truly Magnificent: she is represented in a Niche with our Saviour in her Arms, in the Clouds, all finely finished in White Marble, & the Table & Ornaments & Rails round it are partly various coloured Marble & Copper gilt. Before it hang 6 or 7 silver Lamps, one always burning, from the Roof of the Church. This Chapel, with all its Furniture, was built & ornamented by the late Cardinal de Noailles, Arch-Bp of Paris, who is buried immediately before this Altar, & under these Lamps, under a black Marble with an Inscription: tho' the Chapter, in Consideration of his immense Benefactions to the Church of Paris, gave him 3 small Chapels, by the Side of the Choir, which he laid into one, & finely fitted up for the use of his own Family, as their Place of Interment, over the Iron Doors into which is placed the Cardinal's Heart in a small Urn of Porphiry, or Marble, & by the Side of the Chapel is a long Inscription, reciting the many Benefactions he conferred on this Cathedral. In a Chapel of another Church in this City, *viz*: St Paul's[2] is a very fine Tomb of this Cardinal's Father or Grandfather, as I presume,

[1]Philippe de Champagne, or Champaigne, (1602-74); a Flemish painter.

[2]Demolished during the Revolution.

being for Anne Duke de Noailles, who died about 1670, as well as I remember. The Cardinal's Arms are in the Centre of one of the largest & finest Catherine Wheel Windows in the South Cross Isle, Wch leads to the Archiepiscopal Palace, that ever I saw: he being at the sole Expence of new building this Window, (a Peice of Work not easily done at this Time of Day, when such curious Gothic Work is out of Fashion), together with great Part of this Transept, which was much out of Repair, & almost ready to fall. The other Part of the same Window is filled with painted Glass, & is a most beautiful Sight. A great Part of this Cardinal's Character may be discovered in the *Memoires* of Madam de Maintenon, he being no Friend to the Jesuits; who also on their Part, endeavoured to make him as uneasy as was in their Power, which was then in its Meridian. Happy for them, had they kept more within themselves, & not troubled themselves with Politics & Trade, so much contrary to their Profession, & they might, possibly, have been still in quiet Possession of their Houses, & have maintained that Character in the learned World so justly due to their Merit. [For the inscription see G. Brice, *Description de Paris*, iv. 210.]

On the other Side of the Door into the Choir is another Chapel railed in after the same Manner as our Lady's Chapel, & highly ornamented, at the Expence of the same worthy Prelate: it is dedicated to the Honour of St Denis, the Apostle of France & first Bp of this City, whose Image in White Marble, holding a plain unornamented Crosier, such as a Bishop of those early Times may be supposed to make use of, in one of his Hands, with a plain simple Mitre on his Head.

At the Back of the Choir, in the Stone Work, is let in

a Range of good Carving in a Sort of Alto Relievo,
about 6 Foot from the Floor, in Stone, containing
Histories from the Old & New Testament, Legends &
Lives of the Saints, very well executed for the Time they
were carved in, about the Middle of the 14th Century,
as a Legend or Inscription in large Gothic Letters which
goes round them informs us, & which is not very easy
to be made out: before the East End of the Choir was
new built at the Beginning of this Century, these
Carvings went all round the Choir: the Inscription is
as follows:

C'est Maitre Jean Ravi, qui fut Maçon de N. D. de Paris
par l'Espace de 26 Ans, & commença ces nouvelles Histoires, &
Maitre Jean le Bouteiller son Neveu, les a parfaites en 1351.

On the right Hand, in a Cupboard or Hole worked
in the Wall is deposited, behind the Back of the High
Altar, in the Place where Part of these old Carvings
formerly were, the rich Shrine of St Marcellus,
formerly, I think, Bp of Paris. It is commonly kept in
the Treasury or Sacristy, where I first saw it; but I
afterwards saw it exposed on some Holiday in the Place
I now mentioned.

At the Entrance, by the Door of the 2nd Chapel
round the Choir, on the Outside Stands a Pillar, perhaps
10 Feet high, on the Top of which stands the Statue of
Denis du Moulin, Bp of Paris, Patriarch of Antioch, &
formerly Arch Bp of Toulouse, who died in 1441:
(except I should mistake it for another Statue of Stephen
de Sully, Cardinal de Laon, which is at the Door of a
neighbouring Chapel, which is not at all unlikely; as
my Notes are not very particular). About 2 Chapels
higher up on the same right Side of the Choir, is the
Chapel of St Remy, Arch-Bp of Rheims, in which are

a curious old Monument & a more curious old Picture, both belonging to the Family of the Ursins,[1] now extinct. The Tomb is between 2 & 3 Feet high by the Side of the Altar, of an Altar Fashion, on which, behind one another, are placed two Figures kneeling, the Man in Armour with his Surcoat of Coat Armour flung over it, painted in proper Colours, his Wife is dressed in Black in the Fashion of her Times. On the West Wall, above the Tomb hangs a very curious antient Picture, painted on Board, of a long Form containing the Figures of John Juvenal des Ursins, Baron de Tresnel,[2] who died in 1431, for whom & his Wife the aforesaid Monument was erected, with his said Wife, & 11 of their Children, the first & last of which are habited *in Pontificalibus*, being both Arch-Bp's of Rheims, one after the other. This Picture is so great a Curiosity, that Father Montfaucon has given a Plate of it in his 3rd Volume of *Antiquitez de la Monarchie Françoise*, p. 354. Beyond this, in the same Line in another Chapel, is a very antient Altar Monument of black Marble, on which lies at his Length the Image, in his Episcopal Cope & Mitre, Simonde Bussy de Matifas,[3] Bp of Paris, in white Marble, who died in 1304. In one of the Windows of this Chapel, I observed a very old Coat of Arms of the Family of Courteney, *viz*: Or, 3 Torteauxes: probable of the French Family of that Name, some of whom might be buried in this Chapel, or be Benefactors to it, either by glazing it, or some other Way. In the Chapel close to it, to the East, which is larger than this, & seems to be two laid into one, are two fine Tombs, one on each Side of the Altar, much

[1] The Orsini.   [2] "Trainel", acc. Montfaucon.
[3] 79th Bp of Paris, *ob.* 1304.

alike, being Altar Monuments with Canopies over them supported by 4 Pillars of Black Marble each, & under each a Figure, the one of Cardinal Peter de Gondi, Bp of Paris, who died in 1616, & the other of his Brother, Albert de Gondi, Duke de Retz, both on their Knees before a Desk, on which is a Book. Just before this Chapel is St Marcellus his Shrine, at the back of the High Altar. Further on, on the other Side, is the fine Chapel of the Noailles Family, being 3 laid into one, & finely ornamented by the late Cardinal of that Name, & over the Iron Doors into it, in an Urn, is the Heart of his Eminence, his Body being buried before the Altar of our Lady, in her Chapel in the South Transept, near the Door into the Choir. The Treasury is on the South Side of the Isles of the Choir, (soon after you enter them, thro' a small Room, up a double Flight of Stairs), & seems to have been lately repaired, or new built. In very commodious Drawers, which turn upon a Pivot, are great Varieties of rich Copes & other Dresses for the Clergy on solemn Occasions: & in several Cabinets all round the Room are kept Reliquaries of various Sorts & Sizes, adorned with Jewels, Crosiers of a very antique Fashion, Sacred Vessels of various Sorts, Mitres, Books & MSS. set in Silver gilt ornamented with Jewels —one very beautiful Modern MS. of the Church Service, elegantly written on Vellum & beautifully painted with Landscapes—& some excessive rich Crosses, stuck full of Jewels on both Sides. But that which pleased me as well as all these rich Ornaments were two very antient Curiosities, & of no value but for their Antiquity: the one was an old smallish pointed Knife with an Ivory Handle, about 700 years old: on the Handle was wrote the following Inscription, (the

Chapter holding by Virtue of this old Knife the Parvis
or Square which is before the great Front of the
Cathedral, in the same Manner as the Cathedral of
York was endowed with much good Land by Ulphus,
who gave his drinking Horn of Ivory with them, & by
Virtue of which they hold the same, the Cup being to
this Day in their Possession, a Print of which, with
some Account of the Custom, may be seen in Mr Drake
his ingenious & useful History[1] of that Church p. 481.

Hic Cultellus fuit Fulcheri de Buolo, per quem Wido dedit
Areas Drogonis Archidiaconi Ecclesiae Mariae ante eadem
Eccliam sitas pro Anniversario Matris suae.

That is, This Knife belonged to Faucher de Beuil, by
which Guy hath given to the Church of St. Mary the
Areas (or open Space) before the said Church, which
belonged to Drogo the Archdeacon, for an anniversary
Service for his Mother.

The other Curiosity, in the same Box, is of the same
Kind, being a small Peice of yellowish Wood, like Box,
only it a little worm-eaten, of about 6 Inches long & one
thick, on the Sides of which is cut in gothic Letters,
very unequally, but very easy to be red, this Inscription:

Eberardus et Hubertus de Spedona Villa, Servi scilicet Beatae
Mariae Parisiensis, per hoc Lignum Fulconi Decano Rectum
fecerunt in Capitulo Scae Mariae de Conquestu Antecessorum
suorum quem tenuerant absque Canonicorum Permissione.

"Which is: Everard & Hubert of the Village of
Epona, Servants (or Tenants) of the Church of the
Blessed Mary of Paris, have, by Virtue of this Peice of
Wood, made over their Right to Fulco, Dean of the

[1] Francis Drake (1696-1771); *Eboracum*, publ. 1736. The "horn" is
an elephant's tusk, mounted in gold.

Chapter of Saint Mary, of what they had by the Purchase of their Ancestors, & which they held without
the Leave of the Canons."

In an under Cupboard of the Treasury is a Porphiry
or red Marble Urn, which is destined to receive the
Heart of the present Maréchal de Noailles[1] after his
Death, being like that in which the late Cardinal's
Heart is enclosed in the Noailles Chapel: which
Cardinal's Picture, with that of his Successor in the See
of Paris, Charles-Gasper de Vintimille, & that of Monsr
Antony de la Porte, Canon of this Church, & a great
Benefactor to it, all in half Lengths, hang up in this
small Sacristy or Treasury. The Person who shewed the
Treasury to me was a young Man, very civil & obliging,
& the More to accommodate himself to the English
who came frequently to view it, could speak a little of
their Language, & had a MS. Account of all the
Curiosities in the Church, which he referred me to as he
went along: this he told me was then going to be printed
& when it was published I had it from him, tho' it
came out under the Name of Tho: Berry, Teacher of the
French & English Tongues in Paris, under this Title,
*A compendious & descriptive Memorial of whatever is
curious in Notre Dame, or our Lady's Church at Paris:
particularly inscribed to the English.* 12°, or small 8vo,
containing 48 Pages; being a most trite & superficial
Performance, & more calculated to advantage the
Sacristain, or Under Keeper of the Treasury, than of
any Value in itself: except it may be of Use to take in
the Pocket & by it examine the Pictures more at
Leisure. In this Church I don't remember to have been

[1]Marshall Noailles died in June 1766. [C.]. Adrien-Maurice, Duc
de N., Maréchal de France.

persecuted by Beggars as you are in most others: tho'
in the first North Isle near the lowest End, is a Sort of
raised Stage whereon sit several of the Children of the
Maison des Enfans trouvez, or Foundling Hospital, with
a Nurse or two, all dressed in black Serge & White
Caps & Handkercheifs, their House being in the
Square or Area in the Corner of the Street by the
Cathedral, where is a Bason to receive Alms towards its
Support. I staid here, & heard Vespres very finely &
solemnly sung by the Canons, who are almost the only
Secular ones who rise at Midnight to sing Matines in
the Choir: after which I walked to my Lodgings in the
Petits Augustins Street, thro' the Street of St Andrews des
Arts or des Arcs,[1] & having been on the Tramp all Day
without once getting into a Coach, I was most heartily
tired, & was determined not to fatigue myself so much
again, as the Stones of the Streets were slippery, & there
being no Foot Walk, it was not so safe to walk them as
with us in London.

Wednesday, 30 *October.* Fine Day. At Breakfast Time
Madame Theodora Eynhouts, a Cousin of Mr Theo-
dore Eynhouts,[2] both settled in the Rue de Bussy, as
Milliners & Linen Drapers, & equally related to Mr
Van Mousselle of Antwerp, who has been at my House
at Blecheley in Buckinghamshire, where he was with
my Neighbour Mr Cartwright, came of her own Accord
to offer me Linen: it seems she was sent by Mr
Walpole's Servant to me: but as I had a Sort of Acquaintance with her Cousin, by travelling with him in the
Coach from Cambray, I rather chose to deal with him.
I hired a Coach for the Day, & went first to the Sorbonne College, where I never was more deceived in my

[1]Rue St. André des Arcs.   [2]*See* p. 26, *supra.*

Life: for, from the grand Terms always used by the
French on talking of this House, I expected to have
found quite another Thing than it is in Reality: where,
excepting the Church in the Middle of the Front, both
to the Street & the Court, every Thing seemed mean
& pitiful, The cheif Court in which one Front of the
Church stands, has a large Entrance or Portal from a
Narrow Street, called, I think, La Rue de la Harpe:
this Court is rather oblong & narrow, being only the
Bre[a]dth of Part of the Church, with 5 or 6 Steps,
which run across it to ascend to that Part nearest the
Church, & very irregular, & far from handsome,
Buildings of Stone on both Sides & at the other End of
it for the Apartments of the Students: on the left Hand,
as you go to the Church, is an Apartment or large *Salon*,
called the *Salle des Thèses*, or Hall where the Disputa-
tions are held for Degrees, which is a tolerable large
Room, with Desks for the Disputants, & Benches for
the principal Auditors. Round it are hung a great many
fine Portraits: among the Best, the present Pope, his
Holiness Clement 13; his late Holiness Pope Benedict
14; the Cardinals de Richelieu, Tencin de Fleury,
Soubise, & de Rohan: his present Majesty King Lewis
15, the late King Stanislas of Poland, (then alive).[1] The
Church is not large, but elegant & handsome, in the
Form of a Cross, the two Porticos on each Side, North
& South making the Transept: that to the Court has a
Portico of 10 Pillars supporting a Pediment: in the
middle of the Church is a beautiful Dome, withinside
of which are painted in Fresco the Figures of the 4
Fathers of the Church, & the Statues of the 12 Apostles
stand in Niches against the Pilasters of the Nave &

[1]Stanislaus I died Feb. 23, 1766.

round the Dome, of a Sort of white Stone: The Church seems heavy, from its massive flat Pillars, & its want of Light, & is elegantly paved with red & white Marble, disposed in various Figures: the High Altar is composed of 6 fine Marble Corinthian Pillars, ornamented at Top & Bottom with Brass gilt, with 2 Angels at the Top of the Pediment, & on each Side of the Altar Peice, (which is a very fine & large Crucifix of white Marble, the Back Part of it being black Marble, which shews the Crucifix to Advantage), stand the Figures in white Marble, of our Lady on one Side, & St John the Evangelist on the other. Our Lady's Chapel, on the opposite Transept of that you enter from the Court, & against the South Wall of which is erected the Altar, is very handsome: she is represented in a fine Statue, having our Saviour on her Knees, above the Altar: so that, I suppose, I mistook when I said there was another Portico on this Side: for the other great Front, with 2 Orders of Architecture one above the other, is, as I take it, at the West End of the Church, fronting the Square. But the greatest Ornament of this Church, or indeed of any I ever saw, either here, or elsewhere, is the most elegant & beautiful Tomb[1] of the Founder of the present Church, & the Restorer of the College, the great Cardinal de Richelieu, who lies buried immediately under it, exactly as you enter what is usually the Choir Part of most Churches, in the Middle, before the High Altar: he is represented as half reclined on his left Side rather, looking towards the High Altar, with his right Hand on his Breast, which partly covers the Cross of the Order of the Holy Spirit, & his other pointing to one of his Books of Piety or Controversy, (for he wrote

[1] See *Letters of Hor. Walpole* (Toynbee), No. 15, Ap. 21, 1739.

on both Subjects), held open by a fine Image of Religion,
represented as a Woman behind him, supporting him
with one Hand, & holding the Book in the other, which
it is supposed, he composed in her Defence: at his Feet
sits another fine Figure, bathed in Tears, to represent
the Loss which Science & the Arts have experienced by
his Death: she covers her Face with one of her Hands,
& on her Knee lies an open Book: behind him, on the
Matrass lies the 4-pointed Cap, & at his Back sit two
naked small Angels, one weeping, supporting his
Arms, ensigned by a Ducal Coronet, & above that the
Cardinal's Hat, & behind hang the Collar of the Order
& the Anchor, as Grand Master of the Navigation. In
every Window of the Church is a large Coat of Arms
with the same Insignia, & a Border round the Sides of
the Window in painted Glass in a neat & elegant
Fashion. I did not take the Colours of the Arms, as I
knew I had so many Prints of him & them: yet they
are blasoned by the Engraver of this Monument in 6
Plates, exhibiting the 4 different Views of it, with one
as a Frontispeice, with an Account of the Cardinal's
Tomb, & a Bust of him, & another giving a Plan of the
Crypt or Vault & Coffins immediately under the
Monument, by Simonneau, as Argent 3 Cheveronels
Gules, as I have done them at p. 7 of this Volume: but
at p. 96 of a fine Book painted in their proper Colours,
with this Title, *Creations des Chevaliers de l'ordre du St
Esprit faits par Louis le Grand, ou Armorial Historique des
Chevaliers de l'ordre, tres exactement recherchè, blasonè et
ornè de Suports et Cimiers.* Par le Sieur F. de la Pointe,
Ingénieur & Géografe du Roi. A Paris 1689, 4to, in
which the Arms of all the Members of this Order
created by Lewis 14 are blasoned, they are, Argent, 3

I

Cheveronels Gules for Armand-Jean du Plessis, Duke de Richelieu: so that as this seems to be an authentic Book of French Heraldry, I have given that Cardinal's Arms a fresh Place here, as the other is presumed to be wrong:[1] & for no other Reason; as his Eminence, however great his Character may be as a good Frenchman, yet as an Enemy to England, (tho' his Patron's Sister was on the Throne of it), & an Encourager of the Faction against K. Charles & the Church of England, he cannot be looked upon with that Esteem, due to his general Merit, in this Island, as on the Continent. This Conjecture I find confirmed, since I wrote the last Paragraph, by turning to a little Book of French Heraldry, wrote by Father Charles-Francis Mene[s]trier, Jesuit, entitled, *Abrégé méthodique des Principes Heraldiques*. A Lyon, 1688, 8vo, in the Preface to which, at p. xvii (tho' not figured) these Arms are assigned to Du Plessis-Richelieu: D'Azur à trois Chevrons de Gueles: which *Azure* is certainly a Mistake for *Argent*, as I have noted by my Pen on the Place; otherwise it would be false Heraldry. But enough & too much for so silly a Jargon. The Cardinal is dressed in his Robes, & Scull-Cap on his Head, lying on a Matrass, & under that a large Peice of Drapery, the Sides of which are all round embroidered with his Arms & Cypher, alternat[e]ly, which almost covers the Altar Tomb, which is raised about 3 Feet from the ground, & railed round by a low & elegant Iron Palisade. The whole of this most beautiful Monument is of white Marble, but of a yellowish Cast from Smoak & Dust: the Draperies of all the Figures, & the Figures themselves, with their

---

[1]What C. means is obscure, since he appears to distinguish between two identical coats.

several graceful Attitudes forming a whole not to be met with any where else. It is supposed that Le Brun,[1] the famous French Painter, gave the Model & Design which was afterwards executed by that excellent Sculptor Francis Girardon.[2] A Journey to Paris, merely to see this single Monument, would not be wholly thrown away: at least it pleased me much more than I am able to express. The Taste it is done in, is much superior to the Time in which the Cardinal deceased: accordingly it was not erected 'till 1694, by his Executors. The Inscriptions on the Tapestry hanging gracefully on each Side of the Tomb, are the same. [See G. Brice, *Description de Paris*, iii. 193].

The Cardinal's Death happened on the 4 of December, 1642, a few years after his Design for the Grandeur of this College, which was not finished 'till after that Period: & bating the Church & Monument, I saw nothing at the famous College of Sorbon[ne], (the Library I saw not), which was not exceeded by almost any of our meanest Colleges in Cambridge, whose Situations are infinitely superiour. It is probable the Revenue of it may be considerable: yet I question whether even in that Respect our Foundations at Cambridge do not equal it: as the Buildings are not large, & far from elegant.

From hence I went to the Benedictine Nunnery of Val de Grace,[3] founded by Queen Anne of Austria, Mother of Lewis 14, to return Thanks for the Birth of that Monarch, after 22 years Barrenness, & for that of his Brother the Duke of Orleans. It is situated at the

[1] Charles le Brun, 1619-90.

[2] *c.* 1630-1715; the decoration of the Porte St-Denis was also due to him.

[3] Originally established in Val Profond, near the village of Biérre.

Extremity almost of the Rue St Jacques, having a small
paved Court before it inclosed by Iron Palisades to the
Street, ordinary Buildings on the 2 Sides, & in Front
to the Street also, the fine Frontispeice of the Church,
consisting of 2 Stories, the lowermost having a beautiful
Portico on a Flight of about 16 or 18 Steps, with 4 fluted
Corinthian Pillars, which support a Pediment, on which
is a large Clock; on each Side of the Portico are
Niches, in which are placed Statues of St Benedict & St
Scolastica: & on each Side of the Church is a Pavilion
which reaches to the Side Buildings with an Attic Story
at Top. The Dome of this Church is very beautiful, &
is, with that of the Sorbonne & the other of Cardinal
Mazarine's *Collège de Quatre Nations*, no small Ornament to the View of the City of Paris: tho' the Square
before it has but a mean & pitiful Appearance: Over
the Portico, on a Frize, is wrote in very large Gold
Letters this Inscription,

JESU NASCENTI, VIRGINIQUE MATRI.

Behind the Frize which surrounds the Bottom of the
Dome in the Inside is this wrote also in great Capital
Gold Letters:

*Anna Austria, D. G. Francorum Regina, Regniq. Rectrix, cui
subjecit Deus omnes Hostes, ut conderet Domum in Nomine Suo,
Ecc. A.M.D.C.L.*

The Church is built in the Form of a Cross, on no great
Extent, the Dome seeming to me to be too big for so
small a Building: yet withinside it appears with great
Symmetry, being highly ornamented with Paintings,
Mosaic Work, fluted Corinthian Pillars, & fine
Cornishes.[1] The High Altar is very magnificent,

[1]An 18th cent. form.

somewhat like that of St Peter's at Rome, being an
Oval with 3 twisted Marble Pillars, all over covered
almost with Vine Leaves & Fruit in gilt Brass, on each
Side, which support a Kind of Canopy above, on the
Top of which is a Cross, & Angels, as big as Life, on
the Top of the Pillars, in Front, & on the Sides: this
Altar is ascended to by many Steps, on which are placed
2 fine Images in White Marble, on their Knees & in
Action of Adoration, of the Blessed Virgin & St
Joseph, with the Infant Jesus in Swadling Cloths lying
on the Middle of the Altar between them. Just at the
Back of the Altar is a Grate from whence the Nuns may
see, on occasion, the Holy Sacrament when it is solemnly exposed. The two Transept Isles are grated up quite
to the Top, with Curtains drawn before them: that on
the South Side or right Hand is the Choir of the Nuns,
where they sing their Service: the opposite one is hung
all in Black with Escocheons against the Walls, being
the Chapel of St Anne, where the Queen Mother's
Heart is deposited, with most of the Hearts of the
Royal Family since the Founding of this Royal Abbey.

From this Convent I went to the Grand Carmelites
Nunnery, situated a little lower, in the same Street, on
the other Side of the way, & down a Sort of Lane or
Passage to it. It seemed an old Foundation by the
Gothic Building on the Outside of the Chapel: for as to
the Inside, it is so painted & gilt, & otherways ornamented, that there is no judging hardly what Order it
is built in. We went not into the Convent with the
Coach, but was admitted into the Church by the Sexton
thro' a very crampt & narrow Pair of Stairs, which
brought us into the Sanctuary or Choir. The Church is
one single long Room, with an high Gothic Stone Roof,

as it seemed to me, supported by tall gothic slender Pillars or Pilasters against the Sides of the Wall, between the large Windows: but the Walls & every Part, both Pillars & Roof, were painted & gilt in a most sumptuous Manner, with vast large Pictures in fine Frames, under every Window & between them in the Choir Part, painted by the best Masters, as Poilly, De la Hire, Champagne & Stella [1] & Le Brun. The Roof also is remarkable for its fine Paintings & curious Fore-shortenings: particularly a Crucifix about the Middle of the Roof, which is made to appear, at a proper Distance, as if it stood erect. The High Altar is ascended to by a grand Flight of 20 or more Steps of black Marble, with Balustrades on both Sides of the same coloured Marble covered at Top with Brass, & has a noble Effect from the Bottom of the Church: the Altars of the Carmelites being all so placed by Order of their Founder, to represent the Ascent to Mount Carmel, the Prophet Elias being claimed by them as their Founder of their first Institution.[2] The Altar is supported by 4 grand Corinthian Pillars of a fine Marble. In a Sun, or perforated Ornament of Silver gilt, covered on both Sides by Rock Crystal or Glass, is the real Heart exposed to View of every one, of the very worthy Cardinal de Berulle, the Director of the Nuns of this House, whom he had fetched himself out of Spain, being the first of the Order of Reformed Carmelites according to the Rule of St Teresa, that were introduced into France: this is set in a Hole of the Wall near the East End, on the South Side, by the High

[1]Family name of three generations of French artists.

[2]Actually founded, on Mt Carmel, by a Calabrian pilgrim named Berthold in the 12th cent.

Altar; so that the Nuns also may see it, as well as those
in the Church. On the same Side of the Church, below
the Steps and on one Side of the Flight of Steps up to
this Altar, is an Ordinary Vestry Room; above which is
the Nuns' Choir, with a Grate to the Church: they have
also another grated Gallery at the West End, where
they sit to hear Sermons, on particular Occasions, when
there is preaching in their Pulpit, which also is placed
in the Nave, or outside of the Division from the Choir
by an high Balustrade, on the same South Side: Over
the Door of Entrance from the one to the other, is a
very fine Crucifix of Copper gilt, greatly admired for
the Beauty of the Carving, being the Work of James
Sarazin, an excellent Sculptor. Over the Gallery at the
End of the Church are the Statues of St Peter & St
Paul, & between them on a Pediment is that of St
Michael casting out the Devil, done in a very masterly
Manner. It is difficult to see any of this Order of Nuns,
who are very rigid & recluse: however I bought some
Trinkets of them, as they were offered me by the
Sacristain. In a small Chapel about the Middle of the
Nave on the North Side is an honourary Monument for
Cardinal Peter de Berulle, who is represented in his
Cardinal's Robes in White Marble, on his Knees, on a
square Pedestal of above 3 Feet high of the same
Materials, & seems to be addressing his Devotion to
the Altar, too near before him; for the Chapel is much
too small for the Tomb, there being hardly convenient
Room to pass between it & the Altar, to the other Side.
This beautiful & expressive Statue was done by Sarazin.
But this is not all the Beauty of this Chapel of St Mary
Magdalen, which is painted thro'out by Le Brun, who
has exerted himself particularly in the Picture over the

Altar, where the Saint is expressed as relinquishing the World & its Vanities, & dedicating herself entirely to Devotion: the Expression of Contrition in her Face & Actions is inimitable, & the colouring of the whole exceedingly fine: tho' I was told by a Judge in Painting, that the gaudy French Manner was too glaring, & that a Picture fronting it, against the West Wall, behind the Cardinal's Statue, on the same Subject, I think by Guido,[1] as much excelled that by Le Brun, as the Italian is superior to the French Schole. But of this I am no Judge: & as a Proof of it, I must needs confess, that Le Brun's Performance struck me much more than the other. One, or both, were covered by a green silk Curtain, by way of Preservation from Dust & Accidents. [For the inscription see G. Brice, *Description de Paris*, iii. 115.]

The Abbè le Camus not only erected this Monument to the Cardinal, but was also at the Cheif Expence in the Decorations & Ornaments of this Church: he lies buried under Part of this Pedestal, before the Altar of this Chapel, & has over him a small Square Peice of White Marble on which is engraved this Inscription: [See G. Brice, *Description de Paris*, iii. 116].

I suppose he was some near Relation of the eminently pious John Peter le Camus, Bp of Belley, who died in 1652. The Cardinal de Berulle died in celebrating Mass, Oct: 2, 1629, in the Church of the Oratorians, which he had founded, & where he lies buried, as I shall mention afterwards, with a long Inscription: he was upon the Point of Consecration in pronouncing these Words of the Mass, *Hanc igitur Oblationem*, when he

---

[1]Not overlooked, however, by Walpole; *Letters of Hor. Walpole*, (Toynbee), No. 1644, Sep. 12, 1775.

dropt down dead: so that, says Perrault, in his *Homme illustres*, p. 4, not being able to finish the Sacrifice, as a Priest, he finished it as a Victim: which is elegantly expressed in this Distic:

Caepta sub Extremis nequeo dum Sacra Sacerdos
Perficere, at Saltem Victima perficiam.

It was in this Monastery that the celebrated Penitent, the Duchess de la Val[l]ière, Mistress to Lewis 14, after having lived in it in great Austerity & Devotion 36 years, died in 1710, & was buried in the inner Part of the Convent. Exactly by the Door into St Mary Magdalen's Chapel, in the Nave on a small oblong Peice of White Marble is the following Inscription for an Historian of France,[1] who has been as free in his Censures upon the English, as I have been upon the French, & was on that Account taken to Task by a Bp of the Church of England. [See G. Brice, *Description de Paris*, iii. 120.]

From the Monastery of the Grand Carmelite Nuns I went to the Priory of the English Monks of the Order of St Benedict, in the same Street of St James, at a very little Distance, on the other Side of the Way. It is seated close to the Street, & makes but a very mean & ordinary Figure, as most of the other Religious Houses in this Metropolis, do, to the Street: a Portal, with an extreme small Court or Passage conducts you to a very high Flight of Stone Steps up to the Church or Chapel Door, which is near the High Altar: I suppose 20 or 30 Steps: so that, I suppose there is a Passage under this Part of the Church: for I did not examine it, or made much Enquiries about it, for Fear of being too curious in my

---

[1] See *Reflections on Mr Varillas's History*. By G. Burnet, D.D., Amsterdam, 1686.

Observations about a Society, who are so mal-treated &
worse-spoken of in their native Country: on which
Account, I thought it neither decent, proper, or prudent
to be at all particular in my Observations or Questions,
either in this or any other of my own Country Foundations. On the right Hand is the Porter's Lodge, &
Entrance into the House, which is small & neat, with
Cloysters, & a pretty Garden behind it, from whence
you have a good View of the Feuillantine[1] Nuns'
Convent & Church, which last is a very elegant modern
Building, & stands more detached from the Street than
does our Benedictines, & nearer the City Side. The
Prior's Apartment was small, but very neat & commo-
dious, up one Pair of Stairs, & another Landing Place
from them conducted you to a Door into the Church.
On the Staircase I observed a Picture of Sir Thomas
More, another indifferent one of the worthy Martyr to
the Presbyterian Faction & Cruelty, Arch-Bp Plunket.[2] By this Door you entered into the Choir of the
Church, which appeared to me very singular: the
Monks' old oak Stalls, without any high Backs to them,
just such as we have still in many Chancels of our
Parochial Churches, being placed in the middle, a few
on both Sides, with Passages behind them; I presume,
they being cramped for Room: however it did not look
amiss, as it was placed between the Sanctuary or Part
appropriated to the High Altar, on one side of which
stood a large Image of the Founder of their Order, the
great St Benedict, & the lower Part of the Church, to
which you descended by many Steps. The Nave or

[1] Of the Order of St Bernard; named from Feuillant (Languedoc).

[2] Oliver Plunket, Primate of Ireland; convicted of treason, on inade-
quate evidence, and executed in 1681.

lower Part of the Church, had a Chapel or two on each
Side against the Walls, & was no Ways ornamented.
In a small dark Kind of Vestry, or Chapel, at the North
West Corner of the Nave are the Bodies deposited,
unburied, of King James the second, & his Daughter,
Louisa-Mary who died in 1712, at 19 years of Age,
being a very accomplished young Princess. They both
lye on Tressels or Biers, & are covered by a large
black Velvet Pall on which are embroidered the Arms
of England: but thro' Age, (the King dying at St
Germains en Laye in 1701, above threescore years ago),
it is no wonder that the Pall has suffered thro' Age, &
that it looks very Shabby: the Princess lies in a Coffin on
the right Hand of her Father, whose Face in wax-work,
exactly resembling his Coin & Pictures, dressed in a
real laced Night Cap, & taken after he was dead, is
shewn in a Box at the same Time. Near the Feet of the
Coffins, close by the Door as you enter this Vestry, &
against the Wall in it, is erected a small ordinary Altar,
ornamented with Black, with lighted Candles on it, on
which Mass is daily said for the Repose of their Souls.
Both the Meanness of the Chapel & its correspondent
Furniture, as well as the unfortunate History of the
unlucky, tho' worthy & good Prince who lies in it, is a
very proper Lesson how to value the glittering Scenes
of this World, where those who made the greatest
Stir & Bustle in their Lives, in a few years after their
Deaths, are as soon forgotten, & as much neglected,
as if they never had been. Else how can we account
for the poor, mean & wretched Appearance, both of the
Furniture of the Altar, & Covering of the Coffin, of
this so admired-by-many a Prince, & who suffered so
greatly in the Cause of his Religion? I was told by the

Sacristain, that the late Duchess of Buckingham,[1] his natural Daughter, was used frequently to come & weep her Father's unhappy Fate in this Chapel: yet she never found it in her Heart to bestow any Thing towards the decent adorning her Father's forlorn Habitation, tho' perhaps an 100th Part of the vain Expence of the Funeral of her Son, might have found a new Pall, & more decent Ornaments for the Altar. The worthy Founder of this House was Wm Giffard, of the Family of that Name of Chillington in Staffordshire, who becoming a Benedictine Monk, was first consecrated Bp of Archidal,[2] as Suffragan & Co-Adjutor to the Cardinal de Guise Arch Bishop of Rheims, & on his Death, was himself promoted to that great Dignity, being Primate & Metropolitan of all France, & Duke of Rheims & Peer of France, in which grand Church [Rheims] he lies interred, dying Apr: 11, 1629. This worthy Primate of France, in 1611, laid the Foundation of a small Convent of Benedictine Monks at St Malo's in Bretagne: but that being found Fault with, as being too near the Neighbourhood of the Coasts of England, King Lewis 13 gave him Leave to remove his Foundation to the Fauxbourg St Jacques in St James's Street in Paris, where he became the first Prior, tho' it had not a legal Settlement, 'till many years after his Death, (in 1642), Queen Anne of Austria being a singular Benefactress to it, as were many of the English Nobility & Gentry; as appears by several of their Arms in the great

[1]Lady Catherine Darnley (*ob.* 1743), who married as her second husband John Sheffield, D. of Buckingham. She often visited her father's body, which was kept unburied, that it might some day be interred in England, but refused to buy a new pall for it. See *Letters of Hor. Walpole* (Toynbee), i. p. 332 *n.*

[2]Archidalia, *in partibus.*

West Window of the Church, & in others also; some
of which I took an Account of in an hasty Manner, &
others I neglected. In 1674, the Church was began, the
first Stone thereof being laid by Mary Louisa, Queen of
Spain, Daughter to Philip Duke of Orleans by his Wife
Henrietta of England, (Daughter to Charles I by his
Wife Henrietta of France): but it was not consecrated
'till 1677, by the Arch-Bp of Paris, afterwards Cardinal
de Noailles. The same Arch-Bp Giffard dedicated
himself to God in the Order of St Benedict Dec: 14,
1608, taking upon himself at his Profession the Name
of Father Gabriel de St Mary, in the English Benedictine Priory of Dieulwart, near Nancy in Lorrain,
which he had begged of the Cardinal of Lorrain for
them in 1606, that being the first Settlement the
English Benedictines had Abroad: this House he almost
rebuilt, & in a Manner may be called the Founder of it,
from his great Benefactions to it. In this House my
Friend Father Sympson, Chaplain at Mr Throckmorton's at Weston[1] in Buckinghamshire, had his
Education, who has often talked to me of the Pleasant-
ness of the Situation & Cheapness of the Country.
There were several Monuments of English Gentlemen
in the Church, but I transcribed none of them. Just
opposite to the Convent on the other Side of the Street,
was a public Fountain. When I called at this House, I
enquired for the Prior, but was told by the Porter, that
he was not at Home: I then asked for the late Prior,
Mr Price, who was in the Country: however, as the
Porter desired me to tell him my Name, I gave him that,
with a Direction where I might be found, at the Hôtel
d'Orléans, Rue des Petits Augustins: this I rather did,

[1]Weston Underwood, near Olney.

in Hopes that the Prior, or some of the Fathers of
the Convent would be so obliging as to call on me;
especially as Father Wybourne, the late Prior, had told
me, that he would write to the Prior, & desire him to
let me have what Money I had Occasion for: however I
saw none of their Reverences during my Stay at Paris:
which was the more disagreable to me, as I much
depended upon seeing some of them, who might have
been of great use to me, as I knew no one at Paris:
besides I had a secret Inclination in Favour of this
House, & Religious Order, formerly so flourishing in
England, & had just before I left Cambridge, employed
Monsieur la Butte, a Teacher of the French Language
there, & who was going to Paris, to enquire of Mr
Walmesley,[1] the then Prior, a great Mathematician, &
Friend of Dr Smith, then & now Master of Trinity
College in that University, & with whom he held a
Correspondence, whether it would be allowed for me, a
Clergyman of the Church of England, to have a Lodg-
ing at their Convent: but Mr Browne Willis, my most
worthy Friend & Patron, just then [1753] presenting
me to the Rectory of Blecheley in Buckinghamshire, a
Stop was put to that Project, which had it then taken
Place, might have fixed me there for my Life, as I never
had any other Views in Life, than to live retiredly &
quietly, & pretty much to myself, after the Monkish
Manner: which I yet, tho' more in the World, in paying
& receiving Visits, than many of my Condition, I can't
help, privately & in secret, to prefer to such Dissipation.

In the middlemost Window of the South or right
Hand Side going up to the Altar, are the Arms of

[1]Charles W. (1722-97): F.R.S., resided at Bath for the last forty years
of his life.

Walter Montagu,[1] Abbat of Pontoise [Arms described]. It is most probable that he was a kind Benefactor to this House, as he was of a most remarkable generous Spirit. Having been educated in Sidney College in Cambridge, he went Abroad to finish his Studies, where he was converted to the Roman Catholic Religion; which was the more extraordinary, as his Brother, Edward Montagu, was that noted Puritan Earl of Manchester, who, as Visitor of the University of Cambridge in the year 1643, turned out Multitudes of loyal & worthy Members of that University to make way for as many factious & presbyterian Intruders into their Places, & had the singular Disgrace put upon him at the Restoration, to displace these Intruders into other Men's Property, & put the right Owners into their Freeholds again, which they had been dispossessed of by his Authority. This Earl was eldest Son of Henry Montagu [1st] Earl of Manchester, & our Abbat was his [the 1st E.'s] 2nd Son. Mr Dodd, in his *Catholic History of England*, Vol. 3, p. 94, giving an Account of the Life of the Abbat Montagu, makes a gross Mistake in a Point of Chronology: for observing that Cardinal Mazarine, who during his Troubles, has been under Obligations to the Abbat, yet on his Restoration to public Favour, was forgetful of them, he says, That "while the two Queens [Anne of Austria, Queen Dowager of France, & Henrietta Maria of England] lived, & had any Power, he never wanted Advocates on any Occasion. But after their Decease, Mazarine began to look cool upon him." Now it is notorious, that both these Queens survived that Minister many years, who died in 1661: whereas the Queen Regent of France

[1] c. 1603-77.

lived, if my Memory fails me not, to 1666, & the Queen Mother of England died not 'till 1669: the year after which our noble, honourable & worthy Abbat died at Paris, & chose for the Place of Sepulture the Church belonging to the Hospital of Incurables in that City: an infallible Mark of his great Humility, & true Christian Charity. [References to materials for a Life of Abbot Montagu omitted.]

In the next Window below them on the same South Side, near the West End, are the Arms, with Coronet & Supporters of Wm Herbert,[1] Marquis & Duke of Powis, impaling those of his Duchess, Elizabeth Somerset, Daughter to Edward, Marquis of Worcester, & Sister to Henry, Duke of Beaufort. This most noble Marquis & Duke of Powis following his Royal Master's unhappy Fortune into France, died at St Germains en Laye, June 2, 1696, at the Age of 69 years, & was buried in the Parish Church belonging to that Town & Castle. No doubt but he was a Benefactor to this English Convent, as his Grace's Arms are placed in so conspicuous a Part of the Church. As I have the Honour, at some Distance, by my Mother's Side,[2] to draw my Original from the same noble House of Herbert, (let it be said with much Vanity & Ostentation, for, from the least to the greatest, we have all the Pride & Vanity to mend our Extraction, & probably the lower we may draw it, the Passion to improve it may be the stronger) my Grandmother being Neice of the famous & worthy

[1] 1617-96; created Duke by James II, in exile.

[2] Catherine Cole claimed that Abdias Tuer's wife was sister of George Herbert. But G.H. had, it seems, only three sisters—Eliza, Margaret and Frances, whose married names were Jones, Vaughan and Brown respectively. See *The Life of Lord Herbert of Cherbury*, Strawberry Hill, 1764.

Christian Poet, the rev: Mr George Herbert, Brother
to the Lord Herbert of Cherbury, as famous for his
Infidelity,[1] as his Brother was for his practical Christianity, by one of their Sisters, it was doing such an
Honour to myself in recording this Coat of Arms, that
Self Love & Vanity both conspired to check all the more
humble Motions of Humility in not taking Notice of it
in the Manner I have done. From the English Benedictines I went to the French Convent of the Nuns of
Port Royal, to enquire for Miss Throckmorton,
descended from the same most noble Family of Herbert, Duke of Powis, her Grandmother being Lady
Teresa Herbert, Daughter of [the] Duke [of] Powis:
I was desired by her Mother Mrs Throckmorton to
call upon her here, & see after her Welfare, but was told
by the Portress that there was not one English Lady in
that House. This Convent is at the very Extremity of
the Rue St Jacques, near the Royal Observatory, & the
Feilds: tho' it seemed but an awkward Kind of Place,
being on the same Side of the Street as the English
Benedictines, & not far from them: their Church was
in the Court into which the Coach drove, but I did not
go into it, as the Door was shut. After having tired
myself with viewing so many Sights, I drove to Mr
Walpole's to Dinner at 3 o'Clock, who sent me Home
to my Lodgings in his *Vis-à-Vis* about 7, when he went
out upon a Visit.

Thursday, Oct: 31. Great Fog. I sent Letters this Day
to my Sister Catherine Cole at Hackney in Middlesex,
to my half-Brother the rev: Dr Stephen Apthorp at
Eton College, to the rev: Mr Goodwin, Rector of
Loughton in Buckinghamshire, one of my next

[1] *I.e.* Platonism.

K

Neighbours, & to my two Parishioners, Mr Nathaniel
Cartwright of Blecheley & Mr Tho: Cooke of Water-
Eaton in that Parish. Mr Galand, a true French Barber,[1]
of the Rue Jacob, came to take Measure of me for a
Peruke, & breakfasted with me: he told me that the
rev: Mr Howard, Nephew to the Duke of Norfolk,
lately lodged at his House. A Capuchin Friar came
to me for Alms. Small Rain almost all the Day. I
excused myself from dining with Mr Walpole this Day;
& enjoyed myself by not stirring out anywhere.

Friday, November 1. All Saints. Small Rain. As I was
informed that the Arch-Bishop of Paris was to officiate
pontifically, I went to High Mass at Notre Dame at 10
o'Clock, which was not finished 'till past 12. His Grace
officiated in his Pontificals, with his Mitre on his Head,
which, however, was frequently taken off, & put on
again, by one of the assisting Canons, many of whom
were dressed in very rich Copes; but most of them were
in their Stalls, & I observed that many of them had red
Cassocks under their large black Cowls: they all
attended in a very solemn Procession all round the
Choir & Isle of the Church twice, during which Time
some Anthems were sung, while the Grand Organ at
the West End of it played, the Arch-Bp at Times
saying Part of the Service in the Middle Isle of the
Nave. The Service was very grand, the Epistle &
Gospel being sung on different little Sort of Tribunes
just above the Back of the Stalls, & between them &
the Back of the Altars of our Lady & St Denys, on each
Side of the Entrance into the Choir. A Representation
of High Mass in this beautiful Choir, & just as I saw

[1] "I sent my 2 French wigs to my London Barber to alter them, they
being made so miserably, I could not wear them." (C., Feb. 27, 1766).

it solemnised, may be seen in a fine Print in the first Volume of *Religious Ceremonies of all Nations,* (the Plates of which are engraved by Picart), at p. 313. I was in a Gallery which runs all round the Chapels of the Choir, & looks over that Part of the Church & the Nave at the same Time. The Music, to my Ear, was not near so agreable as the Church Music with us: probably it was by my not being acquainted with it. The Arch-Bishop is a well-looking, tall & fresh-coloured Man, & seemed to me to be of the Age of between 50 & 60 years: his Name is Christopher de Beaumont du Repaire,[1] a Man of Courage & Resolution, who has defended his Church, Clergy & Faith against the repeated Attacks of the Parliament like another St Athanasius. His Arms, embroidered on Silk, are at the Back of his Throne in the Choir, & are, as well as I can remember them, Argent, on 2 Bars Azure 6 Fleurs de Lis: but of this I won't be sure, as it is only by Memory many Months after I saw them. (I write this June 16, 1766). I saw a Print of him in a Shop near the Cathedral, which I intended to purchase, but forgot it.

Saturday, Nov: 2. All Souls. Fine Day. After Breakfast I went in a Coach to the greatest Ornament of the City of Paris, of the modern Kind, I mean the Royal Hospital of Invalides founded by Lewis 14, in the Beginning of his Reign for disabled Officers & Soldiers. It is situated at the Extremity of the Fauxbourg St Germain, in the Feilds, with its grand Front looking to the River, not far from the Isle aux Cignes. It had a large Plantation of poor shabby looking Trees in regular Lines planted before it, with a Court, surrounded by a Fosse & Parapet-Wall before the grand Front, over the

[1]Archbishop of Paris, 1746-81.

Portal of which is a fine Alto-relievo Equestrian Statue
of Lewis 14: the first Court is handsome, but dull &
flat, as there are no Windows, or too few of them in it,
tho' a Sort of Cloyster runs all round it, & an expensive
Sort of Dormer Window at Top, in the Shape of
Military Dresses, go round the whole of it. In the
middle, fronting the Entrance, is the grand Portal of
the Church, which is a long plain unornamented Nave,
with a vaulted Roof, & Organs over the West Door:
in the Church, before different Altars, some kneeling,
others sitting on Forms reading, & all at their separate
Devotions, for Mass was over before I got here, it
being past 12 o'Clock, I saw, what I shall never see in
England, I am afraid, a great Number, 50 Perhaps, of
Officers & Soldiers, in the most recollected[1] Attitudes
at their Devotions: on the left Side, by the High Altar,
you ascend some Steps which leads thro' a Vestry to the
Dome Part of the Church, behind the High Altar: this
Part strikes one the more, as the other Part was so very
plain: here is nothing but the utmost Beauty & Magnificence: exquisite Painting, fine Carving & Gilding,
rich Marbles & Statues, & in short, every Thing that can
please the Eye & gratify the most difficult Curiosity.
The High Altar is so contrived, by 6 twisted Pillars,
3 on each Side, supporting a Canopy, that it serves
both for this glorious Part of the Church, as well as
for that in common Use: for here no one comes but
out of Curiosity; & it seems to be an expensive Room,
of no Use, but for shew & Grandeur only. The Dome
is supported by vast fluted Pilasters, & finely painted:
the Floor immediately under the Dome is a vast Star, or
Estoile, of beautiful coloured Marble, cheifly red, on a

[1]Absorbed in contemplation; see *O.E.D.*

white Ground; & seemed to be much too exquisite to be
trod upon: & indeed the Sentinel, who was on Guard
at the Entrance into this Part of the Church, desired me
not to Walk upon it: you descend some Steps to it; or
rather from it, & the grand Entrance into it, fronting
the Altar, you ascend to the high & other Altars &
Chapels round it: for it being an entire square Building,
the 4 Angles or Corners are so many private beautiful
Chapels, richly ornamented with Paintings, fine Altars,
painted Glass & fine floors of various coloured Marbles,
in Figures of Fleurs-de-Lis, & other Foliages &
Devices, as the initial Letters of the Founder's Name,
crowned with the Royal Crown of France. These 4
Chapels are dedicated to the 4 Doctors of the Church,
whose Statues in Plaister of Paris, greatly bigger than
Life, were formerly in Niches over the Altar, but were
then replacing by very fine Statues in White Marble:
that of St Augustine was putting up while I was there.
The History of the principal Passages of each Saint's
Life was painted in different *Compartiments* of the Dome
of each Chapel, & the Apotheosis or Death of him was
represented in the Summit of each Dome. Besides these
4 principal Chapels with Domes, in the 4 Angles of the
Church, there are 2 very fine Altars between them,
on the N. & S. Sides of the Church, or Transept of it,
against the North & South Walls, fronting each other:
the one dedicated to our Lady, with a delicate Statue of
White Marble on the back Altar, & the other to St
Teresa, with as beautiful a Statue of her, of the same
Materials. These Altars are most richly & sumptuously
adorned, with Carving, Gilding & every Thing that can
contribute to make them rich & beautiful. It is probable
that King Lewis caused them to be so dedicated out of

Compliment to his Queen, Maria Teresa: if that was the
Case, my Friend Dr Pulter Forester, now Chancellor
of the Diocese of Lincoln (by the Bargain made between
Green Bp of Lincoln & him, within these 2 Months)
his Compliment to his Wife was not so singular as I
esteemed it, when the Doctor first told me of it: for he
having, by the Legacy of his Aunt, the late Lady
Monoux,[1] an House in Bolton Street, Piccadilly, which,
after her Ladyship's Death, he, in 2 or 3 of the Winter
Months, used as a Town House, about 2 or 3 years ago,
(to authorize his leaving his Country Parish, as well as
to turn a Penny, & make an Advantage of it), took it
into his Head to build a new Chapel in that Neighbourhood, where new Buildings were daily encreasing, with
a Design to let out the Pews for so much a year: by
which Means he cleared, as he told me himself, about
£100 per ann, & when the Chapel was finished, he had
it consecrated under the Invocation of our Lady, for no
other Reason but because that was his Wive's Name.
The letting out Pews for such a Sum by the year, (tho'
it seems an odd Practice, that People should be forced
to give Money for coming to Church, to do their Duty,
which ought to be left at Large, as well as the Word of
God freely dispensed to them), yet even this paltry &
greedy Custom has Catholic Authority also in its
Favour: for at the Metropolitan Church at Paris are
various Advertisements on large painted Boards
regulating & fixing the Price of Chairs in such & such
Places & Parts of the Church, for those that make use
of them: & I was more than once called upon, as I was

[1]Presumably the widow (*ob.* 1758) of Sir Philip M. the 3rd Bart.
G.E.C., *Complete Baronetage*, makes the widows of the 4th and 5th
Barts. die on the same day.

Kneeling on one at the Abbey Church of St Germa[i]ns des Prez, by the Sexton or Clerk, to pay for the use of it: which I should not have comprehended, if my French Servant had not paid 2 or 3 Sous for me & my Servant. I gave about a Livre, or 10 Pence, for my Place & 2 Chairs in the Gallery at Notre Dame, when I went to High Mass there on All Saints Day. The Dome of this most noble & elegant Church[1] is a great Ornament to this City, as it is seen from every Quarter of it, as it is of a most beautiful Construction, having a Sort of Lanthorn above it, which is terminated by a light Pyramid. After I had examined at Leisure the Beauties of this most complete Church, I drove to Mr Dessein's, a Bookseller, near the Grand Augustins Convent, where I ordered some Books to be sent to my Lodgings, & from thence drove to Dinner at the Hôtel du Parc Royal, Rue du Colombier. This Bookseller I had met at the same Hotel, was a very civil & honest Man, could speak a little English, & had lived 8 or 10 Months in the Strand in London, with a Bookseller of Credit, whose Name I forget, on Purpose to settle a Correspondence & learn the Language; which now at Paris is in no small Vogue & Reputation, I much doubt for no great Good; as is every Thing that is English,[2] even to Politics; which also bodes no great Prospect of their future Peace & Tranquillity.

Sunday, Nov: 3.[3] Fine Day. I walked first to the

[1] *I.e.* the *Invalides.*

[2] To illustrate the *anglomanie* of the time, George Selwyn told Walpole that at " a vast dinner", given by Madame de Villars to the Duchess of Bedford, "a huge dish of hot rolls and a sauce boat of melted butter" appeared at dessert. "Because", explained the hostess, "you English love hot rolls." *Letters of Hor. Walpole* (Toynbee), No. 858, Nov. 30, 1762.

[3] Dec. 3 (MS.).

Church of the little Austin Friers, & passing thro' it,
got into a Boat which carried over Passengers to the
other Side of the River, & went & examined every Part
of the Louvre on the Outside: it being Sunday I could
not have Access to the inner Apartments, where the
Academies are held. The grand Court is a noble &
magnificent Square, of different Sorts of Architecture,
it having been undertaken at different Periods; cheifly
under Lewis 14, who finished that glorious Front
towards St Germain l'Auxerrois, with a single Row of
fluted Corinthian Pillars on a lower Story or Base,
having 3 Pavillions, one in the Middle, under which is
the Grand Entrance, & 2 at the Extremities: the Front
also to the River is of the same Design, only Pilasters
instead of round Pillars range along it between the
Windows, with 3 Pavillions also in the same Manner;
as has also the 2 other Sides of the Square: these
Pavillions were roofed formerly *à la Mansarde*, as it is
called, from the Architect Mansart, who invented them:
which are frightful high Roofs, quite out of all Proportion: as they are now repairing the grand Front, &
new ornamenting it, having laid it also open, by pulling
down Buildings which were too near it, & obstructed a
clear Passage, & good View of it, they have taken away
these preposterous Roofs, only one now remaining at
the Angle nearest the Pont-Neuf; which I suppose is
going to be pulled down, as there were Scaffoldings
about it. A new Story also was newly added, & not yet
finished, with light Pillars on the Inside, on the right
Hand as you enter the Court from St Germain l'Auxerrois. It is supposed that Philip Augustus had a Palace
on this Spot, but certain that Francis I began the
present Building, which the late King had the Honour

to finish. I could not help taking Notice here, as in all other their fine Buildings, that there was a Nastiness, Slovenliness & Filthiness about them, that greatly disgraced them. As the Masons & other Workmen had not finished in this Place what they were about, it may admit of some Excuse: yet great Inequalities & Unevenesses in the Walking Part, & great Heaps of Dirt by the Passages, might surely be removed, & set to Rights, by People who are apt to find Fault every where but at Home, at no great Expence or Trouble.

As I have mentioned Madame Geoffrin at p. 81, & the *White Hall Evening Post* of June 17, 1766, this Moment come by the Post, has the following Article relating to her, I shall give it a Place here, as a Supplement to my short & imperfect Account of that Lady: (I write this June 18, 1766).

"*Paris, June* 2. Madame Geoffrin, Mother to the Marchioness de la Ferté-Imbault, is just set out for Poland, where her Company is much desired by the King,[1] who does not forget, upon the Throne, the Friendship he contracted with her during his Residence in France. This Lady, who is upwards of 60 years old, kept an open Table here for all the *Beaux-Esprits* & Men of Literature; & no Foreigner of Consequence ever came to this City, without being introduced to her. His Polish Majesty, who had an opportunity of discovering the true Value of her Society, wrote several Letters to her, since his Advancement to the Throne, inviting her to come to Warsaw: & as Madame Geoffrin is peculiarly curious with regard to her Furniture, & much

---

[1]Stanislaus Augustus Poniatowski, elected King, 1764; *ob.* 1794. Mme Du Deffand calls him "Prince Geoffrin"; *Lettres de la Marquise du Deffand à Horace Walpole*, i. 102.

attached to her own Apartment, his Polish Majesty carried his Gallantry so far, as to procure, unknown to her, an exact Account of her Furniture, in Order to surprize her with an Apartment in his Palace, perfectly resembling that she had here. The Empress of Russia has also written several Times to this Lady, expressing how much she wishes to be acquainted with her: so that she may possibly go to Petersburg: in which Case, it is said that Monsr d'Alembert will accompany her."

If all this is not put into the News Papers, without any Sort of Authority, & only to Amuse the Public, by filling up their Papers, in Order to make People stare, which is most probable,[1] one may form a Judgement of his Majesty of Poland & her Majesty of Russia, their Principles, from the Choice of their Company. Monsieur D'Alembert's Pride seems to have been gratified by his Refusal of undertaking the Education of the future Emperor of Russia. It would be as happy for the Poles as well as the Russians to be less fond of French Philosophers with their Infidelity: it will hardly mend their People's Morals, but will certainly make them worse Subjects. I remember very well Mr Walpole's mentioning the Peculiarity of Madame Geoffrin's Way of Life, where every one was handsomely entertained, but that she would have her way, & left or came to her Company as it pleased her Fancy: he said that she was not of the Nobility, but was left a very rich Widow. But not to forget my Journal.

After admiring the Louvre I walked to the Side of it fronting the River, & back to the Pont-Neuf, all the way being crouded with People listening to Mountabanks on Horseback, & on Sort of Stages, with Cur-

[1]But see *Letters of Hor. Walpole* (Toynbee), No. 1091, Feb. 8, 1766.

tains & small Apartments behind them, acting Farces
& Interludes, for their own Profit, & diversion of the
People: on the Pont-Neuf I met with Mr Theodore
Eynhouts, who very civilly invited me to dine with him,
but I excused myself & appointed another Day. I then
took a Coach & went all round the new Boulevarts, or
made a Circuit of the City of Paris on this Side of the
River, surrounding the Fauxbourgs of St Germain, St
James, St Marceau, & St Victor, going through the
long Street, after I had got out of my own of the Petits
Augustins, of Du Colombier, Jacob, Sorbonne & de
l'Université, which all form one long Street from the
Rue de Seine to the Palais de Bourbon, (which unluckily
obstructs the View down to the River), & so on a fine
paved Way, lined on both Sides by but indifferent Trees,
by the Hôtel des Invalides, leaving a vast spatious
Building, close to it, called *L'École Militaire*, on the
right Hand, which is a new Foundation, & an Appen-
dage, as I take it, on the Invalides, for the Education of
their young Nobility & Gentry in the Military Art.
There were quantities of Sallad Gardens by the Road
Side, but that was not diversified, as about London,
with pleasant Villages, nor elegant & neat Boxes, with
pleasant Gardens about them: tho' there were 2 or 3
new Houses of this Sort which I took notice of, & not
more. I left the Royal Observatory, on a rising Ground,
on the left Hand, which may possibly be Convenient to
the Purpose in the greatest Degree, but to my Fancy
one of the clumsiest & heaviest Buildings I ever saw: &
can compare it to nothing so well as the triangular
Tower built by the late Duke of Argile[1] on Hounslow

[1]Archibald, 3rd D. of Argyle; see *Hounslow Heath, A Poem*, by
Wetenhall Wilkes, dedicated to the duke (1748).

Heath. Further on you cross the great Post Road to Lyons, & leave the Horse Market, or open Space where these Animals are sold, on the left Hand: not far from which you see the Gobelins & its Church, passing the River that goes to it, by means of which many of their fine Manufactures have been carried on to that Perfection which they have obtained; particularly in Tapestry, the Colours of which have been thought to have been heightened by the particular Property of that Stream. Not far from hence, on the Right, & inclining to the River Seine you discover an Hospital which covers as much Space as a little Town: it is called *Le Salpêtrière* & gives Food & Rayment to between 7 & 8,000 People of both Sexes:[1] such as the Sick, disabled, poor, disorderly Persons, Women of loose Lives, mad People & Beggars: in short all that can give no good Account of themselves are sent here, where, if in Distress & Sick, they are humanely taken Care of, tho' I think lodged too many in a Room, & too close together; if they are well, they are set to various Kinds of Work to earn their Livelihood. I went thro' many of their Wards & Apartments, which were full & kept very clean. Their Church is built on a new Construction, being a real Cross, having a vast heavy Dome in the Middle, with 4 Naves, fronting the High Altar which is immediately under the Dome, & serves for the 4 Churches, as they are in Effect: it being so contrived that the different Sexes & Sorts of Persons in the Hospital should not intermix with each other. It should seem that Cardinal Mazarine was a Benefactor to this Institution, as his Arms in large are over one of the principal Gates into it. The Church as gloomy

---

[1] The hospital assumed its present form (for women only) in 1823.

withinside, as it is awkward & clumsy on the Outside.

Monday, Nov: 4. Rainy. As I catched a sore throat
yesterday either in passing the River in a Boat without
any Great Coat, or in the Coach in having no Glasses,
the Wind passing freely thro' it, as I took an Airing
half round the City, I wrote to Mr Walpole to excuse
my waiting upon him to the Luxemburg Palace, &
staid within all Day.

Tuesday, Nov: 5. Very fine Day. I walked to see the
Abbey of St Germains des Prez, it being, in a Manner,
close to my Lodgings. The Court from St Benedict's
Street is the Cheif Entrance to the Church, & is of no
great Appearance: the Tower of the West Front has the
Look of very great Antiquity & is excessively ugly, in
no Stile of Architecture, but only an awkward great
Tower with no Sort of Ornaments about it: but the
great Portal under it, by which you enter into the Nave
of the Church, very amply makes amends for any
Deficiency elsewhere, by its venerable Antiquity &
curious Imagery of some of the first Race of the French
Monarchs. From the Stile of the Architecture it is easy
to judge that this Gateway was built long before what
we now stile Gothic Architecture was introduced: for
the four Statues in each Side of the Door are not placed
under Niches or pointed Arches, as was the Manner of
the later Gothic Architects, but each on a Pedestal, with
its Back against a Pillar, the Capitals of which are
ornamented variously, some with Acanthus or other
Leaves, others with human Figures, Angels, or Birds;
in the same Manner as some of the Capitals in the
glorious Cathedral of Ely, particularly in the old Part
of the Church, now the Canons' Lodgings, are orna-

mented. Over the Door is a curious alto-Relievo
representing the last Supper, where our Saviour sitting
at a long Table, with St John the Evangelist reclining
on our Saviour's Lap, & 5 other Apostles sitting on
each Side of him, with one other on this Side of the
Table, with one Knee on the Ground Kneeling, &
holding a large Cup, for the Sop. But as this curious
Gate has been often described, & particularly lately by
Dom Montfaucon, in his *Antiquitez de la Monarchie
Françoise* Vol: 1, p. 50 to 54, where he has also given a
Plate of it, I shall say no more about it. The Nave is
large & clumsy, with great heavy Pillars on each Side,
over which are hung several large fine Pictures representing cheifly the History of the Miracles of St Paul &
St Peter. In the middle of the Choir where the Monks
sing their Service, which is now the whole old Choir,
with the Abbat's Stall in the Center, where the old
Altar formerly stood, with handsome Stalls all round
on both Sides, is the raised Altar Monument of King
Childebert, Founder of this Royal Abbey: he is carved
lying on his Back, with a Church in his right Hand &
a Sceptre in his left, & is supposed by Father Montfaucon in his *Antiquitez* (p. 58 & 160 of his 1st Volume),
to be made about the Beginning of the 11th Century;
he has also given a Print of it, as to the upper Part: for
it is now, I suppose, very unlike what it was when it laid
before the High Altar, possibly little raised from the
Ground: the Sides of it now are Marble on which are
Inscriptions to be met with in Germain Brice's *Description de Paris*, Vol: 3, p. 302 &c. This old Tomb is
supposed to be made after the Model of an older, the
original one, broke by the Normans when they rifled &
plundered Paris & its Environs: for this King died in

558. At the Foot of this Altar Tomb, on the Floor, is a
Marble with an Inscription on it for a natural Son of
Henry 4th, Lewis de Bourbon, Duke de Verneuil, who
had been Commendatory Abbat here & Bp of Metz,
but afterwards married: at his Death in 1682 he ordered
his Heart to be buried in this Place: near which is also
another Gravestone of White Marble, I think, for
another very young Commendatory Abbat, Lewis
Caesar de Bourbon, Count de Vexin, who died 10 Jan:
1682, aged between 10 & 11 years, soon after his
Nomination to this Dignity, & lies buried here. The
High Altar is now placed at the Entrance into the old
Choir, being a most stately & magnificent Canopy on
the Top of which is a Cross fixed on a Globe or Mound,
round which a Serpent is twining, & under it hangs,
supported by 3 Angels, the Tabernacle in which is
preserved the consecrated Hosts, all supported by 6
Corinthian Pillars, in a Sort of Circle or Oval, surrounding the Altar, 3 on each Side; so that the rich & curious
Shrine of St Germain, who died Bp of Paris in 576,
held up towards the middle of the Canopy by 2 Angels
in Brass as big as Life, Kneeling, may be seen at the
same Time, equally commodious, both by the Monks
in their Choir, & by the People on the other Side, which
is however the principal Front of the Altar, the Pillars
of which are of a fine *Vert-antique*[1] Marble. This Front
to the Nave, where the People assemble for Divine
Service, is separated from the 2 Transept Isles on each
Side, under the great Arches of the Pillars, which
support the Middle Tower, & in Front across the Nave
from the same Pillars, by a Range of fine Iron Palli-
sadoes, with an Entrance in the Middle from the Nave,

[1]Verd-antique; essentially, serpentine.

which is called the Sanctuary: within which, just at the
Entrance lies a curious old Marble, covered almost all
over with a large Plate of Brass, on which is carved the
Portrait of William, Abbat of this House, mitred & in
his Cope, with Ornaments all about the Plate: which is
the only old Monument of any of the Abbats which I
observed in this Church: but it seems there is a Chapel
in the Abbey, which I did not see, where most of them
are buried, & where it is probable they have their
Tombs. But the most curious Tombs in this Church,
or indeed elsewhere, particularly one of them, are in
this Sanctuary, ranged in a Circular Kind of Manner
round it, 3 on each Side, under the Iron Pallisades,
raised Altar Tomb Fashion, about 2 Feet from the
Ground, of Stone, in a too modern Stile for the Covering
of them at Top, which are the Originals, taken from the
Choir Part of the Church, when that was new modelled
& the new Altar placed in its present Situation. These
curious Tombs are of 3 Kings of France of the first
Race, with their Queens, Chilperic & his Queen
Fredegonde; Chlothaire II & Bertrudis his Consort,
with Childeric II & his Queen Bilihilde: concerning
the finding the Monuments of these 2 last, there is a
curious Dissertation in Vol: 1. p. 173, of Dom Montfaucon's *Antiquitez*, who has also given Plates of the 2
first at p. 162, of the same Volume. That of Chilperic
is much like that of the Founder, King Childebert, & is
supposed to be done at the same Time with it, from
Copies of the Originals, or from Peices of the Originals,
in the 11th Century, broken by the Pagan Norwegians
& Danes, who plundered France in the same Manner
as they had England. Chilperic is represented crowned,
holding a Sceptre in one Hand & his Chin & Beard in

his left: & round the Verge of the Stone is wrote in
half-gothic Letters this Inscription: ✠ *Rex Chilpericus
hoc tegitur Lapide*: but the Tomb of his Queen, the
infamous Fredegonde, is the most curious of any of
them, being certainly the Original which at first covered
her Grave: for it seems as if it was designed to lie flat
on the Ground, or under some Arch in the Wall, it
being in the Shape of a Coffin Stone, broad at the Head
& narrow at the Feet: it is a very curious Stone, & the
only one of the Sort I ever saw, being wholly Mosaic
work, or small Stones joyned together on the Surface,
forming the Figure of a Woman crowned with an
Ornament terminated at Top with a Sort of Fleurs-de-
Lis, as is also the End of the Sceptre in her right Hand:
her Head, Hands, Feet & Girdle are plain, & hollowed
into the Stone, & seem to have been formerly enamelled
with a more precious but slighter Materials, which
thro' Time are perished: the whole Figure is dressed in
Robes very distinguishable by the different Stones &
small Interstices, in which Brass or other Metal is run,
to separate the Foldings & various Parts of the Habits,
& all enclosed by a Border on which are ranged Roses
or other round Ornaments & Flowers in great Numbers.
This very antient & curious Monument I had often
desired to see, & the first Thing I enquired after, in
looking into the Church, of the Lay Brother, who
shewed it to me, was this precious Relic of Antiquity;
but he seemed to be quite in the Dark about it; so I concluded it was removed into some private Part of the
Church: however, on going into the Sanctuary, I easily
discovered it, from its singular Texture. It stands the
first, nearest the High Altar, on the Gospel or North
Side of it, in the North-East Corner, close to the Iron

L

Palisades on one Side of it: but the slovenly condition in which I saw it, gave me no high Opinion of the Cleanliness of the Keepers of the Church, & was a sure Indication that no Father Montfaucon was then among the Monks of the House: for it was in a Manner covered all over with Grease & Dust, by the neglect of the *Sacristain* or Lay Brother who had the Care of keeping the Church clean. Methinks never so much Finery & so much Nastiness were so near together: the truly magnificent, rich & splendid Altar, made up of Jewels, Gold, Silver, beautiful Marble, fine Carving & Gilding, exceeded almost any Thing of the Sort I ever saw: while close to it, as a Foil, stood the most antient Tomb in the Kingdom, for one of their first Queens, all over besmeared with the Oyl for the Lamps, with an old Oyl Pot upon it, from which the Oyl that served the Lamps in the Church, were served: as if this contemptuous Treatment of the Monument of so great a Princess—& one whose Power, in her Time, was uncontrouled—was a just & providential Return in this Life for the Scandals, Violences & Oppressions she had formerly been guilty of, when in the Height of her Ambition & Lust of Power. The Richness of the Shrine of St Germain, in which are kept his Remains, being a Box or Cabinet in the Shape of a Gothic Chapel, of about 4 Feet in Length, & 2 in Bredth, is very great: being entirely covered with Silver gilt & enameled, with Images of Saints all round it, & adorned with Quantities of Jewels. In the Sacristy, besides the rich Habits in great Plenty, & Reliquaries & other various curious Vessels for Sacred Purposes, I admired in particular a Cross of a very large Size, lately new made in Silver, in which the old Relics & Jewels of a former

Cross were set, being full of Emeralds, Amethists, & other precious Stones of a surprizing Bigness & admirable Beauty. Tho' I must needs confess, that most of the Jewels here, & at Notre Dame, as well as others that I have seen in their Churches, did not seem to me to be real Jewels, both from the Muddiness of their Colours, unshapeableness of their Forms & other Circumstances. Perhaps if they were set to more Advantage & better cut, they might appear to be in Reality, what at present they seem to be only Representations of, & those not very good ones. In the South Transept against the East Wall is a fine Statue of St Margaret, in White Marble, trampling on a Dragon, this Part being a Chapel dedicated to her. Near to this to the West is another Chapel lately fitted up, as it seemed to me, having a fine Altar-Peice against the South Wall on which is the Image, in the Clouds, (being Alto-Relievo), of St Maur, to whom the Chapel is dedicated, & close to it are the Monuments of the Cardinal de Furstemberg, Abbat of this House, & his Nephew the Count de Furstemberg. This Cardinal seems to have built the new Brick Part of the Abbey, of which you have a View from an Opening at the upper End of the Rue du Colombier, as his Arms are over the Iron Gates leading up to it. In the opposite Transept is a fine White Marble Monument for the late King of Poland, John Casimir, who after he had abdicated his Throne of Poland, came into France & was Abbat commendatory of this Royal Foundation, (he having formerly been a Jesuit before his Election to the Polish Diadem[1]), & died in 1672, his Body being sent into Poland to be buried in the Royal Vault of those Kings,

[1]He was Cardinal-priest.

according to the established Custom of that Monarchial
Republic, tho' his Heart he left to be interred in this
Abbey. His Tomb is against the North Wall, & very
large, he being represented in his Royal Robes,
Kneeling on a Sort of Sarcophagus, & offering his
Crown to his Maker, extending his Hand with that in
it, & his Eyes being directed to the Altar. In a Sort of
Chapter-House, on the left Hand of the Court going to
the great Door of the Church, are several full Length
Pictures; among the Rest a very good one of King John-
Casimir: when the Lay Brother who shewed it me, he
smiled when he was relating to me Part of his History,[1]
& seemed to be well acquainted with a Part of it
relating to an Amour he was supposed to have with a
certain Lady, after he became Abbat here. But this
might be Scandal, & I report it as such. In a small
Chapel, behind the Choir, there being Chapels all round
it, are 2 handsome Monuments of Wm & James
Douglas, with long Inscriptions before them, & presuming that they were in Print, I did not transcribe
them: they are both large, with their Effigies in Marble,
one against the Side Wall, & the other in Armour,
reclining on his left Side, in White Marble, is against
the West Wall: but they did not seem to be very
excellent in their Kind. The Lay Brother as he was
shewing them, told me that very lately the Duchess of
Douglas,[2] who was then at Paris solliciting a Law Suit
in Relation to her late Husband's Family, had not long
before been to see the Monuments of these two

---

[1] V. *Mélanges d'Histoire et de Littérature*, Tom. 2, p. 468.

[2] Margaret, wife of 1st D. of Douglas, *ob.* 1774. Walpole relates that
she had just left Amiens on her way home, with the embalmed body of
a servant "tied before her chaise". (*Letter* to H. S. Conway, Sept. 12,
1765).

Gentlemen of that Family, of whom she took very little
Notice: that she stalked about the Church like an
Amazon, with her Arms a Kimbow, that she was a large
ungain Person of a Woman, seemed to have a great Deal
of Pride & little Breeding. There is one most remarkable great Bell in the Tower, which requires 8 or 9 Men
to raise it: it has a fine Tone, & is seldom rung:
however, when I was at Paris it had more than ordinary
Practice, as the Prayers of 40 Hours for the Health of
the Dauphin continued many Days before I left it. An
ugly dead Wall, of a most enormous Height, runs all
the Length of the Rue du Colombier, from the new
Iron Gates at the Upper End of it, near the Rue de
Seine, to the Corner of the Rue St Benoit: being the
Back Buildings of Part of the Abbey. The present
Commendatory Abbat is Lewis de Bourbon, Count de
Clermont, of the Condè Family, of the Age of near 60
years, being a well-looking Man, & inclinable to be fat
& jolly.[1] I walked from hence to the most noble Church
of St Sulpice, dependent upon this Royal Abbey,
which is not yet finished: but as I took more Notice of
it upon a 2nd View, some Time after, I shall defer
saying any Thing about it 'till I come to that Part of my
Notes relating to it. From thence I walked to the Rue
de Bussi, to Mr Theodore Eynhout's Magazine,
Warehouse, (or Shop, in plain English), where I bought
me a Dozen of Holland Shirts, & half-a-Dozen Muslin
Neckloths, & as he told me that he knew of a Person
who could make my Shirts as well as in England, I left
them with him to be made after a Pattern I sent him:

[1] 1709-71; though in orders, he was allowed in 1733 to bear arms,
but his military career came to an end in 1758 after his display of
incapacity at the battle of Crefeld.

but such work was never before seen as they made of it; & I was forced to have them all new wristbanded when I got Home: for they are all of a Peice from Beginning to End: all Shew & Outside; & so they have but a little Lace on their Clo[a]ths, Ruffles on their Shirts & Powder in their Hair, they don't trouble themselves about the Fineness & Goodness of the Materials, or whether they are washed once a Month. This Day my French Valet was so drunk that I was quite ashamed of him in the Abbey Church of St Germain-des-Prez: I told him if he was so again, when he was to go out with me, that I would discharge him: he made an Excuse, that he had been at a Cabaret with a Man who owed him some Money & had paid him, & that they had been bargaining together about some of their Lottery Tickets; of which they have so great Variety & so great Plenty, that it is no small Prejudice to the common People, who ruin themselves in gaming at them.

Wednesday, Nov: 6. Tolerable fine Day. Much indisposed with Wind in my Stomach, which was very much out of order. I attributed it to the change of Diet I was fallen into: for whereas at Home I never upon any Account ever Taste a Drop of Ale or strong Beer, (drinking at Dinner only small Beer, when it is small & good & fresh, otherwise Water only), & rarely a Glass of Wine, sometimes not a Glass in a Month; & this not out of Abstinence or Merit, but solely out of Choice, liking neither the Taste of Beer or Portugal or Spanish Wines, I now, one Day with another, drank near a Bottle a Day, as I relished exceedingly both the Burgundy or *Vin de B[e]aune,* a species of Burgundy, I generally made Use of, as well as the Champagne: tho' I did not commonly drink the latter,

as it was above double the Price of the other: but both
excellent in their Kinds. The free Use of what I was so
little accustomed to, together with the excellent & rich
Cyder of Normandy, I apprehend occasioned my Complaint: which I the more readily believe, as my English
Servant, who was near as sober as myself, & as little
used to drink Wine, was taken ill at the same Time, &
in the same Way. The Seine Water is very apt to disorder Strangers on their first coming to Paris, & therefore a too free use of it, without a good Deal of Wine
mixed with it, is not reckoned wholesome: these, with
the Deliciousness of their well ripened Grapes &
Cressan Pears, to a Person who loves Fruit as much as I
do, are more than sufficient to throw one into a Fit of
Sickness, which might have lasted longer than, thank
God, mine did, which was off again the next Day: tho'
I had 2 or 3 other Returns of the same Complaint before
I got Home: for as I did not leave off my usual Way of
Life I had begun since I came into France, so it is no
wonder that I had frequent Attacks of the same Com-
plaint: not having Time to season myself to it. However,
I was not so ill, but I went & dined at the Hôtel du Parc
Royal, where, while we were at Dinner, a Servant came
to inform Mr Walpole, that his Grace the Duke of
Richmond, our Embassador, was just then arrived at
his Hotel, *viz*: the Hôtel de Brancas, as I think, near
the River Side: as soon as Dinner was over, he went to
pay his Compliments to him, which gave me an Opportunity of returning to my Lodgings, which was the best
Place for an indisposed Man. The Duke of Cumberland,
by Mr Walpole's Letters, died suddenly on Friday last:
he was one of the fattest Men I ever saw: on opening
his Head, a sharp pointed Bone, growing out from his

Skull, was supposed to have pricked his Brain, &
occasioned his Death.[1] Dr Barnard was elected Provost
to Eton College October 25, being Friday.

Thursday, Nov: 7. Fine Day. I had determined to
have gone this Day to St Cloud, but not being quite
well, I put it off to another, & so never went at all, &
saw nothing of it further than passing by it in the Road
to Versailles. About Noon I took a Coach & went to see
the Convent of the Grands Augustins, situated on the
same Range with the College of the 4 Nations, on the
Side of the River, below the Pont-Neuf towards Notre
Dame. The Entrance into this Convent is by a Portal
of modern Architecture, over which is a good Statue of
St Augustin, as is also another, much admired, of St
Francis, Kneeling on a Pediment, in the Habit of his
Order, & in the devout Posture in which it is supposed
that he received the Stigmata or 5 Wounds, representing those received by our Blessed Saviour: this stands
in a Corner of the Cloyster, near a Beam, on which is
placed a Crucifix from which the said Stigmata seem to
proceed: it is a Figure much spoken of, & admired for
its Attitude & Proportion: but having been painted
over in its proper Colours, being only the Model of one
at the Louvre, it has an ordinary Appearance. The
Church is one large Room & of no great Beauty,
tho' the Altar is Magnificent, of 8 Marble Corinthian
Pillars: the Stalls on both Sides are very numerous &
handsome, with 2 very stately Thrones on the Entrance
on both Sides, with Canopies in the Form of Crowns of
France, one for the King & the other for the Dauphin,
this being the Church in which the Knights of the Holy

[1]The report of the post-mortem (*Public Advertiser*, Nov. 5, 1765)
does not confirm this statement.

Ghost[1] are installed, there being some magnificent Pictures of an enormous Size, above the Stalls in the Choir, against the Walls, representing the Reception of particular Knights, under the last 5 Kings, the present one being included. The Canopy of the Pulpit is an imperial Crown of France, very large, carved & gilt, & looks very singular: but this being a Church where his Majesty upon solemn Occasions resorts, this Royal Ornament is suitable enough. In 3 moderately handsome Rooms on the ground Floor are Pictures in square Pannels, from the Top almost to the very Bottom, of all the Knights of this Order from its first Institution to this present Time, which entirely cover all the Sides of the Rooms, except the last, where fresh Subjects are put up, as they are created. As I knew that the famous Historian, Philip de Comines, was buried in this Church, I had a Desire to see his Monument, which one of the Friers was so obliging as to go & get a Key, to open the Chapel Door, & shew it me. Was it not that they called it a Chapel,[2] I should have taken it for a Lumber Hole: you descended into this Hole 3 or 4 Steps, where one could hardly distinguish for Dust & want of Light, his Monument, there being hardly Room for a Priest to say Mass at the Altar & 2 or 3 People to hear it, it being so very small & inconvenient. The Tomb consisted of 3 Figures, himself, Wife & only Daughter, who was Countess of Penthièvre. This little Chapel stands close to the East Wall of the Church, on the North Side of the High Altar. The Person who shewed me the Parlours where the Pictures of the Knights are placed, told me, that there were 2 or 3

[1]Created by Henri III in 1578.
[2]De Comines had it built during his life-time.

Englishmen who were Friers in this House, & named
one Father Dillon, an Irishman, & Relation of the
present Arch-Bp of Narbonne, or To[u]louse, Arthur
Richard Dillon,[1] (Brother, I think, to my Lord Dillon).
From hence I went to St Roche's[2] Church, (which I
have described at p. 99) where was a Baptism going to
be solemnized: but I staid so long waiting for the
Priest, that I left it without seeing the Ceremony
performed. From hence I crossed the Pont-Neuf & got
into the good Street St Honoré, one End of which
abuts upon the great Rue St Denis & the other thro'
the Gate St Honoré goes into the Fauxbourg of that
Name. The first Place I stopped at was the Dominican
Convent[3] of the Reformed Jacobins, as the Dominicans
are called in France, on the right Hand of the Street
fronting the Port St Honoré. The Entrance into it
from the Street is by an awkward Kind of Court, the
West End of the Church fronting you, a Thing of no
great Appearance: but the Way we went into the Cloysters & from thence into the Church was by a Passage
on the South Side, close to which was a Sort of Room,
or Parlour, open to the Cloysters, which were painted
all round with the History of the Founder of their
Order, but damaged by Wet & Moisture, in which were
2 or 3 Chairs & a Picture or two: but what Use the
Room was put to, I know not. The Church is of no
great Beauty: on the left Hand of the High Altar, is an
ordinary Chapel, against the West Wall, is a good fine
Monument for the Marechal de Crequi,[4] where he is
represented on his Knees, with an Inscription & his

[1] 1721-1806.   [2] Rocque (MS.).
[3] Later to become famous as the meeting-place of the "Jacobins".
[4] François de C., *ob.* 1687.

Arms in Front. The Library of this Convent is well
furnished with Books, but as it was not open, I did not
see it; tho' the Frier who shewed it me offered to open
it to me any Time that I would call to see it: he took me
into the Chapter House, a long gloomy Chambre, with
a French Roof; that is, the Rafters all bedawbed with
Paint, in Flowers & Leaves & other ornaments, with
no Ceiling. From hence I went to the Convent of the
Feuillants,[1] on the other Side of the same Rue St
Honoré: this is a Reform of the Order of St Bernard,
or Cistertian, Order: it has a noble Portal with high
Walls to the Street & exactly fronts the Grand Place of
Lewis le Grand: the Front of the Church is very
beautiful on the left Hand: but a Swiss Porter took me
into it thro' a Part of the Cloyster in Front, & turning
to the left Hand passed thro' the Chapel of the Family
of Rostaign,[2] being the 3rd on the right Side of the
Church from the cheif Entrance: opposite to which is a
fine Monument with *Medaillons* for the Count & Chevalier de Harcour, Father & Son, of the Lorraine Family.
The high Altar, railed in at some Distance, is of no
particular Beauty: on the right Hand is a very neat
Chapel, against the West Wall of which is a large
Monument of white Marble, being a Sarcophagus,
terminated by an Urn almost to the Top of the Ceiling,
which is not very high, & on which are painted her
Arms, for the Princess de Guémené: a neat Altar fronts
it. The Monks' Choir behind the High Altar is floored
with Wood, & hung round with large Pictures: the
Chapter House is beautiful, being an handsome

[1]Whence the club of the *Feuillants,* opponents of the Jacobins, was
named in 1791.

[2]Rostaing.

Parlour, & well adorned with good full Length Pictures
of Kings Henry 3, their Founder, Henry 4, Lewis 13,
& 2 of Lewis 14, with 2 fine Pictures of the present
King & Queen of France, given to them in 1760,
with the Dauphin's Picture & another or two. The
Cloysters are very handsome, being very near the Back
Part of the Gardens of the Thuilleries, & painted all
round with Histories relating to the Life of St Bernard
& other Worthies of the Cistercian Order: but what
pleased me more than all, was the beautiful painted
Glass in every Window of the Cloysters, painted in
small square Pains,[1] & other Ornaments of beautiful
Foliage, the whole History of the Life of the Blessed
John de la Barriere, who introduced the Reform into
this Order, & established his Convent in this Place,
being called hither by King Henry 3, & made the first
Abbat.

Close to the Feuillan[t]s is the Capuchins' Convent,
founded also by King Henry 3, with high Walls to the
Street, which includes a Court before it, & also fronts
the Street which opens upon the fine Square of Lewis
14, on the other Side of which another Street opens &
discovers the Church of the Convent of the Capuchin-
esses,[2] & may be seen from this Convent in the Rue St
Honoré. This is reckoned the largest Community of
this Order in the Kingdom, there being about 130
Friers maintained in it. The Gardens are large &
spatious, but far from handsome. The Church has
nothing that struck me so much as the Gravestone
before the High Altar, of the famous Duc de Joyeuse,
Peer & Marshal of France, who in 1587, after the
Death of his Wife, quitted his Dignities & Govern-

---

[1] 18th cent. form of "panes".   [2] A coinage of C.'s.

ments, & took the Habit of a barefooted Frier in this
House,[1] under the Name of Father Angel, where he was
buried at the Age of 46 years in 1608, giving an evident
Proof of the Reality of his Contempt for the Grandeurs
of this World, & his Love of Retirement & Christian
Self-Denial.

Near this Convent & so many others which are just
by, is placed a public Fountain with this pretty Distic,
in Allusion to its Situation, put over it:

> *Tot Loca Sacra inter, pura est quae labitur Unda:*
> *Hanc non impuro, quisquis es, Ore bibas.*

This is of the Composition of the famous & ingenious
Poet John Baptist de Santeul,[2] Canon Regular of St
Victor, whose Turn lay this Way. Close to the Grand
Capuchins' Convent, at the Extremity of the Rue St
Honoré, & near the Porte of that Name, stands the
Convent of Austin Nuns, called *Les Filles de l'Assomp-
tion*: their great enormous Dome or Church stands in
the Street, tho' the Grand Entrance is by a little Court,
separated from the Street by a Wall, & on the right
Hand, immediately as you enter it, the Magnificent
Portal, on a Flight of many Steps, strikes your Eye with
Reverence, as 8 noble Corinthian Pillars on these Steps
support the Portico & Pediment above: the Inside of
the Church is only a great massive heavy Building, with
great flat naked Walls, it being nothing but a round
Building, to support an enormous Dome, of no Beauty;
particularly on the Outside; being terminated at Top
with nothing but a clumsy awkward flat Kind of Ornament, which adds to the general Deformity of the whole.

[1]But he left the Order in 1592, took to a military life, and returned
to the Order seven years later.

[2]Santeuil; *ob.* 1597, famed for his Latin poetry.

The Nuns have a Choir separated from this Dome, under which there are four small Chapels contrived between the Pilasters which support it. The Inside of this Church I did not see, as the Doors were shut, & upon desiring to see it, there was some Difficulty, which I don't recollect. I was the more easy, as I was told there was nothing worth staying for: the Dome is discoverable on all the Quarters of the City: but, in my Opinion, adds not much to the Beauty of it.

On the other Side of the Street, exactly opposite to it, is another small religious Community of Franciscan Nuns or Poor Clares, called by the Name of the *Filles de la Conception*: I crossed the Way to see it, as it fronts the Street, but makes no Addition to the Beauty of it, but as the Church Door was shut, I made no further Enquiry to get a Sight of it.

As the Place de Louis le Grand was just by, I walked into it & admired the Beauty & Magnificence of it: this truly noble Square, if it may be so called, as it is rather an octagon, is composed of Buildings of equal Symmetry, Proportion & Beauty all round, with 2 Openings in the Centres of the 2 principal Sides, into the Rue St Honoré, & the other in which the Capucinesses are placed, & is called by their Name Le Rue des Capucines. The lower Story or Ground Floor are rustic Arcades, & has the Look of a Cloyster all round: but the Arches are filled up: so that I suppose this Floor is used for Offices: the 2 upper Stories have Pilasters between the Windows & a Garret terminates the Roof of the Building. In the Middle of this superb Square stands the noble Equestrian Statue[1] of Lewis 14, dressed in the Roman Habit, & both the King & the

[1] Designed by François Girardon and cast by J. B. Keller, a Swiss.

Horse are esteemed excellent for their Attitudes &
Proportion, being of the largest Size: even the Pedestal
on which they are placed is a fine Peice of Work, the
Marbles of it being richly ornamented with gilt-Brass
Decorations: on the Sides are very long Inscriptions, &
the Ends have the Royal Arms, & those of the City of
Paris, which was at the Expence of building the Square,
erecting the Statue & lately repairing the Pedestal of it,
which is surrounded with an elegant Iron Palisade to
keep off Coaches & other Things from injuring it.

From hence I went in the Coach, tho' just by, to the
Convent of Capuchine Nuns, the Front of whose
Church, standing in the Street, exactly fronts the King's
Statue in the Square, & the Convent of the Feuillants in
the Rue St Honoré. This Front is very handsome,
being a Portal of the Doric Order on a Flight of Steps,
which support Pillars or Pilasters, for I forget which,
which support an Entablature above it. The Church
withinside is elegant, but not large, having about 3
Chapels on each Side of the Nave, the Nuns' Choir
being behind the High Altar, the Picture of which,
being the Descent from the Cross,[1] is very fine. The
Nuns were singing their Vespers while I was looking on
the 2 or 3 fine Monuments in the Nave. The first is that
of the Duke de Crequi, Governor of Paris, who died in
1687: he is represented in his military Habit, sitting on
a Sarcophagus, under which stand 2 Figures of Women
representing the Virtues on each Side of the Pedestal
which supports the Sarcophagus, in Front of which are
his Arms, viz: Or, a *Créquier*, or wild Cherry Tree, of
7 Stalks, Gules: behind him is another Figure of a
Woman representing Hope, weeping, all which Statues

[1]By Jean Jouvenet, in 1697.

are of White Marble: & on the Back of the Tomb, under the Arch, is a Peice of Drapery, on which is inscribed a French Inscription: the whole composing a very beautiful & stately Monument. Exactly fronting this, in another Chapel of the Nave is another Tomb of the same Design, tho' of more expensive & delicate Marbles, for the great Marquis de Louvois, Francis-Michael Le Tellier, Son of Chancellor Le Tellier. He was Secretary at War under Lewis 14 & his Prime Minister, & died in 1691. He is represented half reclined on a Sarcophagus, in the Robes of the Order of the Holy Ghost, with his Wives[1] Figure sitting at his Feet, both of which are in Statuary Marble; but Vigilance & Prudence, two fine Statues sitting on each Side of the Sarcophagus of green Marble, or rather of the Pedestal which supports it, & on Front of which is the French Inscription, are of Brass. Just under the Arch, & above the Figures, against the Wall are the Arms of Le Tellier. The very last Chapel on the left Side as you enter the Church from the Street, & close to the Church Door, is a very beautiful & most elegant Chapel, fitting up with fine Marbles, & Compositions to represent Marble, on every Part of it, in which is buried the late great Marchioness de Pompadour, Mistress to his present Majesty: no Part of the Tomb was as yet brought in, nor was the Altar finished: but it bids fair to exceed any of the other Chapels in the Church for Elegance & Beauty. Two fine Giallo-antico Marble Pillars support the Altar Peice: the whole of this Chapel is covered from Top to Bottom with fine Marble. The Monument of Monsieur de Louvois is on the other Side of the Nave, about the Middle, as the

[1]Variant of "wife's".

Duke's opposite to it, is on the same Side with Madame de Pompadour's.

This Rue de Capucines leads in a strait Line, crossing the good Street de Richelieu, to the Place des Victoires, a public Place, which, but for its round or circular Figure, we should call a Square: it is but small, & tho' the Buildings round it are built all upon the same Plan, & much in the Stile of those of the Place de Louis 14, with a rustic ground Floor, & Pilasters between the Windows of the two upper Stories, & a Garret above, yet from the Smallness of the Place or Circle, it has but a mean Appearance, which was much heightened by the Rubbish & great Stones for Buildings & Repairs which laid scattered about it & round the Statue. This beautiful Statue of Lewis 14[1] seemed to me to be too big for the Place it occupied, being an enormous one in Brass, treading on a 3-headed Dog Cerberus, & behind him an Image of winged Victory crowning him with Laurel: this Stands on a vast Pedestal of White Marble, at the 4 Angles of which sit chained as many Slaves in Brass, being a most flattering Compliment to the Vanity of the great Lewis, as if he had conquered & subdued every Quarter of the Globe: four principal Streets terminate in this Circle, besides 3 smaller ones: & from these you may have a good View of this vast Statue, which is all over gilt with Gold: for the Circle or Place is too confined to have a proper View of it; which is surrounded by a Palisade of Iron to keep it from Injury. At the Foot of the King's Statue is this short, glorious & fulsome Inscription:

VIRO IMMORTALI.

[1]Destroyed in 1792.

M

Not far from this Place des Victoires, near the Palais Royal & the Rue St Honoré, is the Opera House: it was burnt down about two years ago, and they are now actually rebuilding it much finer than before: it is built for the cheif Part, & as it is not closed up to the street, the Passengers may be satisfied that they need be under no Dread of a 2nd Accident of that Sort; for the Staircases, Lodges & private Apartments seem all to be built of Stone: I suppose, for Security against Fire. It seems to be a most stately Edifice, & well contrived for the Reception of a great Audience. The Operas are now performed in a Play House in the Palace of the Thullieries. I went from hence over the Pont Royal to see the Convent of Theatin[2] Monks situated upon the Quai which goes by their Name, not far from my Lodgings: the grand Entrance in their Church is upon this Key or Quai, fronting the River, & is an handsome modern Building with Pillars on a Flight of Steps in Front: the Inside is a plain Square & poorly ornamented, it being left unfinished for Want of Money, tho' the great Cardinal Mazarine was their Founder, whose Heart is deposited with them: there are 4 awkward Kind of Chapels in this Square or Nave, above which is a unfinished Dome of no Beauty: behind the High Altar is a very narrow small Choir, for the Religious to sing their Service in: the Entrance into the Convent is by a small Court surrounded by Caryatides or half-human Statues or Pillars supporting the upper Building, & of no great Beauty. I was glad to get Home to sit down to my Dinner, & rest my Legs, as well as to digest &

[2]From Theate, ancient name of Chieti; one of the founders of the order was John Peter Caraffa, Archbishop of Chieti.

methodize what I had seen in the Day. At night we had a good Deal of Rain.

Friday, Nov: 8. Tolerable good Day. Mr Schelling, a Brandenburgher, who called himself *Tailleur du Roi*, brought me Home my black Cloth Coat, flowered black Velvet Waistcoat, black Breeches of the wove Stocking Manufacture I purchased at Roye, & a Great Coat of a Pompadour Colour as we call it, that is a Kind of Colour between a Purple & Red. After I had paid him his Bill, which came to £11. 3s. 0d. I took a Coach & went to Mr Livier's, a Print-Seller who lived in the Rue de St André des Arcs, where I bought several Prints. He was a Middle Aged well-looking Man, who had lived above 20 years in London, where he had married an English Woman, fat, handsome & cross-eyed: she told me that she had Relations who lived at Turvey in Bedfordshire, & that Mr Livier made her the best of Husbands: they had no Children, had been married 20 years, & returned to France about 4 or 5 years: they were well acquainted with Mr Garrick, who had lately been at Paris[1] with his Wife, & had lately dined with them, as also with Mrs Clive, the Actress. They were gentile Sort of People, & lived very handsomely: I went to drink Tea with them more than once on a Sunday Evening when several English People were there to play at Cards, they having always Card Company on that Day: they offered to lodge & board me, Breakfast, Dinner, & Supper, Fire, Candles & every Convenience, for a Guinea & an half a Week, if I should come again to Paris: which would be much more convenient & more easy to me than at an Hotel, where I gave a Guinea a Week for my Lodging only.

[1] In 1763 and 1764.

I then went to the Parish Church of St Andrew des Arcs, situated on the left Hand of the Street, & almost at the Extremity of it, leading to Notre Dame, in a very confined & crouded Situation: the cheif Entrance is to the Street, & has but a mean Look: I did not observe that any of the Churches had Church Yards or Burying Grounds to them, except the famous one of The Holy Innocents; of which I shall make mention in due Time. The Church is not antient,[1] & yet has no modern Appearance, with Isles & Pillars all round it; the Choir is but small, but very neat, & the Nave not extensive; but altogether [it] is an handsome Church, with a beautiful Roof of Stone. About the Middle of the Church, on the right Hand going to the Altar End of it, is a gloomy Kind of Chapel, filled with Monuments for the Family of De Thou, celebrated for the many great Men it has produced. [Arms described.] Against the Wall is an awkward Mural Monument in Marble, containing the Bust of Christopher de Thou, the Father of the famous Historian James-Augustus de Thou,[2] whose Monument is on the adjoyning Wall, where he is represented, in a Marble Statue, on his Knees, between his 2 Wives, with this Inscription in Front, being only a Part of his Epitaph. [See G. Brice, *Description de Paris*, iii, 222.]

I was very glad that I accidentally fell upon the Monument of this Man, not knowing before that he was buried or had any Monument in this Church: tho' it is Pity that the Chapel was not better lighted, & that the Tombs & Chapel itself were not kept in a more

[1]About 1640.

[2]Jacques Auguste de Thou (1553-1617): his *Historiæ sui temporis* appeared 1604-20, and a French translation in 1734.

cleanly Manner, being all over covered with Dust, & in
a slovenly Condition; very different from two very
elegant ones of White Marble in the Choir, on either
Side of it, for Anna-Maria Martinozzi, Princess of
Conti, Neice to Cardinal Mazarine, & of her Younger
Son, Francis-Lewis Prince of Conti, who died in 1709
at the Age of 45 years. The Mother's Epitaph I shall
transcribe, as it shews the Portrait of a Princess so
singularly good in a Station so illustrious, a Time of
Life so inviting & open to Temptations, especially in a
Court so voluptuous & given up to Pleasure & Gayety
as was the Beginning of the Reign of the young &
handsome Lewis 14. This virtuous Princess's Monument is erected against one of the Pillars which divide
the Choir from the Side Isles on the South or right
Hand Side as you go up to the High Altar, beyond the
Stalls of the Canons, (if there are any, as it seemed to
me that there were, as I saw several Priests in Cowls
singing their Vespers in them), where her Figure is
represented in Basso Releif in White Marble, surrounded by the Virtues of which she made Profession,
by the famous Sculptor Girardon,[1] with the following
Inscription below:

A la Gloire de Dieu, et à la Memoire eternelle D'Anne-
Marie Martinozzi, Princesse de Conty, Qui, détrompée du
Monde dès l'Age de dix-Neuf Ans, vendit toutes ses pierreries
pour nourrir pendant la Famine de 1662, les Pauvres de Berry,
de Champagne et de Picardie; pratiqua toutes les Austeritez que
sa Santé peut souffrir: demeurée Veuve à l'Age de Vingt-neuf
Ans, consacra le Reste de sa Vie à élever en Princes Chrètiens
les Princes ses Enfans, et à maintenir les Loix temporelles et
Ecclesiastiques dans ses Terres: se rèduisit à une Dépense très-

[1]François G. (c. 1630-1715): he executed the mausoleum of Richelieu at the Sorbonne.

modeste; restitua tous les Biens dont l'Acquisition lui fut suspecte, jusqu'à la Somme de huit Cens Mille Livres: distribua toute son Épargne aux Pauvres dans ses Terres, et dans toutes les Parties du Monde; & passa soudainement à l'Éternitè après seize Ans de Persévérance le 4 Février 1672, âgée de 36 Ans.

Priez Dieu pour Elle.

Louis-Armand de Bourbon, Prince de Conty et François-Louis de Bourbon, Prince de la Roche-sur-Yon, ses Enfans, ont posé ce Monument.

This last Prince, who survived his elder Brother, & by that means became Prince of Conti himself, at his Death, desired to be buried at his Mother's Feet in this Church, whose Monument of White Marble, containing his Bust in a *Médaillon,* hanging on a Trophy, against the opposite Pillar to his Mother's Monument, is also very elegant & neat: underneath which, on a Table of black Marble is a Latin Inscription in gold Letters, which may be seen in Germain Brice's *Description de Paris,* Vol: 3, p. 227.

The famous Engraver Nanteuil,[1] is buried under the Organ Loft at the West End of this Church: Christopher Thuanus his Monument & Bust is against the West Wall, fronting the Altar of the Chapel, & his Son James his Tomb is under the Window of it against the South Wall, if so be it is the South. Monsieur de Thou's *History of his own Times* is universally allowed to be a most excellent one: yet it has one great Fault, if the voluminousness of so many large Folios for so short a space of Time as a Man's own Age may not be thought another, (for I won't even suppose that his Bias for Liberty & the Hugonot or Calvinistical Party against the League & Popery in its worst Habit, can, in this Age

[1]Robert N. (1630-78).

of Liberty in which we live, ever be thought a Blemish,) which is, his Affectation of latinizing every Name both of Persons & Places; by which the real & true Names of both are often confused, if not utterly lost. Another Advocate for Liberty in the Ecclesiastical way, Sébastien le Nain de Tillemont,[1] the very worthy & pious Ecclesiastical Historian & Annalist, (who died Jan: 10, 1698, aged 60 years), by his Desire to be buried in the Church of Port Royal des Champs, among the great Fautors of Jansenism, sufficiently testifies his Bias to that Party, descended from & cultivated by the Jansenists, & which within these 3 or 4 years has by slow, but sure Degrees, absolutely routed their bitter Enemies the Jesuits, & will, in good Time probably, go further Lengths than many good Men of that Party could foresee, & which, it is also probable, they would do their best Endeavours to prevent. When the Abbey of Port-Royal des Champs in 1710 was entirely erased, with the Church, for being a Seminary of avowed Jansenists, the Bodies of many Persons, who had been there interred, were taken up, & transported to different Churches: that of Monsieur de Tillemont was removed to this Church, which was his Parish, & placed just before our Lady's Chapel in the same. That infamous Wretch, Archibald Bower,[2] the Ecclesiastical Mountabank of this Time, who from being a Jesuit, now stiles himself Esquire, plagiarously gave a Translation of

[1]1637-98: educated by the Jansenists at Port Royal; his *Mémoires Ecclesiastiques* and *Histoire des Empereurs* are mines of wealth for the historian.

[2]This notorious turncoat, who was successively Jesuit (1706-26), Protestant (1726-45), Jesuit (1745-47), Protestant (1747-   ), (but possibly Jesuit all the time), died on Sept. 3, 1766. See his Life in the *Dict. Nat. Biog.*

what he found in this virtuous Priest, Monsieur
Tillemont's Writings, as his own *History of the Popes*;
a Work that was undertaken 20 years ago, & just now
brought to a Conclusion [I write this Saturday, June
28, 1766] by him. This Mr Bower, at the Time I speak
of, above 20 Years ago, when he was much in the
Fashion, & patronized by a Party of a particular Cast,
Family, & Education, & of a Presbyterian Disposition,
put me to no small Difficulty: for the present Earl of
Kinnoul,[1] at that Time Viscount Dupplin, Member for
the Town of Cambridge, had been particularly civil to
me in all his Behaviour, (& especially on my taking
Holy Orders), of his own Motion, without any Sollicita-
tion on my Side, generously procured me a Scarfe, by
putting me on the List of his Father, George Earl of
Kinnoul, his Chaplains, & sent me down the Instruments without any Expence: which, tho' it was at that
Time of no real Use or Advantage, & only a Feather &
Peice of Honour, by intitling me to wear a silk Scarfe[2]
over my Shoulders, in any Place but in the Universities,
was yet done in so gentile a Manner, as to enhance the
Value of it into a real Obligation. Soon after this
happened, my Lord Dupplin sollicited me in so pressing
a Manner to subscribe to Bower's Book,[3] that I never
was so distressed in any Part of my Life: as I was
greatly ashamed to refuse so trifling a Request, after so
gentile a Favour conferred upon me in the easiest Way,
& was conscientiously determined not to assist in the
least Degree a Person for whom I had so early conceived

[1]Thomas Hay, 8th Earl.

[2]The "scarf" usually denoted that its wearer was a nobleman's
chaplain, its colour matching his patron's livery.

[3]*History of the Popes*, which began to be published in 1748.

the most unalterable Aversion. I was forced to do then, what went greatly against the Grain, refuse a Trifle to a Person to whom I was under Obligations, merely from this Nicety, in not countenancing such a Person. Dr. Douglas,[1] Chaplain to the Earl of Bath, & Canon of Windsor, has so evidently laid open this Man's Forgeries & Villainies, that it is wonderful that he has the Assurance to go on still in his Pretences. But he has this grand Fortification to secure him against any the strongest Attacks: he writes against the Popes & Popery: & whoever does that in England, let him be what he will, his Cause will be supported, & his Adversaries treated as Papists. This happened to Dr Douglas: So this will happen to every one who will be bold enough to speak the Truth favourably on that Side, tho' unquestionable.

The End of this Church of St Andrew des Arcs is terminated in a circular Manner, which is the prevailing Taste of most of the Churches in Paris, & indeed of the whole Country, & has an exceeding good Effect: the Choir also is rounded at the East End, & the Altar is very elegant, with 2 Angels on the back Altar, Kneeling & in Adoration of the Crucifix between them. In the North Isle, by the Door on the left Hand looking up to the Altar End of the Church, against the Wall is a small & beautiful Mural Monument of White Marble, for a Monsr Joly de Fleury, (as well as I recollect, for I won't be certain), on which is represented above, the Figure of a Woman in the Attitude of Sorrow & Distress, expressed in the highest Degree of Perfection.

From hence I went to see the Parish Church of St

[1]John Douglas, (1721-1807); successively Bp of Carlisle and Salisbury. A noted controversialist.

Severin, one Corner of which stands in the great Street of St James. This is one of the most beautiful & light Gothic Buildings in the whole City, with 2 Isles & Rows of Pillars from the Bottom surrounding the Whole Church, Choir as well as Nave & *Rond-Point*, as they call the circular finishing of the East End, with neat pretty Pillars, & an elegant Chapel of [our] Lady behind the East End, newly built, & a double Range of Windows all round the Church, finely painted. The high Altar of the Choir is quite new & extremely beautiful, tho' small, being an Arcade or half Dome supported by 8 Pillars of red Marble, ornamented with gilt Brass in an elegant Taste. The famous Stephen Pasquier,[1] as great a Lawyer as Antiquary, is buried in a Chapel, where is his Bust: & the two celebrated Brothers Scevola & Lewis de St Marthe,[2] the illustrious Authors of the *Gallia Christiana* in several Volumes, are also here interred; with Andrew du Chesne,[3] Historiographer of France; Moreri[4] the Author of the Dictionary which goes under his Name, & which gave Rise to that of Peter Bayle; & the no less famous Jansenist Writer, Dr Lewis Ellis du Pin.[5] Round the Iron Palisades which enclose the Choir are several Times the Arms of the celebrated Anne-Mary d'Orléans,[6] Princess de Dombes & Duchess de Montpensier,

[1]Étienne Pasquier (1529-1615), author of *Recherches sur la France* (1560).

[2]This is an error, *Gallia Christiana* (1715) was by Denis de Sainte-Marthe.

[3]1584-1640; author of *Historiæ Francorum Scriptores*.

[4]Louis M. (1643-80): author of *Le Grand Dictionnaire Historique*.

[5]1637-1719: his *Bibliothéque Universelle des Auteurs Ecclésiastiques* was in 58 vols.

[6]A.-M.-Louise d'Orléans (1627-93).

commonly called Mademoiselle de Montpensier; she was only Daughter of John Baptist Gaston, Duke of Orléans, (Brother of Lewis 13), by his first Wife, & was equally famous for her ordering the Cannon of the Bastille to be fired against her Cousin Lewis 14, as for her Amour with the Duke de Lauzun. This Lady died in 1693, & was at a considerable Expence in the Ornamenting this Altar & Choir. This she chose as her Parish Church: see her Reason for it in her *Mémoires*, Tome 5, p. 116, (8°, Paris, 1728, in 6 Volumes).

From St Severin's Church I went to the Convent of Carmelite Friers in the Place Maubert, at the Corner of the Rue St Victor, of no great Appearance to the Street: the Church is one of the most awkward, dirty & gloomy Places of the Sort I ever saw: the Choir Part is large, being the cheif Part of one large Room, without Pillars, & great unornamented flat walls, more of the appearance of a Barn than a Church, except that the High Altar, at the End has the usual Ornaments of a Christian Place of Worship, tho' one of the most heavy & clumsy Things I ever set Eyes on; there being Numbers of Pillars, Niches & Statues, one above another, in as bad a Taste as is possible to conceive. Behind this massive Altar-Peice of Stone, painted like Marble, the Friers have a Choir, tho' there are a vast Number of Stalls all round the vast Choir in Front of the Altar, by the left Side of which & near it, close to the North Wall, on a square Pediment of Stone, is a frightful Statue on his Knees of some Cardinal, but of what Name I am ignorant, as there was no Inscription, & as the *Sacristain* knew nothing of the matter. Perhaps it may be only a Doctor in his scarlet Robes, as it was painted in that Colour, with an Ermine Hood, just like our Cambridge

Robes for a Doctor in Divinity. At the Bottom of the Choir, against the South Wall, in the Nave, is erected an Altar with an Image of St Roch, this Part of the Church being called his Chapel; for it has no Enclosure: just opposite to it [there] is, on the left Side, an Opening or large North Isle, against the East Wall of which is a neat Altar-Peice with Corinthian Pillars, dedicated to our Lady of Mount Carmel, her Image being in the Center of it, to which there is great Devotion on particular Days. On the North Wall by it I observed a modern Monument for the Family of Chauvelin: one of which Family, now in great Rank at Court, & I think an Abbè,[1] has done no small Prejudice to the Interest of the Jesuits in that Kingdom. Their Cloyster is large, but not handsome, & a large Pulpit of Stone stands in the Court of it.

From the Carmelites' Convent I went to the Parish Church of St Nicholas du Chardonnet, seated in the Rue St Victor, at the Corner of another Street, which is a very beautiful modern Structure in the Form of a Cross, with Isles & 2 Transepts: the Crucifix over the Door into the Choir by le Brun,[2] with 2 Statues of our Lady & St John the Evangelist on each Side of it, are very justly admired their Beauty & just Proportions. The Altar is handsome, but has nothing very remarkable about it. In a Chapel on the right Hand of the Nave is a fine Tomb for Monsr d'Argenson;[3] & the famous & learned Abbé Jérôme Bignon[4] has a Bust over his Tomb also in this Church: but what pleased

[1]Henri-Phillippe Ch. (1716-70).
[2]Charles Lebrun (1619-90): Director of the Gobelins from 1660.
[3]Several of the family were buried here.
[4]1589-1656; jurist; used the nom-de-plume of "Théophile du Jay."

me most here, or indeed any where else, was a Monument in a Chapel on the left Side of the Choir, but so
small, & so crouded, & withall so dark & gloomy, that
it is difficult to observe all the Beauties of the Chapel,
or the Tombs which are in it. The whole Chapel was
designed & painted by the famous Painter Charles le
Brun, whose Battles of Alexander have given him a
Reputation which even the natural Envy of the English,
or Jealousy rather, against French Acquirements,
cannot but applaud. Pity it is, that want of Light, & a
general Dinginess or Dirtyness takes away from this
beautiful Chapel the Merit it deserves. The Altar-
Peice, representing the good St Charles Borromeo at
his Devotions, (he being the Patron Saint of le Brun),
before a Crucifix, is an admirable Peice; the Painter
exerting the full Force of his Genius to make it a
Capital Picture. Under this Picture, & above the Altar
is a Basso-Relief in Brass or Copper, the whole Length
of the Altar, in which the same Saint, to whom this
Chapel is dedicated, is represented giving the Sacrament to People infected with the Plague. The Ceiling
also is finely painted by the same Hand. Under the
Window, against the North Wall is the large Monument, on some Steps, of Charles le Brun, who died
Febr. 12, 1690, aged about 69 [71] years: his Bust, on
a Pedestal, rests on a Table at the Foot of a Pyramid of
Marble behind it, & on Front of the square Pedestal
which supports the Bust is a long French Inscription.
But the Monument which struck me most exceedingly
is that for Le Brun's Mother, against the West Wall,
fronting the Altar: this elegant & beautiful Monument
is thus conceived: she is represented in White Marble,
as far as can be seen of her, in the utmost Confusion &

Surprize, as coming out of her Coffin, made of green
Marble, the Lid of which she holds up with her left
Arm & Hand: an Angel in the Air, sounding the last
Trumpet, above the Sarcophagus, of an inimitable
Beauty, adds a Life to the whole which is above
Description. I must own this Monument pleased me as
well, if not more, than any I had seen since I came to
Paris, not excepting the grand one of Cardinal Riche-
lieu at the Sorbon[ne]. I forgot to mention some fine
Statues at the Foot of Le Brun's Monument. What a
Contrast does the Thought of this fine Monument of
Le Brun's Mother make with as expensive an one, &
perhaps more so, which I have described in my 33 vol:
p. 281[1] of these MS. Collections in Maulden in Bed-
fordshire, where a Countess of Oxford & Elgin is
represented in her Winding Sheet, as arising out of her
Tomb, which is shaped like a great Cauldron or Cistern,
with the most unmeaning Insensibility that can be
conceived? This Tomb was erected however not a great
Number of years before the other, *viz*: in 1656; an
Æra not at all propitious for the Arts & Sciences; when
Fanaticism would stamp the Censure of Idolatry upon
any Image but those of the Devil & Oliver Cromwell.
But an elegant Monument of the same Sort & Design,
about the Age of Le Brun's Mother's, will retrieve our
English Taste from the Reproach of Barbarism, in the
Church of Long Stow in Cambridgeshire: I have given
a Draught of it in my 2nd Vol: of these Collections at
p. 128,[2] being the half-Length Figure arising out of his
Tomb, with one Hand catching at & laying Hold of
an Anchor extended from the Heavens; as an Emblem

[1]*Add. MSS.* 5834, 267-283.
[2]*Add. MSS.* 5803, 124.

of Hope. The Figure is to represent Sir Ralph Bovey,[1] Baronet, who died in 1679; he is in White Marble, & his Sepulchre or Sarcophagus of black, & the whole very excellently finished. The only Place that you can see this beautiful Tomb of Le Brun's Mother, is in an inconvenient Corner of the Chapel, the N.E. Corner, between the Altar & her Son's Monument.

In the Evening arrived at the Hôtel d'Orléans where I lodged, a Couple of Gentlemen, Father & Son of the Name of Taylor, as well as I could learn, who were going to Bordeaux; but the Son, a Military Man, having loaded Pistols in his side Pockets, by some Accident or other, one of them went off, & discharged 4 Balls into his Thigh.

He was carried up to his Apartment & was thought to be in great Danger: however before I left Paris he was on the mending Hand.

Saturday, Nov: 9. Fine Day. At noon I went to the Mat[h]urins Convent in St James's Street, between the Ruës des Noyers & des Mat[h]urins: They are called Trinitarian Friers every where but in France, & this Convent is the general Residence of their General, or Head of that Order. The Entrance into their Convent is by a small Court, separated from the Street by an Iron Palisade, with some good Buildings on one Side of it, & fronting them, on the right Hand as you enter the Court is the Cheif Entrance into the Church, which seems to be newly built, being an handsome Portal. I came here with a Design to see some Ceremonies in the Church, but I made it so late, as usual, before I set out, that the Service was over before I got there. The Church is one single handsome Room without any

[1] 1st, and only, Bt.; Attorney; Sheriff of Warwicks. 1652-3.

Pillars, & well roofed. Pretty high against the North or left Wall of the Nave are hung up many Iron Chains & Fetters in Gratitude for particular Deliverances from Turkish Slavery; the Trinitarian Order being instituted for that Charitable Purpose: over the High Altar also, which is very elegant, with beautiful Pillars of Marble to support it, (4, I think), is a fine Statue of the Blessed Virgin, who holds in her 2 Hands a couple of Chains which confine 2 Slaves in Action of Adoration on each Side of her. The Choir is very handsome, as are the Stalls: in the Choir, towards the Entrance lie 3 or 4 ordinary Stones with Arms & Inscriptions on them for as many Ministers-General of the Order, the Arms ensigned with an Hat, like a Bishop's or Cardinal's Coat-of-Arms: one in particular I observed was for one Guillaume, or Wm, le Feure, (Minister General of the Order, who died in 1764), on the South or right Hand as you look to the Altar, near the End of the Stalls. The Choir is separated from the Nave by 6 Pillars which go across it, & over the Door in the middle is a fine Crucifix, with Angels holding the Instruments of the Passion. On each Side of the Nave are Altars, & that on the left Hand is in a Sort of Recess, but neither of these Chapels are inclosed.

After I had viewed as much of this Convent as I thought proper, I drove to the Scotch College of St Andrew, situated in a Street pretty steep of Ascent, called Les Fossez de St Victor, just without the Limits of the University in the Fauxbourg St Victor & between that great Abbey & that other as celebrated of St Geneviève. This whole Street of the Fossez de St Victor, on the right Hand, going down from St Geneviève, consists of 3 religious Houses; the first belongs to the

Fathers of the Christian Doctrine, which I did not see: the middlemost is that of the Scotch College, & close below it are the English Canonesses of St Austin, the House being called Our Lady of Sion. I should not have thought of the Scotch College perhaps, if my French Servant had not told me that he had been often to Mr Gordon, the Principal of it, with some Scotch People he had served: so as I drove by it in my way to St Geneviève, I called upon the Principal, making an Excuse for my Intrusion by telling him that I recollected that our King James 2nd had a Monument in his Church, & that I should be much obliged to him for a Sight of it. The House was so loftily situated on the Side of a Hill, that when I had ascended one Pair of Stairs up to the Principal's Lodgings, I was upon a Level with their Gardens, & on the same Floor with their Chapel. I was carried up another Pair of large dirty Stairs to the Principal, who was a tall, raw-bon'd Man, about 60 years of Age, seemed to be much broken with the Gout, who talked a Medley of a Language between Scotch & French: he received me in his Chamber, which was hung all round with Pictures of the unhappy & unfortunate Family of Stuart;[1] but some Scotch Gentleman of Fashion coming in upon him, I staid with him but a few Minutes, he ordering a Servant to shew me the Chapel. In the Antechamber to the Principal's Apartment were a few old Pictures of no Value: among one of them was the worthy James Beaton, Arch-Bp of Glasgow, without his Mitre, & by him a plain small Cross or Pastoral Staff. He was made Arch-Bp of Glasgow in 1551, & perceiving the mad work of the Knoxian Reformers, in 1560, he very prudently left the King-

[1]See *Letters of Hor. Walpole* (Toynbee), No. 2243, Dec. 1, 1781.

N

dom, taking with him all the Archives of his Church, &
deposited them, partly in the *Chartreuse*, or Carthusians
Convent, at Paris, & partly in the College belonging to
the Scotch Nation in that City, to which last he bequeathed all his Effects at his Death in 1603, on Apr:
24, at the Age of 86 years, & where he was buried: for
on the Entrance into the Chapel by a Door on the South
or right Side of it, is a small mural Monument of black
Marble, with a double Inscription, for David Murray,
Bp of Murray in the 14 & 15 Centuries, who founded
the College, & for this Arch-Bp Beaton: but as I did
not read the Inscription, I won't be positive whether it
was an Epitaph for the last, who is reckoned very justly
a second Founder, or whether it was only an honourary
Inscription recording his Benefactions: especially as I
find in a Book in my Possession, printed at Paris in
Folio in 1625, & wrote by Father Hilarion de Coste,
Minime, at p. 460, that his Grace died in 1603 at Paris
& was buried at St John de Lateran: I suppose the
Church of that Name at Paris:[1] which I think the more
probable, as not one Author that I can meet with
records the Place of his Sepulture, tho' all are circum-
stantial enough in other Points, except this Franciscan;
who living at Paris, & writing so soon after his Death,
could hardly be mistaken in a Fact, that, probably, he
might remember of his own Knowledge. In an History
of Glasgow, printed in 8vo in that City in 1736,
called *A View of the City of Glasgow*, by John M'Ure,
alias Campbell, are at p. 28, the Arms of his Uncle of
both His Names, Cardinal, Arch-Bp of St Andrews, &
consequently his; which are blasoned in the *Biographia*
[*Britannica*] at p. 570. The same Author of the *View of*

[1]Attached to the *Commanderie* of the Order of St John of Jerusalem.

Glasgow, p. 21, says, that the Arms of the See of Glasgow, is a Salmon: but how borne, I know not: sure I am, that in a MS. of my own in Relation to Heraldry, I have entered the Arms of this Arch-Bishopric thus: Argent, St Ninian in Pontificalibus, full-faced proper, mitred & a Crosier in his dexter Hand, Or. When I was at Glasgow about the Year 1749, together with Dr Gooch, now Canon of Ely, Dr Goodall now & at that Time Archdeacon of Suffolk, & Mr Erasmus Earle of Pembroke Hall in Cambridge, (Son to Augustine Earle Esqr one of the Commissioners of the Excise), the Magistracy there did us all the Honour of giving us the Freedom of the City in a very polite & gentile Manner in their Town Hall. I have mislaid the Instrument of my Freedom: but I remember that there is a Salmon also in the Arms of that City. After a tedious Search for this Instrument, I have at last found it. The Arms in its proper Colours are blazoned on the Back of the Parchment, which is about 6 Inches on every Side, & are thus: Party per Fesse Argent and Gules, over all an Oak Tree on a Sort of Ground at the Base of the Sheild, Vert, on the Base or Gules Part is a Salmon[1] on his Back, en Fesse, with an Annulet in its Mouth Argent, on the Top of the Tree is a Bird, & on the sinister Side of the Cheif from the Tree hangs a Bell: but neither the Bell, Bird or Annulet are marked in any

---

[1]One story accounting for the salmon in the arms of Glasgow is this: The Queen of Cadzow had given a ring (the king's gift) to a knight. The ring was found in the knight's possession, and was thrown into the river by the king, who threatened the queen with death if she failed to restore it. She appealed to Bp Kentigern, who told a fisherman to bring him the first fish he caught in the Clyde. This was a salmon, which had the ring in its mouth. *Cf.* A. C. Fox-Davies, *The Book of Public Arms*, 1915, p. 314.

other Colour but Argent; tho' it is probable that is not the proper Colour for any of them.

The Foliages & Ornaments round the oval Sheild were printed & neatly painted, on the Top of which sat 2 naked Boys blowing Trumpets, & holding above their Heads & over the Sheild a Scrole, in which was wrote, "Let Glasgow flourish;" I suppose the Motto to the Arms. Below this & under the Arms is wrote: The reverend William Cole his Ticket of Glasgow, 1749. The Border round the Instrument is neatly engraved, being Shells, Foliages, Flowers & Knot-work, neatly coloured, & within, partly in Print & the rest filled up with Hand-writing, as follows:—

> At Glasgow the twenty fifth Day of August,
> Seventeen Hundered & fourty nine years:
> The which Day In Presence of the Right
> Honourable Andrew Cochran Esqr, Lord Provost
> of the said City, John Broun, Robert Christie
> & Thomas Napier, Baillies thereof, George
> Bogle, Dean of Gild, & sundry of the Gild
> Council of said City, the reverend William
> Cole of King's College in Cambridge is
> admitted and Received Burgess & Gild Brother
> of the said City; & the whole Liberties,
> Privileges and Immunities belonging to an
> Burgess and Gild Brother thereof are granted
> to him in most ample Form, Who gives his
> Oath of Fidelity as Use is. Extracted furth
> of the Gild Books of the said City By
>   Jo McGilchrist *dept Clke.*

As the Arms of the See of Arch-Bp James Beaton gave Occasion to this Deviation, so it is high Time to return to that worthy Prelate, who as he was a Sufferer for his Religion, a faithful Servant to his Prince, & a

Preserver of the Antiquities of his Church & Nation, when almost every one else was robbing & pillaging it, I always conceived no small Esteem for his Character, & occasionally in my Reading put down any Thing I met with relating to him, tho' out of my Plan to trouble myself with Scotch People or their Affairs. [*List of References*.]

Altho' I have tricked out the Arms of the Arch-Bp & his See, yet I won't pretend to say that the latter is properly done: I suppose that what McUre means by surmounted of a Salmon, is, that either the Family Arms or those of the See were born[e] in an Inescocheon.[1] But enough of this matter.

The Front of this College of the Scotch Nation to the Street is tolerably handsome for a French Building, & the Gardens are airy & pleasant, & as it is situated upon so high an Eminence, the Apartments ought to be pleasant, as far as the City of Paris & the Country about it, can make them so. The Principal told me that if I would call at any Time, particularly about 10 in the Morning, he would shew me the MS. Papers left them by Arch-Bp Beaton, the MSS. of the late King James 2nd which he bequeathed to this Seminary & some original Letters of Mary Queen of Scots.

I know not how numerous this Society is, nor the Nature of their Institution: but as I saw several rough, dirty Scotch Boys on their large Staircase, without any particular Habit, I presume it is a Schole or Seminary for the Catholic Youth of that Nation: for I asked no Questions on the Spot, & never thought to do so elsewhere. The Chapel[2] is small, but neat, having an Altar,

[1]An "inescutcheon" is a small shield borne on the escutcheon.
[2]L'Eglise de Saint André des Ecossais.

on which is placed a large Picture of the Crucifixion of St Andrew on his Cross, in a gilt Frame, which is the only Altar Peice, & behind it are 3 or 4 Stalls for the Priests to say their Vespers, in a very crampt and narrow Quire; being hardly Room enough to pass to them. Just opposite the Door into this Chapel, against the North, or left Hand Wall looking up to the Altar, is a very elegant mural Monument, from the Floor, of various coloured Marbles, ornamented with Decorations of gilt Brass: the Bottom Part is a Sort of Pedestal, in Front of which is the following severe tho' exactly just Inscription, which supports a small Pyramid against the Wall, on the Top of which is an Urn; a little below it is a *Medaillon* with the Head of the King, & below that are the Royal Arms of King James the 2nd. On the Floor just below this Monument lie 2 Lozenges of white Marble to denote that the Brains & Entrails of that unfortunate Monarch & those of his Queen are there deposited. The Epitaph or Inscription is as follows:

D. O. M.

Jacobi II. Magnæ Britanniæ, &c. Regis. Ille Partis Terra ac Mari Triumphis clarus, sed constanti in Deum Fide clarior, huic Regna, Opes et omnia Vitæ florentis, Commoda postposuit. Per summum Scelus, à sua Sede pulsus, Absalonis Impietatem, Achitophelis Perfidiam & acerba Semei Convitia, invicta Lenitate & Patientia, ipsis etiam Inimicis Amicus, superavit. Rebus Humanis major, Adversis superior, & cœlestis Gloriæ Studio inflammatus, quod Regno caruerit, sibi visus beatior, miseram hanc Vitam felici, Regnum terrestre cœlesti commutavit. Hæc Domus quam pius Princeps labentem sustinuit, & patriè fovit, cui etiam Ingenii sui Monimenta omnia, scilicet sua Manu scripta custodienda commisit, eam Corporis ipsius Partem qua maximè Animus viget, religiose servandam suscepit.

Vixit Annos LXVIII. Obiit Kal: Oct:
Anno Salutis Humanæ M.D.CCI.
Jacobus Dux de Perth
Præfectus Institutioni Jacobi III.
Magnæ Britanniæ Regis,
hujus Domus Benefactor,
mœrens posuit.

On the Floor, a little to the Head of the 2 Lozenge-
shaped Marbles I just now mentioned, & not far from
the West & North Walls, lie 2 large handsome black
Marble Slabs, such as we have for Grave-Stones in
England, & not common in France, for two Dukes of
Perth, Father & Son, of the name of Drummond, who
following King James's Fortune, lost their real Earl-
doms for an imaginary Dukedom.[1] I did not take any
of the Inscriptions, as it might have given offence. On
the West Wall just above these Gravestones, is a small
mural Monument for the Duchess of Tirconnel, of the
Name of Jennings, Sister to the ever famous Sarah
Jennings Duchess of Marlborough. On the Floor also
on the South or right Hand of the Duke of Perth lies a
Gravestone for a Scotch Gentleman of the Name of Hay.
There were other Monuments in the Chapel, but I
thought it not civil to be too curious in a Place, which
is treated with no Mercy where I commonly dwell. The
Principal of this College accidentally told me, or I
should have passed by it without calling at it, that the
very next House to his, was a Nunnery of English
Ladies, of the Order of St Augustine: this was a little
lower down the Street, but touching the College: so
I walked from one to the other. The Entrance was by a

[1]They were both named James, and died in 1716 and 1720 respectively. For the inscriptions see *Collectanea Topographica et Genealogica*
(1834-43), vol. vii. pp. 32-42.

Pair of great Gates & a Flight of Stone Steps into a very
small & miserable paved Court, with the Church on the
right Hand as soon as you have ascended the Steps,
which may be about 20, & a few more on the right
Hand Side, looking up to the High Altar: before which
under a Grave Stone with a long Inscription, rather
inclining to the right Hand Side of the Chapel, lies the
famous Richard Smith,[1] Bp of C[h]alcedon, who made
so much noise in England in his Time: he was the Cheif
Founder of this House in 1633, where he died March
18, 1655, aged 88 years: for an Account of whose Life,
see Mr Dod's *Catholic Church History of England*, Vol:
3, p. 4 to 17 & p. 76 to 79. As also for an History of the
Foundation of this Convent in the same Volume p. 17,
18, 19, 20. The Church is handsome & tolerably large,
& full of Monuments against the Wall & on the Floor,
both in the Church & in the Nuns' Choir, which is
large & divided off by a large Grate at the West or
lower End. Below Bp Smith's Gravestone was a quite
fresh one for Mr Giffard, who was lately buried there:
by the Side of the Bp were 3 or 4 other large Stones, &
one near the Door for a Lady Aston.[2] On the North or
left Hand Wall rear the Altar were 2 mural Monuments for the Family of Throckmorton; & altho' I had
copied a neat mural Monument for Sir John Yate[3]
Baronet, who died in 1690, & was buried in this Church,
to whose Memory Sir Robert Throckmorton, (who had
married his Sister & Heir), erected it, into my 40th
volume of MS. Collections at p. 224, 225, yet I did not

---

[1]Vicar-apostolic for England and Scotland (1625).

[2]Probably the widow of the 5th Lord Aston of Forfar, who died at
Paris in 1759.

[3]4th, and last, Bt, of Buckland (Berks).

observe it, or overlooked it. But as I observed the 2
aforesaid Monuments of the Throckmorton Family in
this Church, I thought it not improbable but that I
might learn whether the Daughter of my late Friend
George Throckmorton Esqr was not here, or where I
might find her: as her Mother was very desirous that I
should see her before I came back into England: therefore seeing one of the Nuns at the Grate, peeping
behind a Curtain, who, I presume, had let me into the
Church, (as the Person who did so, desired from within,
that we would not enter it 'till she had Time to get into
her Choir), I went up to her, & desired her, after some
Conversation about her Convent & Church, to inform
me where I could find such a young Lady: she immediately told me, that she was in their Convent, & that if I
would go into one of the Parlours, she would wait upon
me there: accordingly I crossed the Court & sat down
in the Parlour, as it was called, being an Hole, about 6
Feet square, with 2 old Rush Bottom Chairs & whited
Walls, till Miss Throckmorton appeared, with the same
Canoness, in another such Parlour on the other Side of
the Grate. She was much altered for the worse, according to my Opinion, since I had seen her: seemed delighted to see a Person she had known in England, &
expressed herself very happy in her present Situation
with these English Ladies; but seemed to dread very
much her approaching Leave of them for the French
Nunnery of Port Royal, where her Grandfather Sir
Robert Throckmorton was desirous she should go
for a Time in order to perfect herself in the French
language, as none but Ladies of the best Families in
France were educated in that Monastery. The Canoness
who was with her, a very pretty little Woman, aged

about 30 years, as well as I could guess, told me her Family Name was Sanders & that she was a Native of Oxfordshire. She also informed me that the present Abbess or Superior of the House was named Lancaster, & that there were not above 16 Professed Nuns in it. After I had been with them about a Quarter of an Hour, I took my Leave of them, & promised to call before I left Paris. The eldest Daughter of Mr Throckmorton died in this House about 3 or 4 years ago, & was buried in the Nun's Choir, about the middle of it, as Sister Sanders told me, shewing me the Place: this young Lady was a great Favourite of mine, & promised fairly to be very gentile & handsome: I had given her a little before she set out for Paris for her Education a curious Peice of Antiquity in their way, being a small gold Cross enameled & Pearls pendant to it: my Sister Catherine Cole had given it to me a few years before. However, the Throckmorton Family is in no great Danger to be extinguished, as my late worthy & humane Friend has still surviving 5 Sons, & 2, if not 3, Daughters. And may that worthy Family never want Heirs to inherit their noble Fortune 'till the latest Generations!

From this Convent of our Lady of Sion I went to the Royal Abbey of St Victor, which gives its Name to a large District or Fauxbourg on this Side of Paris: it is one of the most considerable in that City, & the only Convent of the Sort in the Kingdom, if I understand aright the Canon who was so obliging as to shew me about the whole Abbey; who was a very handsome black[1] Man, with a fresh Colour, more like an Englishman than of this Country, & about 40 years of age: his

[1]Frequently used to mean dark-complexioned, or having black hair.

Habit was very neat, being black, with a short white
Linen Kind of Surplice above it. This Royal Abbey was
founded about 1113, by Lewis the Fat, & was remarkably famous for many Centuries, when Schole Learning
was in Fashion & Repute, for the many great Scholars
it produced. The Revenues of it are so great, that the
Abbat is generally a Commendatory one, & some of the
Cheif Persons about the Court have lately held it;
among the Rest, the Duke of Berwick's Son, who was
Grandson to King James 2, was possessed of it. The
Library is not far from the Church, & you ascend to it
by an handsome Stone Staircase: it is a long Room, but
not very handsome, having Beams running across it, on
which are placed, for want of Room probably, some
Pictures: for on both Sides against the Walls, & above
the Book Cases, are ranged Pictures of all the great Men
who have received their Education in their House, or
any ways belonged to it, as also of their Abbats & other
Religious of their House & Order. Over the Door as
you enter it is a Bust in white Marble of a Lawyer, who
was a considerable Benefactor to the Library: at the
other End of the Room, which is far from being handsome or any Thing extraordinary as a Library, is an
elegant Room or Cabinet, lately fitted up, of a square
Form, with 3 Windows in it to different Views: this has
a very fine Clock & Mathematical Instruments, &
contains besides a vast Quantity of curious & valuable
MSS. One view overlooks their extensive Gardens, &
so to the Seine & the Isle de Louvier, which is at no
great Distance from it, tho' obstructed by Buildings
from any View of it. The Cloyster of this Abbey is large
& handsome, & has more the Appearance of a
Cloyster of any I had seen, having curious antient Pillars

of a round gothic Fashion & small, all round the Inside Division of it from the Court within. The Church is not very large, but regular & handsome, with a very noble Altar; behind which is the Choir for the Religious to say their Offices in: this is esteemed the oldest Part of the Church; for the other Part don't seem to be above 250 years old; tho' it has in the 2 Transept Isles two very handsome Rose or Catherine-Wheel Windows; but not of the Lightness & Beauty of the older Gothic work. As you enter the Canons' Choir I mentioned, on the right Hand close to the Wall & at the very Side of the Door, is a very antient Altar Tomb, under the Wall, of an old Bishop of Paris, dressed in his Pontifical Habit & an old short Mitre on his Head: I did not hear his Name; at least, if I did, I don't now remember it. Exactly opposite to this on the other Side of the Choir under an Arch of the Wall, on the South or left Hand, near the Back of the Altar, is the Tomb, containing the Bones of the famous Schole-Man, Hugh de St Victor, having another old Altar Monument, I think, standing before it, or rather on one Side of it, in the Choir. He died in 1139 & was buried in the Cloyster, from whence his Bones were removed 200 years afterwards to this Place: his Epitaph is as follows:

> Conditur hoc Tumulo Doctor celeberrimus Ugo,
> Quem brevis eximium continet Urna Virum,
> Dogmate præcipuus, Nullique secundus in Ore;
> Claruit Ingenio, Moribus, Ore, Stilo.

In the same Place was buried another great Scholar of those Times, & a Canon of this House, called Adam de St Victor, whose Epitaph, for its Simplicity, Morality & Beauty, (I shall be called a Monk for stiling it so) I shall transcribe, preferring it to the more elegant

Ciceronian Jargon of this enlightened Age, whose Compositions this way are often so perplexed, far-fetched & Bombast, that it is a Question, whether Tully would understand their Meaning, (tho' designed to imitate his Stile), was it possible for him to see them. It is as follows, as I took it from Germain Brice, not seeing it myself:

Hæres Peccati, Naturæ Filius, Iræ,
    Exiliique Reus, nascitur omnis Homo.
Unde superbit Homo? Cujus Conceptio Culpa,
    Nasci Pœna, Labor Vita, necesse mori.
Vana Salus Hominis, vanus Decor, omnia vana:
    Inter vana nihil vanius est Homine.
Dum magis alludit præsentis Gloria Vitæ,
    Præterit, imo fugit; non fugit, imo perit.
Post Hominem Vermis, post Vermem fit Cinis heu, heu,
    Sic redit ad Cinerem Gloria nostra simul.
His ego qui jaceo, miser et miserabilis ADAM,
    Unam pro summo Munere posco Pacem.
Peccavi, fateor, Veniam peto, parce fatenti:
    Parce Pater, Fratres parcite, parce Deus.

He died in 1177, & composed many Hymns, which are still sung in the Church of France. Both this & the following Epitaph are in a Stile of many I have seen in England composed about the 14th Century:

Petrus eram quem Petra tegit, dictusque COMESTOR:
Nunc comedor: Vivus docui, nec cesso docere
Mortuus, ut dicat qui me videt incineratum;
Quod sumus iste fui, erimus quandoque quod hic est.

This last was for Peter Comestor, or the Eater, the Author of an Ecclesiastical History, who died in 1198.[1] Another Church Historian is buried in this Convent,

---

[1] His *Historia scolastica* was printed as early as 1470.

the celebrated Louis Mainbourg;[1] & the no less famous
Poet Santeuil[2] who was a Regular Canon of this House,
dying in 1697, was buried in the Cloyster. The Canon
who shewed me the Abbey was very obliging & desired
me to come again & look over the Church & Sacristy
& amuse myself as often as I pleased in their Library:
he told me that they had lost several volumes lately by
Persons who came there under a Pretence to Study; in
particular a volume or two of the numerous Tomes of
the Acts of their Royal Society: which would, in a
Manner, spoil their whole set, & do no great good to
the Purloiner.

From St Victor's Abbey I drove to the Convent of
the Dominicans, or Friers Preachers, commonly called
the Jacobins in France, seated in the Rue St Jacques.
This is their great Convent at Paris, & was founded in
the Time of St Dominic himself in the 13th Century,
under the Reign of Philip Augustus. The Church[3] is a
large awkward Kind of Building, of no regular Architecture of any Sort, & has more the Appearance of a
great Barn, than any Thing I can compare it to: yet in
this gloomy, slovenly Church lie more of the Royal
Family of France, & contains more curious Monuments
than any that I saw in France, St Denis excepted. It is
composed of one large Room, which was never roofed
with Stone, with one Row of Pillars in the middle of it,
excessively gloomy, dark, dismal & dirty: the right Side
looking up to the High Altar, serves for the Nave &
Choir, & the left Side is a long Isle, at the East End of
which is a Chapel dedicated to Our Lady of the Rosary,
which is close to the High Altar of the Choir on the

[1]Historian: his *History of the League* was translated by Dryden.
[2]Jean de Santeul.   [3]Demolished at the Revolution.

right Hand of it, as another Chapel dedicated to St
Anne, as I take it, is on the left of it, in the same Isle, &
makes a Sort of Transept at the East End of the Church,
where also is a Passage or Door into the Convent. On
the right hand of the High Altar is a dark gloomy Kind
of square Chapel, up a few Steps, dedicated to St
Thomas Aquinas, as I guess. There are private Chapels
on the North Side of the long Isle, in which are many
Monuments: over the Door of one of them is the Statue
of a Bishop on his Knees in full Proportion. The Altar
is on an Eminence of several Steps, & round the large
Choir are the Friers' Stalls: the Pillars of the High
Altar, 6 in Number, are very stately, & of fine Marble.

In the middle of the Choir are 3 or 4 very curious
Altar Tombs of black marble, on each of which lie the
Figures of 2 Persons in white marble, at the Feet of one
another, all along the Choir: one of them was for
Clementia of Hungary, wife of Lewis the 10, who died
in 1328, with a long French Inscription on the Verge of
the black marble Table on which the Figure lies; as is
the Method of them all: the other Tombs in the middle
of the Choir are for Earls & Countesses of Artois,
Evreux & other Sons & Daughters of France. But I
discovered a very curious Monument on the Floor,
towards the Feet of the last of these Altar Tombs in the
Middle of the Choir, near the East End of the Friers
Stalls on the North or left Hand Side, very near a Side
Door, which goes out of the Choir into the Side Isle,
or rather Transept Chapel of Our Lady of the Rosary.
It lies neglected on the Floor & very dirty; being a
large Marble Slab, covered all over with Brass, having
engraved on it the Figure of a Prelate in his Cope &
Mitre on his head. This was the Tomb of Humbert,

Dauphin of Vienne,[1] who, being overpowered by the Earl of Savoy & much concerned for the Death of his Son, who was drowned, gave his Territories to King Philip 6, on Condition that the eldest Son of France should be called The Dauphin; he afterwards quitted the World, took upon himself the Order of St Dominic & retired to this Convent, to which he became a considerable Benefactor, & at Length was made titular Patriarch of Alexandria & perpetual Administrator of the Arch Bishopric of Rheims. On his Tomb is engraved this Inscription.

Hic jacet R. Pater & Dominus amplissimus D. Humbertus, primò Viennæ Delphinus, deinde relicto Principatu, Frater Ordinis Prædicatorum, Prior in hoc Conventu Parisiensi, ac demum Patriarcha Alexandrinus, & perpetuus Ecclesiæ Administrator Rhemensis, et præcipuus Benefactor hujus Conventus. Obiit autem Anno Domini 1355, Die 22. Maii.

Near this, against a Pillar or the Iron Rails by the Door which divides the North Isle, or Transept Chapels from the Choir, hangs a large framed Table on which is wrote an Account of all the cheif Monuments in the Church: but is a dingy, dirty Kind of Thing, much like the Frames containing the Degrees of Matrimony in many of our Country Churches. On the Steps, just before the High Altar & by the Door going into St Thomas Aquinas his Chapel, on the right Hand Side of the Choir, is an elegant Monument of black marble with the Figure of a Man in Armour in black Marble, designed for a Count de Clermont of the Bourbon Family, Son or Grandson of St Lewis King of France: close by him, on the North Side of this Chapel are a Couple more of the same Sort of Tombs, for the same

[1]Viennois, properly.

Family, as I presume. Against the Walls of this Chapel
were fixed 2 Marble Busts, one of a Bishop, the other of
a Dominican Frier: but there were too many Things in
this Church to be observed to fix my Attention particularly on any; so that I do not know for whom these
Busts were designed: but as Nicholas Coeffeteau, Bp of
Marseilles, a learned writer & Friar of this Convent[1]
& Father Noël Alexandre a later writer & Frier of the
same, were both buried in this Chapel, it is not unlikely
but they may be designed for them. The Holy Sacrament was exposed upon the High Altar & Candles
lighted both upon that & St Thomas's Altar, if I
remember right; it being the Festival of Commemora-
tion of all the Saints of the Order of St Dominic.
Opposite the Count de Clermont's Tomb, on the other
or North Side of the Steps was another fine Tomb of the
same Sort of black & white Marble, & near it, on the
Top of a Pillar was the Statue of a Princess of the Royal
Blood of France; but I forget for whom designed: these
are close to Our Lady's Chapel of the Rosary. In the
North Isle also were 3 or 4 black Marble Altar Tombs
with Figures of White Marble on them, with French
Inscriptions about the Time of Our Edward 3, for
Noblemen of this Country: but I made no Notes about
them. I asked a Friar whom I met in the Isle, for Leave
to see their Library: but it being a Festival Day it was
shut up, & [he] desired me to come any other Time. In
short I was very glad not to walk about any more,
having passed backwards & forwards about these
Monuments 'till I was quite tired: there being such a
Collection as scarce to be met with in any single Church

[1] Author of *Tableau des Passions Humaines*, etc.
[2] Author of *Historia Ecclesiastica*, etc.

besides. After having gratified my curiosity sufficiently in this Conventual Church, I passed over the River & the Isle du Palais, & passing by an House near the Pont-Neuf before you come to the Samaritaine, I was invited in to see the Carcase or Skin stuffed of the wild & savage Kind of Wolf that had done so much Mischeif, Killing & devouring Numbers of Men, Women & Children in Auvergne & the Gévaudan[1] all the last year; with Accounts of which our News Papers in England were continually full. It was not bigger than a large Mastif Dog, had very sharp & long Teeth, was of a dirty Cream Colour, & was now just begun to be shewn in Public, after having been for some Time in the Queen's Ante-chamber at Versailles, where Mr Walpole told me he saw it, when he was presented to the King & Royal Family there.[2] I purchased 2 common prints painted in its proper Colours of it while at Paris; neither of which were like the Creature in Shape or Colour: & as this Beast made so much Noise all over Europe, did so much Mischeif & alarmed the Parts he infested so terribly, I will give the Account of him which is printed on both the Plates: together with the Advertisement handed about to draw People to see him.

Avis au Public. Le Sieur La Cote, Garde-general des menus-Plaisirs du Roi, donne Avis au Public, qu'il fait voir la cruelle Bête qui a fait tant de Ravage dans l'Auvergne & dans le Gévaudan, qui a été tuée le 20 Septembre dernier, dans les Bois de la Resérve de l'Abbaye Royale des chasses en Auvergne, par

[1] A former district of Languedoc, nearly corresponding with the Dept. of Lozère.

[2] "He was exhibited to us with as much parade as if it was Mr Pitt. It is an exceedingly large wolf, and, the connoisseurs say, has twelve teeth more than any wolf ever had since the days of Romulus's wet-nurse". *Letters of Hor. Walpole* (Toynbee), No. 1057, Oct. 6, 1765.

M. Antoine, Chevalier Militaire de Saint Louis, seul Porte-Arquebuse de sa Majesté: laquelle a été presentée au Roi & à toute la Famille Royale par M. Antoine de Bauterme, son Fils. La Loze ou on la fait voir est sur la Quai de la Feraille, chez le Sieur Ricci, Italien.

Permis d'imprimer & distribuer, ce 7 Octobre 1765. De Sartine.

The first Print represents him as a black long-bodied Creature, with short Legs & Claws like an Otter, with the King, Queen, Dauphin & Royal Family attended by the Courtiers & one Bishop, looking at him: at the Bottom is this wrote: having a Wound in his left Shoulder & over his left Eye.

Representation de la Bête du Gévaudan qui a fait tant de Ravage dans ce Pays & dans l'Auvergne, &c.

Pour que cet Animal se conservât, dans son Naturel, on l'a disséque, embaume et attache sur une Planche, tel qu'il est ici représente.

The other Print represents him of a dark brown Colour as just shot, two Men being in Persuit of him: & in two small Views in the same Print, are shewn several Peasants as his Persuers into a Wood, the other Mr Antoine shooting him, with a View of the Abbey & Spire of the Church by the Side of the Wood. On it is wrote in 4 different Parts of the Print.

Représentation de la Bête feroce &c: qui a été tiree dans le Bois de Pommieres en Auvergne par Messrs Antoine & Reincherd le 20 Sept: 1765.

Mr Antoine etant averti que cette Bête fesoit des Ravages dans les Bois de l'Abbaye Royale des Chazes en Auvergne, a envoye des Valets de Limiers et les Chiens de la Louveterie de sa Majesté pour détourner cet Animal. On a fait dire a Mr Antoine qu'elle etoit dans les Réserves des Bois de Pommieres: tout de Suite cet Officier est parti de Besset, ou il etoit, qui est eloigne de trois Lieucs de ces Bois: et le 20 Septembre de grand Matin, il a fait fouiller le Bois par ses Gardes, et par 40 Tireurs des Habitans de Langeac, et des Villages Voisins: pour lui, il s'est place dans un petit Détroit au Bout d'un Sentier: la Bête s'est presentee a lui a 50 Pas de Distance, et presentoit le Cote droit et la Tête: alors il lui a tire un Coup de sa Canardiere, qui etoit chargee de 5 Coups de Poudre, de 35 Postes a Loups, et d'une Balle de Calibre. Ce Coup a renverse par Terre cette furieuse Bête, lui a crevé l'œil, et les Postes l'ont frappee sur tout le Cote droit, et l'Epaule. Quoique cet Animal ait été si fortement frappé, il s'est releve, et a couru avec une telle Promptitude sur lui, qu'il n'a pas en le Tems de charger sa Canardiere: ce qui l'obligea d'appeller du Secours: Mr Rainchard, Garde de Msr le Duc d'Orleans, est arrive a Tems; il a tire sa Carabine, sur cette Bête, qui l'a frappee par Derrière. Ce Coup la fait avancer 25 Pas dans la Plaine ou elle est tombee morte.[1]

After this I took a walk in the Gardens of the Thuilleries, reckoned some of the finest in Europe: but a Person must have never been out of Paris, or at least never seen some of the finer Gardens which abound in England, to prefer these to them. The Terrass which runs along the Side of the River would be delightful, was the River like the Thames & covered with Boats of every Sort: however the Walks, Water & Statues more especially render this a delightful Rendevouz in fine Weather: & the Palace of the Thuilleries at the End of it near the Pont Royal is by much the noblest Pile of Building I ever saw, & well worthy of the great Lewis 14, who compleated what was begun by Queen Catherine de Medicis. A Noble Terrass or Flight of Steps runs the whole Bre[a]dth of this Palace, which has now the additional beauty of having his present Majesty's Equestrian Statue in the Central View from

[1]Reproduced *verbatim et literatim.*

it at the other End of the Gardens. Centinels stand at
the Entrances of them to keep out People who are
ill-dressed, & such as are not proper to mix with the
People who resort there: which Centinels also supply
Refreshments of Wine, Coffee & gentile Repasts for
such as chuse it.

Sunday, Nov: 10. Small Rain. Feverish & not very
well: however at Noon I went out in a Coach to see the
Place or Square of Louis the 15. This most beautiful &
elegant Square, when it is finished according to the
Plan, will be superior to any Thing of the Sort in this or
any other Capital: one Side only is built in Part, which
is nearest to the Faubourg St Honoré: for the Outside
Shell only of many of the intended Houses is as yet
erected: but built upon a most superb & rich Design,
with Pillars between each Window & Balustrade at
Top, of a fine coloured Stone: tho' I was told, that the
Houses did not let well, nor were People eager to take
Leases to build on the Spot. The Equestrian Statue of
King Lewis 15 was just mounted on the Pedestal: he
stands with his Face looking to the Palace of the
Thuilleries: many People thought if it had been placed
with its Back to the Palace, & looking towards the
Country its Attitude would have been more proper.
But be this as it will: it is one of the most pleasing
Statues I ever saw. Lewis 15, like his great Grandfather,
Lewis 14, had the Satisfaction of being, as well the first
in Rank, as in Grace & Beauty: his present Majesty
being reckoned one of the most handsome & accomplished Men in his Dominions:[1] his Statue indeed has

---

[1]Walpole, writing to Lady Hervey, Oct. 3, 1765, observes, "The
King is still much handsomer than his pictures, and has great sweetness
in his countenance".

the Look of an Hero & a Caesar, & the Horse is
equally spirited, generous & bold. The Pedestal is not
yet finished as to the Ornaments, & the Scaffolding is
still about that Part of it: 4 Figures of Women in Brass,
as is the Statue, stand as Supporters at each Corner of
the Pedestal. This expensive Statue is a Gift of the City
of Paris, in Honour of their Sovereign, Lewis the well-
beloved. The Square has the Elysian Fields on the
River Side of it: but the Place was so dirty & miry when
I was there, except on some Pavements that crossed it,
that the Horses could hardly drag the Coach out of the
Mire: when the Square is more finished it is probable
that it will be paved. From this I went to that other
noble Square called the Place Royale, quite at the other
End of this Part of the City on the same Side of the
River, near the Porte St Antoine, the Bastille & the
Boulevarts. The Place Royale is a perfect Square, where
the Houses are built all of the same Design with a
Cloyster underneath, not much unlike Convent Garden
in London; the Houses also being built of Brick, which
is unusual at Paris. In the middle of this large Square is
the Equestrian Statue of King Lewis 13,[1] on a Pediment
of white Marble: the King's Figure, with a monstrous
Plume of Feathers on his Helmet, is not much esteemed;
but the Horse is reckoned a most finished Peice of
Sculpture. An Iron Palisade goes all round this Square
& encloses some Grass Walks within.

From hence I went to see the Gate, now stopt up,
thro' which Henry the 4 made his Entrance into Paris,
after his Abjuration of Huguenoterie & Calvinism.
Near this is the Porte St Antoine, at the Extremity of

---

[1]Destroyed in 1792, the Square being re-named *Place des Vosges;*
the horse was designed by Daniel Volterre.

the Rue St Antoine, which is a very broad & good
Street: this Gate was erected in the Reign of Henry 2;
but has been much ornamented & improved in that
of Lewis 14. Notwithstanding, upon the whole, it
appeared to me to be but a heavy Business: it has 3 large
Passages in it; that in the middle being rather the
biggest, & is adorned with Statues, Carvings &
Inscriptions: it has been rendered famous by the
Skirmishes at it in the Civil Wars in the Beginning of
the last Reign; & still more so by the bold & rash
Action of Mademoiselle de Montpensier,[1] the King's
[Louis XIV] first Cousin, who being of the contrary
Faction, ordered the Cannon of the Bastille to be fired
upon the King's Troops as they were endeavouring to
get Admittance into the City thro' this Gate. However
she lived long enough to repent of her Gallantry: as
Lewis 14 is supposed never to have forgot it. Close to
this almost stands the great, heavy & clumsy Castle of
the Bastille, which consists of a sort of Square Building,
with 8 roundish high Towers about it, & none or few
Windows from it: so that it must be a very gloomy
Habitation for the unhappy People who live in it:
except the Court within-side is better lighted. It was
built as a Fortress & Defence of the City in the 14
Century, & now serves as a Prison for State Criminals.
Monsr the Comte de Lally was confined therein when I
was admitted into the outward Courts of it: he is since
executed, about 2 Months ago [I write this July 5,
1766] for a supposed Neglect of his Duty as Com-
mander for the French King in the East Indies, when

[1]Anne Marie Louise d'Orléans (1627-93); during the Fronde she
played an Amazonian part and after the battle of the Faubourg St
Antoine saved the beaten troops of Condé by covering their flight in the
way indicated.

the English gained their point against him. He was of Irish extraction & was immensely rich; which many said was the immediate occasion of his Execution: but with what Justice, I am sure I am no Judge: it is certain his Condemnation was attended with great Squabbles among the French: But I am not qualified to speak about them, knowing little of their Politics, & not daring to take any measure of them from what we say of them in this Country. The Bastille stands on the right Hand of the Porte St Antoine as you go out of the City upon the Boulevarts, which were exceedingly dirty & miry, & hardly fit for a Coach to pass on them at this Time of the year, when they are deserted 'till the fine Season appears: however I went the Round of them again, (notwithstanding the Remonstrances of the Coachman to the contrary, to whom I was forced to give something in order to pacify him), quite to the Porte St Honoré, stopping however to look at the Portes St Martin & St Denis: the first of which is an handsome modern Gate, built in 1674, consisting of 3 Arches, the middlemost of which is thrice as big as the 2 other: above the 2 smaller Arches is some Basso-relievo, & the whole is of a rough rustic work, very noble & handsome, with a rather heavy Entablature above a Cornice at Top, on which is a fulsome Inscription to the Glory of the great Lewis 14, which 2 Angels below on the Basso-Relievo are sounding forth with their Trumpets. Thro' this Porte I entered Paris in my way from Cambray, the Street of St Martin being a very good one, & remarkable for its running in a direct straight Line quite thro' the whole City of Paris: for, beginning at the Porte St Martin, it crosses the Seine at the Pont Notre Dame, then thro' a strait Street across the Isle du Palais, crosses the other Branch of the River at the Petit Pont where it meets the long Street of St Jacques, & loses itself in the Faubourg St Jacques, near the Royal Observatory: being the longest direct Street perhaps in Europe. The Rue St Denis runs parallel with it in the same Manner: for beginning at the Porte St Denis it runs parallel with St Martin's Street through the whole quarter of the City called La Ville, 'till you come near the River, where it unluckily meets with a little interruption, but soon gets into the strait Line again on the Pont du Change, crosses the Isle du Palais & the Pont St Michel, where it joins the long Rues de la Harpe & d'Enfer, & so goes out of the City on the other Side of the same Observatory. The Porte St Denis was built by the City about the same Time as that of St Martin, in the midst of the Glories & Conquests of Louis 14: so Allowance ought to be made for the flattering Inscriptions upon them both: it is by much the most light & elegant Gate in Paris, consisting of a noble Arch in the middle, on each Side of which against the Walls are erected a Pyramid with Trophies & Armour on them, under which, in the Pedestals of both are two small Passages or Doors for Foot Passengers: it is terminated at Top by an elegant & airy Frize, under which is wrote, in great Capitals,

LUDOVICO MAGNO.

In my Progress of to Day I went to look at the stately Portal or West Front of the Jesuits' Church in the Rue St Antoine: but since the Banishment of these Fathers, the Church has been shut up, & only one Mass a Day said in it by the Priests of the Seminary of St Paul, a little way behind it: so as I was here after Mass was over I could not have a Sight of it then: also of the fine Front

of St Gervais his Church, not far distant, in a very
crampt & narrow Situation: which is so much the more
to be pitied, as they reckon it one of the most complete
Peices of Architecture in Paris. This Day Mr Livier,
the Print-Seller, brought me some Prints, particularly
two of Cardinal Pole from a Picture in a Collection in
Paris, & not easily to be had in England, being desirous
to make a Present of one of them to Mr Phillips, the
Writer of the Life of that Cardinal: who, since my
Return, having occasion to write a short vindication of
himself against 4 or 5 warm & angry Antagonists,
which the said Life had raised up against him, took
Occasion to Compliment me, for some trifling Observations I had sent him, but without naming my Name:
by which I escaped most certainly as hearty a Drubbing
from the same Quarter as the Author himself met with:
for such is the Freedom of thinking & speaking in this
falsely boasted free Country [of England], that if a Man
speaks against Popery & in Favour of Presbytery,
Atheism, Deism, any wild Enthusiasm, Republicanism,
& any Sort of Liberty even to Licentiousness, why then
you may speak & write as freely as you please, & even
be applauded for it: but if on the contrary you should
happen to be so old-fashioned to speak candidly in
Favour of old Maxims & even for the Religion of the
Establishment, & hint a Dislike of Innovations either
in that or the Constitution of your Country, you will
most infallibly be stigmatized by these pretended
Lovers of Freedom of Thinking, either as a determined
Papist, which is worse than Devilism, or else for a
secret Fautor & Favourer of them, which is little less
than Diabolical Treachery: when these very Men are
the actual Betrayers of their Establishment to their

artful, cunning & undermining Enemies. It is my firm Belief that we shall be glad to call in the Assistance of those we so grossly abuse, notwithstanding all their Faults, to save the main Chance from Infidelity & Profaneness.

Monday, Nov: 11. *St Martin.* Foggy Day. I had a Design to have gone to Mass to St Martin au Champs, but did not find myself well enough to go out with Pleasure: however, I went to Dinner at the Hôtel du Parc Royal, where Mr Mariette[1] came in the Afternoon. By the Letters from England this Post, News came that his Majesty's Brother, Prince Frederic was so far gone in a Dropsy as to occasion little Expectation of his Recovery.[2] Mr the Duke de Nivernois called on Mr Walpole about 6 o'Clock to carry him on a Visit to his Duchess.[3] On my Return to my Lodgings I was much out of order with my Stomach. I paid Mr Armand, the Taylor, £3. 10s. 0d. for a Coat & Waistcoat for my Servant.

Tuesday, Nov: 12. Foggy Weather. By means of a good Night's Rest I found myself very well this Morning; however I did not stir out 'till about Noon, when I went first to the Gate of St Bernard, situated across the Street which runs by the Side of the River, opposite the Isle Notre Dame: This Porte St Bernard is rather an heavy massive Building, built or repaired in the late Reign, as Inscriptions & Basso-Relievos on both Sides

[1] Pierre Jean M. (1694-1774); collector of engravings; Walpole refers to "old Mariette" in a letter to Thos. Brand, Oct. 19, 1765.

[2] See *Public Advertiser*, Nov. 4, 1765, p. 2, col. 2.

[3] "She is the Duke of Newcastle properly placed, that is, chattering incessantly out of devotion, and making interest against the devil that she may dispose of bishoprics in the next world" (Walpole to Lady Hervey, Nov. 28, 1765).

are addressed to the glorious & real immortal Memory
of Lewis 14. It has 2 Arches or Passages of equal Size:
it takes its Name from a large Convent of Barnardin
Monks at some Distance from it. Near this Gate you
pass over an handsome Stone Bridge of about 5 Arches
into the Isle Notre Dame; so called, because it belongs
of Right & Property to that Cathedral, which is built,
however, on the adjacent Isle du Palais. The Parish
Church of St Louis in the Isle Notre Dame is a very
elegant modern Structure in the Form of a Cross: on
each Side of the High Altar is a fine Statue: one of them
is St Louis, & the other, I think, Charlemagne. In the
North Transept is a beautiful Altar of St Geneviève, &
her Statue upon it in White Marble: the opposite
Transept is the Chapel of our Lady: I think there was
another elegant Chapel on the same Side below it,
where they were Saying Mass while I was there. In this
Church the famous Philip Quinault,[1] a most ingenious
Poet & Writer, tho' no Favourite of Boileau, lies buried.
On the North West Corner of the Church, in the Street,
is a small Tower, on which is just now erected a small
Stone Spire or Steeple, peirced with many Openings, &
built this year, 1765, as appears by that Date upon it.
These Spires are not common in France, which made
me take the more Notice of it. From the Isle Notre
Dame you pass the Seine over the Pont Marie, a Bridge
of 5 Arches of Stone, into that Part of the City of Paris
distinguished by the Name of La Ville; which Compre-
hends all the whole Side from the River on the St Denis
Side of the Seine: when you are over this Bridge you

[1]Philippe Q. (1635-88): "The French still think that ballad-wright
Q. their best lyric poet; which shows how much they understand lyric
poetry!" Walpole to Mason, Oct. 8, 1776.

turn on the right Hand to go to the Arsenal & the
Convent of the Celestins: the first containing a long
Range of Building, with Courts, to which you enter by
a handsome Gate, running along the Banks of the River,
exactly fronting the Isle Louvier, on which are no
Buildings, but only large Magazines of Wood. Close to
this fine Gate of the Arsenal, stands the Entrance into
the large Convent of the Celestin Monks, the cheif
Front of their Church, in the Gothic Stile of Architecture, with Stone Images about the Door: the Cloyster
is close adjoyning on the left hand. The Church is
neither handsome nor light, but ample Amends is made
for any Deformity in the Building, by the Number &
Beauty of the Monuments in it, which exceed any in
Paris for Beauty, tho' probably [those in] the great
Convent of the Jacobins or Dominicans may be more
numerous. The High Altar of the Choir has a fine
"Salutation" in Marble on it, being the Figures of the
Blessed Virgin & the Angel Gabriel. On the Steps up to
it, in an Arch of the North Wall, is a curious old Tomb
of black Marble, & on it lies an Image in White
Marble of Leo de Lusignan, King of Armenia, who
being drove away from his Dominions by the Turks,
retired to Paris, where he died in 1393. Father Montfaucon has given a Print of his Statue in his 3rd Vol. of
Antiquitez de la Monarchie Françoise, p. 189. Just below
this in the same Wall, a little above the Door into the
Choir, in another Arch lies a low Altar Tomb of black
Marble, on which is the Image of a Lady in White
Marble, very neatly carved, & well preserved: it is
designed for Anne of Burgundy, Duchess of Bedford,[1]

[1]Walpole refers to this tomb in a letter to H. S. Conway, Oct. 29. 1774.
[Continued] In a Book called *Histoire de Notre Dame de Liesse*,

Wife to the great John Duke of Bedford, Brother to King Henry 5, & Regent of France in the Minority of his Nephew King Henry 6. This Lady died in 1432. Mr Walpole told me that he would have a Print of it engraved, before he left Paris, as there is no Mention of her in Father Montfaucon, nor no Account of her Tomb in any of our English Historians. However in looking into Tindal's Edition of Rapin,[1] in a short Note, Vol: 1. p. 555, Note 5, is a Blunder or two: 1st he says she is buried in the Orleans Chapel: but that is on the other Side of the Church: & if he means by calling her Tomb black Marble, that her Effigies is of that Colour, it is a Mistake: but I ought not to dwell upon such trifling Oversights in other People, when I am conscious that this very work abounds with much more considerable. I remember some years ago Mr Walpole told me, that the Earl of Bute had more than once mentioned to him, a great Desire that something of the same Sort for England, as the learned Benedictine Dom Montfaucon had done for France, should be set on Foot, Mr Walpole has several Materials towards such an undertaking;[2] & has already, in his Noble Authors, Anecdotes on Painting & elsewhere, obliged the World with some Specimens of such a Design: towards which no one has contributed so much as my industrious, good &

---

p. 42, by Mr Villette, it is said that there is a figure of Anne Duchess of Bedford in the windows of the Church of the Hospital of St Esprit à Paris [C.].

[1] Paul Rapin de Thoiras (1661-1725); N. Tindal translated his *Histoire d'Angleterre*.

[2] Walpole's views on this subject are given in letters to the Rev. H. Zouch and Lord Bute. *Letters of Hor. Walpole* (Toynbee), No. 624 (March 15, 1759), and No. 806 (Feb. 15, 1762).

worthy Friend, the late Mr George Vertue. Just
opposite, on the other Side of the Choir, below the
Altar of the Secretaries of the King, & just as you enter
the Door into the Orleans Chapel, under the South
Wall, lies a very noble Monument of raised or cast
Brass on the Floor, of a Bp in his Pontificals, & mitred:
but for whom designed I know not, as I forgot to ask,
or, what is more probable, the Person who shewed me
the Church, did not know: this is much worn away by
Peoples treading upon it. I observed another Bp mitred
& in his Episcopal Robes, lying partly under the handsome Brass Eagle in the middle of the Choir, tho' rather
towards the lower End of it, being a large Stone covered
with a Brass Plate all over, & carved: I did not discover
his Name, but he was called Episcopus Ebroicensis;
which, I presume, means Evreux.

The Chapel of Orleans is on the South Side of the
Choir or right Hand: it is small, nothing beautiful in
itself, but so full of Monuments that there is hardly any
stirring in it. The Windows of this Chapel are Curious,
containing the Portraits of a great many of the illustrious
Family of Orléans. The first Tomb that strikes you on
entering this Chapel on the left Hand of the Door, & is
equally well seen in the Choir, as it is so placed as to be
Part of the Division between that & the Chapel: it is a
Pyramid of white Marble on which are Trophies &
Ornaments in the same Sort of Marble, with the Sides
of it in black Marble, on the Top of which is a gilt urn,
& standing on a Pedestal of Marble on the Fronts of
which are Basso-Relievos finely executed, & at the 4
Corners of the Pedestal are Statues, in White Marble,
of the Virtues, executed also in an admirable Manner.
This beautiful Monument was erected for 2 Dukes of

Longueville, Father & Son,[1] who died in the years
1595 & 1663, whose Hearts are deposited in this
Chapel; as was the Body of the Son of the latter, the
last Duke of that Family, who was shot by a Dutch
Officer at the Passage of the Rhine in 1672, at the Age
of 23 years, the Duke refusing to give Quarter to such
Scoundrels, as he called the Dutch. Close to this is a
still more elegant & beautiful Monument, consisting
only of a most delicate twisted Pillar of White Marble,
on which are carved Leaves & Foliages in the lightest
Manner, on the Top of which is an urn of Copper
containing the Heart of the Great Constable Anne de
Montmorency, who was killed in the Battle of St Denis
in 1567, fighting against the Huguenots. This Pillar
stands on a triangular Pediment of red Marble, on
which are Inscriptions & Verses, with the Statues of the
3 Cardinal Virtues in Brass at the 3 Corners. This most
elegant Pillar is so singularly handsome that one could
stand looking at it & admire its beautiful proportions
for Hours together. The Altar close to these 2 Monuments is on one Step: over it is an old, but very fine
Picture, with wooden folding Doors to it, representing
our Saviour's Descent from the Cross, painted by
Salviati.[2] Close to it on the right Hand, under the S.
Wall, & below the Windows, is a small Monument of a
very young Princess of the House of Longueville, with
her Effigy in white Marble. In the middle of this Chapel
stands a very noble Monument of Marble of two
Stories, the Uppermost about 4 or 5 Feet from the
Floor, having 4 White Marble Statues lying on the
uppermost Table, of Lewis Duke of Orleans &
Valentine Visconti de Milan his Wife; which 2 Figures

[1]Henri I and II.   [2]Francesco Rosso S. (1510-63).

are given by Father Montfaucon in his 3rd vol: of
Antiquitez de la Monarchie Françoise, p. 180-181, with
2 of their Sons on each Side of them. The Tables on
which the Figures lie are of black Marble, & the 2 Side
Figures lie lower than those of the Duke & Duchess:
this stands just before the Altar & very near it. Just
behind this magnificent Tomb, at the Head of it, is one
of the most elegant & well-fancied Monuments I ever
saw: it is a beautiful Pillar, consisting of 3 Figures of
Women in White Marble representing the Graces, who
with uplifted Hands support a conjoyned Heart of gilt
Copper in which are those of King Henry 2 & his
Queen, Catherine de Medicis. These most elegant
Statues stand on a Pedestal of a triangular Form, as well
as I can recollect, with 3 different Latin Distics on them.
It is one of the most tasteful Monuments I have ever
seen. Close to it stands another of much the same
Design, being a plain white Marble Pillar, on the Top
of which, as well as I remember, is an Urn, with Flames
proceeding from the Mouth of it, in which is enclosed
the Heart of King Francis, 2d Husband to Mary Queen
of Scots: the Column is upon a Pedestal of red Marble,
of a triangular Form also, at the Angles of which sit 3
Virtues weeping, with Flambeaus extinguished, to
represent their Concern for his so premature Death.
Against the South Wall, under the Windows, near the
Door at the West End of the Chapel, in the Monument
of Henry de Chabot, Duke de Rohan, who died in
1655: he is represented in a reclining Posture, on his
left Side, in White Marble: just by him is another Tomb
for one of his Ancestors: & opposite, on the N.W.
Corner of this Chapel is another for Timoleon de Cossà,
Son of a Comte de Brissac, who was killed in 1559, at

P

the Age of 25 years, fighting against the Huguenots,
& was buried here by Order of King Charles 9th, being
one of his Favourites: This Monument is a Pillar of
White Marble, on which, at Top, is a gilt Urn, containing his Heart, supported by a Pedestal of Marble
with Inscriptions. Against the West Wall are other old
Monuments; one of which is a plain Plate of gilt Brass
with a long Inscription in gothic Characters: but I had
no Time, nor Inclination to read it, there being such a
Profusion of Beauties in so small a Space about me.

At the West End of this Chapel d'Orléans, is a Door
into another Chapel of about the same Size belonging
to the Family of the Duke de Tresmes: in it are several
Monuments: one, under the Windows of the South
Wall, just as you enter it, is of a General of that Family,
& opposite to him, in a very exalted Situation, is his
Duchess, in White Marble, in the Dress of her Times,
with Ruff & Farthingale, on her Knees praying &
looking to the Altar just by her, which is finely ornamented. On the opposite Side, under the Windows of
the South Wall, & against it, is a very fine Monument,
near the Door into the West End of the Church, of
white Marble with the Figure very well expressed of a
Duke de Tresmes as if expiring in his Bed.

In the West End of this Isle, on a Line with the 2
former Chapels, are several Monuments: particularly
of Sebastian Zamet, an Italian Partizan, who is mentioned by Boileau, as also his Son of both his Names,
who was Bp of Langres & died in 1655. Close to this
is a small Monument of one Charles Magneus, who is
represented as sitting, with his left Hand supporting
his Head, in Armour & in Stone, as well as I can
remember: on some occasion being imprisoned falsely,

& being discharged, he died of Joy in about a week
after. The Convent is very large, as well as their Gardens
& the former lately rebuilt: & their Cloistre joyning to
the Church very pretty & neat.

From the Celestins I drove thro' the Arsenal, & by
the Walls of the Gardens belonging to it, on one Side,
& those of the Convent of the Celestins on the other,
into some of the Courts about the Bastille, where were
Draw-Bridges & Lodgings for the Soldiery, & so thro'
the Rue St Antoine into a Narrow & crampt Street to
see the fine West Front & Church of St Gervase. Great
Pity it is that so beautiful a Peice of Architecture,
reckoned one of the most perfect of the Sort in Paris,
should be so confined, as to have no very convenient
Spot to take a View of it: indeed there is a little Kind of
opening before it: but even that is disfigured by a
paltry crooked little Tree, not bigger than an Orange
Tree, placed in the middle of it. This Front is composed
of 3 Stories with Pillars; the uppermost terminated by
a Cross, & the middle one having 2 Niches, in which
are the Statues of St Gervase & Protase. The Clergy
were singing their Vespers in the Choir, while I was
there: which Choir is very beautiful, & divided from
the Nave & Side Isles by handsome Iron Palisades: on
each Side of the elegant High Altar were White Marble
Statues of St Gervase & St Protase;[1] the History of
whose Martyrdom is finely painted in 6 oblong large
Pictures by Le Sueur & Champagne, hanging above
the Pillars of the Nave, 3 on one Side & as many on the
other. The Windows are finely painted all over this

---

[1]SS. Gervasius and Protasius, the legendary twin martyrs of Milan:
see Butler's *Lives of the Saints*, June 19; the pictures were removed to
the Louvre.

Church, which is an elegant Gothic Building, with a beautiful stone ribbed Roof, & ended at the East in a Round Point. Over the Door into the Choir a very fine Crucifix, with Images of our Lady & St John the Evangelist on each Side of it, done by the best Hands, are greatly admired. In a Chapel on the North or left Side of the Isle by the Choir, against the West Wall, is a quite new Monument of a late Rector of the Parish whose Name was Francis Feu, who had been Parson there above 60 years, & was so much beloved & regretted at his Death, that his Parishioners erected this expensive Monument to his Memory. It is composed of his Statue in White Marble, on his Knees, his Hands stretched out, & his Eyes directed towards the High Altar of the Choir, just by & almost in Front: he is in his Sacerdotal Habit & Maniple on his left Arm, Kneeling on a Sort of Sarcophagus, & on each Side of him upon it are Urns, rather large, & sending forth Smoak in Abundance by the Sides of the Pyramid of black Marble, which is behind him against the Wall. However, upon the whole, tho' it is a rich & expensive Monument, yet it is not a very pleasing one, being in the French showy Stile, with Robes puffed out & extended, as if a Pair of Bellows had just blown under them to swell them out to an undue Proportion. On the other Side of the Nave, rather more to the West End, in a Chapel, is a very fine Tomb against the Wall for Michel le Tellier,[1] Chancellor of France & Prime Minister to Lewis 14. It is composed of various coloured Marbles: the Chancellor is represented as half reclined, in his Robes of Office, on a Sarcophagus of black

---

[1]François Michel le Tellier, Marq. de Louvois (1641-91); as Minister of War he organised the French standing army.

Marble, with a Boy weeping at his Feet, on each Side
of the Sarcophagus, which is placed on a large Pedestal,
are 2 Statues of Women sitting to represent so many
Virtues, finely executed, & 2 others, to represent
Justice & Prudence, in white Marble also, are placed
quite at Top of the Arch which terminates the Monument. Above the Chancellor's Head, against the Wall,
& under the Arch, is a Table of Marble with an
Inscription. This worthy Magistrate, foreseeing, &
knowing what mad work the Calvinists would infallibly
set on Foot, should they grow so powerful in France as
to gain a Majority, 8 Days before his Death in 1685,
signed the Revocation of the Edict of Nantes, at the
Age of 83 years, at which Time he could not help crying
out in the Words of good old Simeon: *Nunc dimittis
Servum tuum, Domine, secundum Verbum tuum, in Pace.*
How different from this, & from what a different
Principle must it arise, was the Exclamation of his Son,
Maurice le Tellier, Arch-Bp of Rheims, who 3 years
afterwards, seeing our unfortunate King James 2nd at
the Court of Versailles, (after his unnatural Daughter &
Son-in-Law & Nephew, were in Possession of his
Throne, which he was forced to quit upon no other
Score than a sincere Attachment to that Religion, of
which that Prelate made Profession, was at the Head of
in his Country, & which, it is to be feared, he had not,
by many Degrees, the Value for, which this religious
Prince must be allowed to have), could not help saying,
with a licentious & philosophic Sneer, to those who were
near him, pointing to the King, "See there a Man, who
has lost 3 Kingdoms for one Mass!" By the Turn of the
Expression it is evident, that this Arch-Bp would have
been more complying, & not lost his Arch-Bishopric

for so trifling a Circumstance as his Conscience. Indeed, if the scandalous Chronicle says true, his Liberties with the fair sex, might give him a favourable Opinion of a Church, which allowed its Prelates the Liberty of leading about a Sister or a Wife, as they judged proper. This Charles Maurice de Tellier, Arch-Bp of Rheims, dying in 1710, at the Age of 68 years, was buried also in this Chapel, near his Father, where all such Differences in Opinion as these, it is to be hoped, are buried with him.

In this Church lies interred the famous Poet Paul Scar[r]on, who died in 1660, more famous perhaps for being the first Husband of Madame le Maintenon, than for his poetical Qualifications; which were only of the Burlesque & ludicrous Kind.[1]

From the Church of St Gervais, I went to that of St John en Grève, not far from it, & dependant upon it: it stands in a narrow Street, with Steps up into it, at the Back of the Hôtel de Ville, near the broad & open Place called the Grève,[2] near the Pont Notre Dame: the End of it fronts you as you come from St Gervais, in Ronde Point, & is a neat Gothic Building with painted Glass Windows throughout. The Choir is neat, with Joyner's work gilt, & the High Altar very elegant & rich with Marble Pillars: the Stone Roof is very high & neat, & the Arch which supports the Organs at the End of the Church much taken Notice of for its Boldness & Width. I went from hence to the Palais where I bought several Snuff Boxes, Toothpick Cases, Ribands & such Trifles to carry with me into England as Presents for my Sisters & Acquaintance.

[1] A vivacious account of Scarron is given in I. Disraeli's *Curiosities of Literature*.

[2] The place of execution till 1830.

Wednesday, 13 *November.* Foggy Weather. My French Servant drunk before he came to me in the Morning. I walked to the Bureau, near the Pont Royal, & beyond the Theatins Convent, (where Coaches & Chaises are let to go to Versailles), about 10 o'Clock. I got into a Coach with a very civil officer, & a Gardiner belonging to the King's Gardens at Versailles, who told me that he knew Mr Miller,[1] & that he had a Son now in England. I had much Conversation with this old Gentleman, who told me that altho' the Climate of France was much milder than with us in England (which I was thoroughly convinced of by the Ripeness of their Grapes, the Flavour of their Pears, & by a second Crop of Figs now in October, which tho' not absolutely ripe or good, are yet enough so as to be sold in the Streets to the Common People: whereas ours never have the least Tendency to Ripeness in this Season, but are generally as hard as an Apple; except in some remarkable warm Situations, where I have seen a Sort of unripe Pulp in some of them;) yet there were many Things which we had in greater Perfection in England, & which stood the Frost & Winter Season better with us than in France: he instanced, among other Things, that best of Spring Garden Stuff, Broccoli, which, he said, was always killed by the first severe Frost: whereas it is well known, that our Broccoli is never in Perfection 'till a good Frost has nipped it.

The Road to Versailles, which is about 10 Miles, is over the Pont Royal, by the River-Side under the Garden Walls of the Thuilleries, by the Side of the Place de Louis quinze, under the Walls of the Elysian Feilds

[1]Philip M. (1691-1771); author of *The Gardeners' and Florists' Dictionary* and other botanical works.

& Cours de la Reine, on a good paved Way all the Road. About Mid-way, passing over a Wooden Bridge over the Seine at a Village called Sève,[1] is the Palace of St Cloud, about half a Mile distant on the right Hand, on the banks of the River on the other Side of it, very delightfully situated: this Palace belongs to the Duke of Orléans, the Garden Walls & Gate come close up to the Side of the Road, near the Bridge, from whence you very easily discover the Palace. On a very elevated Situation on the left Hand, are several Royal Palaces & Noblemen's Houses, particularly the Castle of Meudon, Belle-Vue & others, which, from their Situation must command a very enchanting Prospect; as the Seine, at a Distance would look as well as other Rivers of the same Capacity, & the City of Paris & Country & Houses about it, must greatly enliven the Scene: which, however, can never be perfect or complete, for that universal Brownness, & want of Verdure, to give a Life & Cheerfulness to a rural Scene so remarkable thro' all the Country, & for the Beauty of which England is as remarkable & beautiful. At Sève is a great Manufactury of Porcelaine or European China, which we generally in England call St Cloud China, from its Vicinity to that Palace or Castle: the House in which it is manufactured is on the left Hand at the other End of the Town in going to Versailles, at a little Distance from the Road, & has the Appearance of a noble Convent or College, it being a Quadrangle of a very great Extent, built in an elegant Taste, with vast Furnaces & Offices for the hardening & baking the China, as also for the storing it up in Magazines for Sale. It is of a most admirable Beauty & Texture: the

[1]Sèvres.

White has no Glassyness, as many of our Manufactures established in England has; but its Whiteness excells that of the true Porcelaine, as much as the Dresden Manufacture exceeds all other in the Beauty & Elegance of its make, Fashion & colouring. Indeed it ought to be superabundantly eminent & excellent, as the Price is excessive. I was with Mr Walpole one Day at a great Shop in Paris, Mr Poirier's,[1] where it was sold, & saw him give 10 Louis or Guineas for a single Coffee Cup, Saucer, & a little square Sort of *Soucoupe*, or under-Saucer, to set them on; they were indeed the highest finished Things of the Kind that can be conceived: perfect Jewels that deserve to be set in gold Frames to be admired & looked at, but never to be used for Fear of breaking them: at the same Time, at another Shop of the same Sort, in the Rue St Honoré, at one Madame Du Lac's, he bought a Chocolate Cup & Saucer for his Nephew, the Bp of Exeter,[2] which cost between 3 & 4 Guineas, & was a great Beauty of a less gaudy Cast. I was tempted to purchase 2 or 3 Things of the lowest Price I could meet with, as Specimens of this beautiful Manufacture: accordingly I bought half a Dozen Cups with Saucers, for Coffee, which cost 9 Livres each Cup & Saucer, the whole 54 Livres, (or above 2 Guineas considerably), for the Set, with a neat Sugar Dish & Cover at 12 Livres: being the lowest priced Things I could meet with in that extravagant & tempting Shop; where the Mistress was as tempting as

---

[1]"I know the faces of every snuff-box and every teacup", writes Walpole to Conway (July 31, 1771), "as well as those of Madame du Lac and Monsieur Poirier". But it is Mme P. alone of whom Mme Du Deffand speaks in connection with china, and this frequently.

[2]Hon. Fred. Keppel (*ob.* 1777), who married the natural daughter of Sir Edward Walpole.

the Things she sold, & where a younger Man than myself would run great Risk of losing what is of more Value than Money, except he was much upon his Guard: so that it is no wonder that such a Shop was thronged with Customers, or that the Mistress of it might boldly set what Price she thought proper upon her Commodities: for both her Person, tho' drawing towards 40, as well as I could judge, voice & manner, were so engaging, that it was almost next to impossible to refuse her what she asked for them, or to go away without purchasing something both to remember where you bought it, as well as the Manufacture itself. The Duke & Duchess of Richmond, who were attended one Morning, while I was at Paris, by Mr Walpole, bespoke a Service of this Manufacture for their Table which was to cost 500 Pounds: I mean Mr Walpole went with their Graces to Sève. I could not help observing the very different Appearance the Face of the Country bore so near the Metropolis & that of the same Distance from London: tho' on the left Hand going to Versailles from Sève there were fine Woods belonging, I think, to the Park or Forest of the Duke of Orleans: hardly a Gentleman's House all the way: no neat & spruce Boxes with Gardens on the Road Side: whereas, go which way you will for 20 Miles round London, & the Country is filled with them: indeed you have as natural Inhabitants of the Feilds in greater Plenty than any where about us, except in some Noblemen's Parks & about their own Habitations, as at Woburne Abbey, Houghton Hall[1] & some other Places, where I have seen them in as full great Plenty as here: I mean Hares & Pheasants: the former of which I saw playing about

[1]Seats of the Duke of Bedford and Lord Orford respectively.

like Rabbits on a Warren all along the Feilds by the
Road Side, both going to Versailles & St Denis, & such
Quantities of Partridge as would surprise one not
accustomed to it, as they are in this Country: & both
Hare, Pheasants & Partridge so tame & gentle, as even
the rumbling of the Coach Wheels over a constant
Pavement of Stone does not frighten them. You pass a
continued Pavement thro' an Avenue of Trees, (every
tenth of which is marked with a Fleur-de-Lis, as
belonging to the King, not only on this, but on the
Roads from Cambray & Calais, & so, I suppose,
thro'out the Kingdom, where there is a regular Avenue
on the Road Side) to Versailles, about half-a-Mile's
distance from which the Avenue is wider, & exactly
fronts the Castle towards the Town; on each Side of
which Avenue, beyond the Trees, the nearer you
approach the Castle, are gloomy ordinary Houses, &
hardly one that one would wish to live in: when you get
into the grand Court or Square before the Castle or
Palace, [there] are in Front of it, on each Side of the
Road from Paris, most magnificent Stables & Offices
for the Attendants on them, ornamented with Statues &
Basso-relievo's of those Animals[1] in various Postures.
Two or 3 Handsome Streets, terminated at their Ends
with Churches, & public Buildings, center in this
Square & give it a noble Appearance, which however is
much abated by the Dirtiness of it, & by a Quantity of
great Stones for Buildings which lie scattered up &
down about it: by no means becoming the Dignity of an
Approach to so celebrated a Royal Palace. What struck
me most among all the dirty magnificence[2] of Versailles,

[1]C. forgets that he has not mentioned horses.

[2]"A mixture of parade and poverty", Walpole calls Versailles,
writing to John Chute (Oct. 8, 1765).

was the Chapel, on the right Hand Side of the Palace as
you look at it from the Town, which had scaffolding
about it, & was repairing on the Outside: for as to the
Inside, nothing could be more splendid, glorious or
heavenly: But I am by no means qualified to give a just
or adequate Description of so much Beauty, order &
Elegance. It is one single Room of a due Proportion,
except that the Height of it seems to be rather excessive,
the Ceiling being painted by the best Masters: a
Gallery goes round it, supported on each Side by 8
Corinthian Pillars of a very White Stone, equal to our
Portland Stone, before which Gallery is a Balustrade of
Marble covered with gilt Copper: behind the Altar is
[an] Organ Loft & Places for the Band of Music
belonging to the Chapel, & in Front of the Altar, at the
West End of the Church or Chapel, is the same Gallery
Continued, but on the 2 opposite Angles or Corners
nearest the Church or Nave, or projecting into it, are
two most rich & elegant Boxes, in the Shape of Lan-
thorns, one of which is for the King & the other for the
Queen, both of which are glazed & all over gilt, but
hang so much by Geometry, that to a Person in the
Body of the Church they look rather dangerous to be in
them: tho' no Doubt, sufficiently able to support any
Weight that is likely to be in them. The Altar is exquisitely fine in Marbles, gilt Brass & other Ornaments,
2 Angels of the last Materials being on it, adoring the
Crucifix, above which is a Glory of the same Metal gilt.
The Pavement is of fine Marble in various Figures, &
a small Dome painted represents the Assumption of our
Lady, whose Chapel on one Side, as also that of St
Theresa's, with the last Saint's Picture over the Altar of
her Chapel, with the Altars themselves, are admirable:

as is indeed every Thing in this most beautiful & elegant
Church, in which I could willingly have staid as many
Hours as I did Minutes, & not have been tired with
feasting my Eyes on so much Beauty. On the outside of
the Chapel were the Statues of the 12 Apostles & the 4
Fathers of the Church, with a small Lanthorn, rather
than Dome, in the middle. I had been over so many of
the Apartments of this vast & capacious Palace as I
thought proper, before I went down Stairs into the
Chapel: so that the Royal Family from their Tribunes
or Gallery at the West End of the Chapel are upon the
same Floor with it. The Apartments are all very royal &
magnificent, with admirable Paintings & rich Furniture
of every Kind. The Gallery that is so much talked of for
its Length & Beauty, did not strike me with the same
Sensation: for neither its vaulted Roof, tho' finely
painted by Le Brun with the Conquests of Lewis 14, in
different *Compartiments*, nor its large Windows down to
the Floor, in the French Stile, no more than its correspondent Looking Glasses on the opposite Side, also
down to the Floor, pleased my Fancy. I thought them
all too glaring & gaudy. The antique Marble Statues
disposed at the Ends of the Gallery & in various Niches
on one Side of it, with the antique Busts on fine Marble
Tables of different Colours & Sorts, pleased me more.
The other Apartments & Salons are truly noble, but to
endeavour to describe them is as much beyond my
Power & Abilities, as Inclination: for it would be end-
less to take Notice of the vast Number of fine Rooms,
capital Pictures, rich Furniture & Curiosities, which
would fill a volume on Purpose. The Gallery takes up,
if I am right, the whole Length of the Cheif or middle
projecting Front of the Palace, & commands the

Fountains & Water Works just before it, & the fine
Terrass all along the Building. This Middle Front is
adorned with all the Ornaments of a most expensive
Structure, as Columns, Carvings & Statues: the two
other long Ranges of Building, which compose the
whole grand Front, at either End of this fine middle
one, & are placed much backwarder, are not so
decorated, but in a plainer Stile, tho' very handsome.
To have a full View of this extensive Front one ought to
go to the other End of the grand Bason in the Centre of
the whole Building: which Bason was wholly repairing
while I was there, it being empty, & the Stone Sides of
it having by Time & Weather, been much broken &
out of their Places, a new Margin of Stone was then
putting on, & other Reparations to the Fountains, &
Jets d'Eaux, the Statues of which were extremely fine,
as of various other Basons in different Parts of the
Gardens, & particularly one on the left Hand Side of it,
in Centre of that Side Front, being the Apartments of
the Dauphin or Dauphiness: the other Side, as well as I
remember, has no Bason before it, but only green
Lawns, & on the Extremity, in a lower Garden, into
which you look by a Balustrade above, is the Orangerie:
by which, down a Pair of Stone steep Stairs, I went to
my Inn, the *Cadran bleu*, or Blew Dial, where a great
Entertainment or Wedding Dinner was preparing, with
Music & Dancing. The Gardens are very extensive, &
sloping down every way from the Palace, & at some
Distance from it, on the Level, which is filled with a
numberless Quantity of various Sorts of fine Basons,
Jets d'Eaux, with their Statues & Devices, Marble
Statues & other proper Ornaments, it gradually &
gently descends, by various cut & clipped Avenues of

Elmes of the Dutch Sort, & exceeding lofty, to give a
Shade for Summer Walks in this hot Soil, to lower Parts
of the Gardens, all equally adorned with Water Works,
Fountains & Statues. I did not wonder at the Dirt &
Confusion of the Part of the Garden before the Castle,
as so many Workmen were making Reparations in it,
taking the Opportunity of the Court's Absence, at that
Time at Fontainbleau; no more than at that Squallid-
ness & Dirt in the Salons & Staircases of the Palace;
presuming that they were not so, when the Court was
here: but I could not help taking Notice of a Contradiction, as I thought, which much struck me: it was
this: when I was at the Opera, then held at a Play
House in the Palace of the Thuilleries, by Reason the
new one in Building was not finished since its Con-
flagration, I observed, in coming out of it, many
People, who had sat there 3 or 4 Hours, had Occasion
to make Water, at a great Distance from the Entrance
into the Opera House, but were not suffered to do so by
the Soldiers or Centinels; as it was in the Precincts of a
Royal Palace: a Peice of Cleanliness the more extraordinary, as at Versailles, even under the Palace Walls,
nay even upon that very Stone Staircase which leads
into the Gardens, & under the Windows of the Royal
Apartments, people were suffered to lay their Nastiness
in such Quantities, that it was equally offensive to the
Sight & Smell, as well as difficult to avoid treading in
it as you went down them.

After I had dined & refreshed myself at the Inn, I
walked down the Town to the Bureau, where a miserable Thing of a close Post Chaise, with a Driver on a
little Box before you, was ordered for me, which carried
me with sufficient Expedition to Paris, tho' quite dark

before I got there. In going from the Castle to my Inne,
I turned down a Street & went into a Convent of Recollet Friers. Neither their Cloyster nor Church were
extraordinary: the latter was hung in Mourning upon
some Occasion or other. I was told by a Person in the
Gardens, that the Dauphin was so ill as little Hopes were
given of his Recovery: the same Person, who took me
for an Italian Abbé, told me that the Queen Dowager
of Spain was dead: but this was premature.

Thursday, Nov: 14. Foggy Weather, & some Rain
towards the Evening. The great Bell of the Royal
Abbey of St Germain des Prez tolled to give Notice of
the Prayers of 40 Hours for the Health & Recovery of
the Dauphin, who received the Viaticum & Extreme
Unction yesterday, & the Holy Sacrament, by Order of
the Arch-Bp of Paris, was exposed on the Altar of every
Church in his Province or Diocese, before which the
Prayers of 40 Hours were to be said. Two Priests are
obliged, by this Institution, to be continually upon their
Knees before the Holy Sacrament saying this Prayer
for an Hour together, & then others relieve them, & so
by Succession 'till the 40 Hours are compleated.
However, at the End of this Term, this most amiable
Prince continuing still very ill, & his Life of great
Consequence to the Church & State, it was thought
proper to continue them for many Days more. However
it pleased God to dispose of him otherwise than we
short-sighted Mortals prayed for; as He took him to
Himself a few weeks after :[1] at the same Time releasing
him of his Pains & delivering him from the Troubles &
Uneasinesses preparing for him by a factious &
turbulent Spirit forming among his Subjects, had he

[1]On Dec. 20.

lived, which, in all Probability, will end in downright
Rebellion, Anarchy & Confusion.[1] As I was a few Days
after this at the Royal Abbey of St Geneviève, where
the following Order or Mandate was stuck up in many
Parts of the Church & about it, I asked the Swiss, who
shewed me the new Church, if he could not procure me
one; which he presently did by running to his Lodge
from whence he brought me the following, printed on a
full sheet of Paper, with the Arms of the Abbey on the
Top of it: & as I have mentioned in this Place the
Devotion of the 40 Hours it may not be out of its Place
to transcribe it here, as it explains more explicitly the
Meaning of it, & at the same Time shews the Love of
the Clergy towards their Prince, & his worthy Son. The
Reason of the Abbat of St Geneviève's printing such a
Mandate by his own Authority, is, that his Abbey is of
exempt Jurisdiction, depending immediately on the
Pope, & not under the Jurisdiction of the Arch-Bp of
Paris, who sent out Mandates of the same Import; some
of which I saw in different Churches, tho' not of so
large Dimensions as this, which is as follows; & which
I thought worth preserving as a fugitive loose Paper, &
of some Curiosity:

"MANDEMENT
"du
"Reverendissime Abbé
"de l'Abbaye Royale
"de Ste Geneviève
"de Paris,
"dependante immediatement du
"Sainte Siége:
"Qui ordonne des Prières publiques
"pour le Rétablissement de la Santé
"de Monseigneur le Dauphin.

[1] Chesterfield's famous prophecy had been made twelve years before.

Q

"Charles-François de Lorme, Abbé de l'Abbaye Royale
de Sainte Geneviève au Mont de Paris, dépendante immédiate-
ment du Sainte Siége, et Supérieur Général des Chanoines
Reguliers de la Congrégation de France, aux Chanoines de notre
Abbaye, & à toutes autres Personnes dépendantes de notre
Jurisdiction Abbatiale, Salut. Hâtons—nous, M.T.C.F. de
désarmer le Bras du Tout-Puissant, deja levé pour nous châtier.
La France est menacée du Coup le plus funeste. Le triste État
où se trouve réduit Monseigneur le Dauphin demande de nous
les Prières les plus ferventes, pour obtenir le prompt Rétablissement d'un Prince, que le Ciel avoit accordé à nos Voeux dans les
Jours de sa Miséricorde, & qu' it a comblè des ses Dons les plus
précieux, pour faire notre Bonheur, & pour nous servir de
Modéle; d'un Prince si cher à l'État par ses excellentes Qualités,
& à la Religion par son éminent Piété. Recourons avec autant de
Zèle que de Confiance à la puissante Protection de notre Sainte
Patrone. Sa Majesté, par les ordres dont elle nous a honorés,
réclame son Intercession, dont elle a éprouvé elle-même les Effets
dans les fâcheux Événemens qui ont pensé nous la ravir. Secon-
dons ses Désirs; suivons son Exemple. Puisse Geneviève, sensible
à nos Alarmes, faire passer efficacement jusqu' au Trône du
Tout-Puissant & les Cris de la Foi du plus tendre de tous les
Pères, & nos ardentes Supplications pour le Rétablissement de
son auguste Fils. Puisse notre Monarque Bien-aimé entendre
bientôt ces Paroles consolantes, addressées par le Sauveur du
Monde à cet Officier de l'Evangile; Votre Fils se porte bien;
(Jean, 4.) Allez, je le rends à votre Foi, à votre Tendresse, & aux
Voeux de tout votre Peuple.

"A ces Causes, pour nous conformer aux Ordres du Roy, & à
l'Arrêt de ce Jour, rendu par la Cour de Parlement, & en même
Tems satisfaire à notre propre Zèle, nous ordonnons que la
Chasse de Sainte Geneviève, Patrone de Paris & du Royaume,
sera découverte ce Jourd 'hui, dont la Ville sera avertie par le Son
de toutes les Cloches de notre Abbaye: que le même Jour on
célébrera une Messe solemnelle à neuf Heures du Matin que
pendant que la Chasse demeurera découverte, on dira au Grand
Autel des Messes depuis cinque. Heures du Matin jusqu' à Midi:

que quatre Chanoines Réguliers de cette Eglise feront successive-
ment de Prières, selon l'Ordre qui leur sera marquè, devant la
dite Chasse, hors le Tems des Messes, qui seront célébrées au
Maitre Autel: que tous les Jours il sera fait, à l'Issue de Complies,
une Procession dans l'Eglise, & un Salut, où on chantera, 1° les
Litanies qui commencent par ces Mots, *Aufer à nobis.* 2° Le
Clergé étant rentré dans le Choeur, le Trait *Domine, non
secundum,* l'Antienne de la Sainte Vierge, *O Maria,* l'Hymne,
Spes magna Gentis. Trois Fois le ℣. *Domine, salvum fac Regem,*
avec *le Gloria Patri,* l'Antienne de la Paix, *Deus meminerit,*
le ℣ & l'Oraison marqués au Processional, *Pro Infirmo.*
   "Donné à Paris en notre Abbaye Royale de Sainte Geneviève
le 13 Novembre, 1765.
   "Signe, De Lorme, Abbé de Sainte Geneviève.
   "Et plus bas—Par mon Reverendissime Abbé.
   "Fr: Regnier, Secrétaire du Chapitre, De l'Imprimerie de
P. G. le Mercier, Im-primeur—Libraire de l'Abbaye Royale de
Sainte Geneviève, Rue St Jacques, au Livre d'Or, 1765."

   At 11 I called upon Mr Walpole, who carried me to
the late Count de Caylus[1] his House, near the Place de
Louis quinze, to see his Antiques, Curiosities &
miniature Pictures, cheifly in Enamel. The Count was a
very learned Man & good Antiquary, as his Writings
testify: he died of the Gout, (in the very Room we sat
in to look over the Seals, Rings &c.) in the neat Canopy
Bed of flowered Silk, still in the Chamber, which was
small, as was the House. A Print of his Lady was in the
same Chamber over a Door: the Count was just a little
turned 60 years of Age, & was lately dead, leaving an
immense Collection of Roman Antiquities of all Sorts
to the King's Library; by which means the Public will
be benefited by them, better than if they were dispersed
in private Hands, as they will be accessible to at stated
Times; these were all numbered & disposed in several

[1]Anne Claude de Lévis, Comte de Caylus, *ob.* Sept. 5, 1765.

small Chambers which the Gentleman who had the keeping of them readily shewed to Mr Walpole, who desired me to put down into my Pocket Book such & such Things, especially a few Miniature Pictures, which he had a Design to bid for at the approaching Sale of the Count's Goods: for all the Paintings & a Room full of other Antiques were to be sold, which were not given to the King: the Things Mr Walpole intended to purchase were as follows: first, Miniature Pictures of

The Duke d'Épernon.
The Princess Palatine.
Monsr Barbesieux.
Monsr de Vendosme.
Madame la Connêtable Colonna.
The Duchess de la Va[l]lière.
The Duchess de Montpensier.

Among the antique Rings & other Antiquities:

No 117. 2 Antique Bottles.
No 135. An antient Writing Box or Écritoire.
No 125. An antient Bottle.

How he came off for these last I know not: but for the Miniatures he told me before I left Paris, that a rich Financier had bespoke them all, & was determined to bid more for them at the Auction than any other Person probably would.[1] After taking an Airing about the Place de Louis 15, we went to the Shop of Madame du Lac, where the Earl of Fife[2] with Mr Sheffeild, Son of Sir Charles Sheffeild,[3] were making Purchases. The

[1]But Walpole, writing to Conway (Nov. 29, 1765), declares that "I am over head and ears at Count Caylus's auction, and have bought half of it for a song".

[2]James Duff, 2nd Earl (1729-1809); married a daughter of the Earl of Caithness in 1759.

[3]1st Bt., *ob.* 1774.

Earl lately came from the Spa with his Lady, by whom
he has no Children: he is a rather undersized thin Man
of about 30 or 40 years of Age, & his Family being
concerned in some Endeavours for the Steward Family,
the Title was forced to be changed from Scotland to
Ireland, in Favour of this Gentleman, who has a very
large Estate, & being a good Oeconomist, is not
likely to injure it; his Lordship was in Mourning, &
bought an elegant Watch of 50 Guineas. Mr Sheffeild
is a young Man of about 20, rought faced, clumsy &
of no very promising Genius, as seemed to me. Mr
Walpole, among other Things, bought 3 most beautiful
Vases for a Chimney,[1] of blew Enamel, set in gilt
Copper, for Mr Chute[2] of the Vine in Hampshire: they
cost 19 Guineas, & were most elegant Ornaments for
the Place they were designed, the middle one being
larger than the 2 others: I bought a few Things here
which are not worth mentioning. From this dangerous
Shop we went to another not a whit less so, Mr Poirier's, where the China & Toys & fine Cabinets were
rather richer & in greater Abundance; being a Magazine of several lower Apartments full of them: Mr
Walpole, among other Things, bought an elegant
Tripod of gilt Copper, in an antique Fashion of about 4
Inches high to burn Incense, or *Pastilles à bruler*, on: it
cost 3 Guineas. I bought a single Coffee Cup & Saucer
of the enamelled Chantilly manufactured China, for
which I gave 12 Livres, or about half a Guinea. While I
was at Dinner at Mr Walpole's the Duchess of Richmond sent to him to go out with her to some Entertainment this Evening; so I left him about 5 o'Clock, &

[1]A recognised equivalent of "chimney-piece".
[2]John Chute (1701-76), Walpole's lifelong friend.

went to the solemn Service for the Dauphin at the Royal Abbey of St Germain des Prez, where the Service was very solemnly chanted, not only by the Monks in their Choir, but by all the Congregation, both Men & Women, tho' in Latin, & who seemed much in Earnest, & very fervent in their Devotions. After a Time, 3 Monks in rich Copes came out of their Choir into the Sanctuary before the High Altar, when the Holy Sacrament was exposed to the Devotion of all the People. I suppose the oldest Monk, who seemed to be about 70 years of Age, & whose Cope was held up & supported by the 2 others on each Side of him, might be the Prior of the Abbey: here they recited some Prayers on their Knees before the Altar, & afterwards rising up, the Prior, if he was so, read aloud, from a Paper, given him by one of the other Monks, a Latin Prayer for the Recovery of his Royal Highness the Dauphin, naming him by Name. During this Service one of the Monks gave the Sun, or *Soleil*,[1] in which the Holy Sacrament was enclosed in the Center, between 2 Glasses, into the Hands of the Prior, who gently turned himself about with this lifted up in his Hands, that all the People withoutside of the Sanctuary, in the Nave & Transept Isles, might see & adore it: after this it was again set on the Altar, & just before the Service was finished, one of the 2 Monks, by a Pair of Steps, getting up upon the Altar, put the Holy Sacrament into the Tabernacle above the Altar, & locked it up, they having all three first adored it prostrate on their Faces to the Ground. The Church was as full of People on this Occasion as it could hold, who all seemed much concerned, & very devout. Many People had small Wax Candles in their

[1]Ostensorium, or monstrance.

Hands to enable them to read their Prayers & sing their Hymns & Anthems on this Occasion: otherwise they must have been at a Loss, except they could say them by Heart, as I observed many of them did; for the Church was but very poorly illuminated. I paid a Trifle for the use of a Rush-bottomed Chair to Kneel on or against, & might have purchased a *Bougie* or Wax Light had I had any use for one. After this Service was over I walked to Monsr Livier's in the Rue de St André des Arcs, & drank Tea there, Madame Livier undertaking to buy me some Things for some of my Acquaintance which she was better qualified to purchase than myself. The Duke of Beaufort gave a Supper & Ball last Night[1] to the Duke & Duchess of Richmond,[2] at which all the English of Fashion were invited: among the Rest, the Countess of Berkeley,[3] & her 2 Daughters, related to his Grace, & lately come to Paris, were the Principal.

Friday, Nov: 15. Small Rain, but tolerable fine Day without any Sun. Mr Theodore Eynhouts brought me my Bill for a Dozen of Shirts & half a Dozen of Cravats, for which I paid him 214 Livres: I gave him a Bank of England Bill of £10, he promising me the Difference when I should dine at his House in 2 or 3 Days Time. I sent 2 Bills of the same Sort to be changed at Mr Foley's, an English Banker. This Day I had some Words with my French Valet, La Pierre, mentioned at p. 33. & was determined to have discharged him, & have taken another, had I not found some Difficulty in

---

[1] "The Duke of Beaufort made a ball two nights ago in the hotel where I lodge, at which we were no fewer than forty-eight. I was forced to go in my own defence". Walpole to Mann, Nov. 15, 1765.

[2] Charles Lennox, 3rd Duke.

[3] Elizabeth Drax, wife of the 5th Earl.

getting one. I staid at Home all Day, had 2 Woodcocks, or a Brace, as Sportsmen call them, an Omelette & Sallad for Dinner.

Saturday, Nov: 16. Tolerable fine Day. Mr Livier brought me several Pair of Pearl Necklaces, & a Pair of 3 Double Ruffles at 17 Livres, for Mrs Holt of Loughton in Buckinghamshire. I then walked to hear Mass about 11 o'Clock at the noble Parish Church of St Sulpice, lately rebuilt & enlarged, being the Parish Church of almost the whole Fauxbourg of St Germain des Prez, the Abbey of which is Patron of the Living, the Rector's Income being much better than many Bishoprics. It is wretchedly situated in narrow Streets, the small Space at the North-West Angle of it, in which stands the Rector's House of 8 or 9 Windows Front, being the only tolerable Point from whence to take a View of it: the whole West End, with vast Pillars & Flight of Steps up into the grand Portico being obstructed by a dead Wall belonging to the Seminary of this Church. This noble Pile of Building was erected by Contribution & a Lottery, & carried to its present Perfection by the Care & unwearied Diligence of the late Rector, Mr Languet de Gergy,[1] whose magnificent Tomb is erected in a Chapel on the right Hand or South Side of the South Isle, he being represented in his Sacerdotal Habits, Kneeling on a Sarcophagus, with his Hands extended out to, & his Eyes directed to the High Altar in the middle of the Church. It is composed of very fine Marbles, & his Robes are in a very flowing & airy Position. On the Tomb are these Arms, *viz*: Azure, a Triangle & a Mullet at each Point of 6 Points, Or: it is ensigned by a Mitre, & has both a Cross &

[1] He was also Abbé de Bernay.

Pastoral Staff or Crosier by it: but what Right a Rector
of a Parish has to these Insignia, except he might be
possessed of some Abbey, I know not. His brother the
Comte de Gergy is buried in another Part of this
Church. At the West End over this grand Portico, are
2 octagon Towers, & several fine Statues disposed in
proper Places still further adorn it: but you must almost
break your Neck to take any View of it, there being so
little Space before it. Both the North & South Porches
are very noble, but not to be mentioned with the grand
one. The Nave is separated from the Side Isles by most
noble Corinthian Pillars, & fine Chapels surround the
Church & Chapel of our Lady behind it, which is a most
finished round Building, with delicate Paintings: on
the beautiful Altar, in a Niche is a rich & most complete
Statue in Silver of the Virgin Mary: but I never saw it,
a fine Picture of her being placed before it the 3 Times
I was there, & I never asked to see it, by having the
Picture removed: besides I never loved to interrupt
People's Devotion; as there were always, even after
Mass was over, Numbers of well-dressed People at
their Devotions in every Part of the Church: so that you
could not move from one Place to another in these
Churches without having an Hundred Eyes upon you;
which was always disagreable to me: whereas in London you might go very quietly into every Church of the
City & Suburbs, & not be interrupted by one single
impertinent Looker-on. The High Altar is immensely
fine, being built according to the Stile of St Peter's at
Rome in the middle of the Church, under the Dome,
with an exceeding beautiful Canopy of gold carved
work hanging over it. By the Sides of the Choir, which
is separated from the Side Isle by Iron Palisades, Pews

by the outside of them, are Stairs to go down into the vast & capacious Vaults under the Church. At the Bottom of the Church, near the grand Organ Loft, against the 2 last Pillars on either Side of the Nave, are two of the most sumptuous & largest Sea Shells,[1] edged with gilt Copper, & fixed against the Pillars, for Holy Water Basons, or *Benitiers*, that ever were seen: they were sent as a Present 2 Centuries ago by the Republic of Venice to the King of France [François I], & were 'till lately, always kept in his Cabinet of Curiosities, when King Lewis the well-beloved bestowed them upon this Church for that Purpose. This is the Purport of an Inscription on the Pillars above each of them. Near the Choir & High Altar against the Pillars are some Statues of our Saviour, the Blessed Virgin, Apostles & Saints, with Angels in Brass by the Altar, done in an exquisite Manner. The Windows are of beautiful stained Glass with elegant Bordures. In short, the Inside of this Church, to my Fancy, greatly exceeds that of St Paul's at London: & I much doubt whether it is not as capacious: tho' nothing I ever yet saw exceeded the Outside of St Paul's. In this Church the Holy Sacrament was exposed on the Altar, with Lights burning, on Account of the 40 Hours' Prayers for the Dauphin's Recovery: as indeed the same was observed in every Church I afterwards entered during my whole Stay at Paris; as the Time was lengthened from Time to Time. This was my Parish Church, the Rue de Petits Augustins being situated in it.

From St Sulpice I took a Coach & went to the great Convent of Cordeliers, at no very great Distance from it, in a narrow confined Street, with a good old Portal

[1] *Tridacna gigas.*

with Images on it, to the Street. The Church[1] is large, dismal, dark & dirty, but the Altar is very handsome on several Steps. On the South Side of the Choir, is a narrow Passage or Isle, between that & the Side Chapels, towards the Entrance from the Nave, or West End, against the Wall, being the Back of the Choir, on the left Hand, (close to an Image of our Lady in a Niche in one of the Pillars, under which is wrote, *Consolatrix Afflictorum, ora pro nobis*, & by it, on the Wall in vast gold capital Letters lately done, *Consolatrice des Affligez, priez pour nous*), is a small mural Monument of white Marble in a Frame of red Marble, very plain, & at Top these Arms with Supporters, *viz:* a Castle, impales, Or, a cross Gules, & in the first Quarter a Lion rampant Sable, for Burke or Burgh, of the Clanrickard Family, & on it this Epitaph.

> Cy dessous git le corps
> du tres noble Dame,
> Milady Honoria Burke,
> Fille de Milord Jean
> Comte de Clanrickard,[2]
> Nièce du Maréchal
> Duc de Berwick,
> Epouse de Messire Jean
> Kelly, Gentilhomme,
> Seigneur Irlandois, décé-
> dée le XXIX du Mois de Juin
> l'An M.DCC.XLII.
> Agée de trente cinque Ans.
> Requiescat in Pace.

In the *Irish Compendium*, p. 70, printed in the year 1735, is no Mention made of the Husband of her

---

[1]Long ago demolished.   [2]John Bourke, *ob.* 1722.

Ladyship, who possibly might not then be married, tho'
those of her 3 Sisters are recorded.

On the South or right Side of the Choir, near the
Door into it from the Isle, & not far from the High
Altar are two antient Altar Tombs of white Marble; the
one upon the Steps above the Door of a Man in Armour
lying on it, & the other just below the Door of a Lady
of the same Sort, in the Dress of her Times. On the
opposite Side, below the Door into the North Isle, &
touching the End of the Friers' Stalls in their large
gloomy Choir, is a Table Monument of black Marble,
on the Top of which is carved the Figure of a Religious:
& above the Door on the Steps or just at the Foot of
them, for I forget which, is a very beautiful Altar
Tomb of a Man in Armour reclined on his right Side
reading on a Book open by his Knees, with a Couple of
Books on the other Side of him at his Feet, all in Cast
Copper, & exquisitely finished: this elegant Tomb is
designed for Albertus Pius, Marquis of Carpio, who
being despoiled of his Estates in Italy retired into
France & was Governor of Piedmont, & dying at Paris
in 1535, was buried here in the Habit of St Francis.
Behind the Altar, on either Side, in the rounding of it,
& inclosed by Balustrades, lie 2 very old Monuments,
quite close to the Back or Sides of it: that on the right
Side is of a Bp mitred, with his Crosier in his Hand, in
White Marble on an Altar Tomb: but both the Tombs
& the strait Places they are confined in, are very dirty
& slovenly. In this celebrated Franciscan Convent,
founded in the Life Time of St Francis himself, lie
buried 3 of its most celebrated Doctors, Nicholas de
Lira, John Scot the subtil Doctor,[1] & our Countryman

[1] Duns Scotus.

Alexander Hales[1] the irrefragable Doctor: but their Tombs being in the Chapter House, I did not see them: no more than I did that of the Prior of Crato, Don Antonio who called himself King of Portugal both in England & France, where he died in 1595, after King Philip of Spain was in real Possession of that Kingdom. Several of the respectable Family of Lamoignon have also Monuments in this Church, from whence I went to the Parish Church of St Cosme,[2] in the Ruë de la Harpe, & not far from this Convent, which is very small & squat, the Choir also being very small, which has been lately repaired with very gentile & neat Decorations: the Altar is very elegant, in a round Figure & composed of blew & white Marble.[3] In this Church the famous learned Brothers of the Name of Du Puy,[4] Authors of the *Gallia Christiana* or *Sacra,* lie buried, with long Epitaphs, & against a Pillar of the left Hand of the Nave, near the Door into the Street is a very elegant mural Monument with his Bust & Medallion in white Marble for the famous Surgeon Monsr la Peyronie. At no great Distance from this in the Rue St Jacques or near it, stands the Parochial & collegiate Church of St Benedict, which is a Gothic Building, with 2 Isles on the right or South Side, with neat Pews in them, according to the English Manner—which, however, disguises a Church, & only serves for sleeping Places. The Choir is very beautiful & newly fitted up, with Corinthian Columns about the Altar in an elegant Stile, & very different from every other Part of the Church.

[1]Alexander of Hales, *ob.* 1245.   [2]Suppressed in 1790.
[3]The church, as such, was closed in 1813.
[4]Pierre and Jacques, Royal librarians; but the *Gallia Christiana* is by D. de Ste-Marthe.

From hence I drove to the Parish Church of St Hilary,[1] which is small & nothing extraordinary: & as I was coming out of it, being told by my French Servant that an English College was just by, I walked down a Street just opposite to it, & a little way down, on the right Hand, entered into a very tolerable Quadrangle with good & lofty Buildings all round it: the Chapel, directly in the Centre of the Front as you entered the Court, was a new & elegant neat Building both within & withoutside, something like several of our Chapels at Cambridge, with several Monuments in it on the Floor & Walls: but as I had asked Leave to see their Chapel of a Priest in the Court, where were about 20 of them in their Habits, & as they had called the Principal, a very tall old Man, thin & paralitic, who introduced me into it, where 2 Priests were on their Knees before the Holy Sacrament in their Sacerdotal Vestments on Account of the 40 Hours' Prayers for the Dauphin. I did not think it decent or proper to be inquisitive either by my Words or Looks when they were so solemnly engaged in that Place: so that I know not for whom the Monuments were erected. This was a Seminary for the Irish Nation;[2] the Principal whereof was named Devereux, who was very obliging & civil, & intreated me much to go with him to his Apartments: which I should certainly have done had my Time allowed it: but as I was going to the great Monastery of St Geneviève, just by, where I expected to be much taken up, I excused myself to him.

Before I went into the Abbey Church of St Geneviève, I stept into the Parish Church of St Stephen du Mont, they standing close together in an open trian-

[1]Demolished in 1795.
[2]Séminaire des Prêtres Irlandais, in the Rue des Carmes.

gular Space, with their Fronts upon a Line with one
another: the Abbey Church having but a very mean
Appearance. The Front of St Stephen's, which stands
to the left of the other, on a Flight of many Steps, but
without any Columns before it, is very rich in Statues,
Niches & other Ornaments in Stone Work, but without
any Sort of Taste in either Gothic or Roman Architecture, but a Jumble between both, which is worst of
all: however, the Inside of it, even in this Stile, is a very
beautiful Building, & very large, the Pillars of which
are constructed in a very particular Stile, a Gallery
running from one to the other, & a neat round Gallery
in Stone Work round each of them. The Arch going
into the Choir from the Nave of Stone is very finely
carved, & of a curious Design, but rather heavy, over
which stand the Crucifix & Figures of our Lady & St
John the Evangelist very well executed. The Choir is
large & very beautiful, with a very rich Marble Altar
Peice: & the Chapel of our Lady behind it is a very
finished Peice: as is the Pulpit in the Nave of a most
curious Design, with Angels sounding their Trumpets
on the Top of it. Racine the Poet, & Pascal[1] the
Jansenist & cutting Writer of the *Lettres Provinciales*,
are buried in this Church, from whence there is a
Passage in the Nave on the South or right Hand, by a
Groupe of Figures in the East Wall representing the
History of our Lord's being laid in his Tomb, (the
Figures as big as Life), into the North Isle of the Abbey
Church of St Geneviève, which is a dull, heavy, gloomy
Building, & of no great Capacity for so Royal a
Foundation:[2] I take it St Etienne du Mont is both
longer & wider. In this North Isle you ascend many

[1]Paschal(MS.).   [2]The Church, except a tower, was demolished in 1807.

Steps into the Chapel where the Shrine of St Geneviève
is placed, & beyond which is a very handsome Chapel,
in which are preserved, as I suppose, the Relics of St
Clotildis, Wife of Clovis, Founder of the Church: on
the right Side of which, by the Side of the Shrine of St
Geneviève, which is exactly behind the High Altar, is a
neat Chapel, against the Eastern Wall of which is
placed a most sumptuous Tomb of Francis, Cardinal de
la Rochefoucault, Abbat of this Monastery, who died
in 1647 at the Age of 87 years. He is represented in
white Marble, in his Cardinal's Robes, kneeling on a
Sarcophagus of black Marble, & admirably executed.[1]
The Shrine of St Geneviève may be seen above the High
Altar, in the Choir, being a very antient & rich Chest or
Gothic Church, ornamented with Jewels of great Lustre
& Value: it was raised upon 4 fine marble Pillars, which
stand on a Marble Base or Pedestal, & the Shrine itself
being supported by the Figures of 4 Women in full
Proportion, I thought its Situation much too elevated:
at least I should not have been pleased with the office
which I saw executed by 2 of the Canons or Priests of
the Church, who were mounted on Ladders & Balustrades, lighting the Wax Candles about the Shrine,
which the 4 Women's Figures held in Branches in one
of their Hands. The Organs were playing all the Time
I was there, on Account of the Shrine's being uncovered,
& the Holy Sacrament's being exposed. Multitudes of
People were there at their Devotions on this Occasion
which prevented my taking more Notice of an old
Marble covered with Brass, which lies in the Choir near
the Entrance into it, being the Figure of a Religious,
probably one of the Abbats, tho' it had no Mitre on his

[1] By Phillippe Buister.

Head. Just by this stands the most elegantly designed
Brass Eagle I ever saw: the Support of it being an
antient Lire or Harp on which 3 Angels at the 3 Angles
of it are playing with their Fingers, & seem to touch it
so lightly & delicately as to draw Harmony from it. A
little higher up, in the middle of the Choir, is the
curious old Tomb of King Clovis, the first Christian
King & Founder of the Church, now called St Geneviève in Paris, who died in the year 511. This Tomb is
very well preserved, except that some of the Fleurs-de-
Lis on his Crown are broken: tho' I don't think they
were ever such perfect ones as Father Montfaucon has
represented them in the Draught he has given us of the
Figure on the Monument, in his 1st vol: of *Antiquitez
de la Monarchie Françoise*, p. 58. No more than that at
the End of the clumsy Sceptre in his right Hand. But
however that may be, this can determine nothing in
Respect to the Antiquity of the Fleurs-de-Lis being
originally affected to the French Monarchs & Monarchy: I have copied into my various Volumes of
Antiquities, cheifly in Regard to Cambridgeshire,
Hundreds of old original Seals, & have seen Thousands
of them, where the Impress was an awkward Kind or
Fleur-de-Lis; used by Men & Women of a very
inferior Rank. In short, it seems to me, that the Form of
that Flower, especially what is usually drawn for it, is
the most obvious & natural of all Forms for the
Termination of a Sceptre, or the Device of an oblong
Seal, such as they used when Seals first came in Fashion:
for Instance, a Point with 2 Curves on the Sides of it, to
give it an Air: & this I take the original of the Fleur-de-
Lis to be.[1] Besides, this Tomb is confessedly no

---

[1] Usually now regarded as representing the head of a weapon.

R

antienter than the 12th Century, when the Canons
rebuilt their Church, which had been destroyed by the
Normans, who, it is supposed, broke the Tomb of
Clovis in order to rifle the Body, which used to be
interred with many Jewels of rich Ornaments about it,
at that Time: & it is probable the new Tomb was made
according to the Fashion which then prevailed, rather
than after the old Figure, if there was any, that was on
the original Tomb: & for this Reason: because the old
Statues which the French Antiquaries assign to King
Clovis, are all of them dressed in the loose Habit,
thrown over their Shoulders *à la Romaine*, & not in a
Sort of Cloak as this is at St Geneviève. He is represented lying on a black Marble Table, in white Marble,
crowned, with a thick Beard & long Hair, with a Sort
of Cassock buckled round his Body with a long Belt, to
which hangs on his left Side a Satchel; his right Hand
holds a Sceptre of Brass or Copper, & his left Hand
takes hold of an open Cloak which falls down behind &
on both Sides of him, by a String or Riband which joins
it at the Neck or before his Breast. That this was the
Fashion of dressing Persons of Distinction on their
Tombs about the 11th or 12th Century, is very evident
from a most curious one of this Sort still in Being in the
Parish Church of Ramsey in Huntingdonshire, where
I took a Draught of it in the year 1744,[1] & may be seen
in my 5th Volume of MS. Collections, p. 103. where
Ailwin, Cousin to King Edgar, Alderman of all England, & Founder of the Abbey of Ramsey, who died in
993, is habited much in the same Manner as Clovis, &
his left Hand holding the String which fastens the
Cloak or Robes over his Shoulders. I have a Print of

[1] *Add. MSS.* 5806, p. 102.

Ailwin's Tomb, drawn by the late ingenious Dr
Stukeley in 1719 & inscribed to his Friend & Brother-
in-Law Samuel Gale Esqr. I have also a Drawing of it
in Indian Ink, which I met with by Accident: but
neither of them are exactly like that which I took on the
Spot: tho' both, perhaps, may be more like the Original
than my poor rough Sketch of it, where I have made
his left Foot rest upon a Bird, an Eagle perhaps; which
is taken no Notice of in the 2 others, which also make
the Shape of the Stone to be nearly parellel on the
Sides: whereas if mine is right, it is in the Shape of an
old Coffin Stone, much broader at the Head than at the
Feet. (As Dr Stukeley was an excellent Draughtsman,
he having shewn me at his own House near Queen's
Square, several Volumes of Drawings, both of Antiquities & Views of Countries & Buildings, I am at a
Loss to account for so manifest a mistake either in his
or my Drawing of the same Thing). But to return to
King Clovis his Tomb, which 'till within about 100
years ago, laid very near the Floor, but was then raised
about 3 Feet from the Ground, & is now an Altar
Tomb,[1] on one of the Sides of which was then added
this Inscription in Honour of their Founder, the first
Christian King of France: tho' from the Turn of it, it
might formerly have been an Altar Tomb, then of
ordinary & common Stone, which was by the Abbat &
Canons converted into Marble.

> Clodovaeo Magno, Regum Francorum primo Christiano
> Hujus Basilicae Fundatori
> Sepulchrum vulgari olim Lapide structum,
> Et longo Ævo deformatum,
> Abbas et Conventus meliori Opere,
> Cultu et Forma renovaverunt.

[1] Removed during the Revolution and in 1816 transferred to St Denis.

Just above this Tomb are the Steps up to the High Altar, which is very elegant & handsome, on which stands a most beautiful & rich Tabernacle with Pillars of Marble & composed of all Sorts of rich Marbles of various Colours, with Ornaments of gilt Copper & Images about it, with those of St Peter & St Paul, to whom the Church was originally dedicated, on each Side of the Altar, which is surrounded by a Balustrade of Marble covered on the Top with Brass: and behind this Altar, which may be surrounded, stands the Shrine of St Geneviève upon 4 very high Pillars: of which I had a better view than standing below, as an officer of the Church carried me up into a little Tribune or Gallery on the right Hand of the Altar, & near it, from whence you have a good view of the Shrine & its Richness. St Geneviève is the Patroness of Paris, & her Shrine is carried in Procession round the City, & to Notre Dame on any public Calamity. In the Nave, on each Side two, are 4 most magnificent Pictures in Frames of great Price, representing as many Deliverances thro' the Intercession of this Saint: those on the North are for Deliverances from Dearth & Dryness: one on the other Side is to represent a Deliverance from a rainy Season, & the other to return Thanks, as well as I can recollect, for the Recovery of the Health of his present Majesty, thro' the Prayers of this Saint, & to which the Abbat's Mandate at p. 241, as I take it, alludes. All these fine Pictures were Vows, given by the City of Paris, to this Church, in Return for Benefits received thro' the Mediation of its Patroness. Her original Tomb, a great clumsy Thing, of no Kind of Beauty, is in a Crypt just under the Altar above, which is on many Steps, & the Chapels beyond, & about it: at the Head of it, which

stands in the middle of this Crypt, & by 2 Pillars which
support the Roof, between which, is a small Altar, on
which is a curious Cross & an *Ecce Homo* made out of a
single Peice of Coral, & given to this Altar by Father
Claud Molinet,[1] a Canon Regular of this House &
Author of the beautiful Book, called, *Le Cabinet de la
Bibliothèque de Ste Geneviève*, printed at Paris in 1692,
in Folio, with his own Print, & several Views of the fine
Library in this Abbey & Plates of all the Curiosities &
Medals then contained in it. On this Altar at the Head
of St Geneviève's old Tomb, (which has no Part of her
Relics remaining in it, all being put into her Shrine,
even to the Boards of her Coffin), is the first Mass said
in this Church every Morning at 5 o'Clock. I understood this old Tomb was for St Clotildis, Queen to
Clovis: but the *Description of Paris*, p. 496, Vol: 2. says
otherwise, & I might, & certainly did, misunderstand
the Man who shewed me this Crypt: which was
presently as full of People as it could hold, it being
always lock'd up: but the Man as quickly voided it, that
I might see it at my Leisure. Beyond this Crypt &
Tomb is another small Chapel of our Lady, also under
Ground, at the Entrance into which, on both Sides, in
Arches, in the North & South Walls, & not far from
the Foot of the aforesaid old Tomb, are 2 others seemingly of as great an Antiquity, being plain ordinary
monuments of Stone or Cement over it, looking like
great old fashioned Boxes or Chests, with round or
arched Covers: the one is for St Prudentius,[2] & the
other for St Ceranus, both antient Bps of Paris. That
on the right Hand in coming in, has had an Hole broke

[1]Claude Dumolinet.

[2]Bp of Troyes; not admitted as a saint by the Bollandists.

in the Top of it. In the North Isle, by the Side of the Choir, against the North Wall, is a mural Monument for the famous James Rohault,[1] the ablest Mathematician of his Time: & not far distant, against a Pillar of the Nave, nearest the Choir & this Tomb of Rohault, is a Bust above the mural Monument of white Marble, for the more celebrated René Descartes. I also went all round this celebrated Convent, first by a Sort of Court, leaving a large Statue of St Geneviève on the left Hand in a Nich[e], of white Stone, & near a Fountain, into the Cloysters, which are new & stately, as their Dormitory also is, & much more their magnificent Library, in the Form of a Cross, with a Dome in the middle; (Plans of which may be seen in Father Molinet his Book): the Staircase up to it is truly noble. Their Gardens are very handsome, & one Hall by them with Pillars in the middle, full of the Portraits of Popes, & called the *Salle des Papes*, pleased me very much. In the Cloysters is a very handsome & large Chapel, called *La Chapelle de la Miséricorde*, with a Vestibule or Passage before you go into it: the Altar of it is very handsome with a large Crucifix on it of wrought Copper with Figures by it: & in the middle of the Chapel, about a Foot from the Ground lies a most beautiful Tomb of cast Copper, being an Abbat of this House, called Joseph Foulon, in his Mitre & Cope, who died in 1607, & to my Mind, I hardly ever saw a more finished Peice: To say more of the Library & Cabinet of Curiosities would be needless, as there is so exact an Account of them in the Book by Father Molinet. The old Church is to be pulled down as soon as the new one, now in Building, & already raised about 20 or 30 Foot

[1] 1620-75; a zealous Cartesian.

from the Ground [is completed]: it stands to the North
West of the present Church some 20 or 30 yards & is
built of a fine Stone of a yellowish Cast, like that with
which Clare Hall in Cambridge is built: the Vaults &
Chapels underneath this glorious Church, supported by
vast Pillars & Arches, & which are divided into Isles,
(Part of it being designed for sacred use), look very
nobly: & the Church, in the Form of a Cross, with a
fine Dome in the Middle, according to a Plan which I
saw hanging up in a Window of the Library, nearest
the Church & looking upon it, when finished, will be
one of the noblest & grandest Piles of Building in Paris.
I went from hence to the Palace of Luxembourg, whose
Gallery on the right Side of the Court as you enter it,
painted by Rubens, is so justly famous. It is a very
magnificent Pile of Building, of one single large
Quadrangle, with an Ascent of a few Steps towards the
further End of it across the Court, which conducts you
thro' the Front Arch, by dirty & ill-looking Staircases,
to the spatious & fine Gardens behind it. It was built by
Queen Mary of Medicis, whose Statue, with those of
her Husband Henry 4th & her Son Lewis 13, are in the
Front nearest the Street or open Place before it.[1] The
Front of it stands in the spatious Street called La Rue
de Vaugirard & fronts the Rue Tournon: it has very
spatious Gardens & Walks, which are public for the use
of the City.
   At the Back of these Gardens, are the very large ones
also of the Carthusians, in the Faubourg St Michel, at
no vast Distance from the Royal Observatory, by the
Rue d'Enfer, which runs parellel a great Way with the

[1] It is now uninhabited since the death of the late Queen Dowager
of Spain. [C.]

Rue St Jacques. The Entrance into the Carthusians Church or Chapel, (for it has no Isles), is a long Room, with a small Antechapel, is by a very ordinary-looking Porch: there are a few Stalls in the Antechapel, (for the Lay Brothers), which are very handsome, of modern workmanship; as are those of the Monks on both Sides of the Chapel, which are plain, without any Elbows or Pillars between them; but like those in Trinity College in Cambridge, the whole Chapel being very like it, except not near so large, elegant or handsome. The Altar is neat, & there are very fine Pictures against the Walls, above the Stalls. But the Paintings which are most famous in this Convent are those in the small or lesser Cloyster, round which are painted in different *Compartiments*, with long Copies of Latin Verses in adjoyning Partitions explaining each Picture, the Life & Death of the good St Bruno,[1] the Founder of this rigid Order, by the Pencil of Le Sueur. They are not near so big as Life, & are most excellently painted: but I must needs own, to my Confusion in Painting be it spoken, that had I not been before told of their Excellency & Perfection, it is more than probable that I should have passed them by without much Observation. The Weather has injured the Painting in many Places: for which Reason they have folding Doors to cover them & preserve them from injury. The painted Glass Windows in this Cloyster, with Bordures & Devices, are very neat & elegant. The great Cloyster at the Back of the Monks' Cells is rather ordinary, & the great green Quadrangle within it, in which the Monks are buried, (there being several Graves & Crosses on the Turf), is kept very slovenly. Each Monk has a small

[1] 1030-1101.

House & Garden, which he cultivates himself, to his own proper use. These Houses you see in the Quadrangle, & have upper Rooms & are divided from one another. I saw them all at their Devotions in their Stalls, where their Comportment was very affecting: there seemed to be about 40 in all, or perhaps not so many. After seeing so many Things, & walking about so much, I was glad to get Home after 4 o'Clock to Dinner, & while I was at it, a Frier of the Hospital *de la Charité* called upon me for Something for his Hospital, which being given to him, he told me very civilly, that if either myself or Servant should be so unfortunate as to be ill, & have Occasion for their Service, he desired me to send to them & one of the Friers, who are of the Order of St John of God & are dressed much as the Franciscans are, except in darker Habits, would attend me. Their House is just by, in the Rue des Sts Pères, which goes down to the River, & runs parallel to the Rue des Petits Augustins.

Sunday, Nov: 17. Fine Day, but no Sun. I did not stir out 'till 3 o'Clock, when I went to Dinner to the Hôtel du Parc Royal. While we were at Dinner a Message came from the Duchess of Richmond to desire Mr Walpole to go with her Grace this Evening to the French Comedy: but he was engaged to be in the Evening at Madame Chabot's,[1] an House which he shewed me in a Square the first Time I went out with him, as also the House where the celebrated Madame de Sevignè [lived], (a Corner House, which he carried me on Purpose to see, not far from the Port St Antoine,

---

[1]Lady Mary Howard, daughter of the Earl of Stafford, who married Comte, afterwards Duc, de Rohan-Chabot. *Cf. Letters of Hor. Walpole* (Toynbee), No. 1060 (Oct. 15, 1765).

or the Entrance upon the Boulevarts, as well as I
remember). He received a Letter from Calais from the
Comte de Guerchy,[1] the French Embassador in England, & another from Mr Thomas Gray of Pembroke
Hall in Cambridge.[2] When I left him I took a Coach &
went to the Opera in the Thuilleries. Mr Walpole's
Swiss Servant Louis went with my Servant, & I paid
for their Admission: but on their not being able to get
Places in an uppermost Gallery, they were admitted,
(as both were well-dressed & not in Liveries), into a
Box or *Loge* on the other Side of the House, exactly
fronting where I sat myself. Here I could not but observe the gay & sprightly Turn of the French: in the
same *Loge* where I was, & in those on each Side of me,
were several Ladies & Gentlemen, the Ladies painted
most frightfully without any Art, on their Cheeks with
red, & all of them, both Men & Women singing aloud
with the Actors & Performers on the Stage: which
provoked me exceedingly, & I heartily wished them
further from me: for they absolutely spoiled, by their
indifferent Howling & Noise, the whole of my Entertainment: as it was impossible to distinguish the better
Voices on the Stage.

Monday, Nov: 18. Tolerable fine Day, & no Sun.
Mr Walpole agreed to call upon me to go with him to
the Palais Royal, or House of the Duke of Orleans, near
the Rue St Honoré, where is the choicest Collection of
Pictures in Paris; he was to have been with me at 11

---

[1]Claude-Louis-François de Regnier (1715-67); Walpole held him
in high esteem; *cf.* W.'s *Memoirs of the Reign of George III* (1894),
i. 240.

[2]For this (undated) letter, see *Correspondence of Gray, Walpole, West
and Ashton,* edited by Paget Toynbee, 1915, ii. 236.

o'Clock, but his Cousin Mr Walpole[1] being just arrived at Paris from England, & after he was gone, Madame Geoffrin calling also upon him, detained him 'till near 1 o'Clock: which was the more unlucky, as I had promised M[r] Theodore Eynhouts, to dine with him in the Rue de Bussy at 2 o'Clock: so I sent & begged he would not expect me 'till towards 3. The Front to the Street is very regular & handsome, with a good Opening before it, & on one Side of it the new & stately Opera House now in Building. You enter the Palais Royal in your Coach into the first Court, which I suppose are cheifly Offices on the Ground Floor, & a second Court had Coaches in it. We ascended to go to the Guard Chamber, by a Staircase in the right Hand Corner of the first Court: I suppose a private Way: for I hardly ever saw so dirty, nasty & stinking a Place for such a Purpose: however, when you had passed this rather Approach to a Gaol, than a Prince's Palace, you saw nothing but Carving, Gilding & the utmost Finery, both in the Building itself & its Furniture. In one of the first Apartments I saw a full Length Picture of Cardinal Richelieu, the first Builder of this Palace; & in another near it one of a Duchess of Richmond, in the same size, I think the celebrated Frances Howard, with a long Cane in her Hand, & a Bell on a Table by her.[2] I think in the same fine square Room was another of Sir Thomas More, Lord Chancellor of England, & in another fine Room, fronting the beautiful Gallery, was a vast large Picture of King Charles I. sitting in a Chair,

[1]Hon. Thomas Walpole, *ob.* 1803; merchant and banker; son of Lord Walpole of Wolteston.

[2]For a lively account of this remarkable woman see Arthur Wilson, *The History of Great Britain* [or rather of James I] 1653, pp. 258-9.

with his Family about him, said to be painted by
Vandyke: but Mr Walpole, whose Judgement in these
Matters, as well as in most others, I would sooner
depend on than any one else, assured me, after a mature
Examination of it, that it was only a good Copy of the
famous one in England at one of the Royal Palaces. I
could with Pleasure have remained here for many Days,
& therefore my being obliged to hurry over the few
Apartments I could look into, was very unfortunate.
The Pictures by the most Capital Masters are alone
worth a long Journey to come & look at; & indeed I
never was more entertained in my Life. The Furniture
also, & Proportions of these fine Apartments are well
worthy of a Stranger's nicest Observation: the Lustres,
vast Looking Glasses, Cabinets of various Sorts, some
painted in Miniature, choice Tables of the finest
Marbles, on which were Bronzes & Busts of exquisite
Workmanship, all made me regret the Shortness of my
Time: for after I had been to the further End of the
most beautiful Gallery painted by Coypel with the
History of Virgil's *Enead* & admired the Chimney at
the End of it, I was obliged to take my Leave of Mr
Walpole, who sent me to the Rue de Bussy in his *Vis-à-Vis*, designing to stay there 2 Hours longer. The cheif
Thing that displeased me in these fine Apartments, was
the Slipperiness of the waxed Floors, on which I was
afraid of falling down every Step I took. When I got to
Mr Eynhouts I made the best Excuse for my making
them wait Dinner: but was told, that Madame was but
just come in, & was not yet come down Stairs; & we
waited a full Quarter of an Hour before Madame
appeared in the Shape of one of the most uncouth, short,
fat, squab Personages I ever met with: yet with all these

Disadvantages, added to as plain a Visage, & as much
wrinkled as her Fat would allow it, for I suppose she
was turned of 60, she aimed at the Airs which would not
have became her 40 years before. She was dressed in a
Quaker Colour brownish Silk Sack, with no Stays, &
quite at her Ease; & tho' the Room we dined in was
rather a dark Closet than any Thing else, with a very
large Fire in it, yet Madame had a Pot with Embers in
it (a Convenience used very commonly by the Ladies in
Paris, as I saw by the Quantities of them exposed to Sale
as you passed by the Shops) to put under her Petticoats,
to keep her Feet warm. After a good Deal of foolish
Noise & Parade as she came down Stairs & into the
Room, I suppose, to make herself taken Notice of, which,
had she had a Grain of good Sense she would have
avoided, she placed herself in her Chair without taking
the least Notice of any of the Company, which consisted
only of her Husband, who I observed was only a Cypher,
tho' a good large one; her Neice, a young Woman of
about 25 years of Age, handsome & well-behaved, a
native of Lyons, & only dressed in an ordinary Linen
Gown, like a common maid-Servant in England, (where,
thank God, every Degree in Life, except the very
highest, are dressed, & look better, than those of the
same Degree in France), & myself. During a good Part
of the Dinner the same Contemptuous Behaviour was
Continued; when observing that these grand Airs made
no Impression upon me, but [were] possibly to her
Disadvantage, she veered about, & began to be wonderful civil, & very inquisitive, & at last, to complete the
Scene, to be very abusive of her Husband, & Contemptuous of his Country : while he, poor Soul, was obliged
contentedly, as well as myself, to sit, & hear her talk her

Nonsense, & expose herself, while she thought she was
exposing him, & setting out herself to Advantage in the
Estimation of a Stranger: during which Time he sat
eating his Victuals & drinking his Goblets of Wine, with
as much Composure as if she had been asleep, or saying
nothing: which was a sure Sign to me, that it was no
new Scene, but had been repeated so often as to have
lost all its Effect. Among other Things she was pleased
to tell me before him at Table, one was, That she really
believed she was the first Parisian that ever married a
Dutchman: that she had been deceived absolutely in his
Country & thought that he was a Fleming, who, she
said, had more Politeness & wit, (*Esprit* was the Expression she made use of) than the Hollanders or Dutch,
who were, she said, the greatest Clowns, & Blockheads
under the Sun. I sincerely say not a Syllable more than
she uttered. I was quite shocked at her Grossness, &
could not tell how to behave: so did as the 2 others in
Company did, take no Notice of her: but had she been
mine, as she was Mr Eynhouts' Wife, I should have
thrown a very good Soupe into her Face, Dish & all.
We had a very good Dinner, one Thing at a Time, &
good Wine: a Maid Servant only waiting, & my
English Servant in the Kitchin: for the Room was not
big enough to contain any more. One Thing I observed
worthy of Imitation, which was, the Practice of setting
a large Silver Tumbler or Goblet of about half a Pint
by the Master & Mistress's Plate, & others of Glass
or Plate for the Rest of the Company: which cleanly
method entirely avoids the disagreable Circumstance of
drinking after other People: but however well contrived
this Practice might be, that of having coarse ordinary
Table Linen, & hardly clean, with dirty Spoons &

Knives, was not so laudable: but what offended me more
than all their Dirt, was the Beastliness of Madame, who
with all her affected Airs, was constantly hawking, &
spitting upon the Floor, during the whole Time of
Dinner. However disgustful this may be to an Englishman, he must away with it, or keep at Home: even the
greatest Ladies & Men of the first Fashion are continually doing so, or what is still nastier, pulling out
their white, or rather whitish Hankercheifs, &
spitting half Snuff & half something else, into them:
for every Frenchman is a Snuff-taker. An Instance Mr
Walpole gave me of the Nastiness of their Conversation,
which would be highly offensive to any English Company, & which I should not have believed, had I not
been told it by him, who never exaggerates, was this: I
was giving him a Description of my Entertainment at
Madame Eynhouts, & particularly of her continual
hawking & spitting about at Dinner Time: he assured
me it was the same in better Company, and told me that
not two Days before dining at one of the greatest Tables
in Paris, with a Great Deal of French Nobility, it was
the same during the whole Course of their Dinner, &
that in particular, a blind Lady of Fashion & great
Distinction for her Wit & Understanding,[1] in the
Middle of Dinner, while they were talking of the
Dauphin's little Prospect of Recovery, assured the
Company, that His Royal Highness had a greater
Chance than they were aware of: that she had received
a Letter that very Morning from Fountainbleau, giving
her an Account that he had happily had a very stinking
& faetid Stool the Evening before, & that in great

---

[1]Mme Du Deffand; *cf. Letters of Hor. Walpole* (Toynbee), No. 1070
(Nov. 12, 1765).

Abundance. It is possible that we carry our Delicacy in this & many other Points to too great Lengths: (particularly in the Decency of not going to necessary Conveniences, especially among the Ladies, when it is dangerous often to abstain from it): but surely nothing can countenance bringing such nasty Ideas into Question, at Meals more especially, but the having a Stomach callous to all Sensation & Feeling of a delicate Texture. I should not have dwelt so long upon so filthy a subject, but to shew the French in their true Light, of despising all Mankind, when none deserve it more than themselves, & of giving poor Mr Eynhouts his Revenge in exposing his conceited Wife. I suppose he might some 20 or 30 years ago have been a very portly & handsome jolly Dutchman, & thereby excited the carnal Part of his Parisian Wife's Affection, who, I apprehend, may be some ten years older than him: who, notwithstanding his Bulk, & Carbuncle Face, is still as pleasant an Object as herself. I paid him for my Dozen of Shirts & 6 Cravatts, £9. 14s. 6d., & taking my Leave of them as soon as decently I could, I walked to the Abbey Church of St Germain's des Prez, where I staid Vespers & *Salut*, performed as before at p. 241 for the Dauphin's Recovery.

Tuesday, 19 *Nov:* Fine Day. After Breakfast I called upon Mr Livier in the Rue St André des Arcs, whose Wife went with me to the Sainte Chapelle, where she heard Mass, & afterwards to a little Shop exactly before the great West Door, upon the Steps, where she cheapened for me a Necklace of Marchesite[1] for Mrs

---

[1]Marcasite and fire-stone are forms of iron-pyrites, popular as ornaments in the eighteenth century. *Cf.* Goldsmith, *She Stoops to Conquer*, Act III: "The ladies . . . carry their jewels to town, and bring nothing but paste and marcasites back".

Goodwin of Loughton in Buckinghamshire, Mrs Holt's Daughter, with a Pair of Ear-Rings of Fire-Stone, both which cost £3. 13s. 6d., a Pair of Ear-Rings for my Neice Apthorp which cost 17s, a Hoop Marchesite which I intended for a Present to Mrs Sanderson, (Daughter of Sir Christopher Hale, Baronet, & just then married to Mr Sanderson, Rector of Newton-Longueville), with other Trifles. After I had set Mrs Livier down at her House, I drove over the Pont-Neuf into the Ville & Quartier de St Honoré, & went to see the Parish Church of St Eustace, which is situated in a very crampt & narrow Street: the South Side of which, to the Street, is much ornamented with Sculpture, especially about the Portico. It is a large & handsome Church, built in a Stile between the Gothic & Roman, yet far from being ugly: it has a double Row of Pillars & 2 Isles on each Side all round the Church, which is terminated with a *Rond Point* or semi-circular End, & very handsomely vaulted all over with Stone, & of a great Height. In the Nave stands the elegant Pulpit against one of the Pillars, very finely carved, & on the opposite Side, *viz:* the North, is a very large Pew with a Canopy above it, in a *Compartiment* of which I observed the Story of St Eustace on his Knees by his Horse & before a Buck which has a Cross between its Horns. The High Altar in the handsome Choir has 4 very fine Marble Corinthian Pillars to support it, & behind it on the left Hand or North Side, under an Arch made on Purpose, being Part of the Monument, stands the very fine & noble Tomb of the famous Minister of State to Lewis 14, John-Baptist Colbert,[1] of various coloured Marbles: his Statue, on his Knees, dressed in the Robes of

---

[1]Jean Baptiste Colbert (1619-83); Minister of Finance.

s

a Knight of the Holy Ghost, is of white Marble & finely
executed, he kneels on a Sarcophagus of black Marble,
& before him, on it, is an Angel, holding an open Book,
in which he seems to be reading, & his Hands closed,
as directing his Devotions to the Altar of the Chapel of
our Lady, just before him, or rather in a Slanting view
of it. About the Tomb are several Devices & Inscriptions descriptive of his Character & Virtues, & at the 2
Ends of it, on round Pedestals, are 2 very fine marble
Statues representing Religion & Abundance. In a very
small Chapel behind, or rather on one Side of this truly
elegant & noble Monument, in Part of which it is
erected, are 3 or 4 Marble Tables of Inscriptions for
some of the same Family. Among many other great
Men interred in this Church are John de la Fontaine, &
Voiture. From hence I went to the Fathers of the
Oratory in the Rue St Honoré where there is a good
Portico to their Church,[1] with Columns on several
Steps: but not being able to get Admission there, I went
down a Street under the Walls of their Church &
Convent, & passed by several of the lower neat Apartments of these Oratorians, into their Church; which is
a modern handsome Building, with a very singular
Altar towards the End of it, on which is placed a very
beautiful Tabernacle of various marble Pillars which
support an elegant Dome: the Altar may be surrounded[2]
on every Side: at the Back of it, towards the Choir in
the East Part of the Church is a Front of black Marble
on which is engraved the Names & Dates of Decease of
4 or 5 Generals of their Order, the last of which was
buried in 1733. On the left Side of this Altar in a very

[1]Became a Protestant Church in 1802.
[2]*I.e.* "circumambulated".

dark & gloomy North Chapel, in a Manner close to it, is a very beautiful Statue & Tomb of the pious Cardinal Peter de Berulle, whose Statue is also at the Carmelite Nuns as described at pp. 134, 135, who is represented Kneeling upon a Sarcophagus, as I have it in my Notes, but I think it is on a large plain Altar Tomb of White Marble, or Pedestal, as well as I can recollect by my Memory, with a very long Inscription in Front in Latin: the Cardinal is in his Robes, the Drapery of which is very finely executed, as well as can be distinguished in so gloomy a Situation, with Hands extended towards the adjoyning High Altar, & looking in a Book which an Angel holds open before him, if my Notes are right, & I have not jumbled this Circumstance with that of the same Sort on Monsieur Colbert's Tomb:[1] for I do not recollect the Angel on this last, which, as well as I can remember is only a single fine white Marble Statue of the Cardinal on the Pediment. It is great Pity it has not a better Situation, as it well deserves it. Perhaps when the Eastern Part of the Church is finished a more becoming & lightsome Place may be found for it. In the Fathers' Choir behind the Altar, on the Walls above the Stalls, are three very large & gaudy Pictures, which may be very fine also, but did not please me.

From hence I went to the Church of St Honoré,[2] which gives its Name to this Street & Quarter of the City, on the opposite Side of the Street, & at no great Distance from the Fathers of the Oratory: it is rather small & dark, having no Pillars in it, being a single Room, the Choir or Sanctuary Part of it being divided by Balustrades, the High Altar being handsomely

[1]The angel, or genius, was on Colbert's tomb.   [2]Demolished in 1790.

ornamented with Pillars, & a good Picture of our Lord
in the Temple disputing with the Doctors, by Philip
Champagne: near which, on the South Side or Right
Hand lies the Body of Wm du Bois,[1] Cardinal Arch-Bp
of Cambray, who, while only Abbé du Bois, had been
employed by his great Patron, Philip D. of Orleans,
Regent of France, as Minister into England, to George
1st. His Tomb however is in a small Chapel on the same
Side of the Church, just as you enter it from the Street,
being a very elegant Statue of his Eminence on his
Knees, (in white Marble, on a Pedestal of the same
Materials) in his Cardinal's Robes, & very like a fine
Print which I have of him, in my large Collection of
Prints, painted by Rigaud in 1723, the year in which he
died, & engraved by Drevet[2] in the year following: on
which Print are these Arms assigned him, Azure 3
Trunks of Trees reared from the Ground & their
Branches without Leaves, in Allusion to his Name of
Bois or Wood, Or, on a chief Gules 3 Mullets of 6
Points peirced, argent. This Bearing Colour on Colour
is what the English Heralds term False Heraldry: but
it is not unusual in the French Blason, who are not so
exact & accurate in the Heraldry as the English:
witness the same Colours in the Feild & Cheif for the
Family of Le Tellier: neither are their Coats so simple
& plain, (a great Merit in Coat Armour), as the English
nor so well-proportioned in their Bearings either of
Ordinaries or Animals, which are usually too large &
out of Proportion, as well as very complicated & too

[1]Guillaume Dubois (1656-1723); negotiated the triple alliance of
England, France and Holland in 1717.

[2]Pierre Drevet (1663-1738); his sons, Pierre Imbert and Claude,
were also engravers.

much like Devices. The Reason of the Cardinal's
Tomb being placed in a different Part of the Church
than where his Body lies interred, as the *Sacristain*
informed me, was, that the Wall was judged too weak
& feeble to support any Ornaments or Parts of the
Monument, & the Place too narrow & circumscribed
for so stately a Tomb; however, where it is now placed
is not much to its Advantage either for Shew or
Neatness: for the Place being dark, tho' in a Manner
close to the Door as you enter the Church, so that it is
not so conveniently seen as it deserves to be, & besides
is all over covered with Dust from its Situation so near
the Door of so frequented a Street: altho' it is a new
Monument, it has already the Appearance of an antient
one, from its dirty Hue. His Hands are extended &
Eyes as looking towards the Altar. The Cardinal was
an Honorary Canon of this Parochial & Collegiate
Church. For some Account of whom you may see in
Baron Polnitz's[1] *Mémoires*, Vol: 2 p. 292, who says that
his Brother was one of the Canons of this small but rich
Church, erected this Monument for him, & added this
Inscription on the Front of the Pedestal. [See G. Brice,
Description de Paris, 1752, i. p. 241.]

In a Chapel opposite to where the Cardinal's Tomb is
placed, but rather higher, is a very beautiful Picture,
over the Altar, of the Adoration of the Shepherds. I
forgot to mention at the Fathers of the Oratory, that
their Altar is of a beautiful & ingenious Contrivance,
representing the Ascension of our Blessed Saviour,
holding in one of his Hands a small plain Cross, under
an Arch or Semi-Circle of Marble supported by 4 fine

[1]Karl Ludwig von Pöllnitz; his *Lettres et Mémoires* published in
1738-40.

red marble Pillars, & the Images below, as well as that of our Lord, are admirable[1] well executed. From hence to the Hospital of the Quinze Vingt, (I mean from the Church of St Honoré), is no great Distance, being on the other Side of the Rue St Honoré, almost opposite to the Palais Royal: the Church is a very old Building, as is evident from the Lowness of its Situation, the Ground being removed at the Entrance into the Church on the Side from the Street, & going down several Steps to the great Portal on one Side of it, which is ornamented with Statues *à l'antique:* it was founded by St Lewis for 300 Blind People, which gave it its Name, 15 Twenties making that Number. The church is small & dark & dismal, & very dirty & ill-lighted: Palisades divide the Nave from the Choir. I observed a most curious Peice of old gothic Sculpture in Stone, at the upper End of the Isle against the East Wall, representing some History, of which I knew not the Subject, in many small Stages, one above the other. Over the Door as you enter this gloomy Church is a small Statue of St Lewis[2] with other Images round about him. By the Ground being removed so much about the Church, it evidently shews how much the City of Paris had been raised in its Streets since the Foundation of this Edifice in 1254.

From this gloomy, I went to the light, elegant & airy Church of St Thomas du Louvre, seated in a very private Corner of a Street, between the 2 Royal Palaces of the Louvre & the Thuilleries. This Collegiate Church was founded in Honour of St Thomas Becket, Arch-Bp of Canterbury, by Robert, Count de Dreux & Clermont, 5th Son of King Lewis the Fat in 1187; but

[1]For "admirably" (*obsol.*).
[2]Removed in 1779 to the *Hôtel des Mousquetaires Noirs.*

being much gone to Decay it was within these few years
taken down, & this beautiful, but small Church built in
its Room, which has indeed more the Appearance of a
large Chapel than a Collegiate Church, tho' very lofty,
it having no Isles or separate Choir in the Building,
being one single Room termined[1] at the East End by a
Semicircle. The High Altar is erected in the Middle of
the Church, surrounded by elegant Balustrades, & on
it is a small gilt Pillar or Support, on which rests by one
Foot an Angel in the Attitude of going to fly, with
Wings expanded, & holding the Tabernacle by a Chain
or Cord in one Hand which hangs over the Altar.
Behind this is the Choir of the Canons, which does not
seem finished, the Walls all round being bare & naked
above the Stalls, except that there are two very antient
Shrines fixed against the Wall by Iron Cramps to
support them, but which don't seem to be in their
proper ornamented Repositories. The first to the left is
very antient, & resembling the old small Shrine of St
Thomas the Martyr at Mr Walpole's House at Strawberry Hill in Twickenham in Middlesex, of which I
have given an imperfect rough Draught in my 40th
Vol: of MS. Collections at p. 151.[2] It is probable this
antient Shrine contains some Relics of the Martyr. The
other on the right Hand of it is Silver gilt, [and] like an
old gothic Church. I did not ask the *Sacristain* to whom
these belonged, as he seemed to be an ignorant Fellow,
as most of those who looked after their Churches
seemed to be. There are 3 Chapels, or Divisions only,

[1]Terminated (*obsol.*).

[2]*Add. MSS.* 5841. "A most curious and venerable piece of antiquity,
in Enamel on Copper, representing the model of the shrine of St
Thomas. . . . Mr Walpole had this curious piece out of the collection
of Thomas Barnet of Kent, Esq." (Perhaps "Barrett" is meant.)

for they are all against the Side Walls, on each Side of
the Church. The first, fronting you, by the Door I
entered it, on the North Side, is the Chapel of St
Thomas Becket, being the nearest on the South Side of
the Church to the High Altar, & very near it; he is
painted on the Altar Peice as being martyred by 2 or 3
Men before the Altar, with a Choirister on one Side by
him. The middle Chapel on this Side, which is deeper
in the Wall, & to represent a Transept or Cross Isle,
but which goes but a very little backwards, is that of our
Lady, & is one of the most superb, beautiful & elegant
Things of the Sort I ever saw. Our Lady is represented
on her Knees in half Relief, or great Basso relievo, with
the Angel saluting her, with a Basket of Peaches,
Apples & other Fruit on the Floor by her, the whole
Marbles & Stucko, (as Part of it appeared to me) of
different Colours, very lofty & exceedingly beautiful &
delicate. This Fronts Cardinal Fleury's Tomb on the
opposite Side. A little below this fine Altar is a small
neat Chapel, near the West Door or grand Entrance, in
which stands a Confessional, & in the same is a very
beautiful modern Picture of St Mary Magdalen on a
Mattrass, before a Crucifix. On the other, or North,
Side opposite to this Chapel of Penance, near the great
West Door also, is another neat Chapel of the same
Sort, used as a Baptistery, in which is a Font, & a
modern Picture of St John the Baptist, baptising our
B. Saviour in the River Jordan. The middle Chapel or
great Arch, which is as the opposite one, a Sort of
Transept Cross Isle, & fronting the Chapel of our Lady,
is quite taken up by a vast large Monument for the late
Cardinal Fleury, Prime Minister of France, at the Time
when the great Sir Robert Walpole, afterwards Earl of

Orford, was in the same station in England, during
whose good (in Comparison of later Administrations)
& happy Administration, tho' maligned & railed
against, England knew & enjoyed the Blessing of
Peace: since which Time we have been in constant
Faction & eternal Wars; or else delivered up into the
rapacious Claws of German Princes: beggarly Princes,
whose cheif Support & Dependence is in their Mer-
cenary Forces, which are ready to fall foul on friend
or foe, just as their Pay & Interest is increased or
withdrawn. No greater or more shameful Instances can
be produced than in the great Protestant Hero, as our
Dissenters & their Friends affected to call the Deistical
King of Prussia.[1] Such another Friend, who has filled
his Coffers pretty well with English Money, is the
wonderful Knight of the Garter, Ferdinand, Uncle to
his Highness the Hereditary Prince of Brunswick, who
married our King's Sister,[2] & is now said, after well
lining his empty Pockets with English Guineas, to be
going with his Prussian Majesty to assist the French
against us & attack Hanover, as usual, in Order to
beggar the Country that is fated to defend it. Never sure
was that just Italian Proverb more certainly verified:

> Da miei Amici mi guarda Dio!
> Da miei Nemici mi guarderò ben'io.

God Almighty defend me from the Designs of my
Friends: from those of my Enemies I will try to defend
& keep myself. Cardinal Fleury is represented as dying,
lying on his left Side, with a Crucifix in one Hand, &
in his Pontifical Robes, with 3 large Statues standing
about the Tomb, which has a Pyramid of fine red
Marble at the Back against the Wall of ye Arch. The

[1]Frederick the Great.   [2]Princess Augusta.

Statues are not yet finished or polished: they were putting them in their Places while I was there, & a large Sackcloth was hung up before them. The Statue of the Cardinal, with the other Figures seemed to me to be vastly too big for their Situation, which is just above the Floor, & that of his worthy Eminence but a little raised above it on a Sarcophagus. The Face, tho' not quite finished, was like his Pictures, particularly one which I have of him painted by Rigaud & engraved by G. Roy, where he is represented as held in a Frame by Diogenes, & a Candle & Lanthorn in his other Hand, with this wrote under him:

Andrè Hercules, Cardinal de Fleury, Grand Aumonier de la Reine, Ministre d'Etat, Grand Maitre & Surintendant des Postes.

> Quem frustra quaesivit Cynicus olim,
>   Ecce inventus adest.
> Dans Athénes jadis tu le cherchois en vain,
> Ridicule Cynique, il devoit naitre en France:
> Cet Homme si parfait, si rempli de Prudence,
>   Nous l'avons trouvé pour certain,
> Sans avoir, comme toi, la Lanterne à la Main:
>   Sufit de voir Son Eminence.

[A print by J. B. Scotin is also described.]

The Collection of Prints in a great Number of Folio Volumes at Strawberry Hill is designed by the Honourable Possessor of them, as he told me about 3 years ago [I write this July 20, 1766, Sunday Evening] at his Death for the Library of Eton College: not that he has any particular Value for that Place, or its Inhabitants, tho' he was the Cause I suppose, of Dr Ashton's being elected Fellow there;[1] but because it is

[1]Ashton became Fellow of Eton in 1745, but that his election was due to Walpole seems to be only a conjecture of Cole's.

a more safe Repository than the University Libraries, & has already a fine Collection of the same Sort, in the Drawings of Mr Topham, whose whole Collection are there deposited. For some Part of the Character of this worthy peaceable Cardinal [Fleury], see Pölnitz's *Memoirs*, Vol: 2, if any Dependance is to be laid on any Account given by so venal & worthless a Writer & Man: for an Account of whose Knaveries & Stratagems, if not exaggerated by some English Writer, on Account of his turning Roman Catholic, Reason more than sufficient for the grossest Abuse in this free Country, see the *Annual Register*, by Dodsley, for the year 1765, Part 2, p. 64.[1] Just above the Tomb of Cardinal Fleury, by the Door as you enter the Church on the North Side, but below the said Door, is another neat Chapel against the North Wall, & just opposite that of St Thomas of Canterbury on the other Side, over the Altar of which, in a modern handsome Picture, he is represented in his Mitre & *Pontificalia* in some sacred office.

When I got Home, over the Pont-Royal I found Mr Armand, a very plain & honest Taylor, who lived at the Sign of *La Folie* in St Germain l'Auxerrois, at my Lodgings to fit my Coat & Waistcoat, & paid him by a Bank of England Bill of 10 Pounds: so readily did these pass in Paris.

Wednesday, 20 *Nov:* Fine Day, cold & Sunshine, with a little Hail for a very short Time at 2 in the Afternoon. At Noon I took a Coach & went to the Convent of English Benedictines in the Rue St Jacques, at the further End of it: for altho' I had heard nothing of any

[1]An elaborate attack on this "Composition of wit, irreligion, odd principles, and baseness of soul".

of them, yet I thought it not civil to Father Sympson, who had recommended me to them, to leave Paris without asking if they had any Commands into England. I found Father Welch, the Prior, at the Convent, who was very pressing for me to dine with him. He was about the Age of 40, an handsome black[1] Man, with a fresh Colour, & 6 Foot high, & was just come to reside here, from a Gentleman's Family in Cumberland, after an Absence of 13 years, when, he told me, he found the French People much altered both in their Religion & Morals. He shewed me his Apartments, up one Pair of Stairs, out of their Cloyster & near the Church, which were neat, small & convenient: their Gardens are small, & from them you discover on one Side the Val de Grace,[2] & on the other a new built Nunnery. In a Window on the North Side or left Hand looking up to the High Altar near the Chapel in which lie the Bodies of King James 2 & his Daughter, are these Arms, *viz:* Gules, a Lion rampant, & a Border engrailed Or, for Talbot, Ensigned with a Green Hat, & a Cross behind the Sheild, from whence descends 2 Dogs or Talbot's Chains, holding 2 of these Animals on a Ground couchant under the Sheild. All very neatly painted. This was designed for the most Reverend Father in God Peter Talbot,[3] Lord Arch-Bp of Dublin, Brother to Richard Talbot, Duke of Tyrconnel, whose Duchess was Sister to Sarah Jenyns Duchess of Marlborough & lies buried at the English Canonesses of St Austin as I have observed at p. 199. This Arch-Bp Talbot had been educated a Jesuit, but had a Licence to quit the Order, & was made by Pope Clement IX,

---

[1]Black-haired.   [2]The church and monastery; see p. 131.
[3]1620-80; he died in Newgate Prison, Dublin; see *D.N.B.*

Arch-Bp of Dublin. (See Dod's *Catholic History*, Vol: 3 p. 284.) My Lord Clarendon in his own *Life*, wrote by himself, 8vo, Edit: 1760, Vol: 1. p. 497 & Vol: 2. p. 269, gives but a very indifferent Account either of his Understanding or Morals. Perhaps he was a Benefactor here, & might be here interred: for not a Soul knew whose Arms they were, no more than they did those of a French Bp's which were in a Window of the same Side, in several Quarters, as well as I can recollect, for I did not so much observe them as I did the English Coats.

In the great West Window are several English Coats of Arms, some of which are much broken: I observed among the Rest, those of the Family of Sheldon, *viz:* Sable a Fesse inter 3 Shell-Drakes Argent, being the Arms of the worthy Family of that Name of Byley in the County of Worcester, always a Roman Catholic Family, as also those of the Family of Latham of Lancashire, *viz*: Or, on a Cheife indented Azure, 3 Plates: which Arms & Family are now ingrafted into the noble Family of Stanley Earl of Derby. The other Arms I did not so particularly observe, as I was not so well acquainted with them, as also for Fear of giving Offence by being too inquisitive & particular in my Observations: which also prevented my asking the Name of a present English Bp of the Benedictine Order, whose Picture was hanging up in the Parlour together with Bonaventure Giffard, Bp of Madaura, his Picture, as the Prior did not name him to me. Bp Giffard's Picture I knew very well, as I have seen a Copy of it at my Friend Mr Throckmorton's at Weston-Underwood in Bucks hanging up in a Bed Chamber which I have often lain in: he is dressed in his Purple Capuchin &

Cross before him, with a large Mitre on a Table by him.[1] From the English Benedictines I went on the same Errand to the Abbey of Port Royal, just by, to take my Leave of Miss Throckmorton & to ask her if she had not a Letter to send to her Mama. The Parlour I was introduced into was a wretched dirty Room up one Pair of Stairs & hung with 2 or 3 different Sorts of ordinary woollen Hanging, near 60 years old at least, & full of Rents & Rags: it had 2 or 3 different Grates all of a Row on the same Side of the Room for different Companies; & the Room where the Nuns or Pensioners were, was a long Slip of a Room, equally dirty & ill-furnished, except that it had a large handsome Crucifix in it; in both Rooms was an Harpsichord; one in the Outside Parlour where I sat, for the Music Master, & the other for the Learners on it. One of the Nuns came to the Grate with her, but soon after left her with me. As soon as the Nun was retired, & she was alone with me, she began to let her Tears fall in Abundance: she said, that she hoped her Mama would not let her remain in that Convent for a long Time, where she had not one Mortal to speak to in her own Language, (there being about 30 Pensioners in it, all of great Families, for they took no other: whereas the Ursuline Nuns took Pensioners of all Sorts). I told her I would have her make herself as easy as the awkward Situation of being a Stranger in the midst of Foreigners would admit: that it was upon this very Account of being bred up with Persons of the first Distinction, who consequently spoke their Language in its Purity, that she was placed there, where I told her, I apprehended she was not to stay long.

[1]If this is the picture of which there is a print by T. Burford in the British Museum, it is by H. Huysing.

She regretted leaving the English Canonesses of St Austin on the Fossez St Victor, & seemed to think it long that she had been at Port Royal, tho' she had not been there a week. These Nuns are Reformed Bernardines, & are stiled Bernardine Nuns of the Perpetual Adoration. The Convent is a Branch of the Famous Jansenistical Seminary of Port-Royal des Champs, which was distant from Paris about 20 Miles, near Chevreuse, of the Cistercian Order, & which was entirely suppressed in 1710, on Account of its Restless & factious Behaviour. The Church of this Parisian Abbey of Port-Royal, is a tolerable handsome Building on the Outside, (for as to the Inside I saw nothing of it), & stands in the Court on the Entrance into it, fronting you, & rather on the right Hand.

From this Convent I went to the elegant & beautiful Parish & Collegiate Church of St Jacques du Haut-Pas,[1] in the Rue St Jacques, the Portico of which is adorned with fine Columns, & the Body built in the Form of a Cross. Over the Door at the Entrance into it is a very excellent striking Picture of the Martyrdom of St Bartholomew:[2] the Choir is most beautiful & the *Chevet*[3] or *Rond Point*, or East End is supported by 6 or 8 fine red Marble Pillars: the Altar itself is of green Marble, & on it is a small golden Pillar on which are carved all about it, Grapes, Vine Leaves, Ears of Corn, to represent the Materials of the great Sacrifice on the Christian Altar & a Branch from the Top of the Pillar supports by a golden Chain the *Ciborium* or Tabernacle, in which is enclosed the consecrated Hoste: the whole most elegantly imagined & executed. Our Lady's

---

[1]This church survived the Revolution.
[2]By Laurent de la Hire.   [3]Dome.

Chapel behind the Altar is very handsome: & in a Chapel on the South Side of the Nave are the Hearts of several of the Family of Longueville, with Inscriptions: on the same Side above, & near the High Altar, in a narrow Side Isle & small Chapel, is erected against the South Wall a very elegant Mural Monument of White Marble, but partly covered towards the Bottom by a Sort of Pew or Reading Desk in Front of the small Altar in which the Tomb & Pew are placed, having a large Urn & by it the Figure of an Angel, holding the Medallion of a Lady, with a Cross on her Bosome, the Monument being constructed of black & White Marble, & not far from the Ground, with these Arms, *viz*: a Cross engrailed between 4 Fleurs de Lis, for Banks, on the Urn, & this Inscription on the Marble Tablet; with this Motto also round the Medallion:

Moriendo Vivo.
Quisquis es, Siste paulisper ad Caelestis
Gratiae Miraculum.
Hic jacet nobilissima Da. Alicia Banks,
Supremi Angliae Justiciarii Filia,
Clarissimi Johannis Borlase, Baronetti, uxor;
quae Corpori Medicinam ad Borbonias Aquas quaerens,
Salutem Animae in Ecclesia Catholica felicius recepit.
A Patria sponte Exul
Tribus Annis ferme Sexagenaria,
Dei Monitu atque Ductu,
per Galliam, Belgium,
Italiam, Palestinam, Ciprium
peregrinata est;
ut plures Fidei et Pietatis suae Testes haberet.
Romae ac Hierosolymis, ceu nova Brigitta, Admirationi fuit:
Barbaris etiam venerabilis;
Summis Terrâ Mariq. Periculis intrepida;
Ubique Spectaculum illustre Virtutis praebens et Exemplum.

Tandem susceptis pro Christo confecta Laboribus,
Meritis plena, ad aeternam Requiem et Coronam evolavit
Die XVI Novembris An: M.DC.L [XXXIII].
Cum Testamento cavisset ut inter Pauper[es]
quorum Nutrix fuerat tumularet[ur].
Johannes Borlase, Baronettus . . .
amantissimae e Regione Tumuli h . . . [sic]
Maerens posuit.

I can find no Account of this religious Lady in Mr
Dod's *Church History* of Catholics, in the Article of
Famous Women, where she seems to have merited a
Place.[1]

From hence I went to take my Leave of the Canonesses of St Austin of Sion House, & received a Letter
from Sister Sanders for England. I went once more
into their Church, where I observed a Monument for
George Throckmorton, 2 for Yates, one for Gifford,
another for Lady Aston: all these in the Sanctuary, or
Parts near the High Altar, as before described at p.
200 of this Volume: but the same Lady pointed out
to me in the middle of their Choir, at the West End of
their Church, a black marble Slab, which I understood
her was designed for Elizabeth Teresa Throckmorton,
late Lady Abbess or Superior of this House: except I
should mistake for the eldest Daughter of my late
honoured & worthy Friend, & accomplished Gentleman, George Throckmorton Esq. who lately died in
this Convent, & whose Grandmother's Name was
Theresa, Daughter of Herbert, Duke Powis. In the
common Dining Parlour at Weston-Underwood are 3
modern Pictures of 3 Nuns in their proper Habits as

[1]See *Borlase of Borlase,* by W. C. C. Borlase, 1888, p. 59. Sir John
Bancks was L.C.J. of Common Pleas. The inscription seems to contain
all that is known of this remarkable woman.

T

Canonesses of this House: two of them at work, young, handsome & dressed, one in the Summer & the other in the Winter Dress of the Order: the 3rd is an old Lady who was Abbess here, as I take it, for her Habit is the same as the two others, who were Canonesses of St Austin, holding a Seal in her Hand, sitting in a Chair; the Seal being the Badge of her Office. See my Volume 40 of these MS. Collections p. 216.[1] The present Superior Abbess, as Sister Sanders informed me, is Dame Lancaster.

Thursday, Nov: 21. Fine Day, frosty & cold. This Day I had the Dispute with Madame Mean, the Mistress of the Hotel d'Orleans, where I lodged, mentioned at p. 35 of this Volume. I took a Coach about 11 & drove by the College Mazarine, or *des Quatre Nations*, into the Rue Guenegaud, to Mr Pascal's, a very civil & well-behaved Coach-Maker, where I picked out a Post Chaise to carry me to Calais, for which I agreed to give 3 Guineas for the use of it so far, & paid him a Guinea Earnest, to be in Readiness on Monday Morning following. From hence I drove over one of the Bridges into the Rue St Antoine, to see the Grands Jesuites, or the Great Professed House of these Fathers.[2] It is seated on the right Hand Side of the Street as you go out of the City, in an open Place, fronting a good Street, & has a Fountain in Front of it, which, in my Opinion, would be better removed. The cheif Front of this noble Church, to the Street, is very magnificent, the Columns with the Portico standing on a large Flight of Steps: over the Pediment are the Arms in large of Cardinal de Richelieu, under whose Administration & Patronage it was founded by Lewis 13

[1]*Add. MSS.* 5841.   [2]*Maison Professe des Jesuits.*

& in Niches are the Images of St Ignatius de Loyola &
St Francis Xavier: whose Statues also, with those of St
Charlemagne, as the French call him, & St Lewis, are
in Niches on the enormous High Altar, whose upper
Story is terminated by a fine large Crucifix, with the
Images of the Blessed Virgin & the Beloved Disciple
on each Side & another of St Mary Magdalen at the
Foot of the Cross weeping. Very fine marble Pillars
support the different Parts of this Altar, whose rich
Furniture, (in Part only, as I suppose), was shewn to
me by a Sacristan, a dirty Fellow from St Paul's
Seminary, at a little Distance behind it, who are now in
Possession of this Church & College, a Priest from
whence, once in a Day says Mass in this once so frequented & celebrated Church. One great Fault in this
stately, tho' not pleasing Altar, is, that it is placed on
so few Steps, that when it was crowded, on any great
Solemnity, the People at the Bottom of the Church
could not see the officiating Priests. It grieved me to see
its present forlorn & desolate State. However, if a too
worldly Disposition, too eager grasping after Power &
Dominion, a Contempt of their Brethren of other
Orders, an intriguing Temper of Mind, & a Running
into Trade, all very discrepant from their pious
Founder's Institution, as their Enemies alledge against
them, they must e'en thank themselves that they are no
longer in France & Portugal. But if these are Falsities,
& only brought against them by their inveterate
Enemies the Jansenists & Deists, & those who have an
Eye to the Robbing of Churches, it is great Pity so
useful & laborious a Set of Men should be so hardly
treated & basely maligned. The Silver Tabernacle was
rich, but in an ill Taste, being, as I judge, made in

Lewis 13th's Time: a small Picture of the Virgin in Blew, holding our Saviour in her Arms, serving by Way of Door to discover the Tabernacle, was, to my Taste, very well painted on Board. On the left Hand or North Side of this vast Altar, is a small Chapel, under the fine Arch into which the Heart of Lewis 13 is suspended in the Air supported by Images of 2 Angels, who seem flying, about 4 Feet high each, & all of Silver, as is the Box in which the Heart is enclosed, & gilt, & crowned with a Royal Diadem: on a Marble Scrole is this Inscription:

Augustissimum Ludovici XIII, Justi Regis,
Basilicae hujus Fundatoris magnifici, Cor:
Angelorum hic in Manibus, in Coelo, in Manu Dei.

In the same Place of the opposite Arch & Chapel on the South Side of the High Altar is the Heart of Lewis 14, in the same Situation & Design: Against the Sides of the Pilasters, supporting these Arches on both Sides, are black Marble Tablets with Inscriptions relating to both these Kings. Just between, or rather below these Chapels, is a fine Dome, painted in Brown Colour. Below these 2 Chapels is a Transept or Cross Isle, very large & spatious: that on the South is the Chapel of St Francis Xavier, over the Altar of which he is painted as preaching the Faith to the Chinese, Indians or Japonians. Against the Walls above the Altar & on each Side of it, are 4 large & beautiful Pictures in Marble Frames, representing the Life of St Lewis, painted by Simon Vouet:[1] these Pictures, as the *Sacristain* told me, were lately sold; as was another most excellent Picture of a Crucifix, placed on the South Wall or Corner Pilaster, just opposite the elegant Pulpit

[1] 1590-1649; an able but too prolific painter.

on the North Corner Wall, of wrought Iron & finely
gilt, near the Bourbon-Condé Chapel, which occupies
the North Transept, & is, more properly speaking, the
Chapel of St Ignatius de Loyola, who is represented on
his Knees before a most beautiful large Crucifix, both
that & the Figure of St Ignatius being of cast Copper,
& above half projecting, or more than alto-Relievo:
this is instead of a painted Altar Peice, & has a very fine
Effect, the back Part of it being of black Marble: on the
Summit of which sit 2 Angels in Copper holding a Sun,
or *Soleil*, with Rays, in the Centre of which is these
Fathers' Device, the ever adorable Name of JESUS. But
the most superb Ornaments of this beautiful Altar
Peice, are the Statues on the Corners of the Balustrade
which surround it, with the Balustrade itself & Basso
relievos on it, all of cast Copper, & of the most exquisite Taste & Workmanship, cast by one Perlan, &
designed by the famous Sculptor James Sarrazin.
Fortitude, Prudence, Justice & Charity, in Statues as
large as Life, occupy the 4 Corners of the Balustrade,
& at the Entrance of the Enclosure of the Altar sit 2
smaller Images holding, one the Arms of the Condé
Family, & the other this Inscription, on a Tablet:

> Henrico Borbonio Condaeo, Primo Regii Sanguinis
> Principi, cujus Cor hic conditum, Johannes
> Perrault, in Suprema Regiarum Rationum Curia
> Praeses, Principi olim a Secretis, quærens de Publica
> Privataque Iactura parcius dolere, posuit
> Anno M.DC.LXIII.

The Heart of the Prince of Condé is in an Urn, held
by Angels, under the Arch which Communicates with
the Side Chapel where Lewis 13 his Heart is preserved;
which Arch is the East Side of St Ignatius's Chapel.

This is one of the finest Things I saw at Paris, & is well worth a Stranger's nice Examination. In a South Chapel, near the South Transept, are several Tombs for the noble Family of Bouillon, & one among the Rest for the celebrated Neice of Cardinal Mazarine, Mary Mancini.[1] A little below, on the same Side, is another small Chapel, near the great West Door, under the magnificent Organ Loft & fine Organs, dedicated to St Stanislas Kostka,[2] who is represented in the new Picture over the Altar, as a Novice, in his black Cassock, attending another Saint of the Order in his Surplice. This Chapel was fitted up & ornamented by the present Queen of France, Daughter to Stanislas late King of Poland, in Honour of St Stanislas a Polish Saint of the Jesuits' Order: as was that other opposite to it, near the West Door on the North Side, dedicated to St Francis Borgia,[3] who is depicted on the Picture over the Altar as visiting a sick Person in Bed. This virtuous Princess, if she is a Friend to the Order, as it should seem she is, by these Benefactions to their principal Church, had not Power or Credit enough, if she had Inclination, to keep them on their Legs: & indeed, to all Human Appearance, the Order seems to be for Ever extinct in this Kingdom, where the Torrent against them seems too strong ever for them to have any Footing there again. The Nave of this stately Church is long & spatious, & a Gallery, with Iron Palisades gilt, runs all round the Church, over the Side Chapels: for as well as

[1]1640-1715; became wife of Prince Colonna; her *Mémoires* appeared in 1678.

[2]1550-68; buried at Rome. (F. Sacchini, *Vita St Kotskae*, Cologne, 1617).

[3]General of the Jesuits; *ob.* 1572.

I can remember, there are no Pillars to make Side Isles.
Under the Dome & Sanctuary are large Vaults for the
Interment of the Society.

From this Church I went to the Parish Church of St
Paul[1] at no great Distance from it, which has a very
curious & antique West Front to the Street, with
Carvings & Images in Niches; which Front was
repairing when I was there: the Structure of it is in a
beautiful Gothic Stile, & the Choir well ornamented
with Stalls & an elegant Eagle, with Figures in Brass
all round it: the High Altar is very beautiful, under the
Chevet or *Rond Point*, & entirely gilt over at Top. On
the right Side of the High Altar, in the Isle by it, is
erected a Mural Monument of Marble, with his Medallion, for Mansart the great French Architect: a little
beyond this further East, to the right is a Door into the
Communion Chapel, which is no very extraordinary
Room, with a Pillar or two in it to support the Roof;
the Altar of this Chapel is very handsome & vaulted: &
close to it in the South East Corner, against the East
Wall, (if it be the East), is a very fine Tomb of White
Marble for Anne, Duke de Noailles,[2] who rests on his
left Arms & lies on a Sarcophagus, with a Statue by him
of Hope holding out a Crown to him, & is an excellent
Peice of Sculpture. I observed some Monuments of
the Noailles Family in a Chapel on the right Side of the
Nave of the Isle. Out of a Door on the left Hand of the
Communion Chapel you go into the very spatious &
large Cloysters belonging to this Church, which serve
as a Burial Place for this large Parish, as well as the
Quadrangle within, as I conceive. I never saw more

[1] Long ago demolished.
[2] 1650-1708; Anne Jules, Duc de N.

perfect or more beautiful painted Glass in my Life, with
the History of the Holy Scripture. In this Church lie
buried the learned & worthy Peter-Daniel Huet,[1] Bp
of Avranches, the more famous Rabelais,[2] & Adrian
Baillet, the Antagonist of Monsieur Menage. The
painted Glass all round the Windows of the Cloysters is
most perfect & beautiful: but the Cloyster itself dirty
& dismal enough.

From hence to the Collegiate small Church of Petit
St Antoine is but a Step, whose Portal is antique,
ornamented with Statues to the Rue St Antoine, being
the South Side of the Church, & is a poor little Church,[3]
of one single Room, and which does not Answer the
Trouble of getting out & into the Coach to look at it;
especially as the Canons, who were then at Vespers in
their Choir, have modernized an old Gothic Building,
& consequently have spoiled what little original Beauty
it might formerly have been possessed of. The Canons
who own this Church are of the Order of St Austin.

From this Church I went to the old gothic Church of
St James de la Boucherie, standing in St Martin's
Street, at some Distance from the Pont Notre Dame
& the Grève: its cheif Front, in a very little Sort of
Opening, for it cannot be called a Square, is antient,
adorned with Statues, & has a large Tower over it, with
3 darkish Kind of Isles on the South or right Sides with
2 Ranges of Pillars to divide them asunder. The Church
was hung in Mourning throughout, & a Grave was
open in one of the Isles, & a Coffin with Lights about

[1] 1630-1721; an eminent scholar.

[2] Rabelais was actually buried at the foot of a large tree in the grave-
yard.

[3] Originally built as a hospital.

it in the Choir. The *Sacristain* told me that the Wife of a Grocer, *un Epicier*, & a Grocer also of the Parish were then dead, & that the Blacks were on this Account. Behind the Choir, on the left Hand or North Side of the Chapel of our Lady, in a little awkward Chapel, was a Tomb of about 300 years Antiquity, being an Altar Tomb & on it two Statues in Stone Kneeling in an Arch of the Wall, of a Man & his Wife behind him, but I saw no Epitaph about it. By this Chapel in another nearer our Lady's Chapel were two other Stone Statues on Foot of St Denis & St George: & still lower in a darkish Isle by the North Side of the Choir, over a Door Way into the Church, is a large Figure of St George on Horseback, armed & slaying the Dragon.

From St James de la Boucherie I went to the Church & *Cimetière* of the Holy Innocents in St Denis's Street: one of the most filthy & nasty Places I ever was in. The Church is small & antient & very gloomy: the Clergy with several Choristers were in the very small Choir singing their Vespers. In the Isle on the right Hand of the High Altar, against the East Wall, stands a very old Statue of a Woman, seemingly a Nun, with a Cord about her Waist, which has the Appearance to have formerly laid on an Altar Tomb, but now stands erect: I asked about it, but could learn nothing of it: it is of cast Brass. From the Church I stepped into the Church Yard,[1] which is, of all the Places I ever saw in my Life, without the least Exaggeration, the most shocking to mortal Pride & Vanity, the most stinking, loathsome &

[1] Rabelais had gibbeted this disgrace to Paris more than two centuries before. Pantagruel "said it was a good town to live in, but not to die in, for that the grave-digging rogues of St Innocent used to warm their backs with dead men's bones". (*Pantag. II.* vii.). The Church was demolished, and the bones carted away without the city in 1784.

indecent. Not but so shocking a Place as this, in every its worst Aspect, & Appearance might have a good Effect on human Delicacy & Pride: I am sure if this would not humble & mortify such Passions, nothing would: for here the last End of Humanity, whether set off by Titles, Learning, Beauty, Power or Riches, is exhibited in its most disgraceful, but necessary Appearance: & as most People in higher Life, generally pass thro' it without ever being acquainted with, or seeing such mortifying Sights, I am persuaded a Visit to this Place, preferably to any other I ever saw, now & then, would have a most salutary Effect upon their towering & lofty Passions, however otherwise it might endanger their bodily Health, by the unwholesome & deadly Steams issuing from every Quarter of this Palace of Death & Mortality. I was tempted to go to this frightful Place by an Account I had formerly red, in the Description of Paris, of a curious Groupe of Figures in one Part of it, representing one Nicholas Flamel, an Alchimist, with his Wife Perronella, & other Figures, which, while I was looking at in the North West Corner of the Church Yard, as I came out from the Church, under a Covering & close to the Wall, my smelling Faculty was so powerfully offended that I could stay there no longer, & thought of leaving a Place so necessarily unwholesome: but observing my two Servants very busily employed, at a good Distance from me, towards the South West Corner, or rather more to the Middle of it, inclining to the West End, in peeping into a Cave or great Hole, I went up to them, & saw such a Scene as might do much Good to the Soul, but smelt such a Stink as was enough to poison one, & to frustrate all the good Effects arising from sober

Reflections upon the Equality that Death makes of us all, & the necessary unavoidable Consequence of Putrefaction, Rottenness & Corruption, after a fleeting & short Life of Delicacy, Luxury & Dissipation. In this Cave, about 30 Feet Square, cheifly covered over by Boards & Planks, were a great Variety of Coffins of different Sizes & most of them ordinary ones, ill jointed & sadly made, according to French Joinery; so that it was unavoidable but that the Smell should find its way out of such ill jointed Boxes: indeed it is inconceivable what a Stench issued from such an Aggregation of mortifying & putrifying Carcases: enough to give the Plague to the whole City: the Smell, literally speaking, did not get out of my Head or Fancy for many Days after. In this Manner do the polite French bury their Dead, leaving them above Ground to poison the Living! for when one Stage is full, they cover it over with a Layer of Sand, as I conceive, & then lay another Pavement of Coffins upon that, which is also covered with Sand when the Floor will hold no more; & so on 'till the Cave is quite full to the Top. This I conceive to be their Way, as another such Cave was open on the right Hand Corner as I entered the Churchyard, which was very deep, & had no Coffins in it, but the Bottom was entirely covered by a fine yellow Sand: so that this Cave was no otherwise offensive than from the general ill Smell of the whole, arising from the other I just now mentioned, at a good Distance from it; from the Melancholy Appearance of every Object in the Place; & more especially from the Sides of this Cave, which from Top to Bottom was made up of nothing else but human Spoils, & a few rotten Remains of Coffins: for here you might see the almost perfect

Skeletons of Men & Women sticking out from the Sides of it, their Bodies & Ribs being still joyned together, & partly hanging from the Sides of this rough, unseemly & unpleasant Cave: the Refuge & last Resort of French Politeness, Nastiness & Indelicacy.[1] The whole Church yard indeed at my first Entrance into it, gave me a thorough Disgust, & a sufficient Specimen of their indecent Treatment of the Dead: for wherever you trod on this shocking Ground, & last Place of Rest & Quiet, as it ought, properly, decently, & as much as it lies in our Power to let it be, you trampled upon the loose & lately dug up Bones & Ashes of our Predecessors: an Action utterly repugnant to the vulgar Feelings of Human Nature, even of English Savages; yet consistent enough to the false Delicacy of French affected Politeness! In this Scene of Death & Desolation, were a few tall high Crosses & Crucifixes of Brass & an old decayed wooden Building: & all round the Square, if I may be allowed the Expression, against the Walls which surrounded it, was an old wooden Gallery built, which was piled up, & crammed as full as it could hold, on every Side of the Churchyard, with Human Sculls & Bones, which were whitened by the Weather. Above these Galleries or Habitations for the Dead were the Backsides of Houses, with Windows looking into the Churchyard above them: whose Situation, in my Opinion, must be equally offensive & unwholesome, as unpleasant & dreary: insomuch that the constant & repeated Greetings of *memento mori*, used by the mortified Carthusian Monks one to the other, compared to the settled abode in such an Habita-

[1]See *Annual Register*, 1767, p. 191 and 1768, p. 177, in a letter from Voltaire to M. Paulet, with reference to the spread of small-pox.

tion may be looked upon only as a Salutation of good
Breeding & civil Respect. I have dwelt the longer upon
so dismal & gloomy a Subject, as the Impression it
made upon my Servant's Fancy was so strong & powerful, that he was terrified & shocked in such a Manner,
that for the few Nights we stayed afterwards in Paris he
could not sleep in a Chamber by himself, but removed
his Bed to another Room where another Servant was
lodged. Brice in his *Description de Paris*, Vol: 1, p. 517,
says that this has been the Public Burying Ground for
the City for more than a Thousand Years: as that is
the Case, one need not be surprized at the Depth of the
Caves, the Fulness of the Sides of them with Bones, &
the seemingly little Earth mixed with them: for the
Place did not seem to me to be an Acre of Ground: &
I observed hardly any Churchyards to any of their
Churches: which however are full of Dead; but we must
suppose those to be of the better Sort: so that the
Populousness of this great City must necessarily, at all
Times, have more than properly crowded up so small
a Cemetery as this of the Holy Innocents. I was
informed that there has been a late Order for no Burials
in the City, & that Burying Grounds are filling up
apace beyond the Suburbs: I had a Mind to have gone
to have seen them several Times, & talked of it to my
French *Valet de Louage*, but was disappointed: & after
the Sight of that of the Holy Innocents, my Curiosity
was more than satisfied. Indeed I never was more
shocked & scandalized in my Life than in seeing so
much Indecency shewn to the Human Species: so I
quitted it as soon as I could, & left the most stinking,
indelicate & indecent Place I ever was in, to cleanse my
Ideas at as elegant a Fountain, called by the same Name,

La Fontaine des Saints Innocents, as any in Paris.[1] It stands
at the Corner of the Street of St Denis & the Rue aux
Fers, & almost opposite to the beautiful old Gothic
West Front of the Church of the Holy Sepulchre, quite
full of Carvings & Statues: as the Door was shut to this
Church, I could only admire the Beauty of the Outside
of it, which to those who have a Contempt for every
Thing that is not Grecian or Roman, would perhaps
appear to be the Height of Barbarousness: However I
had my Revenge on these great Connoisseurs: for being
directed by my *Valet de Louage*, (who are a Sort of
Ciceroni or Antiquaries, by serving various Masters,
who come here out of Curiosity), to look at this Fountain, which, however beautiful & elegant it may be, I
should infallibly have passed by, without any Observation of it, so much was my Attention struck by the more
striking Beauties of the old Gothic Church. Not but
I can allow that the Fountain may have its Beauties &
Attractions: I own it did not strike me: it is a Stone
Building about 40 Feet high, ornamented with Carvings
in Bas Relief & Statues, both above & below the great
middle Story, which has a fine Arch, & Balustrade
before it, between 2 fluted Corinthian Pillars on each
Side of it. It has a double Arch, the Front of it being as
long again to the Rue aux Fers, as that to the Rue St
Denis, which has only a single one. But however fresh
& good the Waters from this Fountain may be, they
derive their Source so near such a contaminated a Place,
that I should never have any Relish for them: it being
close to the Cimetery of the Holy Innocents. Which

[1]Removed, about 1784, to the centre of the market-place which
replaced the cemetery. The sculptures were mainly the work of Jean
Goujon.

Subject I can't dismiss without taking Notice of a Practice I observed, the last Time but one, about 2 years ago, that I was at Hackney, in Relation to the Burial of the Dead in their Church Yard: which being found too small for the great Number & Encrease of Inhabitants, about 3 Years ago, the Parish applied to the late Bp of London, Dr Osbaldiston,[1] for Leave to encrease it, by adding Part of a Feild at the South-East Corner of their Church yard, (& close to my Brother--in-Law Mr Hector Mawdesley's Garden Wall), to it. Accordingly his Lordship had a Tent erected on the Spot, it being a rainy Season, & consecrated it for the Use of Christian Burial. It is the finest Gravel I ever saw: for I went to look at the new Method they were in, to save opening their Ground on every Occasion, & to husband it to best Advantage. On the East Part therefore, close to the new Wall, they drew a Line about 7 Feet from it, & in that Line had all their new Interments: digging one Grave, in which, it being very deep, several Coffins were put, till it was full, & then filled it up, raising an usual Grave Mount over it; & then opened another in the same Line; so that as this new Part & first Line of it may contain above an 100 Corpses, besides those which are buried in other Parts of the Church, & Church-yard, it may be above 20 years before they will be obliged to begin at the said first Range of Graves, there being Room enough for several other Rows of them at their Heads, nearer the Church. And altho' the Grave was kept open in which the Coffins were laid one on another, yet I did not perceive any Offensive Exhalation from it: which may be owing in a good Measure from the more nice joyning

[1] Richard Osbaldeston (1690-1764).

& workmanlike putting together even of our more ordinary Coffins & Boxes than those of our polite & unskilful Neighbours. But however convenient this Way may be for the more easy stowing & great Number of dead Carcases of the Human Species, yet I think it at best but indecent, & can't but lament, that we are outdone in Point of Humanity & all tender Feelings & concern for the Dead by those whom we affect to Stile by no better Name than Barbarians: I mean the Turks; for whose cleanly, decent & religious Respect for the Dead, see what has been said at p. 113 of this Volume.

Having already more than once taken Notice of Madame Geoffrin, at pp. 81 and 153 of this Volume, & reading the following Article in the *White-Hall Evening Post* of yesterday, *viz:* July 22, 1766, relating to a Lady I had the Pleasure of being in Company with when I was at Paris, I shall give it a Place here:

"Warsaw. June 22. The Sieur Leonard Euler, one of the greatest Mathematicians in Europe, has been here some Days with his Family, & during his Stay, the King has given Orders, that he shall be entertained at his Expence. His Majesty lately did him the Honour to invite him, & some other learned Men, to his own Table. Madame Geoffrin, Mother to the Marchioness de la Ferté-Imbault,[1] is likewise arrived here from Paris. Tho' this Lady is 60 years of Age, she performed this long Journey at the King's Request. She has an Apartment allotted for her in the Palace, & is treated with the greatest Respect by the King, who visits her frequently: & the Persons of the highest Rank are assiduous to be in her Company, on Account of her distinguished Talents."

After having left the Church, Cimetery & Fountain of the Holy Innocents, I drove to the Hôtel du Parc Royal, where I dined & drank Tea, & coming Home

[1]Marie-Thérèse (1715-91).

about 9 o'Clock, my Taylor Mr Armand came to me
about my Cloaths, & speaking of his own Account of
Religion, I observed that he was half a Protestant,
altho' he told me that he was educated in the Country
with an Uncle of his, who was a Parish Priest: I
suppose also that he was somewhat infected by the
Malady which now possesses the French; I mean a
Spirit of Free-thinking: that is, a milder Word for
Deism: for I remember he made Use of this Expression,
which probably may be a French Proverb:

Que les plus grands Docteurs, sont les plus grands Douteurs.

He was also a vehement Stickler against the Jesuits;
whom I defended as well as I could: observing, that their
Enemies were also generally the Enemies of Christianity.

Friday, 22 *Nov:* Fine Day & Cold. I paid Mr Armand for my Coat of Cotton Velvet, & black Velvet
flowered Waistcoat 176 Livres, 15 Sous, which is near
8 Guineas. Mr Walpole called upon me about 11
o'Clock to carry me with him to the Royal Abbey of St
Denis, about 5 Miles from Paris. We went in his
Vis-à-Vis Coach & 4 Horses, & got there in less than
an Hour. He was in Hopes of seeing the Church, &
Treasury, (for the other Parts of the Abbey we had
little Curiosity of Examining) much at our Leisure, &
at a Time when they were not crowded with People to
see them, as he had a Letter to the Prior of the Abbey,
Father Chretien, for that Purpose: but we were sadly
disappointed, as the Prior sent his Excuses to Mr
Walpole, that he had a good Deal of Company with him,
who staid Dinner, & therefore sent one of the Monks
of the Convent who would shew us every Thing about
it. But what was most distressful, he hurried us over the
Tombs in the Church, which we most wanted to see, &

u

examine & then carried us into the Treasury, which was full of People, who were looking at the Curiosities contained in it, & shewn to them by another Monk. As the Church, Tombs & Treasury have been so minutely described by Dom Michael Felibien, a Monk of the House, in a Folio Volume, printed at Paris in 1706, I shall say little or nothing of this beautiful Church & its venerable Contents:[1] especially as I begin to be sufficiently tired of writing so much. However I shall put down here a few Things I recorded in my Pocket Book. In the Treasury I met accidentally with 3 or 4 German Gentlemen, with whom I crossed the Sea from Dover to Calais: but as I had no Conversation with them in the Vessel, they being all of them very sick, I took no Sort of Notice of them. Mr Walpole had been informed by Mr Mariette, that in this Treasury were several Wax Figures of some of the later Kings of France, & asked one of the Monks for Leave to see them, as they were not commonly shewn, or much known: accordingly, in 4 Cupboards, above those in which the Jewels, Crosses, Busts & Curiosities were kept, were 8 ragged Figures of so many Monarchs of this Country, to Lewis 13, which must be very like, as their Faces were taken off in Wax immediately after their Decease.[2] The Monk told us, that the great Lewis 14, his face was so excessively wrinkled, that it was impossible to take one off from him. The grand

[1] For a detailed account of the violation and destruction of the contents of the royal tombs at St Denis, in 1793, see *Monographie de Saint Denis*, par le Baron de Guilhermy, Paris, 1848.

[2] "The countenance of Charles IX is so horrid and remarkable, you would think he had died on the morrow of the St Barthélemi, and waked full of the recollection." *Letters of Hor. Walpole* (Toynbee), No. 1572 (Oct. 29, 1774).

Entrance into this most beautiful & light Gothic
Building is from an open Part of the Town, in the
middle of which stands a Cross, & where, I suppose the
Market is kept: it has a high Wall with a great Pair of
Gates before it, between which & the West Front is a
very poor & narrow Sort of Court: so that there is no
tolerable Place to take a full View of this Part of the
Church; which is very antient by the decayed Appearance of the Stones: there are two noble Towers in Front,
on the North one is a neat Stone Spire, surrounded with
Pinnacles: over the great middle West Door is a fine
Catherine Wheel Window, as there are 2 others in the
two Transept Isles of the Church. Three fine Doors of
Gothic work give Entrance into the Nave & Side Isles,
which are descended into by a few Steps, the Ground
being risen about the Church: the curious Figures of
antient Kings & Queens of France under the Arches of
these 3 Doors are given us by Dom Montfaucon in his
Antiquitez de la Monarchie Françoise, Vol: 1, pp. 193,
194, in 3 Plates, representing the Statues of 20 Kings
& Queens, 6 a-peice on the 2 smaller Doors into the
Isles, & 8 under the Arch in Niches of the grand
middle Door; & all very like the original Statues, as
well as I can call them to my Memory: for I examined
them all very minutely at 2 different Times, having
often looked at them with Pleasure in Father Montfaucon's Books, which I have in my own Study: as well as
that other very curious Statue of King Dagobert 1, the
2nd Founder of the Abbey, who is represented as sitting on a Throne or Chair, with his 2 Feet on so many
Lions, both his Hands being broken off, & crowned, &
dressed in a flowing Robe, thrown over his Shoulders.
This mutilated curious old Statue is fixed against the

North Wall of the North Isle, immediately as you enter
the Isle, & under the Tower, very high, in Order to
preserve it from Injury: a Draught of which Statue is
given by the same learned Benedictine in the same
Volume at p. 162, as also at pp. 164, 165 of the same
Volume, a Description & Draught of the very curious
old Tomb of the same Monarch; being a large Arch of
a brown hard Stone or Marble under which he lies on
his left Side with his Queen Nanthilde's[1] Statue at his
Feet & his Son King Clovis at his Head, as a Youth:
the Top of it is ornamented with Gothic Spire Work, &
under the Arch against the Back of the Tomb is a
fabulous History of the Deliverance of the King's Soul
out of Purgatory. This very curious Monument is on
the South Side of the High Altar, against the South
Wall, upon the Steps going up to it, and is covered by a
Tapestry Hanging before it, to keep it from Damage.
It stands just above the Side Altar, against a Pillar of
the Choir, on which a daily Mass is said for the Repose of Lewis 14th's Soul, whose Coffin, covered with
a large Pall is just below it on the first Landing
Place or Steps ascending to the High Altar: tho'
it is supposed that this is only a Representation
to remain there 'till his Successor's Coffin takes its
Place, & that his real Coffin & Body is already in its
proper Place in the long Vault under the Altar & *Chevet*
behind it. Just below this, opposite the Entrance from
the South Isle into the Choir, lies the Stone or Marble,
which is lifted up to go into the Bourbon Vault. In the
middle of the Choir, towards the East End of the
Monks' Stalls, is a beautiful raised Tomb of Copper for
the Emperor Charles the Bald, King of France, who

[1]Or Nantichilde; *ob.* 642.

is represented lying on a Table, supported by small Pillars about 2 Foot from the Ground, or rather more, with his Effigies in above Half Relievo, all in Cast Copper, with the Figures in small of 4 Bishops at each Corner of the Table. He is dressed in his imperial Robes, crowned, with a Sceptre in one Hand & a Globe in his left: & round the Borders of his Robes are Ornaments & Jewels of Steel let into the Copper; which has a very pretty Effect. On the Edge of the Table on which the Emperor is laid, is this Inscription in Verse, & wrote in Characters half Roman & half Gothic, but very legible:

> Imperio Karolus Calvus, Regnoq potitus
> Gallorum, jacet hac sub Brevitate situs.
> Plurima cum Villis, cum Clavo, cumq Corona
> Ecclesie vicus huic dedit ille Bona.
> Multis ablatis nobis fuit hic Reparator
> Secanii Fluvii, Ruoliiq Dator.

A Print of this elegant old Tomb is given by Father Montfaucon in his 1st Vol: of *Antiquitez de la Monarchie Françoise* p. 306, but without the Figures of the Bps at the Corners of it. This Emperor died in 878: but his Monument is supposed to be no older than the 12th Century.

Against the South Wall of the South Isle, under the noble Arch of the vast Organs & Loft, hung several large Bones of a Whale: a Curiosity hardly worthy of so noble a Repository. The Nave is not very long: but the Pillars are light & lofty, & the Stone Roof to the *Chevet* or *Rond Point* very elegant: & all the Windows full of small *Compartiments* of painted Glass, in various & distinct Histories & Fashions. There is a very small South Transept Isle, if it may be so called, & hardly any on the North: so that it has more the Appearance of one long Room with Pillars, than of a large Cathedral Church in the Shape of a Cross. The Iron Work which divides the Choir from the Isles & Nave is very expensive & ornamental. There are no Side Chapels in the South Isle, except one or two at the East End: whereas the North Isle has near a Dozen from one End of the Church to the other. The High Altar is ascended by several Steps, & is very magnificent: behind which is the *Rond Point*, *Chevet*, or Eastern Part of the Church rounded off in a Semicircle; round which are 9 small Chapels, with very gothick antient Shrines & Altars & as antique Furniture: at the East End of the Choir Part of this *Chevet*, against the Pillars which support the Roof, (for the said 9 Chapels have an Isle running between them & the Pillars,) stands the Shrine or great Altar of St Denis. In the North West Corner of this *Chevet*, below the first of the 9 Chapels which surround it, & more to the North, (being the last or most Easterly Chapel of those running in a Line by the North Side of the North Isle), is erected under an Arch of the North Wall, (this whole Chapel being fitted up *à la moderne*, with fine Marbles), the most beautiful & expressive Monument of Marshal Turenne,[1] who is represented as lying in Roman Armour, with a *Battoon*[2] in his right Hand, on his right Side, & expiring in the Arms of Immortality, who, sitting on Cannons & an Urn, from which issues, it being overturned, Quantity of Coin, representing his generous Disposition, supports him with her right

[1] His body was found to be so well preserved, when the tombs at St Denis were violated in 1793, that it was exhibited in a glass case for some eight months. It was ultimately removed, with the tomb, to the *Invalides*.

[2] Baton.

Hand & holds out a Crown of Laurel with her right:
an affrighted Eagle sitting at his Feet, to signify his
Victories over the Imperialists: behind him is a beautiful Pyramid of green Marble terminated by a *Fleur-de-
Lis*, on a black Marble Ground behind it: all these
Figures & Emblems are upon a double Sort of Sarcophagus, covered in part by a Lion's Skin, to represent
the Marshal's Valour & Courage, & are of white
Marble: but the Basso-relievo representing a Battle in
Front of the Sarcophagus, & his Arms & Ornaments
about them below, are of cast Copper, very artistly[1]
performed: the Sarcophagus stands on a Marble
Pediment of 2 or 3 Feet high; beside which sit two most
delicate & beautiful Figures in white Marble: that at
the Head, lifting up her Veil, as surprized at his sudden
Death, represents Prudence or Wisdom, with a Cor-
nucopia from whence falls Plenty of Money; the other
at the Feet, is to represent Valour, & is armed & dressed
as Minerva or Pallas, & seems weeping for his Loss.
Under the Sides of the Arch are Trophies, Armour &
Branches of Laurel, expressive of his Profession &
Abilities in it. There is a small Dome which gives a
Beauty to this elegant Chapel, whose Altar under the
East Window, close to the Tomb, is very beautiful, &
the whole paved with black & white Marble. I did not
see any Inscription about the Monument: so that was
it not for his Arms, & the fresh Tradition relating that
he was buried here, the Knowledge of it might be
forgot. Marshal Turenne was killed by a Cannon Ball,
July 27, 1675.

From this Chapel, at the West Side of it, in a manner
close to the Tomb, is a large Arch, or Opening, which

[1]Recorded form.

looks down into the Isle on the North Side of the Church: for the Chapel & *Chevet* are much higher, perhaps by 18 or 20 Steps, than the Rest of the Church: under which Arch, on a Pedestal, stands a White Marble Image of our Lady with her Babe in her Arms, being Part of the Altar-Peice, if I do not mistake, of the Chapel below, with her Back to the Chapel in which Marshal Turenne's Tomb is placed: on each Side of which Image you look down into the Chapel below it, in which lie, one on one Side, & the other on the other, at the West End, the two white marble Figures of King Henry 2 & his Queen Catherine de Medicis, in their Royal Robes, much worked & ornamented with Flowers, & dressed after the Mode of their Times. In the North East Corner of the said Chapel stands a most curious & valuable Vase of Porphiry, reckoned a great Curiosity. Out of this Chapel was formerly the Entrance into the Rotundo, or circular fine Chapel of the Valois Family, built to receive the Tomb of Henry 2, by his Queen: which magnificent Chapel, being never absolutely finished, & found inconvenient, Leave was given by the Crown to the Abbey to pull it down: & the stately Tomb of Marble, with the Fine Figures in Brass as big as Life standing at the 4 Corners of it, representing the 4 Cardinal Virtues, is now placed in the North Isle of the Choir: this beautiful Monument has a large Pediment, on the Sides of which are fine Basso-Relievos, which support about a Dozen Marble Corinthian Pillars & Pilasters; on the Top of which is an Entablature, on which are the beautiful Figures in Brass, on their Knees before 2 Desks, of King Henry 2 & his Queen Catherine de Medicis; whose Portraits, as dying, & naked, in white Marble lie on a raised Bed

on the Pediment between the Pillars & below the
Entablature, & are so artfully expressed as to shock one
to look at them. This is one of the finest Things in the
Church: a Print of which is in Dom Felibien's *Histoire
de l'Abbaye Royale de Saint Denys*, at p. 565: as is another
of Marshal Turenne's at p. 569 of the same Book.

In the Chapel next below that in which lie the White
Marble Statues of Henry 2 & Catherine de Medicis,
which were originally placed in the principal Chapel of
the Rotundo for the Valois Family: but when that was
pulled down, removed to the Places where they now
remain, as before described, on the North Side of the
North Isle, & parallel with the Pillar in that Isle, on
which is the Kneeling Statue in his Cardinal's Robes, of
the Cardinal Charles de Bourbon, who was proclaimed
by the League, King of France, by the Stile of Charles
10th, if I am not mistaken: which Column or Pillar in
the North Isle stands almost Close to one of the great
Pillars of the Church, which supports the Roof &
divides the Choir from the North Isle, just where the
East End of the Monks' Stalls finish: in that 9th
Chapel from the West End of the Church, stands the
magnificent Tomb, all of White Marble, erected for
King Lewis 12, & his Queen Anne de Bretagne. It is
a most stately Mausoleum on 2 Steps, whereon stands
a large Pediment, the Sides of which all round are
elegantly adorned with Basso-Relievos, containing the
Victories of that King in Italy, & at the Corners of this
Pediment sit the beautiful Statues as big as Life of the
4 Cardinal Virtues, Fortitude, Temperance, Prudence
& Justice, represented by so many Women, each with
its proper Symbol to express her Character. Above this
Pediment rises another on which are placed a Dozen

Pedestals which support a large Entablature, on which are the Kneeling Figures of Lewis 12, & Anne of Brittany, with Cushions on a covered Desk for each of them, & their Hands in a suppliant Posture. Under the Arcades formed by the 12 Pedestals, against each of which are finely carved Corinthian Pilasters, sit the beautiful Figures, about 3 Feet in Height each, of the 12 Apostles: & behind them, within the Mausoleum, on a raised Bed or Altar Tomb lie the naked Figures, as dying, of the said King & Queen, who died, the first in 1514, & his Queen a year after. The whole of this truly Royal Monument is of white Marble, & finished in the highest Taste of antient Rome.

In the South Isle, just opposite to the Place wherein Lewis 12th's Monument was described, is another most sumptuous Mausoleum for King Francis 1, & his Queen Claudia of France: it is all of White Marble, somewhat heavy, & in the Shape of a Cross, the 2 Wings which come from the Sides of it, forming two smaller Arches, on the Sides of which are 2 others to look into the great Arch in the middle, under which, on 2 Sarcophagi, lie the Figures of the King & his Queen: above the Entablature, which is supported by fluted Ionic Pillars & Pedestals against the Arch work, are their Statues also Kneeling before 2 Desks, with 3 of their Children by them. Although this is a most magnificent Sepulchre & in great Taste, King Francis 1st being the Patron, Encourager, & Introducer of Arts & Sciences into his Kingdom, yet its Heaviness did not please me so much as the 2 others in the same Stile: I mean those of Henry 2 & Lewis 12.

There was another Monument in the Choir which struck me much: it was designed for King Charles 8,

who died in 1498. It is all of black Marble, & is placed
on the first Landing Place or Steps approaching the
High Altar, by the Side of the fine & rich Balustrade of
the Sanctuary on the North Side of the Choir, & in a
parallel Line with the white Marble Statues of Henry 2
& Catherine de Medicis in the Chapel on the Outside
of the Choir. King Charles is placed on his Knees in his
Royal Robes, before a Desk on the middle of this Altar
Tomb, at the Corners of which are 4 Angels in the same
Posture, each holding an Escocheon with the Arms of
France & Jerusalem quartered, he having conquered
the Kingdom of Naples; by which means he became
King of France, Sicily, & Jerusalem. This is a very fine,
handsome large Monument.

Other Tombs which I took more particular Notice
of in this charming Church, were, besides a vast
number of Altar Tombs, all of white Marble & in the
same Taste, for Kings, Queens & the Royal Family,
1st a very old grey Marble with a Man in Armour
engraved on it, lying on the Floor, on the North Side
of the Choir, & not far from the West End of the
Monks' Stalls, which was designed for Hugh le Grand,
Father of Hugh Capet, King of France. This Hugh le
Grand, married an English Princess, Daughter to
Edward, King of England, & holding the 3 great
Abbeys of St Denis, St Germain des Près at Paris,
& St Martin at Tours, he was called also Hugh the
Abbat, & dying in 956, he was buried in this his Abbey
Church, under this Stone.

Very near the North West Corner of this Stone, &
almost touching the back ending Stall, & the great
Pillar of the Church, is a neat white Marble half
column on which is an Image: but for whom I know

not, or forgot to enquire. Exactly in the Middle of the
Choir, touching the Foot of the first Steps ascending
the Sanctuary up to the High Altar, lies a large grey
Marble covered all over with a Plate of Brass on which
is engraved the Figure crowned & holding a Sceptre in
her right Hand under a Canopy, with Saints in Niches
on both Sides of it, of Margaret of Provence, Wife to
Saint Lewis, King of France, round the Edge of which
is this old Inscription:

Icy gist la noble Reyne de France Marguerite, qui fu Fame
Monseigneur Saint Loys jadis Roy de France, qui trespassa le
Mercredy devant Noel, l'En de la'Incarnation Nostre Seigneur
Mil 2 Cens quatre vinz & quinze.

> Priez pour s'Ame.

In a Line with this, close to the Door into the Choir
on the South Side in that Isle lies another Stone, like
the former, covered over with a large Plate of Brass,
having an Abbat mitred, with his Crosier, under a
Canopy: this was for the Abbat Matthew de Vendosme,
who died in 1286.

Very near this, a little more to the East, on the other
or South Side of the South Isle, at the Foot of the great
Steps up into the *Chevet* or East Part of the Church
behind the High Altar, against one of the great Pillars,
is erected a fine Altar, enclosed with Rails, & over it a
large fine Statue in white Marble of the Patron Saint of
the Order, the Holy St Benedict; this being called his
Chapel. Close to this, on the South, is the Entrance into
a Chapel quite full of Tombs: the Altar of it being
parallel to the High Altar in the Choir, & of that in the
Chapel in the North Isle in which lie the White Marble
Statues of Henry 2 & his Queen Catherine de Medicis.
The first in entering on the left Hand, the Head almost

touching the great Pillar, on the other Side of which is the great Patriarch of the Benedictine Order his Altar & Statue, & the Side touching the Wall on the North Side of the Chapel, is an Altar Tomb all of cast Brass, on which lies the Brasen Figure of a Man in Armour, under a Canopy, with a slight Support to it: this was erected for Arnold de Guillem, Chamberlain to Charles 7th of France, who died in the 15 Century & for his Probity was called, The Chevalier sans Reproche. The Tomb is plain, but handsome & well preserved. Close to the Feet of this, but in an Arch deeper in the Wall, & under the Steps up into the Chevet, lies a black Marble Altar Tomb, on which is the Figure of a Man in Armour in white Marble, under a plain Canopy above his Head & nothing to support, & on the Rim of the black Marble Slab on which he lies, is this Inscription:

Cy gist Loys[1] de Sancerre, Chevalier, jadis Mareschal de France, & depuis Connestable & Frere Germain du Conte de Sancerre, qui trespassa le Mardy VI. Jour de Fevrier l'An Mil C.C.C.C. & deux.

Quite on the other Side of this small Chapel, at an equal Distance from the West & South Walls & Foot of an Altar before it, there being but little Room to pass round it, stands a very large & high Altar Tomb of black Marble, with the Statues, under Canopies of white Marble, finely ornamented with Saints in Niches on the Outermost Part, of King Charles 6 & his Queen Isabella of Bavaria, the Father & Mother of our King Henry 5th's Wife, who gave Title by that Marriage to King Henry 5th & 6th's assuming the Gouvernment of the Kingdom of France. About 3 Foot from this, in a

[1]Louis.

Line with it, stands another black Marble Altar Tomb,
rather higher & taller than the last, so that you are
obliged to get upon the Steps of the adjacent Altars to
examine the Figures upon it, which are those of King
Charles 7th & his Queen, Mary d'Anjou, in Alabaster:
but I forget whether there are any Figures on the Sides
& Ends of it, as there are upon that of Charles the 6 &
his Queen Isabella of Bavaria, under Canopies, some of
which are fallen & the Canopies broke: one Figure
among the Rest at the Feet seemed to be a Bishop in his
Cope & Mitre. About 4 or 5 Feet more to the North,
but in a Line with the 2 others of Charles 6 & 7th,
about the Middle of the Chapel, is another such Tomb,
Altar Fashion, of black Marble & on the Table of it lie
2 Statues in white Marble of King Charles 5 & his
Queen Jane de Bourbon: He deceased 1380. The Top
of it is richly adorned with Canopies & Statues in the
Niches of their Supporters. This Tomb lies exactly
before the cheif Altar of this Chapel, on the large &
broad 2nd Step of which lie, between that & the Altar,
which covers the Bottom Parts of both, two handsome
Marbles on the Floor, covered with Brass, & much used
by Peoples constantly treading on them, to look at the
3 Royal Tombs already described: one of which was
for a Chamberlain of Charles 5, & the other, Close to it,
for Charles, Dauphin of France, Son to King Charles
6. Very near these two Brasen Tombs, on the South
Side of the cheif Altar, is another smaller & lower Altar
Tomb of black Marble on which lies the Statue in
Armour, in white Marble under a Canopy with no
Supporters to it, of the famous Warrior against the
English in particular, Bertrand du Guesclin, with this
Epitaph engraved round the Edges of the Tomb:

Cy gist noble Homme Messire Bertrand du Guesclin, Conte de Longueville, & Connestable de France, qui trépassa à Chastelneuf de Randon en Iuvaudam en la Seneschaucée de Beaucaire, le XIII. Jour de Juillet l'An M.CCC.iiii. Priés Dieu pour lui.

I shall take Notice of only 2 more Monuments, both of them the first you see, if I express myself aright, as you enter the South Isle by the Choir: the first that you meet with is the last erected in this Church, & is placed against the first Pillar of the South Side of the South Isle, being an elegant Mural Monument of various coloured Marble, with a Bust & Pyramid behind it, for the Marquis de St Megrin: at no great Distance from which, on the same Side, & touching the noble Mausoleum of Francis 1. at the North West Corner of it, stands the beautiful Gothic Tomb of Margaret Countess of Flanders, Daughter of King Philip 5 of France. She is represented in White Marble lying on a Tomb of black Marble, under an Arch or Canopy of Gothic Spire work, & surrounded with an Iron Palisade. Near this is the Door which leads up into the Treasury, which is a good square Room of no great Beauty: on the right Hand as you enter it, are large Cupboards with Folding Doors before them, in which the Relicks & Jewels are kept, & a Monk standing behind a Counter, like our Shops, points out to you every Curiosity in its Turn. In the Room hang several indifferent Pictures, as they seemed to me: one of them representing, as well as I can remember, Joane of Arc. In the middle of the Room is a Marble Pillar to support the Roof, & a Lamp hangs up in it always burning, in Reverence to the Holy Relics in the Treasury: among which a very rich Cross, stuck over with Jewels, & containing a large Peice of the true Cross, was very remarkable for its Beauty: as is also for its real Value one of the 5 Nails which fastened our Lord to it: some curious old Mitres & Crosiers; a most valuable & curious Cup or Vase of one entire oriental Agate: old Books, Buckles or Claspes, Reliquaries of great Price, Crowns & Sceptres, Patens & Chalices, & various other Antiquities & Curiosities, which are minutely described in his [Felibien's] *History of St Denis*, at p. 536, &c. Above these Cupboards were the others in which the wax Figures of some of the later Kings of France are kept, (already described at p. 306 of this Volume). In another Cupboard were kept some very fine Crosses & modern *Soleils* for the Exposition of the Holy Sacrament. After the Monk had hurried us over the Tombs in the Church, & shewn us the Treasury, he seemed to be impatient to be leading us all over the very stately & noble Convent, every Part of which seemed to me to be lately rebuilt: the Cloysters & Dormitorys were most stately & fine walking Places in hot or wet weather: the Apartments for the Monks decent, neat, & convenient, & an Apartment for Strangers of Quality, elegant & well furnished: their Kitchin large & convenient; their Apothecaries' Shop & Apartment well furnished with Drugs & other proper Appurtenances: we were also shewn an elegant & neat small Chapel above Stairs for the Conveniency of the Sick & Infirm: in the long Chapter House I observed the Arms of the Abbey to be carved on the Wainscote, which are France & a Nail in the Centre between the Flowers de Lis: in Honour, as I guess, of their being in Possession of one of the Sacred Nails that fastened our Lord to the Cross. The Pictures at the 2 Ends of the long Refectory, one being the History of the Descent of the Holy Ghost, painted in 1758, by Restout,[1] did not please me. I took particular Notice of a most extraordinary large & fine Lavatory, of 12 Feet in Diameter, it being quite round, & of one single Stone, with neat leaden Statues, at the Bottom of a very fine Staircase that leads up to their Apartments above Stairs. In an handsome lower Parlour were 3 fine full Length Portraits of the Duke de Penthievre, the Count de Tholoux & the Princess of Roche-sur-Yon, with the Busts of Marshals Saxe & Lowendahl on Marble Tables: & over the Chimney was the Picture, which Dom Felibien has given as a Frontispeice to his *Histoire de l'Abbaye Royale de Saint Denys*, representing the Procession made by King Philip the Hardy, who helped to carry the Body of his Father St Lewis from Paris to St Denis, on Friday, 22 May, 1271. Here was also a fine Green-House with Exotic Plants, & other Halls of great State, with good Gardens to walk in.

A young, short & thick Officer of the Regiment of Conti followed Mr Walpole & me into the Church & all over the Convent: he took occasion to speak a little English to me, & upon Enquiry, he told me he was a Native of France, but of Irish Extraction & that his Name was Mac-Cartney. On each Side of the paved way from St Denis to Paris is a Double Row of Trees, & about 7 or 8 Stone Gothic Crosses, some of them very beautiful, on either Side of it; being the resting Places where the Body of St Lewis stopt, when his Son, Philip 3, carried it in Procession from one Place to the other. After dining at the Hôtel du Parc Royal, I went in the Coach to Mr Foley the Banker's in the Rue St

[1] Jean R., 1692-1768.

x

Sauveur near the Rue de Montorgueille, not far from St Eustace's Church, where I changed two Bank Bills of 20 Pounds each for Louis d'Ors, & had 222 Livres 15 Sous for each. Mr Foley was gone into England.

Saturday, 23 *Nov:* Great Frost, excessive cold, & the greatest Rime & Fog I ever saw. In passing over the Pont-Neuf it was so thick, that hardly was the Equestrian Statue to be seen. I paid my *Valet de Louage* his Bill, Monsr Cartier the Wine Merchant's Bill, & the *Traiteur,* or Cook, his Bill. At Noon I walked out, it being hard, dry & frosty, first to the Church of the Petits Augustins, & went out thro' our Lady's Chapel on the South or right Hand Side of the High Altar: from thence I walked once more to take a View of the Saint Chapelle, the Parliament Halles by it, near which I bought several Trinkets, such as Snuff Boxes & Tooth-Pick Cases, & walking from thence by Bye Passages to the Cathedral of Notre Dame, I wanted to get into the Church of St Denys du Pas, which was shut up, so that I could not get in. It stands very low, the Streets being raised above it, & very near the Cathedral: it was a very antient Structure, & has the Image of St Denis holding his mitred Head in his Hand, on the Outside of the East or *Rond Point* Window to the Street. The Church of St Bartholomew is near the Palais & Ste Chapelle: it is an antient Fabric with a *Chevet* or *Rond Point*: the Choir & Nave are very much confined, but neat & handsome, & the High Altar is elegant, 2 Columns supporting a Story above it: there are Chapels all round it, & a double Isle on the right Hand Side: in a Chapel on this Side is a very beautiful white Marble Monument against the Wall for Monsr

Chlerselier,[1] an eminent Mathematician, as it should seem by the Emblems about it. I went to take my Leave of the glorious Church of Notre Dame, where near 100 Canons chanted Vespers most solemnly & harmoniously in their black Cowls, with two Chanters on a Form near the Choir Door, dressed in rich Copes, walked backwards & forwards to the Eagle & then to their Seat, which was richly covered & making several Congées to one another at different Pauses. I could not help admiring more & more this most elegant, beautiful, grand & stately Gothic Pile, which has double Isles all round the Church & *Chevet*: In the very antient Cloyster full of flat Stones for the Clergy of the Cathedral at the East End of it, I observed on the left Hand, soon after you entered it, a Door, which by an Inscription above it, informed me that it was the Chapter House of the Cathedral.

When I came out from the Cathedral I stepped into the Chapel of the Hotel-Dieu, which is close to it, in a Manner, occupying a Corner of the Square before it on the left Hand Side, the Arch-Bp of Paris going between that & the South West Door of the Cathedral to his Palace. The Hospital is an old, but a mean Building to look at: & the Chapel up a few Steps in the Street, was low, dark & dismal, with a Pair of small Organs over the Entrance into it: & as it was pretty much crowded I did not chuse to stay long, but putting my Mite into the Poors Box at the Door, I left it to look at the fine Hospital fronting it, called the Hospital *des Enfans trouvès*, or Foundling Hospital, which is a very handsome modern Building to the Street: but how furnished withinside I know not, as I did not go into it: which

[1]Claude Clerselier (1614-84); an ardent Cartesian.

was the last Observation I made of any public Building in Paris.

Sunday, 24 *November*. Fine Day & cold, but the greatest Rime on the Trees I ever saw any where. The Father Prior of the English Benedictines, Mr Walsh, sent me a Letter of Excuse for not calling on me, with a Packet of Papers, which he desired I would deliver as directed: another also from Dame Frances Sanders, the Canoness of St Austin, with a small Packet to Mrs Bienfait, a Milliner in London. I then paid Madame Meàn for 4 Weeks & 4 Days Lodging at her House, 4 Louis & an half, with which she was well contented. My Servants packed up my Maille & Portmanteaus, while I went to Dinner at the Hôtel du Parc Royal, where Mr Walpole gave me some Letters & small Parcels to carry into England; particularly a beautiful Snuff Box of 5 Guineas, a little Parcel for my Lady Hervey, another for my Lady Littleton[1] & other Things. On taking Leave of him I went & drank Tea at Mr Livier's where were some English at Cards; but I did not know them, & not being very well I did not play, but got Home about 7 o'Clock, & was excessively ill, being taken with a Purging & vomiting all of a sudden: but getting into Bed, I had a very good Night's Sleep, & was well enough, thank God for it, in the Morning. However, as the Weather was remarkably cold, I did not think it safe or proper to begin so long a Journey as from Paris to Calais, immediately after so strong Evacuations, for Fear of catching cold.

Monday, Nov: 25. Fine Day, but severely cold: so much so, that I found no Difference in the Sharpness of our Climate & this of Paris. My Post Chaise came into

[1]Elizabeth Rich, Baroness Lyttelton.

the Court at 8 o'Clock in the Morning: but for the
Reason already alledged I did not chuse to make Use
of it, & staid by the Fire Side all the Day. Mr Eustace,
an Irish Gentleman, who lodged in the Apartment
opposite to me, sent to know how I did. He has
Relations settled in France, where he proposes also
living, being of the Religion of the Country. I paid
Monsieur Pascal 3 Guineas for the use of his Post
Chaise, which was a Close one, & very small, there
being hardly Room for me & my Servant to sit conveniently in it. I paid him also Half-a-Guinea for a Pint
of the best Varnish to new varnish my own Post Chaise
or Chariot at Home, our own not being comparable to
it,[1] & 3 Livres for a Couple of Blereau's[2] or Camel's
Hair small Brushes to do it with.

Tuesday, Nov: 26. Not a very good Night, sleeping
but little. Very fine Day, & excessive hard Frost: so
that I was not a little frightened at the Postilion's going
such a Pace over their slippery Stones thro' the City of
Paris. Mr Walpole sent his Servant Lewis to me, to let
me know that he was coming to see me: I sent him back,
begging he would not give himself that Trouble, for
that I was just going to get into my Chaise; which I did
about 9 o'Clock in the Morning, after a good Breakfast
of Chocolate & Coffee. As there were 2 Persons in the
Chaise I was obliged to have 3 Horses to the Post
Chaise, which go all abreast, the Postilion riding the
outside Horse on the left Side as you sit in it, the middle
one being in the Shafts, & a *Bidet,* generally a little
Stone Horse, in Traces made of Ropes & the most
ordinary Materials, running on the other Side, with his
Bridle fastened to the Shaft Horse. The Postilion went

[1]*See* Add. MSS. 5835, 268.   [2]*Blaireau.*

thro' the Rue Colombier, Bussy, then turned down the
Rue Dauphine & so went over the Pont-Neuf & so got
into the long Rue St Denis, & all this so fast, that I
wished myself out of his Chaise twenty Times, expect-
ing every Moment that the Horses would slip down
with me, as the Chaise & Baggage were very heavy, &
laid with a vast Weight on the Shaft Horse. But the
Horses went very safe, being either very sure footed or
much used to their slippery Pavement. In less than an
Hour I got to St Denis, the first Stage, being a Poste
Royale, for which you pay double, tho' it is not above
5 English Miles: for from the Metropolis or where the
Court resides, as Versailles or Fontainbleau, they make
every first Stage a Royal Post: their Stages being
generally between 5 & 6 Miles: which makes it rather
inconvenient to be so often shifting your Horses: which
in general are very good strong Stone Horses of an
under Size, with a little *Bidet* on the off Side. Their
Postilions are generally great rough, rude, Fellows, of
no Sort of Behaviour & are never contented with what
you give them. I was informed that a 12 Sous Peice was
very sufficient for a Common Stage & 15 Sous for a
Poste Royale: but I found that would never do: so that
I generally gave them for a single Post 18 Sous & for
a Post & an half, a Livre, & the same for a Poste
Royale: which is hardly so much as we give our English
Postilions: who are Cleaner & cleverer Fellows, in the
same Degree as our Equipages exceed those of France
for Lightness, Ease & Convenience. The Price for each
Horse to your Equipage for a single Poste is 25 Sous
each, so that for the 3 Horses it is 75 Sous, which makes
it 3 Livres 15 Sous per Poste: & for a Poste Royale you
pay 8 Livres 5 Sous. I never saw more clownish, brutal

People in my Life than the Postilions & Post-Masters:
they take your Money, hardly vouchsafe you a Look, &
never thank you for it: & of all the People I ever saw
they seem to be the most incurious: I have been for a
Quarter of an Hour at the Door, while 10 or a Dozen
People were busy in lifting up the Chaise with you in
it, others in getting the Horses in, others taking those
away who brought you there, & not a Soul would look
into the Chaise to see if any one was in it, 'till the
Postilion came & demanded his Fee with his Hat on, &
usually took the Pay for the Horses: while Numbers of
Beggars were teising you all the Time for Charity. The
Post-Houses are generally very miserable looking
Buildings, with large ordinary Stables, & none of them
Public Houses: they are contrived for Single Posts or
Posts & an Half according as Towns & Villages lie
convenient for such a Distribution; & where these are
wanting Houses on Purpose are built. While they were
changing my Horses at St Denis, I went for an Hour to
refresh my Memory with the Tombs in that beautiful
Church, which a Swiss shewed to me: & I had more
Satisfaction in looking over them now by myself than
when I was here some few Days before on Purpose to
examine them. The Altar by the Side of the High
Altar, & between Dagobert's Tomb & the Coffin &
Pall of Lewis 14, I observed was not for the Soul of this
last King, but for his Father, Lewis 13. There were
some Monuments in the Chapels on the North Side of
the Church, which I had not observed before, but
which for want of Time I could make no Memoran-
dums of.

From St Denis to Escouan [?] was a single Post,
thro' a flat Country: as is the Country from Escouan to

Chantilly, pretty much like the worst Part of Cambridge-shire, being two Posts & an half, it being only one Post from Lusarche, a little Market Town, to Chantilly. Here the Prince of Condé has a most magnificent Palace, Gardens & Stables: but as Mr Walpole in going to Paris, while he went to look at these Things had his Portmanteau taken off from before his Chaise, with all his Linen & wearing Apparel in it,[1] & I not liking the Looks & Behaviour of the People at the Inn near the Palace Gates, where I changed my Horses, & must have lain all Night, had I gone to have seen every Thing worth looking at, I determined not to go there at all, & only took a Glass or two of Wine & some Bread & never got out of the Chaise. The Town of Chantilly is but a small Place: the Church was a small, elegant Building of modern Architecture, standing in the Street with its West Front, which I left on my right Hand. On the other Side of the Town was the greatest Quantity of Game, Hares, Pheasants & Partridges, that ever I saw: indeed beyond any Bounds of Probability, even to become a Nuisance to the Neighbourhood by their prodigious Abundance. I did not like the Situation of so splendid a Palace as Chantilly, in so low & flat a Country, which rather demanded the more lofty & Princely Situation of an elevated Point of View, from whence the Beauties of it might be admired at a Dis-tance, as well as command from it the adjacent Country. From Chantilly to Lingreville or Creille[2] sur L'Oise, is a Post & an half: this Town is very prettily seated upon the Oise, or Ouse, as we should term it in England, a

[1]"My portmanteau, with part of my linen" are Walpole's words, *Letters of Hor. Walpole* (Toynbee), No. 1051, Sept. 18, 1765.

[2]Creil.

very good River, which runs into the Seine at a good
Distance below Pontoise. Over it at Creille you pass 2
good Bridges; on the Banks of the River you leave in
the Town on your left Hand, a fine old Castle, with
Turrets & Battlements in as great Plenty as in the
Prints of Pomfret & Richmond Castle & Palace,
published by our Antiquary Society, but very ruinous
& out of order, with a neat pretty small round Tower by
it, which looks as if only one Person could get up into
it at once: being like the Towers, mentioned by
Writers, in many of the Cathedral Church Yards in
Ireland; or the Minarets in the Turkish Mosques. The
Parish Church I left at some Distance on my right
Hand, the Tower of which was very large, & I think
had a Spire on it of Stone, but very old & ruinous. In
going out of the Town on my left Hand I saw an old
small Chapel so ruined & desecrated, that a good large
Tree was suffered to grow in the Body of it, the
Branches of which came out at the Roof, which was
fallen in: so that the same Appearance of a ruined &
dilapidated Church, which, I when a Boy used to
frequent, being then esteemed a very handsome one,
in the Entrance into Cambridge by the Castle, ought
not to shock Foreigners, (as they may see the same
Sight in their own Countries), however it may the
Natives; especially when we consider the Incumbent of
it, who thus patiently suffers it to run to Ruin, his being
a Person who has wrote as severely & turned into
Ridicule the common Desecrators of Sacred Edifices in
our Civil Wars, as any man now living: tho' a very
worthy Man for all that: & which only shews the
Inconsistency of Human Weakness: & how differently
we can write & think when the Case is our own. This

Town is pleasantly situated in a Valley surrounded by Hills: & it was a Mile beyond it that the Post House was seated, where was only a few wretched Houses, from whence to Clermont en Beauvaises, which was situated on a very high & beautiful Eminence or Hill, was only a single Post: but it growing dark before I arrived there, I could see less of the Town & Country about it than my natural Curiosity could have wished. I lodged at the Sign of the *Swan*, at a tolerable good House, the Master of which had been a Trooper, whose Name was Caron. As this Journal is only designed for my own use, & to refresh my Memory with what happened in my Journey to & from Paris, I shall put down here my Bill of Expenses, as in other Places, to compare them with those in England: which, notwithstanding all the noted Boasting of French cheapness, will be found to be pretty much the same in one Kingdom as in the other: tho' perhaps our English Profuseness on this high Road from one Metropolis to the other, may occasion the Dearness on this. I had only myself & Servant, which generally I have observed, in an English Inn, without paying for Horses, comes to about 12 or 14 Shillings for Supper & Breakfast: & when the Servants are paid, half-a-Crown more: which is nearly the same in France, on this Road; but at Versailles much dearer; in the same Manner as they make People pay more extravagantly at Hampton Court or Richmond. I have several of my Bills which I shall transcribe as a Specimen; which may also be a Curiosity if these Papers should have the Hap to survive longer than they deserve. My Dinner at Versailles Nov: 13 for myself:

						lv	sous
Potages et Bouillie	-	-	-	-	1.	10
Poularde -	-	-	-	-	-	5.	0
Pain	-	-	-	-	-	-	0.	5
Vin	-	-	-	-	-	-	1.	5
Bois, 2 Peices	-	-	-	-	-	0.	10

TOTALE	-	-	8.	10

Cigne, à Clermont, Nov: 27.

			lv	sous
Fricassèe des Poulets & Canards	-	-	4.	0
Pain & Salade	-	-	-	-	-	0.	16
Vin -	-	-	-	-	-	-	4.	0
Bois	-	-	-	-	-	-	1.	10
Lits -	-	-	-.	-	-	-	1.	0
Pour le Dejeunè	-	-	-	-	1.	0

TOTALE	-	-	12.	6

Wednesday, Nov: 27. Fine Day & Thaw. After Breakfast I left Clermont le Beavoisis, situated on a very loft Situation, & very steep down the Town; which as the Ice was thawing made it still more dangerous: but an Hosteler going by the Side of the Chaise & Horses, made it less frightful. I cannot omit one Circumstance, as it is Picturesque[1] of the French Manners & Cleanliness, which made me laugh, at the Inn at Clermont, where they have an Iron Manufactory. While I was at Supper a very lively Boy, who spoke a little English very imperfectly, came into the Room & was very pressing to sell some neat Knives for the Pocket: as they were very neat, I bought 2 of him, & as he was somewhat entertaining with his French Forwardness, Familiarity & bad English, the Boy telling me that he had had a great Desire of accompanying an English

[1]Apparently, "typical"; but this sense is not recorded.

Gentleman into England, but that his Parents would
not let him go, merely from their Observation of the
common & bad Practice of the English in larding their
common Conversation with Oaths & profane Swearing
at almost every Word: an Observation but too just, &
not much to the Credit of those who practice it! I had
just done Supper, having had a Couple of roasted Teal
or small wild Ducks; one of which I had eat very little
of, tho' I had carved the Wings & Legs, & left them in
the Dish; this I observed the Boy had a liquorish Eye
upon: so sending the Servant of the House out of the
Room, I told the Boy to take a Knife & Fork & eat
what he pleased; which I observed was no unpleasant
Thing to him: but how to use the Fork, tho' he was a
Cutter by Trade, was the great Difficulty: for having
always been used to eat with his Fingers *à la mode de
France*, he was at an utter Loss to handle the Fork, &
made several Essays about it in a most awkward
Manner, & all to no Purpose: so that he was e'en
forced to let it alone, & give up his Duck & Supper; to
his no small Mortification: for he was ashamed to eat
with his Fingers, & in their own beastly Manner, as he
saw me eating with a Fork & wiping my Mouth with
clean Napkins & Table-Cloth, as the English are used
to do upon this Road so frequented by them. After I
had enjoyed for a very little while the poor Boy's
Distress, I told him that he had better take the dis-
jointed Duck Home with him: little suspecting the
way he meant to convey it. This was a Peice of Luck so
little expected that I saw his Eyes sparkle upon it; &
immediately, for Fear of the Servant returning into the
Room before he had secured his Supper, turning aside
his dirty black leather Apron, & opening his greasy

Waistcoat Pocket, he soon put the Carcase of the Duck with its Legs & Wings, Gravy & all, into it, & marched off with it. It was with great Difficulty that I could keep my Countenance during this Operation & Contrivance: for I was unwilling to disconcert the Enjoyment of the Boy in his intended good Supper; yet could hardly contain myself: & I should have been the more sorry to have done so, as the Boy's Gratitude appeared the next Morning, by attending the Chaise all the way down the Hill, & even out of the Town, thanking me for his good Supper the Evening before. Indeed this Circumstance of his going out of the Town with me, brought the Circumstance to my Remembrance, which otherwise would have been forgot. I think the way thro' Beauvais on the left Hand, being a paved way, divided at this Place, & we turned off to the Right, leaving the Causey for a more dirty Road. After you have got about a Mile from Clermont, in a low flat Valley, with Rivulets, stands the large but not elegant or handsome House of the Duke de Fitz-James,[1] with fine walks, Gardens & Woods all about it: you leave his Stables on the right Hand, over the great Entrance by an Arch [let] into which are the Royal Stewards' Arms of England, & the Castle is on the left Hand, very near the great Road, which winds about under his Garden Walks, & is made like some of our new English Roads, with Gravel & Flints, & rising up in the Middle. Very little of the Road from this Place to Boulogne was paved, & the Cheif Part of it very indifferent. The Country between Clermont & Amiens was very like that Part of Cambridgeshire which joins

---

[1]Charles, Duc de F. (1712-1787). Walpole describes both the chateau and its owner in a letter to H. S. Conway, Sept. 12, 1765.

to Hertfordshire; being Chalky, open & champaign.
From Clermont to St Juste, a good Village, was a Post
& an half: & from St Just[1] to Wavigny,[2] a small little
Place, a single Post; & from Wavigny to Breteuil,
(where in a miserable Village, was a small Mount, on
which was built a neat Summer-House), a Post & half.
From Breteuil to Flers was a Post & a half, being a
Parcel of miserable Cottages; & from Flers to Hébécourt, just such another Place, another Post only; as it
was no more from Hébécourt to Amiens. This City is
in a fine Plaine, & the Cathedral, at a Distance & as
you approach it, seems but a small Pile of Building of
the Sort: but when you get to it, its Magnificence &
Grandeur surprize one. The City itself is rather handsome than otherwise, with a tolerable Market Place in
the middle of it, across which I passed to go to my Inn,
& the Houses are passable, as well as the Streets,
standing upon the River Somme, which, about this
Place, branches out into many Streams, & waters the
greatest Part of Picardy, Amiens being the Capital of
that Province. The Master of the Inn that I was
directed to, was a very civil & obliging Man & his Sign
was *Les bons Enfans*, or "The Jolly Topers;" a very
ordinary looking House, tho' I had a very good Chamber below Stairs, with 2 good Beds in for my Servant &
Self. As soon as I got out of the Chaise, I was shewn the
Way to the Cathedral Church, which, of all that ever I
saw, pleased me most. It is the most airy, lightsome,
elegant & pleasing Gothic Structure that can be seen:
I was only concerned that the Day began to close &
that I should not have Time to examine the Inside at my
Leisure. The great West Front is on a Flight of a great

[1] St J. en Chaussée.   [2] Wavignies.

many Steps; which is different from all the Gothic
Churches I have seen, with a large & broad Walk upon
them to the Doors: the Place before it is not open or
large enough to give you a good Prospect of it: which is
so much the more to be lamented, as it deserves it the
best of any I have seen. It is most like the Front of
Peterborough Cathedral of any in England; having 3
large & magnificent arched Door Ways into the Nave &
Side Isles: these Arches or Doors are fuller of perfect
Statues than either Notre Dame or St Denis; and the
whole West Front is most richly adorned with fine
gothic Sculpture of every Sort possible: it has 2 West
Towers, & in the Middle of the Church a most light &
elegant Spire of a great Height. The South Transept
Entrance is also most richly adorned with Statues &
Carvings, as Images in Niches fill up the whole South
Side on the Outside between the West End & the
South Transept; & might do more, had I examined it
more at my Leisure. The Stone Vaulting of the Church
up to the *Chevet* or *Rond Point* is very elegant & nice, &
of a vast Height, with very light neat Pillars, which
surround the whole Church, *Chevet* & all, there being
Isles all round the Nave & Choir; both of them being
entirely paved with black & white marble. The Organs
at the West End of the Church are in an Organ Loft
immoderately high: under which, on each Side of the
Door by the Pillars, lie 2 very fine Monuments in Brass
cast, of two Bishops in their Mitres & Episcopal Robes:
but who they were for, I know not, it beginning to grow
dusky, so that I could not see to read, had there been
any Inscriptions: it is probable they were removed from
the Choir, or some other Part of the Church, when it
was new paved, for as I had only a Boy with me whom I

took from the Inn to shew me the Way, & saw not a
Soul in the Church, I could have no Information: these
Tombs were alike of the Altar Sort, tho' not raised much
from the Ground, & I should suppose they might have
lain in Arches under the Walls near the Altar in the
Choir. In an Arch of the Wall on the Outside of the
Choir on the South, lies an old Statue of a Bishop, & a
little higher, at his Feet, in another Arch lies the Statue
of a Clergyman. Another Bishop in White Marble in an
Arch of the Wall, lies at the East End of the Choir on
the Outside in the Isle. In the West Front & 2 Transept
Isles are 3 beautiful Rose or Catherine Wheel Windows.
The Bp of Amiens, I was told, was a very worthy, good
old Man, who laid out most of his Revenue in Charities
to the Poor, & was much beloved in his Diocese: he
returned only Yesterday from a Mission in the Country
to his Palace in this City, which is situated close to the
East End of the Cathedral: I went into a very small
Court, when I came out of the Church, but saw nothing
of any Consequence to denote any Thing magnificent:
perhaps the Cheif Front or Entrance was by some other
way. As I left the Cathedral to go to the Inn, I met a
large Funeral, which I let pass by me, & then went into
the old Church of St Remy where they were singing
Vespers, the Church being quite full; & as I had Time
enough, not ordering my Dinner or Supper till 6
o'Clock, I staid the whole Time. It seemed a dark &
gloomy Church, the Choir was small, but the High
Altar very much ornamented with gilding: it had 2
Isles with Chapels, larger on the North Side, where
stood a fine Pulpit, all of Brass. It had also a Tower on
the North West Corner of the Church, whose West
Front was ornamented with Statues. Amiens is seated,

like the Duke de Fitz-James's House, in a rich Valley
surrounded with beautiful Hills about it. When I was
at my Inn a Franciscan Frier came to beg Charity for
the Love of good St Francis.

Thursday, Nov: 28. Fine Day. My Bill at Amiens
was

	lv	sous
Pour le Souper - - - - -	5.	0
Deux Bouteilles de Vin de Bourgogne -	4.	0
Bois - - - - - -	1.	15
Pour Logement - - - - -	2.	0
Ratifia - - - - - -	0.	12
Pour le Poste de Hébécourt - - -	4.	19
TOTALE - -	18.	6

I set out from Amiens at 7 o'Clock, without any
Breakfast, & found the Roads intolerably bad from
thence to Pequigny, being a flat fenny Country, & a
Post & a half, leaving the River close on the right Hand,
& Cliffs or Hills on the Left, for a long way. The
Somme is a tolerable good River in this Place, & the
Town of Pequigny but a shabby one: the venerable old
Castle stands on the Side of the Hill commanding the
Town, & seemed to be much out of Repair, tho' in a
pleasant Situation: it belongs to the Duke de Chaulnes.
It was at this Place that the famous Interview & Peace
was made in 1475 between our King Edward 4 &
Lewis II. King of France, mentioned by Philip de
Comines in his *Chronique*, p. LX. of my old Edition of
that Historian printed at Paris in 1529. About a Mile
beyond the Town of Pequigny on the left Hand, at half
a Mile's Distance from the Road, you see a very fine &
noble Abbey of Benedictines called Du Gard, as well as
I could understand the Postilion, just as you pass up

Y

Hill thro' a miserable Village in the Way to Flix[e]-court, being only one Poste, soon after which you discover the next Poste called Ailly le Haut Clocher, from its large Tower on a high Hill, being only one Poste more: & from Ailly le Haut Clocher to Abbeville is a Post & a half, thro' very bad Roads. I was sorry I did not lodge that Night at Abbeville, an excellent fortified Town, seated very low, upon the same River Somme which runs thro' it, tho' we did not pass over it, leaving it on the left Hand, but went over a Bridge at the other End of the Town nearest Calais, which was built over a Stream that runs into it. The Town of Abbeville is very large and well built, & I passed by 2 or 3 very famous churches: but not getting out of my Chaise I went into none of them. The Post House was a very fine one, the very best I met with, at the End of the Town nearest Paris. I saw a great Shew of the Woollen Manufacture as I passed thro' it, & it seemed to be a very flourishing trading Place. From Abbeville to Nonvion was a Post & a half, which was a miserable Village; & from No[n]vion to Bernay one single Post & from Bernay to Nampont, down a steep Hill another Post only. At this miserable Village I experienced as much Barbarity as I could have done in the most un-civilized & savage Nation upon Earth. As it was getting dark, & we had a Post & half to Montreuil, thro' Woods & bad Roads, I began to think it best to enquire whether we should be able to get to that Place by the Time the Gates were shut; being informed that they were shut at this Time of the year at 6 o'Clock, & it was now four, when I had near 8 or 9 Miles to go: Mr Walpole having told me that he was obliged in his way to Paris to lie at a wretched Inn in the Suburbs of

Montreuil, coming after they were shut up. Which
Suburbs on the Calais Side are splendid to those on the
Side I was on, where the very worst Cottage in England
was superior to any House I saw there: which had I
known as well then as I did when I passed by them
afterwards, I should not have hesitated a Moment about
going further than Nampont. Accordingly when I got
there I sent for the Post Master to the Chaise Side,
desiring to speak with him: but he not appearing, a tall
well-looking Woman, near 60 years of Age, but of an
ill-tempered Physiognomy came to me, to whom, in the
civilest Manner & Expressions I could make Use of, I
addressed myself, desiring her to be so kind as to advise
me what Course I had to take; when the old Carrion,
with the greatest *Sang froid* & most cool Indifference,
shrugging up her Shoulders, made Use of this petri-
fying Expression, *Vous êtes le Maitre*: that is, it is no
Affair of mine, & you may do as you please. I then
entreated her, as I was a Stranger in the Country &
unacquainted with the Roads & Hours of shutting up
their Gates, that she would be so kind, as to give me her
Opinion, whether it was safe & adviseable for me to go
any further: when, as if on Purpose to distress one, she
had the same malicious Answer ready, That she knew
nothing of the Matter, & that I might judge for myself.
Upon this, seeing what an Animal I had to deal with,
& observing the Servants about the Horses & Chaise
keeping a profound Silence as their Mistress was talking
to me, I thought it best to proceed no further, & immediately asked if I could be accommodated with
Lodgings at this Post, when I was told that there was
an Inn over the way: upon which I ordered the Postilion to drive me there. Upon seeing me resolute to

stay, the old Bitch, God forgive me, going just into the House, assured me I might go very safe, for that they told her in the House, that the Gates were not shut up till 9 at Night: upon this I desired her to change me a Louis to pay her for her Horses, & while she was gone in to get Change, I heard the Servants talking among themselves, that the Gates would be shut before I got there: & upon my asking them if they had not heard what their Mistress had just said, they made Answer immediately, That notwithstanding her Assurances I should find it as they said: whereupon I told the Woman this Representation, which she said they only chattered among themselves, that the Horses & Postilion might not set out 'till next Day. So relying on this Assurance & wanting much to get to Montreuil, where I knew there was a good Inn & much frequented by English, I determined to set forwards, tho' between 4 & 5 o'Clock. But when I got on the Road, which was bad, & all thro' Woods & Forests, I began to wish myself at Nampont, tho' the most detestable Place I ever was in: for I thought myself very unsafe, even from such a Pack of wretches as I had just left at the Post House, who, if they had a Mind to have followed me, in the Dark, might easily have robbed & murdered me & my Servant, who could make little Resistance without any Arms to defend ourselves: & I could not help thinking the worst of a Pack of People I had just left behind me. However, tho' I was very safe, as the Police is so good thro'out all the King of France's Dominions, as never to hear of any Robbery on the High Way, yet I passed as uneasy two Hours, as ever I did in my Life almost: not only from the said Fears & Apprehensions, but from the Dread of not getting into the Town: for not

a Soul had given me the least Intimation, that it was
possible to get the Gates opened, even after they were
closed above an Hour; so my Distress seemed to be
complete: for the Houses or rather Hovels were such
as there was no Thoughts of getting out of the Chaise,
which I had determined to have slept in, had I not had
the better Fortune to get into the Town. For, without
knowing that it was ever practiced to attempt getting in
upon such an Occasion, when the old Postilion, at some
Distance stopped, & told me that we were too late to
get in, I made him, much against his Inclination, as it
seemed, go up to the very first Draw Bridge to see with
my own Eyes that it was as he told me: & when we were
there, of his own Accord he set up such a Yell as I had
never heard before; which he repeated two or 3 Times
before any Answer was made to him: at last a Centinel
from the Parapet Wall at a Distance from the first
Intrenchment appeared, & demanded, who was there
& what was wanted; when the Postilion answered, that
an English Nobleman was at the Gates & beg'd it as a
Favour to be admitted into the Town; to which the
Centinel replied, That he would go to the Commandant
& try to get the Keys. All this was transacted between
the Postilion & Centinel, without my putting in a Word:
& when the Soldier was gone to the Governor, I told
the Postilion, that I did not use to personate Characters
that did not belong to me; that I was no Nobleman, or
any Person of Quality, or Fashion, but only a plain
common English Gentleman: to which the Rogue of a
Postilion immediately returned me this shrewd Answer;
That if I had a Mind to sleep in the Chaise or in one of
these Hovels a little behind us, I might e'en tell the
Officer what I had told him: for that not long before he

had brought two Persons who were in my Situation, &
who honestly but ignorantly had told the Officer to
whom they applied for Admission, both their Names &
Profession: for they were Tradesmens to whom the
Commandant sent this Message by the Centinel, who
had been dispatched to him for the Keys: *Que l'on
disent à Messieurs les Negocians, qu'ils viellent à leurs
Merchandises:* Pray tell these Mercantile Gentry, to
mind their proper Business, & if they have a Mind to
lodge in fortified Town, to come before the Gates are
closed. This sensible Remonstrance stopped my Mouth,
& I had no Answer to make to it: besides, my Apprehensions of lying out of the Town, began even to
reconcile the Cheat of passing myself off for a Person of
some Distinction: for it rained as hard as it could pour
all the Time of this Parly with the Centinel, & during
the Time of his going for the Leave of Entrance:
insomuch that the poor man was forced to get under his
Horses' Bellies for Shelter. At last the decisive Minute
arrived that was to determine whether I was to lie in
clean Sheets, in a warm Bed. & to have a good Supper,
or lie in the Chaise, in a very stormy, rainy Night: for
it is to be observed that I had had neither Breakfast nor
Dinner all that Day, & had taken nothing but Bread &
Wine & Water. The whole Day was uneasy, from the
Badness of the Roads & the Fears of not being soon
enough at Montreuil but the Landlord at Amiens was
at Fault, in not telling me to set out sooner. The
Suspense I sat in for the full half Hour while the Centinel was gone, made it appear at least treble the Time:
& I don't hardly ever remember to have felt more
exquisite Pleasure than when I heard, at a good Distance the Port Cullice drawing up, & the Draw Bridge

letting down; which was a certain Token that the Keys
& Leave was obtained. When I had passed the outer
Draw Bridge & passed thro' the first Fortifications, 3
or 4 Soldiers came to the Chaise Side & demanded my
Name: I told them fairly & honestly, That my Name
was Cole, an English Gentleman who was returning
from Paris, where I had been merely for Curiosity:
This they wrote down to give to the Commandant, &
having given about half a Guinea to them & the
Centinel, I was let pass the other Gates, with only being
demanded the same Question again at the last. No one
surely could be more happy than myself in a very small
dirty Room, which had not been washed I dare venture
to say of a Twelvemonth, for it was floored, a Thing not
usual in France, & in which were two very handsome &
elegant Beds, on each Side of the Fire, where I ordered
a good Fire & a good Supper, to refresh myself after so
much Uneasiness. And here it will not be amiss to
observe, That many of our Difficulties, which occasion
so much uneasiness, are more in our Fancy, than in
Reality: & that the Pleasure we receive after Suffering
them, is abundantly made up to us after having got over
them. So that in the Main, I ought to think myself
obliged to that old Carrion of a Post Mistress at Nampont, who, undesignedly, was the Occasion of so
sensible a Pleasure to me: for had she been kind enough
to have told me the Truth, in informing me, that I need
not be under any uneasiness about getting into the Town,
even tho' the Gates were shut: for should that be the
Case when I got there, I need only give a Fee to the
Soldiers, & might be admitted, I should have been much
more at my Ease, than I believe, she desired I should be.
That this was often the Case, I was fully satisfied, when

I heard at 9 o'Clock another Post Chaise come driving
into the Inn Yard: which was repeated at 1 o'Clock in
the Morning, while I was abed & asleep, when a Coach
& 4 Horses came there also: & upon Enquiry in the
Morning, I found it was a very common Practice, &
that it was the Thing in the World that the Soldiers
upon Guard wished for, as it was their Harvest. After,
having my Sheets aired at my own Fire, a Precaution I
always took, as the French never air either their Shirts
or Sheets, which are generally as wet & damp as if they
were just rained upon, & getting an excellent Supper
& a few Glasses of Wine extraordinary, I went to Bed,
& slept very soundly. Certainly the French are a more
hardy People than we are: they never air their Linnen,
but constantly go to Bed in damp, or rather wet Sheets,
& put unaired Shirts on their Backs without any
Danger of catching Cold: whereas the same Practice
would give an Englishman, if not his Death, at least the
Rheumatism. But Custom is every Thing: & it is
probable our sitting on Carpets & using ourselves so
tenderly & luxuriously is the Occasion of many
Disorders among us. I could not help observing the
inconsistent Behaviour of our good Neighbours in this
Respect. When the excessive cold & sharp Weather
came in about a week or two before I left Paris, I
observed on a sudden all the World got into Muffs:
some so ridiculously large & unweildly as to oblige
them to have a Sort of Belt of the same Skin come over
one Shoulder, as the Order of the Garter is worn, to
support their Enormity: this is the constant Method of
the Parisian Coachmen, who are not dressed if they
have not a great Muff, as big, literally speaking, as a
Mastif Dog, hanging in their Laps before them on

their Coach box: & you meet in the Streets & in
Coaches Muffs of as extraordinary a Size, tho' of
better Materials: for the Gentry wear Sables & fine
Skins: whereas the Coachmen & more ordinary People
are contented with those of their common rough Dogs'
Skins.[1] Even Beggars & Mumpers in the Streets had
their Muffs on, & the Delicacy of the common Carters,
who drove the Carriages out of the Country into Paris,
a Race of People, whatever we may think of them at
this Distance & in our Admiration of the French
Politeness, as much more clownish & loutish than our
own Sort of People of that Standard, as our tight smart
neat young country Lasses, & well-looking Country
Women or Cottagers Wives, & spruce Maid Servants,
exceed the Dowdyness, Awkwardness, Clumsiness &
Unsightliness of the French Women of the same
Orders; I say these doltish Carters had all of them their
Hands covered with Gloves furred within with Rabbit
Skins. In walking from the *Célestins* into the Arsenal I
observed my *Valet de Louage* go into a second Hand
Shop & cheapen an old Muff: I had the Curiosity to
ask him what they would have for it, & he told me 9
Livres. But with all this Delicacy about their Hands,
they seemed to be as little concerned for the well-being
of their Heads: & so that was kept in Order, & the
Curls & Powder not disturbed, all was well. Nay even
to such a Niceness are they come on this Head, that
both Men & Women never put an Hat on their Heads
for Fear of discomposing their well adjusted Hair:
which, indeed, to do them Justice, they admirably
set off to Advantage: & so that a Woman has her

---

[1]Gray, writing to his mother on Apr. 1, 1739, speaks of "a [French]
Countryman with his great muff."

Head well dressed, *frizè* & powdered, they don't seem to take so much Care about their other Ornaments. It is indeed grown to such an Excess, that they have introduced a new & most troublesome Invention to save the Beauty of their Head Dress, tho' at the Expence of always carrying in their Hand, Winter & Summer an Additional Peice of Furniture: I mean, a Parasol or Umbrella of Silk,[1] which opens by Springs & covers them in the Summer from the Sun & in the Winter from the Rain: & without this additional Implement you meet no one: My Taylor, Shoe-maker & every other Tradesman always came with them: so that a Frenchman has enough to do to take Care of & carry all his necessary Gears about him: for first he must have an Hat, tho' it now become an useless Part of Dress, & for this Reason most Gentlemen have flat slight Peices of black Stuff to represent it, & which they may easily wear under their Arm, it not being possible to put it on their Head, 2nd he is not dressed without a Muff, & that a good large one: & 3dly this now necessary Article of an Umbrella. Enough sure to employ their present Set of Hands, & would not be too much if they had another Pair also. The Gentry, who are supposed to go in Coaches & Chariots, I believe, seldom use these Umbrellas; except to get in & out of their Equipages in rainy Weather. I was much surprized, considering the Enormity of the Size of our Ladies' Silk Hats, of various Shapes & Sizes, which

[1]Though umbrellas had long been known in England, (Gay in his *Trivia*, 1716, speaks of the "umbrella's oily shed"), its use was exceptional. James Wolfe, writing from Paris in 1752, says "The people here use umbrellas in hot weather to defend them from the sun, & something of the same kind to save them from the snow and rain. I wonder a practice so useful is not introduced in England."

every English Woman wears on her Head, to keep them
from the Sun, which is even carried to such an Excess by
the better Sort, & has been now for these 20 years, as to
wear them in the House, at Meals, & all Day thro', &
even at visits, except when highly dressed; I say I much
was surprized in landing in France, where the Sun is
certainly more intense [and] consequently Hats more
useful, to find no such Thing in the Whole Country as
a Woman's Hat: but they all go stalking on with their
tanned Faces & nothing on their Heads but their
awkward coarse Caps. So that our being taxed as following the French in all their Fashions, is certainly unjust:
as nothing, in this Respect, can be more opposite the
one to the other: & I could instance the same in an
Hundred other Examples.

My Bill at Montreuil was as follows:

	ll	sous
Memoire pour le Soupe de Monsieur - -	6.	0
Pour une Bouteille de Vin de Bourgogne -	2.	10
Pour le Déjeûné - - - - -	1.	10
Pour les Bois - - - - - -	1.	5
Pour les Lits - - - - - -	1.	4
TOTALE - -	12.	9

The Inn at Montreuil was *La Cour de France*, the
Landlord's Name was Varein or Warren; he had been
a Gentleman's Servant in England, & one of his Sons
was just returned to him from my Lord Peters's[1]
Family in Essex, where he had been to learn a little
English.

Friday, Nov: 29. Fine Day. At 9 o'Clock I left
Montreuil, which seemed to be a very good large Town;
& the Suburbs towards Boulogne one long Street, with

[1]Baron Petre of Writtle.

good Houses & Inns in it. From Montreuil to Cormont, only a House or two, was a Post & a Half, & from Cormont to Samer one single Post. Samer is a small Market Town, seated on an Eminence, & a small River or Stream rather, by it. As the Springs of my Chaise were broken in getting to it, I was forced to stop near two Hours to try to get them mended: but the Blacksmith was such a Bungler that he could do nothing to them: so after a great Deal of fruitless Pottering, they were forced to fasten it up with Cords. While they were thus employed, I went with a young Lad, whose Name was John Lamb, whose Parents lived at Dover, & who had sent him here to learn the Language, (& who, with other Boys were got round the Blacksmith), into the Parish Church, close by, on the Market Place, to which you ascended by many Steps, & was as ordinary within as it was on the Outside: being a gloomy, dull & heavy Building, of no Sort of Architecture, either modern or antient. In the South Isle in a Niche in the Wall was an ordinary Image of a Man on Horseback: there was no left Isle at all, but it had a very large & square North Chapel parallel to the Choir or Chancel, in which, among other ordinary Tombs, I observed the 3 following for as many Priors of the adjacent Abbey. On the South Wall, above the Rails of the Altar was fixed a very ordinary Sort of Picture on Canvas, as I take it, in a Frame, of a Benedictine Monk on his Knees before a Crucifix on an Altar, with these Inscriptions on it, above his Head:

Cy gysent Adrien la Poterie, Prieur de l'Abbaye de Samer, mort le 14. Sept: 1635. Et Antoine la Poterie, son Frere, aussi Prieur dudit Lieu, mort le 6 de Juin, 1649.

On the opposite or North Wall of the said Chancel was another of the same Sort of Tombs with this In-

scription, which was imperfect in the Date at the latter
End:

Cy gyst Roboam Sar, Prieur de l'Abbaye de ce Lieu, decedè
le 22 Xbr. . . .

This was the most unadorned, naked walled Church
I had seen in this Country: how the Priors came to be
interred here preferably to their own Church, close by,
I know not: for not a Soul was in it but the Boy &
myself. I then went with him to the Abbey, on the
South Side of the Church, which seemed to be a good
Building with a neat paved Walk to the West Door of
their Church, which was also open, but no one in it.
On the South Side of the Church was a good Cloyster,
to which you descended near 20 Steps. The Abbey
Church was small & neat, with the Altar of White
Marble, very elegant, in the middle of the Church, &
the Monks' Choir & Stalls behind it, but without any
Separation or Division, *à la Romaine*: there were also
2 very beautiful Altars of White Marble in the 2 Transept Isles. The Cloysters & part of the Abbey seemed
to be newly rebuilt. I suppose the Priory has the
Patronage of the Parish Church, which might occasion
the Interment of the Priors there. It is probable the
Monks were at Dinner or in their Apartments, for I
saw not one of them. In going out of Samer, about half
a Mile, descending a pretty steep Hill, on a slippery
Pavement, the Middle or Shaft Horse fell down, &
broke one of the Shafts of the Chaise: however, we
joyned it together as well as we could with the Assistance
of some Men & Women, whose Cottages were just by,
& went with it to Boulogne, which was only a Post &
an half: had not this Accident happened, with the other

which detained me at Samer, I designed to have got to Calais this Evening: which, probably, would have prevented the Ugly Accident which befel me at Dover & detained me there a Month confined to my Bed: for had I been at Calais this Night, it is more than probable that I should have got a Passage to Dover the next Day, & might have escaped getting into their ugly Boats in the Dark; as the Tide would probably have carried me into the Harbour. But this was as it pleased God, & might be designed me for my Benefit: & considering all Things, I have great Reason to be thankful that it was not worse. It was wonderful to me that these Accidents of the Horses falling down on their slippery Pavement, (considering how fast they go, & how heavily the Shaft Horse is laden, with a heavy clumsy Chaise, & great Luggage), don't happen continually: in which Case it is almost impossible but the Shafts must be broken: tho' they are made as strong & heavy as possible. I was in continual Fear of it from my first setting out from Paris, & many Times excepted it would happen before; & was constantly calling out to the Postilions to go gently down Hills especially. However I got to Boulogne at 3 in the Afternoon, whose upper Town stands most deliciously on a Cliff, & commands the Ocean: the lower Town lies under it, by a steep Descent by a very broad & good Street, at the End of which was another very good long Street which conducted to my Inn, the *Golden Lion*, kept by two Irish Men of the Names of Jacques & Dogharty, & was a very excellent Inn, & civil People. According to an abusive Letter in the *White Hall Evening Post* of about a Month ago, (I write this July 30th, 1766, in a most gloomy Day & very Melancholy Season, with

Deluges of Rain, Day after Day, when the Roads are worse than in Winter, the Country all over-flown, & Quantity of Hay rotting upon the Ground) the Boulonnois Noblesse of the superior or higher Town give themselves great Airs, & won't mix with the Gentry of the inferior Town, tho' one is as poor as the other. But perhaps that, & other Sarcasms upon them, may be unjust: as it seems to have been wrote by a prejudiced & warm Pen against them. As soon as I was got out of my Chaise & ordered my Dinner, or rather Supper, I took a Walk into the Town, but did not go to their Harbour. I observed that many of the Children & People spoke broken English, & that most of the Signs had French & English upon them. On the right-Hand Side of the High Street, where a Fish & other Market was kept, going up to the upper Town, stood a very large Parish Church, dedicated to St Nicholas, which is large, heavy & gloomy, with an high Stone Spire in the middle, having two Isles, with Chapels round the Chancel or Choir: & nothing handsome or elegant in any Part of it that I could discover. Higher up the Street on the same Side of the Way was an handsome public Building erecting, but having only a Boy with me to shew me about, who was of a stupid & heavy Genius, I could make nothing of him by my Enquiries. At the upper End of this steep, broad & fine Street stood the Citadel & Parapet Walks in it on the right Hand Side, with a most noble & beautiful View over the Lower Town to the Harbour & main Ocean: so that I can't conceive a more delicious Situation: tho' bleak & cold in bad weather. You enter the upper Town thro' a large fortified Gate, on the right Hand of which is the Citadel & Walks aforesaid, & on the left, above an high

Wall, an exceeding large Crucifix, finely gilt & painted, with its Face looking down the Street & commanding the Sea, & our Island. When you have got thro' this Part, leaving a Convent of Ursuline Nuns on the right Hand, in a Sort of Square or Market Place, you go up a Street on the left Hand, which brings you to the most awkward, ill-built & least adorned Cathedral Church I ever saw. The West Front has a poor small Opening before it: & indeed it does not deserve a good one, which would be thrown away upon so poor and clumsy a Thing. It has two small Turrits at the West End, over the great Door of which I observed an ordinary coarse Peice of Carving in Stone, well worthy of the Rest of the Building, which had been defaced by some Bigot: & there was a Spire of no Beauty, on a squat, short, thick, clumsy Tower in the middle of the Church, whose Pillars in the Nave were large & antient, & the Arches circular. The Choir was very beautiful & elegantly fitted up, & the Canons' Stalls very much resembling those in King's College Chapel in Cambridge, with small turned Pillars supporting a Gothic Sort of Canopy over Head, in Oak unpainted: the Bp's Throne was plain & simple, at the East End of the Stalls, & Arms carved on them. [The arms depicted and described.] I have 2 different Prints, in my Collection, of Victor Bouthillier Arch-Bishop of Tours, one of them a very good one, painted by Champaigne & engraved by Nanteuille in 1651, with the same Arms on both. Perhaps he might have been first Bp of Boulogne before he was translated to Tours: or they might be the Arms of some other of the same Family: or of one who gave the same Ordinary. I observed the handsome Altar was built in 1653, & was composed of

black Marble with gilt Ornaments about it; at the
Corners were 2 Cherubims, & in the Middle an Holy
Dove in gilt copper or Brass. The Pillars which sur-
round the Choir near the Altar, & divide it from the
Isles, or rather a large Balustrade on a Pediment are of
a whitish Marble. Behind the High Altar was an
Inscription under a Basso-relievo in white Marble,
fronting the beautiful Chapel of our Lady; the whole
Church being paved with black & white Marble. The
Episcopal Palace is a new handsome Building of white
Stone, sashed in the French ugly Manner, which spoils
the Beauty of the Building. This Palace is on the left
or North Side of the Cathedral, & there is a Passage to
it thro' the North Transept. As it was the Eve of St
Andrew, there were many People in the Church at their
Devotions, & the Music in the Church was tolerable:
tho' I must needs say, that to my Ear & Conception
our English Church Music is infinitely superior &
preferable to any I heard in the French Churches. In
descending the Street in the lower Town I observed the
new Building near St Nicholas his Church was The
Seminary. I got to my Inn about 5 o'Clock, & at 6,
while I was at Supper, the new & elegant English
Coach, with 4 Postilion Horses, with a Post Chaise, in
which were two Negroes, dressed as fine as Hands
could make them, with Silver Lace in Profusion on
their fantastical Caps & Cloaths, & white Silk Stock-
ings, came into the Inn, with another French Servant.
One Mr Milles, a West India Gentleman, with his
Brother were in the Coach: both very young Men; the
elder Brother was the fattest Man I almost ever saw,
being very large & tall withall, & the finest Face that
can be conceived: I saw him at Paris, but not in his

z

Company, with his fine Blacks, visiting Mr Eustace
who lodged in the Hotel d'Orléans, in an Apartment
opposite mine: his Brother had but just come over to
accompany him Back: he was as little & ill-looking as
his Brother was portly & handsome: they seemed odd
Sort of People, & quite frenchified with their Muffs &
other Accoutrements. According to my Servant's
Report, who saw more of them than I did, (as he sat
with the Blacks two or 3 Times), they were very sottish
& drunken, & one of them, the little one, somewhat
disordered in his Head. When their Coach was put into
the Ship at Calais, it was absolutely crammed with
French Pyes, Woodcocks, Hares & Partridges: as the
Weather was cold they might keep; but it was impossible for a single Family to consume so much Provision
in a Week: it is probable they intended the cheif Part of
them for Presents to their Friends. These Gentlemen
followed me all the way from Paris, & came into the
Cour de France at Montreuil at one in the Morning, &
awaked all the House. One of them had been ill on the
Road, which occasioned their travelling no faster. The
arms on their Coach were, Ermine, a Millrind[1] Sable,
2nd & 3rd Gules, 3 Cinquefoils Argent. There were no
Side Chapels in the Nave of the Cathedral of Boulogne,
neither did I observe one Tomb of any Bishop of the See,
in any Part of the Church. My Bill at Boulogne
was:

					ll	s
Postilion from Samer	-	-	-	-	6.	17
To Ratifia	-	-	-	-	0.	6
Fricasè of Chickens	-	-	-	-	2.	0
Brace of Woodcocks	-	-	-	-	3.	10
A Dish of Whitings	-	-	-	-	1.	4

[1]Millrine, *fer de mouline*, iron-clamp of a mill-stone.

Bread	-	-	-	-	-	-	0.	4
To a Bottle of Burgundy	-	-	-	-	3.	0
To Fire	-	-	-	-	-	-	2.	0
To Lodging	-	-	-	-	-	-	1.	12
To a Pot of Coffee & Toast	-	-	-	-	1.	10
Paid for a Bottle of Ratifia	-	-	-	-	2.	5

	TOTAL	-	-	24.	8

By this Bill it is easy to see that an Inn at Boulogne was as dear and expensive as any in England: & notwithstanding the immense Quantity of woodcocks which I saw taken as I passed by the Sides of the Woods near Boulogne, yet they were charged me here as dear as at Paris. I will put down here a Note which the Cook at the *Hôtel D'Angleterre* sent me up on a Peice of Paper, on my sending to know the Prices of some Things I had a Mind to take with me to Blecheley, as the Weather was cold & they would easily keep, having bespoke a Woodcock Pye of 4 Birds only in it, which was put in the Bill when I came away, as it will shew the Plenty of these Articles, when you can buy them at that Price at an Inn.

							ll sous	
Le Couple des Bécasses—(that is—a Brace of								
Woodcocks)	-	-	-	-	-	-	2.	10
Le Couple des Perdreaux[1]—(Partridges a Brace)					2.	10
Une Poularde—(a fine fed fat Poulet)	-	-	3.	0
Un Liévre—(a Hare) -	-	-	-	-	2.	10
Un Dindon—(a Turkey)	-	-	-	-	2.	10

Every Article of which we should pay double for in England, except for the Poularde, which we know nothing of.

Saturday, Nov: 30. St Andrew. Frost, then misling Rain & Fog: & afterwards a fine Day. As I was getting

[1]Young partridges.

into my Chaise in the Inn Yard, a Coach-Maker, whose
Name was Du Four, & who mended & repaired all
Mr Pascal's Carriages, observed to me, that it was
dangerous for me to go any further with the Chaise I
had taken from Paris, & which was so shattered by the
Fall at Samer, that it would infallibly break down with
me before I reached Calais: he moreover told me, that
he had then in a Coach House in the Yard one of Mr
Pascal's own Chaises, which would hold me only, &
that my Servant might go upon a *Bidet*. I thought
myself very lucky in getting another Carriage so oppor-
tunely; so had my Things all put into this new Chaise,
& left the other to be mended at Mr Pascal's Expence
with Monsr Du Four at Boulogne. A French *Valet de
Louage*, who attended Mr Mills from Paris to Calais,
whose Name was Chapline, who lived in the Rue
Colombier, near the *Hôtel de Saxe*, in the second Story
towards the Street, (if I translate aright his Address,
which he gave me, in Order to recommend any Master
to him who was going to Paris), was very helpful to me,
in changing my Valise; & taking my Part against the
Brute of a Postilion, who wanted to be paid for his 3
Horses, which he had brought for my first Chaise,
which held 2 Persons, tho' I now wanted only two,
according to established Rules, as my new Chaise only
held myself, & altho' my Servant was to ride on the
Bidet, which was brought for the former, I would have
given a Livre to this Servant for his Civility, which he
as civilly refused, saying, he had done nothing more for
me than what every one ought to do for a Stranger.
This I mention in Honour to his good Behaviour. He
desired me only, if I had it in my Power, to recommend
him to any of my Acquaintance who should be coming

to Paris; & run & wrote the following Address on a
Scrap of Paper that I might not forget his Name:
Chapline, Rue Colombier, près de l'Hotel de Saxe, au
seconde sur le Devant, Faubourg St Germain. As I had
often drank a most pleasant Dram at the late Mr
Samuel Shepheard's at Bottesham in Cambridgeshire,
(Father to the present Lady Viscountess Irwin,[1]) which
he used to call by the Name of Boulogne, & was nothing
but a Ratify which they made there, I asked for some of
the same, & brought away 2 or 3 Bottles with me into
Buckinghamshire: & have one Bottle remaining now
untouched in the Cellar. [I write this July 30, 1766.]
The new Chaise I got into was one of the gentilest,
easiest & prettiest Things I was ever in. It held only
one Person, but that so snugly & comfortably, that I
have repented myself forty Times that I did not
purchase it. It was a small Chariot, with a Door before,
which let down before to get in at, like our Post Chaises
when they first came into Fashion about 25 Years ago:
two of which Sort I built while I lived in College: but
this was the most elegantly fitted up that can be
imagined: it was thoroughly lined with Crimson Velvet,
with thin stuffed Cushions on the Sides to lean your
Head against, of a rich Crimson Silk, with which the
Pockets were lined, & hung all round with a rich &
beautiful Silk Crimson Lace & Fringe. It had 3 large
Glasses, 2 on the Sides & one whole one before. The
Varnish of it was yet very handsome, tho' used as a
Hackney Chaise. The Chaise had not been ill used, &
I am heartily sorry I did not purchase it. If I had stopt
at Abbeville, I was recommended to the *Ecu de Brabant.*
When I went thro' the City of Boulogne & left the

[1] Or Irvine, wife of the 9th Visct. Irvine.

Cathedral close on my left Hand, it was so thick a Fog
as hardly to distinguish the Postilion: so that I lost the
Beauty of the Sea Prospect; which I was much concerned at, as I had seen nothing of it, tho' I had
travelled many Miles on the Sea Coast in this Part of
Picardy: however the Sun broke out at last, & discovered a very beautiful Country, with Hills & Vales
all the Way from Boulogne to Calais, till you come very
near the last Place, when it begins to be low & swampy.
The other Part was the prettiest Country I had seen
since I left England, & was a good Deal like Barham
Downs, between Dover & Canterbury. From Boulogne
to Marquise, a very small Village, was a Post & a half,
which Village we left on one Side of us; & from
Marquise to Hautbuisson, a Post House only, and that
a new well built one, was a single Post, as it was another
from Hautbuisson[1] to Calais; where I arrived about 3
o'Clock in the Afternoon: & as the Chaise was Con-
signed by Mr Pascal to Mr Dessein at the *Hôtel
D'Angleterre*, who was his Correspondent for Carriages
between Calais & Paris, I remained at his Inn, which
was new built, & was a fine large Quadrangle, with
most sumptuous Apartments & elegantly furnished:
&, which was preferable to all, the Master of it a very
civil & obliging Man. As there was a Packet Boat just
going out, hired by one Mr Trevannion for himself &
Family, I took the Liberty to write a Line to him, as he
was at the *Lion D'Argent*, to beg the Favour that he
would allow me, a single Gentleman only, with my
Servant, to go over in the same Packet with him: but
he sent me a civil Excuse, that he should be very glad
to accommodate me, had he not had some Ladies in

[1] Probably le Buisson.

Company with him, who were apprehensive of being sick in the Cabin, & did not care to have any Persons with them on such an Occasion: but that he was ready to carry any Letters or Parcels that I should entrust him with. On this Message I made myself easy, & gave Orders for my Dinner, my Servant going with my Baggage to the Custom House. However I agreed soon after with the Master of another Vessel to carry me over on the Morrow: but before I went to Bed I was given to understand, that his Grace the Duke of Beaufort, who was to set out from Paris on the same Day with myself, had sent a Servant before him to hire a whole Vessel for himself & Suite, & that this Master, with whom I had agreed for my Passage, had promised his Packet to him: he accordingly came to me, & told me the Case, advising me to ask the like Favour of the Duke, who was expected at Mr Grandsire's every Moment, as I had of Mr Trevannion: but my ill success with the one had discouraged me from any further Application. Yet had his Grace been at the same Inn with myself, & had I known certainly when he arrived at the other, I should have waited on him; especially as I had had the Honour of meeting him at the *Hôtel du Parc Royal;* & I make no Doubt, but his Curtesy would have granted me that Favour. I rested very ill this Night, & was not well all the next Day.

Sunday, Dec: 1. Fine Day, & Frost. I never stirred out of the Inn all the Day, as I found myself not very well, nor much otherwise. This Morning Messrs Mills came to the *Hôtel d'Angleterre;* as did in the Afternoon my Lord & Lady St George,[1] with their Daughter, a Child of about 6 Years old: they had 6 Servants with

[1] 2nd Baron (Irish), *ob.* 1775.

them: an English Footman, & a French man, who was their Cook, with 4 Maids, one a French *Gouvernante* for Miss, my Lady's own Maid, who was an Irish Woman, a young French Girl, as a Companion to Miss, to talk French to, & an ordinary French Woman, who was to be under the Cook in the Kitchin.[1] My Lady seemed to be turned of 30, was one of the prettiest & gentilest Women I ever saw, & talked French in Perfection: her Lord was turned of 50, & a well-looking, well-behaved Man. Besides these, there were several other Gentlemen who waited for a Passage, which I was assured of next Day: so that I made no further Enquiries about the Duke of Beaufort; especially as the Master of the Packet told me, that his Servant had orders to him, not to admit any other Person on Board.

Monday, Dec: 2. Fine Day & excessive hard Frost. My Box & Portmanteaus were searched at the Gates of the Town, & I had a Permit from the Governor to go on Board; which I did at High Water in the Harbour at 2 o'Clock in the Afternoon, taking a Cold Partridge & Bread with me to eat in the Passage. I had also a Hare, a Brace of Woodcocks & a Woodcock Pye in a Basket, & 3 Bottles of B[e]aune Wine, or Burgundy, which I had brought with me from Paris, & a Neat's Tongue or two, thinking to have eaten them on the Road, with the Wine: but as I never touched them, I got the Mate of the Ship, to whom I gave a Guinea, to take Care of these Things, with 2 or 3 other Bottles of Ratify from Boulogne, with the Parcels I had from Mr Walpole, with many Trinkets of my own, & some Books & Things of no great Consequence which might have been

---

[1]Almost always spelt thus by Cole.

stopped at the Custom House at Dover, & put them aside, & bring them to me, when I was ashore: which he did very faithfully by little at a Time: my Box & Portmanteaus being sent to the Custom House by my Servant, where I paid about 5 Shillings Duty for a few Things which were in them. We had a most delightful Passage, the Sea being beautiful & not too rough, & the Sun Shining, 'till its setting, very pleasantly, & all the Company on Chairs on the Deck. When the Sun set, & it grew Cold, an additional Great Coat I had made at Paris, like a Cloak, with a good Glass of Brandy from the Mate, made me as warm as I desired to be. The Captain's Name was Baxter, a youngish Man, & his Mate's Name was Barber: & we had above 40 Passengers. It may be Superstition, but I have often observed it, that after a more than ordinary Jollity & superabundant Laughter, I have generally suffered for it by some Disaster. I never was more in that Predicament than this Day, when I laughed immoderately for a great Part of the Passage. For the French Kitchen Maid, notwithstanding she sat opposite to her Ladyship on the Deck, at a very little Distance, sitting close to my Servant, began to take to him very much, tho' he could not understand a Word that she said to him; & was, in short, the oddest Mortal, said some of the drol[l]est Things in her Way, with a true French Assurance, that ever I came near. She soon addressed herself to me, guessing, as I suppose, at my Profession, & told me that in Case of any Danger, she should depend upon me for Assistance: & some Time after was wishing for something to eat & drink. I told my Servant to give her a Loaf & a little French Brandy in a Bottle which Mr Dessein had given him to drink in his

Passage: & this she drank almost up: so that, I believe, that made her more talkative, pert & forward, so that her tongue ran at an immoderate Rate; & at last something else: however she had the modesty to address herself to me, as understanding her Language, to desire me to beg one of the Sailors to give her a Chamber Pot: upon which, thinking she was sick, as many were upon the Deck, I advised her to go to the Side of the Ship, & my Servant should hold her by her Gown for Fear of tumbling over Board: but she directly told me, that however practicable such a Situation might be for us, it would not suit her at all; & without more ado, or further Ceremony, *sans Façon, à la Françoise*, she plainly told me she wanted a Chamber Pot, *pour faire lacher l'Eau;* these were her Words: so I forthwith got her accommodated with one, which she, with as little Shame as Decency & Ceremony made immediate use of, before all the Company, & then gave it with the utmost *Sangfroid* & Indifference, to my Servant to empty it over Board for her: while, the Irish Maid was crying out "Jesu Maria," & the two other Maids quite abashed at the Woman's Impudence. I observed her Ladyship took no Notice, but seemed thoroughly vexed & chagrined at such Indecency, &, I guess, would not take her with her to Ireland upon this Account: for my Servant told me he saw her at Dover, after all the other Part of the Family were gone for London. The Woman, when she saw me, & some others of the Company laughing at her Action, talked reasonably & sensibly upon the Occasion, as any one could: asked, in plain, *gras*, & indelicate words, what any of us would do, if a sudden Griping should take us, & we should want to go to the Necessary House.

But tho' the Woman's Argument's were right in the main, yet she mistook only in this single very material Point: that altho' what she had done was absolutely necessary, yet she might have made an Excuse to have gone under Deck, & have done privately, & by herself, what she chose to do before all the World. But such is the Difference between English & French Education & Customs! We carry to an Excess our Delicacy in these Matters, while our Neighbours exceed in the other offensive Extreme.[1] A proper Medium would certainly be the Best. In the same Ship were the 2 Messrs Mills & their Blacks; a very large & tall old French Gentleman, who wore the Cross of St Lewis; & several other French People of a meaner Quality. But however pleasant the Passage & Company were, it ended very unfortunately for me: for being at a Mile or two's Distance from Shore, tho' we could see the Lights in the Houses at Dover, at about 7 o'Clock at Night, with rather a tempestuous & rough Sea, the Captain declared he could not get into the Harbour for want of Water; & so ordered a large Boat to the Ship's Side, which was to Conduct us ashore. Accordingly scrambling to get out of the Ship into the Boat, which the Waves tossed up & down against the Sides of the Vessel, quite in the Dark, with near 35 or 40 Persons in it, in slipping down the Sides of it, the Edge of the Boat struck against my right Foot, & gave me such a jar as I thought must have lamed me for ever: for my Foot, Leg Knee & Thigh were quite stunned by it, so that I had no Use of them: however sliding down into the Boat I sat in my Place as quiet & contented as if

[1] Sterne's *Sentimental Journey* did not appear until 1768, or C. would have been reminded of Mme de Rambouliet.

nothing had happened; & took no Notice to any Body
of my uneasy Situation: for my Man was at the other
End of the Boat: who had he been nearer could have
done me no Good: as it was as dark as Pitch, & the
Boat crouded so full of People, as most of us thought it
very dangerous: many also of them being excessively
sick, who had been well all the Rest of the Passage: but
the Waves were so high & rough as made a very
sensible Difference between the one & the other
Situation: besides that they dashed over us at every
Minute, & before I got ashore I was as wet as if I had
been dragged thro' a River. I sat in great Pain all this
Time, for above half an Hour, not only from the
Torture I endured, but from the Apprehensions I was
under of the Difficulty I should have in getting ashore;
& accordingly my Apprehensions were not ill grounded:
for I was utterly unable to help myself: & had not a
Sailor, my Servant, & the Mate assisted me, I must
have been left to the Mercy of the Waves, which came
dashing on the Shore with great Violence. My Stick
was of very little Use, or none at all, as it rather made
me worse; there being no Footing for it on the Shingles,
or loose small Stones which the Shore was composed of:
& so leaning on my Servant & the Mate, with the
utmost Difficulty, Labour & Pain I got some tolerable
Way from the Sea Side, before I fell down thro'
Weakness, & Fatigue, & so wrenched the same Knee
that it was the greatest Mercy that ever I had the Use
of it again: for there was Light enough to see that it was
bent outwards, as I lay on the Ground in my Boots, at
a very considerable Distance from the strait Line it
ought to be in: & this, I take it, was the greatest
Misfortune of the two: for by this Wrench, the Sinews

& Muscles of my Leg, Knee & Thigh were so distended & strained, that it is no wonder that the outward
Side of my Thigh some Days afterwards appeared as
black as my Gown, and that both that & my Knee were
in great Pain for so many Weeks. On this Fall I would
not attempt to go any further: but sent away the Mate,
who was over & above Civil & obliging, to get a Chair
& Help to carry me to the Inn: accordingly I was
carried in that Method to it, at no vast Distance, & so
up into a Chamber with 2 Beds in it, that my Servant
might lay in the Room to help me as Occasion served.
Had I thought of being blooded as soon as I got to the
Inn, I make no Doubt but that I should have been well
half as soon again as I was: but it never entered my
Head all the Time I was there: & perceiving, when my
Boot was off, that nothing was broke, I was in great
Hopes that in 2 or 3 days I should be well again: so
getting into Bed as soon as I could have it ready, &
with doing nothing to it, but bathing & rubbing the
bruised Parts with Rum or Brandy, I composed myself
as well as I could; little thinking that it would be a
Month before I should be able to get out of my Bed
again. However, I was Heart-whole & eat a very good
Supper, ordering a roast Chicken & some Whitings: as
I had touched nothing since my Breakfast at Calais, &
the Sea creating generally a good Appetite; which, I
suppose, I should had the less Occasion of gratifying,
could I have thought my Case had been so bad. The
Inn at Dover where I lodged, was the *White Lion &
King's Head*, united, tho' on opposite Sides of a narrow
Street: & my Chamber was up one Pair of Stairs, with
3 sashed Windows in it, to the Street, consequently
very noisy as Pacquets were continually coming in, at

all Times of the Night, & Coaches & Chaises for ever rattling under my Windows, at the *White Lion*. It is 32 Posts from Paris to Calais to Paris: which comes to about 150 Livres, including the Postilion's Fees: consequently, with the 3 Guineas for the Hire of the Chaise, makes it near 10 Pounds in the whole. I had once a Thought of going by the Calais Coach, which goes thro' Beauvais: but it was 7 or 8 Days on the Road, & I had experienced such great Inconvenience in the Straitness of sitting in their Public Voitures, that I was disposed to go by Post Chaises, tho' considerably dearer, rather than suffer such Uneasiness again. The Master of the Inn at Dover was called Hubberd: he had been Servant to some Gentleman, & was an illiterate, ignorant, stupid, drunken, but civil Man; who laid so long in Bed in the Day, after sitting up & drinking at Nights that his Pocket must considerably suffer by it, as he left the Cheif of his Business to Servants, the dirtiest, most disorderly, & worst of both Sorts, except the Drawer, who wrote all his Bills, that I ever saw. His wife was also an ignorant, low Woman, who took as much Care as her Capacity allowed her. Tho' I was so ill in their House, & the Woman passing by my Door 20 Times a Day, yet she never came in once all the Time I was there to ask me how I did: nor did the Master of the House above 2 or 3 Times in the last Week, when I sent for him about hiring his Post Coach to carry me to Blecheley. Yet this was more out of Ignorance & want of knowing better, than any Thing else: as they were always very inquisitive to know every Morning of my Servant how I had passed the Night: & were otherwise always very Civil. Yet so great was their Ignorance & Inattention, that sometimes I have been

forced to stay an Hour in a Morning before they had
any Bread in the House: they bought their Cheese, tho'
a large & frequented Inn, by the Pennyworth at a
Time, & she rarely had a Fowl or any Thing of
that Sort for my Dinner, tho' proper in my Situation:
& the Man was so sottish & ignorant as to be without
Mountain Wine,[1] the only Sort I could relish at that
Time, for Days together, tho' spoke to about it continually by the Drawer & my Servant: so that had I not
happened to have had some Wine by me, that I could
drink, I must e'en have gone without it: tho' 3 or 4
Glasses in a Day, the Utmost I ever chose to drink, was
almost necessary in my Situation. I mention these
Things to shew how improper some People are for their
Professions: & that a Plane to saw with, or a Saw to
plane with, would be almost as proper as such People as
these to do themselves or their Customers any Good in
a public House.

I shall put down my Bills at Calais & elsewhere upon
the Road to compare the Difference between one & the
other.

Novembre 30, No 13, à Calais.

À Dinè à Monsieur

	ll	sous
viz. a Fricassee of Chickens & Sweetbreds. A Couple of Teale, a Soupe, Almonds, India Sweetmeats & Cheese - - - -	4.	o
Une Bouteille de Vin de Bourgogne - -	3.	o
Feu, 8 Pieces de Bois - - - - -	2.	o
Pour un Domestique - - - - -	1.	o
Logement - - - - - - -	1.	10
Une Patèe de 4 Becasses - - - -	8.	o
Carry forward - -	19.	10

[1] A variety of Malaga.

	ll	sous
Carried forward - -	19.	10
2 Becasses - - - - - - -	2.	10
1 Lièvre - - - - - - -	2.	10
2 Paniers - - - - - - -	1.	4
Le 1. xbre à Dejeunè pour Monsieur - -	0.	15
À Dìne à Idem—(viz: Soupe, Fricandeau of Veal & Spinage, a fine Poularde & Sweet-meats &c.) - - - - - -	6.	0
Une Bouteille de Vin de Bourgogne - -	3.	0
10 Pièces de Bois - - - - -	2.	10
Logement - - - - - - -	1.	10
Pour le Domestique - - - - -	1.	0
Le 2 à Dejeunè - - - - - -	1.	7
Feu - - - - - - - -	1.	0
	42.	16
Plus Perdreaux 2 Pains ensemble - - -	2.	0
2 Pièces de Bois - - - - - -	0.	10
TOTALE - -	45.	6

My Bill at Monsr Grandsire's at the *White Lion* at Calais, as I was going to Paris was as follows: tho' my Dinner is not in it, having dined with 2 Gentlemen & paid my Reckoning with them.

Ce 17 d' 8bre 1765. La grande Salle.

	ll	sous
À Soupè pour Monsieur - - - -	1.	0
Pour une Pinte de Vin de Bourgogne - -	1.	10
Pour le Dinè & Soupè pour le Domestique -	1.	0
Une Bouteille de Vin pour le Domestique -	0.	18
Les Dejeunèz—0. 15 sous—Les Lits— 1 ll 4 s	1.	19
	6.	7

My Bill at a very decent clean House at Lille, where I laid two Nights, & had 2 Suppers, one Dinner, &

one Breakfast, for on the Morning I left it, I had some Chocolate from a Coffee House, was this:

Lille, au *Nouveau Monde*, du 19 8bre 1765.
Mèmoire de Monsieur Cole.

	ll		
Trois Repas et une Bouteille de Vin -	7.	5.	0
Les Logement & Bois - - - -	2.	14.	0
Trois Repas de Domestique - - -	2.	12.	6
	[Liards[1]		
Totale -	12.	11.	6

Tuesday, Dec: 3. Fine frosty Weather. Not a moment's Sleep all Night from Pain in my Knee: & foreseeing that I might be confined here a Week or two, I thought it best to send the Packet of Mr Walpole's Letters to his Servant in London, as I heard him say some of them were on Business that required an Answer soon: so I wrote a Line to my Lord St George, excusing myself to him for the Liberty I took, begging him to take the Care of them to London: which his Lordship very kindly undertook.

Wednesday, Dec: 4. Fine frosty Weather. My Leg & Thigh very uneasy.

Thursday, Dec: 5. Fine Weather & hard Frost, I sent on Monday by the Post, my Letters which I had wrote at Calais to my 2 Sisters, my Brother Apthorp, Mr Goodwin of Loughton, in Buckinghamshire, Mr Cooke & Mr Cartwright of my own Parish.

Friday, Dec: 6. St Nicholas. Fine Day. The Night before I had a most terrible Night: not one Minute's Sleep or Rest. Terrified with the Apprehension that something in my Knee was broke or dislocated, & that

[1]Liard, practically a farthing.

I must have my Leg cut off above the Knee, so that I was determined to send for a Chirurgeon in the Morning, & to make my Will: however after Breakfast I found myself much easier.

Saturday, Dec: 7. Rain. I was much better yesterday towards Evening, at which Time I got out of Bed wrapt up in a Blanket to have my Bed made, but could hardly set up 'till it was done; having lain 4 Days & as many Nights without being able to be stirred.

Sunday, Dec: 8. Fine Day. No Sleep, but easy. Mr Gordon, our Agent at Brussells came to the Inn in his way to that Court. Had my Bed made again.

Monday, 9 *Dec:* Fine Day, but windy. Little Sleep, & but an uneasy Day, with a good Deal of Pain in my right Foot & Toe, which was much swelled & inflamed, & which had been perfectly easy & well 'till now: so I thought it a slight Fit of the Gout; which I still believe it to have been, occasioned partly by my drinking so freely of Burgundy as I did, while in France, & drinking hardly any Sort of strong Liquors at Home, which now having the Humours much stirred by my Fall appeared in its proper Shape: for I have long thought & been told, that the Complaint in my Stomach, with Flatulencies & Acidities, with which I have been troubled more or less these 10 or 12 years, was of that Family: which I should not at all wonder at, as both my Sisters have had slight Touches of it, & as my Father had it in a very severe Manner.

Tuesday, Dec: 10. Much Rain. Better Sleep. I wrote to my Sister Catherine, & sent her by the Coach the Woodcock Pye which I brought from Calais: as also to Wm Wood, my Clark, & Father to my Servant, to go to Mr Gibberd, the Curate of Whaddon, to desire him to officiate twice a Day on a Sunday in my Church of Blecheley, 'till I should return: which was very uncertain, & as my Neighbours, who had undertaken to serve my Church in my Absence, had all been their Turns.

Wednesday, Dec: 11. Windy & rainy. Good Sleep, but restless. I wrote a Letter to Mr John Howard, Priest, & a near Relation of the Duke of Norfolk, who lodged at Mrs Crow's, a Milliner in New Bond Street, touching the Packet of Papers which the Prior of the English Benedictines at Paris had desired I would deliver into his Hands: as also to Mr Favre,[1] Head Servant to Mr Walpole; that I would send by the Coach to Mr Cartwright the aforesaid Packet, with those directed to Ladies Hervey & Littleton, who would, I was assured, deliver safely the one to Mr Howard, & the others to Mr Favre.

Thursday, Dec: 12. Fine Day, & a good Night's Sleep.

Friday, Dec: 13. Fine Day & severely Cold. Tolerable good Night but very uneasy all the Day: never being able to turn myself on either Side in my Bed, the Muscles & Sinews of my Leg & Thigh having been so much wrenched & distended. However I could not persuade myself, or be persuaded by my Man, who all along pressed it, to send for a Surgeon, or Apothecary: for my constant Opinion of them, with their Cheifs, the Physicians, was, that they were all of them only necessary Evils, & to be sent to in the last Extremity: many of them, in order to keep a Patient in Hand for a longer Time, would not scruple to put him to agonizing Pain; & that all that they regarded was to get as much

---

[1] Walpole's trusty Swiss.

money out of your Pocket as they could: besides, that I had ever a contemptible Opinion of their Judgment, & that the Reputation many of them acquire is only Fashion & Accident; & that, except in some particular Cases, where a good Physician, who is an honest Man, must, by Experience & practice, if he has any Judgment & Observation, know how to apply Remedies better than one quite inexperienced; & where a Surgeon's Help is necessary, as in Fractures, Amputations & some other Cases, where they are particularly usefull: I ever thought a good honest Apothecary a much safer Person to apply to, than half the Physicians & Surgeons in the Kingdom. But here is the Difficulty: an Apothecary, by the Influence the Physicians have over them, dare not prescribe for Fear of the Physician: tho' he may know in his own Judgement that the Physician has mistaken the Case, & knows little of the Matter. And to such a Pass are we come, that the Fees to these Gentry are so exorbitant & excessive, that, to a Family who have a better Opinion of their Sagacity than I have, who believes that in Cures Dame Nature is generally to be thanked, tho' all goes to the Physician, as well as the Money, & who are sickly, & will needs die in Form, it is well that they do not ruin it in the Money they squeeze from it. So that if a Parliamentary Enquiry into the Conduct of the 3 learned Professions was to be set on Foot, I am certain, that which is most cried out against, the Church, ought to be the last thought of. It is a Shame & Scandal for a Country which boasts of its Laws, to be so maltreated by them & their Interpreters, as the English are: who, with an excellent Constitution are the greatest Bubbles this Day on Earth: more especially to our Lawyers, who, carry

every Thing before them in the House of Commons,
where they swarm, & get Titles & Estates above all
other Professions. But to leave Things as they are, I had
not Mind to be further plagued with their Jargon, Bills
& Medicines: & as was pretty sure that nothing was
broken, but that I suffered from a most violent Jar,
wrench, & Contusion, left Nature to work its own Cure:
which, had I at first thought of assisting, by losing
some Ounces of Blood, had been much more speedy.
I therefore used no other Quackery than now & then
sending to the Apothecary for a little Oppadeldock,[1] &
rubbing the bruised Parts with it. I received Letters
from Mr Cartwright that all was well at Blecheley, &
that my Ticket[2] was just turned out a Blank: another
from my Brother Apthorp that the Vice-Provost[3] was
likely to take the Living of Warplesdon; & another
from my Sister Catherine, that she was very desirous
of coming to me at Dover, if I would give her Leave,
& that she was so fortunate as to have her Ticket in the
Lottery turn out £500 on the first Day of its Drawing:
so that she has been very lucky this year, as not six
Months before my Brother-in-Law; Mr Hector
Mawdsley, left her near £1200 by his Will, in a very
generous, & friendly Manner.

Saturday, Dec: 14. Fine Day, but very sharp & Cold.
Good Sleep in the Night, but rather restless in the Day,
& uneasy.

Sunday, Dec: 15. Fine Day & very Cold. Uneasy in
the Day & tolerable good Sleep at Night. I wrote to my
Sister Catherine Cole to desire her not to give herself
the Trouble of such a Journey in such a Time of the
year, & to such an Inn, as I was in Hopes of getting

[1]Opodeldoc.   [2]Lottery ticket.   [3]Of Eton.

better daily; but could not fix any Time when I should be able to move Homewards, as I was not yet able to be stirred from my Bed. Wrote also to Mr Cartwright.

Monday, Dec: 16. Fine Weather, & tolerable good Sleep, tho' very uneasy with my Knee, & Sinews & Muscles above it. I sent Mr Walpole's fine Snuff Box & other Parcels to his Servant, to deliver them as directed.

Tuesday, 17 *Dec:* Fine Day & frosty. No Sleep in the Night, having desired that the Matrass under the Feather Bed, might be laid upon it: &, I believe, this was too hard for me in my present Situation, tho' always used to it at Home.

Wednesday, 18 *Dec:* Fine, frosty, cold weather. Little or no Sleep, & very uneasy. Letters from Wm Wood; from Mr Cartwright; from my Sister Catherine; from my Brother Apthorp, advising me to come to Eton, & try my Interest with the Fellows of the College for the Living of Maple-Durham in Oxfordshire; from Mr Knapp out of Shropshire; from my Lord Montford,[1] inviting me to Horseth-Hall[2] to meet Mrs Cadogan, his Sister, who was coming to stay a Fortnight or 3 Weeks with him before his Grand Ball on 30 Octob: & desired me to come & stay all the Time his Sister was to be with him; from Father Bedingfeild, *Récollet,*[3] speaking in a Sort of Stile as if I was going over Sea with a full Resolution of turning Catholic; in which he was much mistaken.

Thursday, Dec: 19. Fine Day. Bad Night: little Sleep & very unquiet. I wrote to my Sister Catherine at Hackney; to Mr Cartwright; to my Brother Apthorp,

---

[1]Thomas Bromley (1733-99), 2nd Baron Montfort.
[2]Or Horseheath.   [3]Monk of a very strict order.

telling him that I was no good Sollicitor in begging: that I never should have thought of Burnham or Maple-Durham, if he had not kindly proposed it to me; so that I left it to him to manage that Point as he saw proper: but that I had no Thoughts or Intentions of applying for it myself.

Friday, 20 *Dec:* Tolerable good Weather, & very cold. Little Sleep, & very restless.

Saturday, 21 *Dec: St Thomas.* Great Deal of Rain. Restless & very little Sleep. Letter from Mr Cooke that old Mrs Hanmer of Simpson died on Wednesday last. Since this happened, my Neighbour & Friend Job Walden Hanmer Esq. has met with a worse Misfortune, if the losing his Mother, who put him in full Possession of his Estate at Simpson of about £200 per an. or under, which he had already the Management of, & who had an Annuity of about £60 or £80 per an. from a Company in London, which went away on her Decease, was reckoned a Misfortune by him. For his Cousin Humphrey Hanmer Esqr of Hanmer Hall in Flintshire, & who, I remember, a Fellow of Catherine Hall in Cambridge above 25 Years ago, (where he was always looked upon to be somewhat disordered in his Head), after living single 'till he was arrived at the Age of near 60 Years, about a Month or 6 Weeks ago [I write this Aug: 1, 1766] took it into his Head to marry a common Woman of the Town, by whom, it is thought, he will have an Heir to his Estate: as that was one of the Motives for Humphrey's Marriage. This is the greater Disappointment to my Neighbour, who is of the most sanguine Expectations in every Thing, as he has talked to me, & every other Person that would give him the Hearing, for these 10 years, that his Cousin Humph-

rey's Estate of £1500 per an. when the 2 Joyntures are
fell in, was ready to fall into his Possession; it being
entailed, & he the next in the Entail; for that he was
well assured his Cousin Humphrey would not live a
Fortnight to an End: for that he was far gone in a
Dropsy: & when he told the same Tale again, this
Dropsy was sure to kill him in a very short Time, for
that now he had an Asthma, joyned to it. In short, all his
Acquaintance were stunned with the News of his Cousin
Humphrey's dying Condition; which, according to my
sanguine Friend's Account could not be exceeded but
by the very bad state of Health of his Wives[1] Aunt, Mrs
Warner, in Suffolk, who, by his Report, has been dying
in his Favour almost as long. So that this Matrimony of
his Cousin must needs be no small Mortification to
him, as he has so often told me, that his new House of
Simpson, which last Christmas, or Whitsuntide, as I
well remember, he christened by the Name of Simpson
Place, (as I saw it wrote by him in a Letter to Mrs
Willis, for the very first Time, he having put a Park
Pale about 2 years ago, about a few Grounds lying
round his House, & which he now calls a Paddock, &
told me this year that he intended to stock it with Deer,
& that he hoped to send me some Venison in a Year or
two), was only designed for his 3rd Son: the elder Son,
lately of Catherine Hall in Cambridge, & formerly of
Eton Schole, being to inherit the Shropshire Estate; his
Son Job, now at Sea with Admiral Stewart, to have the
Suffolk Estate, which he actually got his late Aunt
Warner to settle so, upon a Presumption of the Welch
Family Estate soon coming into his Family, & upon
that Account the elder Son much to be pitied: so that

[1]Obsolete form of "wife's."

this Estate at Simpson, which came by his Mother, would do very well for a third Son. Mr Hanmer is a very handsome, well made Man: was Schole Fellow with me at Eton, & thence removed to Baliol College & the Inns of Court, where he is a Barrister, as was his Father. As Sir Thomas Hanmer[1] was his Relation, & took Notice of him, he being often with him in Suffolk, he there fell in Love with his Wife, one of the finest Women I ever saw, when she was Miss Nanny Graham, & Daughter of Colonel Graham of that County; one of her Sisters marrying Sir Wm Bunbury,[2] & another Mr Warren, Minister of Hampstead in Middlesex: but much altered since her Marriage. She makes him a very prudent & good Wife & has not only brought him a good Fortune, by the means of her Suffolk Aunts, with whom she lives continually, but also a great Number of Children: I think they have 7 Boys & a Girl. [I write this Aug. 2, 1766.] Mr Hanmer, tho' an acting Justice of the Peace for Buckinghamshire, by which, it is said, he makes as much or more than suits the Character of a Gentleman, resides for the most Part with his Aunt Warner & Wife in Suffolk: which does not at all interfere with his Business here as a Counsellor: for altho' I know no Man who has a greater Command & Flow of Words, or express himself more to the Purpose in Common Conversation, yet, I know not how, some way or other, his Judgement as a Lawyer is no more depended upon, than his Veracity: for altho' he is a most good tempered Man & one who lives easily & quietly with his Neighbours & Family, being an excellent Husband & Father, yet such is his Turn for the

[1] 1677-1746; 4th Bt., known as an editor of Shakespeare.
[2] Rev. Sir William B., *ob.* 1764, 5th Bt.

Marvellous & surprizing, that very little or no Dependence is to be laid on what he says: not that he
delights in making Mischeif, or other People uneasy;
but such is the Force of Custom & Habit with him,
that I really believe he often thinks he is telling Truth,
when it is the very reverse of it. His predominant
Passion is Vanity: this led him some 3 or 4 years ago,
tho' unqualified by Estate, & in very pinching Circumstances, to offer himself a Candidate for the Town of
Bedford, on some Vacancy, & oppose the Duke of
Bedford in his favourite Borough. He made an Agreement with my Lord St John, one of the Duke's Antagonists in that County, (for I had it from Mr Hinde of
Bedford, his Lordships Factotum, who was By at the
Bargain in Writing), that they were to go equal Shares
in the Expence, which Mr Hanmer was to pay only
when he came into Possession of his Cousin Hum-
phrey's Estate. However, this brought him into
Difficulties which were uneasy to him. It is supposed
that he had an Eye to be made a Judge, if he could get a
Seat in Parliament: for Mr Robert Lowndes of Great
Brickhill, told me this year, that he had lately wrote a
Letter to his Brother, the Member for this County of
Bucks, desiring him to use his Interest to get him made
a Welch Judge: to which Mr Lowndes very sensibly
returned Answer, that in the first Place he had no
Interest to procure such a Favour: & if he really had
any, it ought rather to be employed in recommending
his Brother, who was bred a Counsellor, as well as Mr
Hanmer. This Mr Richard Lowndes said by way of
Banter: for altho' my Neighbour at Brickhill was bred
to the Law, yet it always avoided him, or He it: for tho'
he is a very worthy Man & a good Neighbour, a much

better Character than being the best Lawyer without it,
yet he is designed by Nature for any Thing rather than
a public Orator & a Decider of Controversies. He is
reckoned to sit on Horseback as true as any Man in
England: & so far he judged wisely & accurately, in
not mistaking his Talents & Profession: for soon after
he was in Possession of a younger Brother's Fortune,
he took to drinking with Mr Selby, Mr Tho: Willis,
Senior, Sir Butler Charnock, his Brother Richard, &
that Set, more than was good for his Constitution &
Fortune: the latter of which he set to Rights again by
marrying one of the Sisters of Barrington Shales Esqr
of Morden in Cambridgeshire, & of Hertfordshire, a
most worthy good Woman, who makes him an excellent
Wife, the older, I suppose, by 10 years than her
Husband, who is equally good & affectionate to her; &
are as Worthy a Couple as can be met with. They have
no Children; but Mr Richard Lowndes's Son, Wm
Lowndes Esqr, Major in the County Militia, who lately,
this Spring, married a Daughter of Mr Goosetree of
Missenden, an Attorney of great Eminence & Fortune,
will probably inherit his Fortune: for he is equally
related to his Uncle & Aunt Lowndes of Brickhill; as
his Mother was own Sister to his Aunt: & what is more
extraordinary still, another of Mr Barrington Shales's
Sisters, I think, married another Brother of Mr
Lowndes, who is seated at Chesham, as I apprehend.
Mr Robert Lowndes of Brickhill, keeps a Pack of Hare
Hounds, & often hunts with his Neighbour Mr Selby
of Wavendon with his Fox Hounds, when their Health
will admit it: particularly the latter's, who pays now
with Interest for the Liberties of the Bottle in earlier
Days: for both Mr Selby & Mr Lowndes ever since I

have been in this Country, these 14 years, & perhaps
before, have lived very regularly & soberly: & if they
had began Life so, they would have enjoyed it more to
their Satisfaction, now they are in Prime: especially Mr
Selby, who is continually almost laid up with the Gout,
& so severely suffers in it, that it is a Miracle that he
gets over so well one Year after another, & one Fit of
the Gout after a less severe one: as they grow worse
every Return: & his Life in continual Danger for these
six or seven years last past. He is a very worthy Man,
does a great Deal of Good in his Neighbourhood, &
very sensible: he lives very retired, seeing none in the
Country but a few hunting Gentlemen, & being never
married, (keeping a Mistress, one Mrs Vane, by whom
he never had Issue, a very good Sort of Woman in her
way, & very handsome, as I am told, for I never saw
her), it is a Matter of Speculation where his great
Estate will settle on his Death: for he has no Relations,
that are known, by his Father's Side; a cunning,
artfull & sharping Serjeant-at-Law, who cheated Mr
Browne Willis,[1] as he has often told me, of the best Part
of his Estate in Whaddon Chace: which Father, it is
supposed, was the Son of a Man, who came out of
Yorkshire, & was for a Time, as Mr Hanmer told me,
Servant to the Family of Charnock of Holcote; where
getting a little Money, he purchased a small Estate, &
settled at Wavendon; & breeding up his Son to the
Law, he had the good Fortune to raise a large Estate
out of it; & afterwards married a Daughter of a
Baronet of Bedfordshire, of the Name of Alston;[2] which

[1] 1682-1760; the antiquary; he presented Cole to the living of
Bletchley.

[2] Sir Rowland A., 4th Bt., *ob.* 1759.

Family being rather disordered in their Intellects, Mr Selby has no Communication with it: so it is supposed that some of his nearest Acquaintance will be the better for it. I know the late Mr Tho: Willis,[1] senior, thought he had a good Prospect for it, for his Son: & if it was to go partly in that Channel, it would be doing Justice to a Family which his Father had injured, & would be making a reasonable Restitution. Mr Lowndes, as the Country judges, stands the best Chance, as both the Brothers were his original Acquaintance, are alive with him to cultivate their Interest, which, it is said, they do not neglect; the Major often spending a great Part of his Time with him: & if it was to go there, no one could blame him, or grudge Mr Lowndes the good Fortune: for he is a very worthy Man, & his Family Estate not very great, considering he has represented this County in Parliament, so many years: but the true Reason why a Man of £1800 per an, of no great Interest in the County, has been continued so long in that Station, is the Jealousy between some of the larger rival Nobility & Gentry in it: particularly between the Earls Temple & Fermanagh,[2] who care not to draw their Swords against each other, & can hardly keep them in the Scabbard: so that Mr Lowndes's Seat in Parliament is from the Fear of making a Confusion in the County, which at present is very quiet. Mr Browne Willis told me, that old Wm Lowndes of the Treasury, Grandfather to these Gentlemen, & who raised a great Estate, which he divided into 3 or 4 Parcels, settling so many of his Sons in different Parts of the County, with handsome

[1] Son of Browne Willis.
[2] Ralph Verney, 3rd Visct. Fermanagh, *ob.* 1791.

Estates, (rather than making his eldest a great Gentleman with the whole of his Fortune), was the Son of an
Inn-Keeper at Winslow: at one End of which Town,
the old Gentleman built an handsome House, which
is now occupied by the elder Branch of the Family in
the Person of Mr Richard Lowndes the Member for
the County; who losing his Wife some 8 years ago, &
having only 2 unmarried Daughters, besides his Son,
is now going to quit this House to him & his new Wife,
& retire to an hired House in the Neighbourhood, with
his 2 Daughters. When I came first into Buckinghamshire, Messrs Lowndes, with Mr Tho: Willis, were of
the highest Order of Tories, called by the other Family's
Name: Mr Willis, I suppose, died in that Opinion: but
both the Messrs Lowndes have been veering with the
Stream: especially since the Accession of the present
King, who seems to unite in his Person the Affection
both of Whigs & Tories: yet I cannot but own, that to
hear People argue in a Stile quite different from their
original Opinion to me is quite offensive; & that has
now & then made a Coolness between Mr Robin
Lowndes & myself: tho' generally we have altercated
in a laughing Stile only. But as to Politics, I have ever
been of Opinion, that the greater only use the less as
their Tools to their own Advancement: & this more
especially, when the late Sir John Hynde Cotton,[1] the
most determined Jacobite, to all Appearance, in the
Kingdom, accepted of a Place at Court in the late
King's Time; who, however, had such a particular
Prejudice against him, that he was soon disgusted, &

[1] 4th Bt. of Madingley (Cambs), *ob.* 1752. Forced upon George II
as Treasurer of the Chambers in 1744. *See Letters of Hor. Walpole*
(Toynbee), No. 165 (Dec. 24, 1744).

quitted his Post: on which Account, I heard my Friend
Soame Jenyns[1] say, soon after, that it was the wisest
Thing the Ministry could do, to give Sir John a Place:
for it was like pulling out the Sting of a Bee: which
might Buzz & make a Noise; but could do no Mischeif.
I am in great Hopes the giving the great Patriot Mr
Pitt an Earl's Title, with a Viscounty of Pynsent, will
be equally effectual in displaying that Man's true
selfish Character. For I red in the Yesterday's Paper,
that after all this Stir, Bustle & Confusion which he has
made, with a constant Opposition to the King, he has
been pleased to accept of the Title of Earl of Chatham
& Viscount Pynsent: his Wife, Earl Temple's Sister,
another such Patriot, having formerly been created
Baroness Chatham, to descend to his Son, with a
Pension from the Crown. The affecting to be stiled
Viscount Pynsent,[2] seems as if he meant to reflect some
Gratitude & Honour to the half-witted Fool that left
him his Estate,[3] in Prejudice to his own Relations: one
of which, who now enjoys the Title only, is an un-
beneficed Clergyman in Ireland. If this very disinter-
ested Patriot, as the Bubbles his Admirers have always
chose to represent him, had acted the Part the late
worthy Bp of London, Dr Gibson,[4] did, (tho' not talked
of & little known, tho' a certain Fact), it would have
been an unequivocal Proof of his Integrity, Honour &
Disinterestedness: but as that was not the Case, I shall
never alter my constant & invariable Opinion of this
Man, & that is, that his factious, popular & busy
Disposition, was only put in Motion to obtain Honours,

[1]1704-87; at this time M.P. for Cambs.
[2]Properly, "Visct. Pitt of Pynsent."
[3]Sir William Pynsent, 3rd Bt.   [4]Edmund G., 1669-1748.

Titles & Wealth: & that a most selfish Temper was at
the Bottom. Bp Gibson's Case was this. He had a large
Family both of Sons & Daughters, & no very large
Fortunes to give among them: he had been very kind to
Dr Crow, a London Divine, whom he had not only beneficed, but dignified: when Dr Crow died, out of Gratitude to his Patron, tho' he had several poor Relations,
he by Will gave every Farthing he was worth to the Bp
his kind Patron & Benefactor: who, with a truly real &
generous, & not affected Spirit of Disinterestedness &
Honour, would accept of not a Penny of it, but divided
it properly among the Doctor's Relations. When such
Actions as these are designedly concealed, because done
by a Clergyman, & the contrary magnified to the
Clouds, as I well remember his Abettors did, when he
took a Pension, & his Wife a Title, it is by no means
unreasonable to set the two Characters in opposition, &
draw a Parallel between them. But to leave Politics &
return to my Journal; first observing, that Mr Hanmer's
Father, as I had been told in the Family, being a
younger Brother, & bred up to the Law, was travelling
out of Flintshire to one of the Inns of Court, when he
was stopped at Fenny-Stratford on some Account of his
Baggage or Horse: while he was there he heard some
Talk of a young Lady who had £10,000 to her Fortune,
who lived at Simpson, which was the Parish to half of
Fenny Stratford, as Blecheley is to the other half: on
this occasion, he took an Opportunity to be introduced
to her, & being a tall well-looking Man, as is his Son,
he soon got into the Lady's good Graces, & married
her, he having no Fortune to speak of of his own. She
was Daughter to one Mr Walden, a Tradesman of
Coventry, as I take it, whose Brother had raised a

Fortune, such as it was, in trading to Italy, as it should seem to me, as I have seen some very fine Italian & French Prints in a single Volume of his collecting: among which I remember one in particular that I never saw elsewhere; which was of the famous Dr Owen,[1] Oliver's Dean of Christchurch, which had been engraved at Mr Walden's Expence, with his Arms also under the Print: for they were Dissenters, either Presbyterians or Independents, as I observed in a Note which I have seen in Mr Browne Willis's Hand, & that this Mr Walden was buried among his Friends in the Dissenters' Burial Ground in Bunhill Feilds: & I remember on telling this Circumstance to Mr Hanmer, he was so uneasy at it, as thinking it reflected some Stain on the antient Blood of the Hanmer's to be mixed with that of a little trading Presbyterian, that he often desired me to obliterate that Note which I had entered in one of my Books, & was one Day so earnest about it, as to desire to see whether I had really done as I had promised: This Uncle of Mrs Hanmer made the Purchase of the Estate at Simpson, of about £160 per an: which the present Gentleman has increased by his Wife's Fortune, buying, within these 3 or 4 years, another little Estate to it: & he also purchased the Advowson of the Living, in order to give it to his Son Graham; but to reimburse himself, soon sold the next Turn to my Neighbour Mr Reddall,[2] the present Rector of Simpson, formerly of St John's College in Cambridge, & Son to Mrs Reddall who keeps the *Queen's Arms* Tavern in St Paul's Church Yard; as fine a Woman of her Age as ever I saw, & a Native of

[1]John Owen (1616-1683); ejected from deanery, 1660.
[2]Dixon Reddall, *ob.* 1772.

2 B

Worcester. Mr Reddall's Cousin of Eversholt in Bedfordshire, an Attorney of good Fortune, lately married
his Daughter to Sir Philip Monoux[1] of Sandy, Baronet,
who was educated at Christ's College in Cambridge.
Mr Hanmer has been also very unfortunate in his
Application two Sessions in Parliament in Relation to
inclosing his Parish, which he had affronted by carrying
it in too high a Manner with them: when, had he done
it smoothly, & not so cavalierly, he might easily have
managed that, & any other Point with them: But
having raised an Enemy in one Mr John Goodman, a
Farmer in the Parish of some Property, (whom to
distinguish from the numerous other Goodmans of the
same & neighbouring Villages, they call Gentleman
John Goodman), he spirited up a Party against him, &
had such Influence, that, after putting Mr Hanmer to a
great Expence, he got it laid aside in the Committee
of the House of Commons. And being flattered that he
could gain his Point, the year following, *viz:* 1764, after
gaining over his cheif Antagonist, by some disingenuous
& tricking Management of his own, in wording the
Bill, (a false Copy of which was shewn to the other
Parishioners), they again bestirred themselves, &
prevented the passing of the Bill. I don't think it
improbable that, after all, if the Duke of Richmond,
whose Sister Lady Sarah Bunbury, who is Wife to Mr
Hanmer's Wive's Nephew, Sir Charles Bunbury,
educated at Catherine Hall in Cambridge, whose
Father Sir William, of the same College, & a very
decent Clergyman, after he arrived to his great Estate,
left him by his Uncle Sir Thomas Hanmer, Baronet, it
is whispered made away with himself: but of this I have

[1] 5th Bt., *ob.* 1805. (*Also* Mounox and Mounoux.)

no other Authority than common Report; than which nothing is more false in the general. But however that may be, it is more certain that a neighbouring Clergyman of the same County, Mr Davers, (Son of my Lady Davers,[1] & Rector of Rushbrook, a young Gentleman of an amiable Character), was, within this Month, [I write this Aug: 2, 1766] found by his Mother's Gardener, in the Green-House at Bury, (where her Ladyship now lives, since the Death of her Husband), sitting in a Chair, with a loaded Pistol lying by him on a Table, & one discharged in his Hand thro' his Mouth, & came out at his Head [*sic*]. That this is not un-fashionable in Suffolk with the Clergy, there is another recent Instance in one I knew: Mr Gilbert Affleck, Son to Mr Affleck of Dalham in Suffolk, & member in one Parliament for the Town of Cambridge, who was found in the same Situation at his Father's House at Dalham in the necessary House, about 5 years ago, & was a Person of an unblameable Character. I could give another Instance, to be impartial in my own Family, of one of the same Profession, about as many years ago, who vainly attempted the same Thing: but this is to be said in his Alleviation & Excuse; that he had been absolutely scared out of his Wits, by a Gang of High-waymen of Smug[g]lers, who broke into his House, gagged him, & locked him up in his Cellar, & then rifled his House: some of which Gang were afterwards hanged for it. But I will now return to my Journal, after a most tedious Digression, & unthought of.

Sunday, 22 *Dec:* Stormy Weather. Uneasy, but tolerable good Night's Rest. I wrote to Father Charles Bedingfeild at Mrs Markham's at Somerby Hall near

[1]Wife of Sir Jermyn D.

Grantham in Lincolnshire: to Mr Pomfret of Newport-Pagnell, & Mr Cooke of Water-Eaton in Blecheley Parish. This Day a couple of Sir John Fielding's[1] Emissaries, the trading[2] blind Justice of Westminster, took a Bankrupt who had defrauded his Creditors, & who had been in the House ever since Friday waiting for a Passage into France, but could not get one on Account of the bad Weather, & took him to London, guarded, in the Machine or Stage Coach.

Monday, 23 *Dec:* Stormy & rainy. No very good Night, but very uneasy in my Knee. This Day a young Man was arrested for Debt in the House, but immediately was released on paying the Debt.

Tuesday, 24 *Dec: Christmass*[3] *Eve.* Fine Day. No Sleep till 6 o'Clock in the Morning till 9. I got out of Bed at 11 o'Clock, for the first Time I had been so bruised, to Breakfast, & sat up till one o'Clock, & was a good Deal tired: however I would get up again at 4 o'Clock to eat my Dinner, & did not go to Bed till 10 at Night, hoping that the Fatigue would make me Sleep, & that it was better for my Leg, tho' very uneasy, to be moved about a little, than constantly to lie in Bed. My constant Method thro' Life having been to eat one Meal only in a Day, & always preferring a late Dinner, I seldom breakfasted here till near 11, nor dined till near 5 in the Afternoon, & had my Candles put out about 11 at Night. However I had very little Sleep in the Night the Bell-Man with Boys coming about, about 1 or 2 o'Clock singing the Christmass Hymn: but

[1]Half-brother of the novelist. *Ob.* 1768.

[2]In the sense of making (illegitimate) gain through his official position—as was alleged.

[3]Always thus spelt by C.

whether they rang the Midnight Peel, at 12 o'Clock, as
they do all over Buckinghamshire & Northampton-
shire, I know not; the 2 Parish Churches being quite
at the other End of the Town, towards Canterbury,
near a Mile off; so that if they rang them I could not
hear them. Dover is one long Street built under the
White Chalk Cliff. As I passed by the Church I should
certainly have got out of the Coach, had it been easy
for me, to have seen whether the infamously great Mr
Churchill, who died at Boulogne 2 or 3 Years ago, &
was brought over to be buried at Dover, had any
Monument[1] erected to his Memory, as the Papers said
there was one designed for him. I got to Sleep about 4
or 5 o'Clock, & waked at 9 very uneasy in my Knee.

Wednesday, 25 *Dec:* 1765. *Christmass Day*. Fine
Morning. Rain at Noon, when I got up, & sat up 'till
10 o'Clock. Altho' I had terrible Apprehensions, first of
getting down Stairs, & then into the Coach, which I
was afraid I never should be able to contrive so as to sit
in at my Ease, as also of the Motion of the Coach,
which I dreaded more than any Thing besides, yet I
sent for my Landlord & made an Agreement with him
for his Post Coach, with 4 Horses & 2 Postilions, to
carry me in five Days from Dover to Blecheley, 46
Miles on the other Side of London: for which I was to
give him 9 Pounds, & he to find the Horses their
Provision: only I told him, if I was able to perform my
Journey, that I would take care of Men & Horses when
I got to Blecheley. I received yesterday a Letter from
Mr Pomfret of Newport-Pagnell. As it was Christmass

---

[1]It bore the inscription: "Here lie the Remains Of the celebrated
C. Churchill. Life to the last enjoy'd, here Churchill lies. The Candidate." The old churchyard of St Martin's where he was buried has
long been closed.

Day, I had a very fine Turkey for my Dinner. I agreed with Mr Hubbard, that if I could not proceed in my Journey, that I was to pay him for as far as I went according to the Proportion of 9 Pounds for 5 Days. I was eager to be gone from so noisy & dirty a Place, & should have been happy even to have got as far as Canterbury. In order to sweeten up my Landlord, that I might have a very sober orderly Fellow to drive me, for I found some Difficulty in that Affair, & in my Situation dreaded every Obstruction to my getting away, I made a Purchase of a very beautiful grey Parrot, who sung & talked the best that I ever heard, & which used to amuse me in my Chamber as I lay in Bed, for which I gave an exorbitant Price:[1] & it turned out the more so, as the poor Creature died this Day month following; altho' he was as well as ever I saw him the Day before: so that I am afraid they gave him something in the Kitchen, when they took him out to Clean his Cage, that did not agree with him.

Thursday, Dec: 26. St Stephen. No Sleep 'till 5 o'Clock & then for 3 Hours only, 'till 8: which however was a great Refreshment. I wrote to my Sister Catherine that I would lay at her House at Hackney in my way to Blecheley; to my Brother Doctor Apthorp, & told him of my Intentions of moving on Saturday: & Tom[2] wrote to his Father to prepare Things for me, I designing, in Case no other unlucky Accident intervened to prevent it, to be at Blecheley on Wednesday Evening, & to send my Boy, his Son Jem,[3] upon my little Favourite fat Dun Horse to meet me at Dunstable that Day about 12 o'Clock at Noon.

[1]Four guineas, *v. infra*.   [2]Tom Wood, C.'s factotum.
[3]*i.e.* Tom's brother.

Friday, 27 *Dec: St John the Evangelist.* Fine Day.
Not one Wink of Sleep, & rather uneasy in my Knee.
Letter from my Sister Catherine.

Saturday, 28 *Dec: Holy Innocents.* Fine Day. Excessive hard Frost; insomuch that I was much afraid that
the Hardness & Roughness of the Road [might cause
delay]: Tom packed all my Things, & tho' I ordered
the Coach to be at the Door at 12 o'Clock, yet it never
came 'till 2; & then without Glasses on either Side,
they having been broken, & sent to be mended: so that
I sat in the Coach in the Street waiting for them above
an Hour: so careless & negligent was the Man about
them. However I was happy in getting down Stairs, &
into the Coach very easily, with the Help of a Crutch;
& more happy still that the Coach being roomy & easy,
as I could desire, I sat much more at my Ease than when
I lay in Bed, & never felt the least uneasy Jolt or
Motion during the whole Journey: tho' the Roads were
as hard as a Rock all the Way, & very rough till we
came nearer London. I got to the *Red Lyon* at Canterbury at 5 o'Clock, the Coach going at a great Rate, near
8 Miles in an Hour: which I had no Conception I
could endure before I made a Trial of it: & the Horses
& Postilions being so used to that Place there was no
preventing them going so fast. But before I go any
further I will put down my long Bill at Dover, as a
Memorandum of my Misfortune.

[Cole devotes the last three pages of his "Paris Journal" to
a detailed reproduction of his hotel bills at Dover, Canterbury,
Rochester and St Albans. They merely possess interest as
records of prices, and of these a brief summary will suffice.

Among the daily items are: Lodgings, 2s., Fire, 1s., Bread
and Beer, 6d., Breakfast, 1s. 2d., Wine, 2s. The following dishes

appear occasionally: Fowl, 2s., Wild Duck, 2s. 6d., Boiled Cod and Oysters, 2s. 6d.; "Nuckle of Veal, Bacon and Greens", 3s., Roast Turkey, 5s. (but this lasted for three days). At Rochester, "Servants' Eating & Drinking" costs 4s., and at St Albans, "Shoulder of Mutton for Servants", 3s. 6d.

For "a Parrot and Cage" four guineas was paid.]

ADDITIONAL NOTE

P. 54.—Cole was mistaken in supposing that Walpole was 'never on a horse's back in his life', for, writing to Sir C. H. Williams, Sept. 19, 1744, Walpole tells him that "I have found riding so necessary for my health . . . . that I go coursing constantly every morning . . . letting nobody go with me but my own footman who knows no more of it than I do. . . . How I shall do to-morrow, when I begin hunting, I cant tell, for I cant make that a tete a tete affair!" *Supplement to the Letters of H. W.*; by Paget Toynbee, Vol. III, pp. 373-4.

INDEX

393

PRINTED IN GREAT BRITAIN
BY ROBERT MACLEHOSE AND CO. LTD.
THE UNIVERSITY PRESS, GLASGOW.